1982
The Supreme Court Review

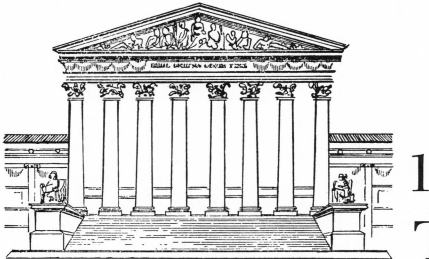

1982
The

"Judges as persons, or courts as institutions, are entitled to
no greater immunity from criticism than other persons
or institutions . . .[J]udges must be kept mindful of their limitations and
of their ultimate public responsibility by a vigorous
stream of criticism expressed with candor however blunt."
–Felix Frankfurter

". . . while it is proper that people should find fault when
their judges fail, it is only reasonable that they should recognize the
difficulties. . . . Let them be severely brought to book,
when they go wrong, but by those who will take the trouble
to understand them."
–Learned Hand

THE LAW SCHOOL

THE UNIVERSITY OF CHICAGO

Supreme Court Review

EDITED BY

PHILIP B. KURLAND

GERHARD CASPER

AND DENNIS J. HUTCHINSON

 THE UNIVERSITY OF CHICAGO PRESS

CHICAGO AND LONDON

INTERNATIONAL STANDARD BOOK NUMBER: 0-226-46435-0

LIBRARY OF CONGRESS CATALOG CARD NUMBER: 60-14353

THE UNIVERSITY OF CHICAGO PRESS, CHICAGO 60637

THE UNIVERSITY OF CHICAGO PRESS, LTD., LONDON

© 1983 BY THE UNIVERSITY OF CHICAGO. ALL RIGHTS RESERVED. PUBLISHED 1983

PRINTED IN THE UNITED STATES OF AMERICA

To
GERALD GUNTHER
*For whom the Constitution is a guide and
not a tool*

CONTENTS

WALTER V. SCHAEFER

PROSPECTIVE RULINGS : TWO PERSPECTIVES

In the closing days of its 1981 Term, the Supreme Court of the United States handed down two opinions dealing with the future impact of its decisions. The first opinion, *United States v. Johnson*,[1] is surprising because it upset, or attempted to upset, a pragmatic result which the Court had reached after much travail. The second opinion, *Northern Pipeline Construction Co. v. Marathon Pipe Line Company*,[2] is surprising because it reached a pragmatic result at the expense of a good deal of previously accepted legal theory. And surprisingly, although the two opinions were announced only a week apart, neither referred to the other.

I

Legislatures normally look forward. When a legislative body changes a rule of law, the new rule ordinarily governs only conduct that occurs after its enactment. If the effective date of a particular statute is to be deferred, the precise effective date is stated. The *ex post facto* clauses of state and federal constitutions prevent or prohibit the retroactive application of criminal statutes. And in civil matters the constitutional prohibition against impairment of contracts, judicial rules of construction, principles of estoppel, and,

Walter V. Schaefer is a retired Justice of the Supreme Court of Illinois and is now of counsel to the Chicago law firm of Rothschild, Barry & Myers.

[1] 102 S. Ct. 2579 (1982).

[2] 102 S. Ct. 2858 (1982).

ultimately, considerations of substantive due process combine to limit the retrospective application of statutes.

Courts normally look back. They apply rules to conduct that has already occurred. Normally, judicially announced rules of law apply retroactively, because they are assumed to be applications of preexisting principles. It is only in recent years that techniques of prospective overruling have been developed.

The retroactive impact of an overruling judicial decision is the same as the impact of a judicial determination of statutory invalidity. "When judges announce new rules of law they are making new law for their time, and it should be no more applicable retroactively where there has been prior reliance on old decisions than when new statutes are enacted by a legislature. Both should be prospective in their operation."[3]

There had been sporadic instances of prospective judicial rulings in the state courts during the nineteenth century.[4] The availability of the technique had been pointed out by Wigmore[5] and Kocourek[6]

---

[3] Leflar, *Appellate Judicial Innovation*, 27 OKLA. L.R. 321, 342 (1974).

[4] See, *e.g.*, Bingham v. Miller, 17 Ohio 445 (1848).

[5] "If a Supreme Court to-day holds that a contract is formed by deposit of an acceptance in the mail box, changing from the rule that arrival of the acceptance forms the contract, may not this leave valid all relations effected before the promulgation of the decision? In other words, stability is wanted for the sake of the concrete relations of individuals, not for the sake of the abstraction; and the former can be preserved, by exception, without preserving the latter." Wigmore, Editorial Preface to SCIENCE OF LEGAL METHOD xxxvii–xxxviii (9 Modern Legal Philosophy Series) (1917).

[6] Kocourek, *Retrospective Decisions, Stare Decisis and a Proposal*, 17 A.B.A.J. 180 (1931). Professor Kocourek proposed the following statute:

AN ACT DECLARING THE EFFECT OF JUDICIAL
DECISIONS OF THE SUPREME COURT

Sec. 1. The final judicial decisions of the Supreme Court are
   (*a*) Decisive of the rights of the parties.
   (*b*) Declarative of the rules of law for future application which govern the questions raised on the facts presented and decided.

Sec. 2. (1) If the Supreme Court believes that a declaration of rule of law theretofore made by the Supreme Court or by any inferior court is unjust, it will decide the instant case in accordance with the juster rule except
   (*a*) Where the former rule is a basis of reasonable and justifiable reliance applicable to the facts of the instant case, or
   (*b*) Where application of a new rule in its judgment will be unduly disturbing to a standard of reasonable and justifiable reliance as to the existence or non-existence of legal relations of other persons not then before the court.
   (2) When the Supreme Court refuses to depart from an existing rule in favor of what it pronounces a juster rule on the questions adjudicated, the expression of that view is evidence for future cases of the existence of reasonable reliance.

Sec. 3. Nothing herein shall abridge the duty of inferior court to apply the declarations of law made by superior courts.

during the early 1900s, but it was not until after 1932 that use of the technique became widespread. In 1932, Benjamin Cardozo, then Chief Judge of New York's highest court, building upon the work of Wigmore and Kocourek, described the technique and advocated its use in his address to the New York State Bar Association.[7] And later in that same year, after Cardozo had moved from the New York Court to the Supreme Court of the United States, he wrote the opinion in *Sunburst Oil & Refining Co. v. Great Northern Railway Co.*[8]

A decision of the Supreme Court of Montana had allowed a shipper to recover the overcharge when a tariff approved by the Board of Railroad Commissioners was subsequently invalidated. In *Sunburst*, the Montana Court overruled that earlier decision and held that the approved tariff was effective until it was invalidated. Nevertheless, Sunburst was allowed to recover because it had relied upon and followed the former opinion. In the Supreme Court of the United States, the railroad claimed that it had been deprived of due process of law by the judgment of the Montana Court. Writing for a unanimous Court, Justice Cardozo held that the Montana decision, which protected those who had acted on the faith of its earlier but now overruled opinion, denied no right protected by the national Constitution. "We think the federal constitution has no voice upon the subject,"[9] he stated.

Once the constitutional doubts as to the propriety of the procedure had been removed, state courts throughout the country employed various forms of prospective overruling in a host of cases involving all fields of law, common, constitutional, and statutory.[10]

II

The concern of the Supreme Court of the United States for the retroactivity of its own decisions can fairly be said to date from

---

[7] Cardozo, *New York State Bar Address*, 55 N.Y.S.B.A. REP. 263, 294 (1932).

[8] 287 U.S. 358 (1932).

[9] *Id.* at 364.

[10] The literature is voluminous. For general discussions, see Mishkin, *Foreword: The High Court, the Great Writ, and the Due Process of Time and Law*, 79 HARV. L. REV. 56 (1965); Schaefer, *The Control of "Sunbursts": Techniques of Prospective Overruling*, 42 N.Y.U.L. REV. 631 (1967); Schwartz, *Retroactivity, Reliability and Due Process: A Reply to Professor Mishkin*, 33 U. CHI. L. REV. 719 (1966); Haddad, *"Retroactivity Should Be Rethought": A Call for the End of the Linkletter Doctrine*, 60 J. CRIM. L. C. & P. S. 417 (1969); Beytagh, *Ten Years of Non-Retroactivity: A Critique and a Proposal*, 61 VA. L. REV. 1557 (1975).

1965, when the Court decided *Linkletter v. Walker*.[11] In 1949, in *Wolf v. Colorado*,[12] the Supreme Court had held that the States were not required by the Constitution to exclude illegally obtained evidence in the trial of criminal cases. Then in 1961, in *Mapp v. Ohio*,[13] the Court overruled *Wolf v. Colorado* and for the first time applied the exclusionary rule to state court convictions. Expansion of the scope of federal *habeas corpus* had made possible the review in the federal courts of state court convictions that had long since become final. A host of state court convictions after *Wolf v. Colorado* were thus potentially subject to a new and unanticipated challenge. *Linkletter* limited the retroactive effect of *Mapp v. Ohio* to those cases in which the judgment had not become final when *Mapp* was decided, saying: "By final we mean where the judgment of conviction was rendered, the availability of appeal exhausted, and the time for petition for certiorari had elapsed [or a petition for certiorari finally denied, all] before our decision in *Mapp v. Ohio*."[14] Whether a defendant would receive the benefit of the ruling in *Mapp. v. Ohio* was thus made to depend upon the rate of progress of his case through the trial and appellate state courts and the Supreme Court of the United States. Whether the search had actually occurred prior to the decision in *Mapp v. Ohio* was completely disregarded.

Shortly after its decision in *Linkletter*, the Court considered the retroactive effect of its decisions in *Escobedo v. Illinois*[15] and *Miranda v. Arizona*,[16] which dealt with the rights of a suspect prior to arraignment on a criminal charge. In those cases, interrogation had occurred in the absence of counsel and without a warning of defendant's right to be silent, and the resulting admissions or confessions had been received in evidence. Because of the disruptive effect of retroactive application of those decisions on the administration of criminal law throughout the country, the Supreme Court limited their effect to trials that took place after each of the decisions.[17]

It was quickly pointed out that the selection of the date of trial to

---

[11] 381 U.S. 618 (1965).

[12] 338 U.S. 25 (1949).

[13] 367 U.S. 643 (1961).

[14] 381 U.S. at 622 n.5.

[15] 378 U.S. 478 (1964).

[16] 384 U.S. 436 (1966).

[17] Johnson v. New Jersey, 384 U.S. 719 (1966).

measure retroactivity was unfortunate. Professor Beytagh has recently observed:[18]

> Had the Court thought more carefully about the consequences of its approach, it is doubtful that it would have applied these decisions to cases where *trials* were begun after they were decided. A sounder approach, it was soon recognized, would have focused on when *violations* of these rules occurred. The new rules would then govern fact situations arising after the date of the decision but would have no application where the pertinent event—here, interrogation without a lawyer or without the prescribed warnings—happened before that date. . . . More attention to this problem could have averted the aborting of pending trials by lower courts which spoke testily of the uncertain wisdom of the Court's holdings in *Escobedo* and *Miranda* themselves.

The Court took note of the criticism of its earlier ventures in retroactivity. In 1967 when the Court considered the retroactivity of "the lineup cases" in *Stovall v. Denno*,[19] it fixed upon the date of reliance on the earlier rule as the determining factor in retroactivity. It did so by providing that its new decisions should be applicable only to lineups that took place after the dates of the *Wade*[20] and *Gilbert*[21] decisions. It thus moved the focus from the neat but irrelevant factor of the rate of progress of a case through our dual system of courts, and centered upon the real life factor of the date of the precipitating event.[22]

In *Stovall*, the Court described the considerations to be taken into account in determining questions of retroactivity as: "(*a*) the purpose to be served by the new standards, (*b*) the extent of the reliance by law enforcement authorities on the old standards, and (*c*) the effect on the administration of justice of a retroactive application of the new standards." The Court then said:[23]

> We also conclude that, for these purposes, no distinction is justified between convictions now final, as in the instant case, and convictions at various stages of trial and direct review. We regard the factors of reliance and burden on the administration

---

[18] Beytagh, note 10 *supra*, at 1565, 1566.

[19] 388 U.S. 293 (1967).

[20] United States v. Wade, 388 U.S. 218 (1967).

[21] Gilbert v. California, 388 U.S. 263 (1967).

[22] See Jenkins v. Delaware, 395 U.S. 213, 218 (1969).

[23] 388 U.S. at 300.

of justice as entitled to such overriding significance as to make that distinction unsupportable.

And in order to avoid the objection that a purely prospective decision, with no impact on the parties before the Court, would be an advisory opinion and so violate the constitutional requirement of a case or controversy, as well as fail to provide an incentive to challenge existing doctrine, the prevailing party was given the benefit of the ruling in his case.

In spite of continuing dissents, based upon widely divergent considerations, the *Stovall* approach became the "orthodox rule." In 1971, it was adapted and applied to civil cases in *Chevron Oil Co. v. Huson.*[24] There the Court considered the retroactivity of *Rodrigue v. Aetna Casualty and Surety Co.*,[25] involving the timeliness of an action brought by a workman injured while working on an island oil drilling rig on the Outer Continental Shelf. *Rodrigue* had held that the Louisiana statute of limitations, rather than the admiralty rule of laches, governed such actions. Under the state law Huson's action would have been barred before *Rodrigue* was decided. The Court pointed out that "*Rodrigue* was not only a case of first impression in this Court . . . but it also effectively overruled a long line of decisions by the Fifth Circuit Court of Appeals holding that admiralty law was applicable." The Court then continued:[26]

> When the respondent was injured, for the next two years until he instituted his lawsuit, and for the ensuing year of pretrial proceedings, these Court of Appeals decisions represented the law governing his case. It cannot be assumed that he did or could foresee that this consistent interpretation of the Lands Act would be overturned. The most he could do was to rely on the law as it then was. "We should not indulge in the view that the law now announced has always been the law and, therefore, that those who did not avail themselves of it waived their rights." *Griffin* v. *Illinois*, 351 U.S. 12, 26 (Frankfurter, J., concurring in judgment).

Describing the status of nonretroactivity as it existed in 1973, Professor Beytagh said:[27]

---

[24] 404 U.S. 97 (1971).

[25] 395 U.S. 352 (1969).

[26] 404 U.S. at 107.

[27] Beytagh, note 10 *supra*, at 1588.

For practical purposes, then, the shaky and shifting majority that subscribed to the doctrine through the years of its development has now become a substantial and dependable majority likely to give more stability to the concept, and, perhaps, to be receptive to suggested remedies for those remaining defects.

In 1975, *United States v. Peltier*[28] followed *Stovall* and held nonretroactive the 1973 decision in *Almeida-Sanchez v. United States*[29] outlawing "border searches" made without a showing of probable cause. In the same year *Bowen v. United States*[30] followed *Peltier* in refusing to apply *Almeida-Sanchez* retroactively to fixed point searches conducted at some distance from the border.

III

So matters stood when *Payton v. New York*[31] came before the Court in 1980. *Payton* involved the constitutionality of New York statutes which authorized police officers to enter private residences without a warrant, and with force if necessary, to make a felony arrest. At 7:30 A.M. on January 15, 1970, police officers who had probable cause to believe that Payton had murdered the manager of a gas station two days earlier went to his apartment to arrest him. Light and music emanated from the apartment but there was no response to the officers' knock on the metal door. They summoned emergency assistance and broke open the door and entered the apartment. A thirty-caliber shell case which was in plain view was subsequently admitted into evidence at Payton's murder trial. He was convicted and sentenced to death. The Appellate Division affirmed,[32] and so did the Court of Appeals.[33] The Supreme Court of the United States first heard argument on March 26, 1979, but the case was not decided until April 15, 1980, after reargument. The Court characterized the arrests in Payton's case and in a companion case as "routine" felony arrests, and held that in the absence of exigent circumstances, the Fourth Amendment prohibits police

---

[28] 422 U.S. 531 (1975).

[29] 413 U.S. 266 (1973).

[30] 422 U.S. 916 (1975).

[31] 445 U.S. 573 (1980).

[32] 390 N.Y.S.2d 769.

[33] 45 N.Y.2d 300.

officers from entering a suspect's home to make a felony arrest without a warrant. Justice White dissented, and the Chief Justice and Justice Rehnquist concurred in that dissent. Although the Court's opinion acknowledged that its judgment was contrary to the weight of authority throughout the country, it said nothing as to the retroactive or prospective effect of its decision.

Not until two years later, in *United States v. Johnson*,[34] did the Supreme Court consider the retrospective effect of the rule announced in *Payton*. After reviewing the course of decision since *Linkletter* in 1965, the *Johnson* opinion turned to the dissenting and concurring opinions of individual justices in cases involving the retroactivity of various decisions. A footnote cited fourteen cases in which Justice Douglas had dissented or concurred specially, six in which Justice Black had dissented, four opinions of Justice Marshall, five dissenting opinions of Justice Harlan, three of Justice Powell and one each of Justice Fortas and Justice Stevens.[35] Justice Harlan's criticisms of the *Stovall-Denno* approach, expressed in picturesque rhetoric—"ambulatory retroactive review,"[36] "fishing one case from the stream of appellate review,"[37] were quoted, and this portion of the *Johnson* opinion concluded: "We now agree with Justice Harlan that '[r]etroactivity must be rethought.' *Desist v. United States*, 394 U.S. at 258 (dissenting opinion)."[38]

Johnson reiterates the refrain that characterized the dissents of Justice Harlan—"the goal of treating similarly situated defendants similarly,"[39]—a goal which according to Justice Harlan, the *Linkletter* "final judgment" approach would achieve. No one can quarrel with the goal. But the question is, Similarly situated with respect to what? The *Linkletter-Harlan-Johnson* approach considers similarity with respect only to the rate of progress of cases through the judicial system. It disregards entirely the element of reliance and the events of real life that gave rise to those cases. That single characteristic, finality upon direct review, is entirely fortuitous, as both

---

[34] 102 S. Ct. 2579 (1982).

[35] *Id*. at 2585 n.9.

[36] *Id*. at 2585.

[37] *Id*. at 2586.

[38] *Ibid*.

[39] *Id*. at 2590.

the Court and commentators have pointed out, and indeed, as the *Johnson* opinion rather grudgingly concedes in a footnote:[40]

> We are aware, of course, that many considerations affect a defendant's progress through the judicial system, and that the speed of appellate review will differ from State to State, Circuit to Circuit, and case to case. Even under our approach, it may be unavoidable that some similarly situated defendants will be treated differently.

The search in *Johnson* occurred in 1977, while the *Payton* case was not decided until 1980. Under the *Linkletter* approach, not only "may" it be unavoidable, it is in fact inevitable that similarly situated defendants will be treated differently.

The Court describes "three narrow categories of cases" in which retroactivity has been determined "through application of a threshold test."[41] The first and third of these categories do not involve any problem of retroactivity. The first includes those cases in which settled precedents are applied to new and different factual situations. The third consists of cases in which the court lacked jurisdiction or, as *Johnson* put it, "a trial court lacked authority to convict or punish a criminal defendant in the first place."[42] Only the second category presents a true question of retrospective or prospective effect. Those are the cases in which the "Court has expressly declared a rule of criminal procedure to be a 'clear break with the past.' "[43] In most of them, the *Johnson* opinion points out, retroactivity depended upon "reliance by law enforcement authorities on the old standards and effect on the administration of justice of a retroactive application of the new rule."[44]

Having established these three categories, the opinion in *Johnson* goes on to apply them to *Payton* and finds none of them applicable. It is obvious that *Payton* was not within the first or third categories, for *Payton* neither applied settled precedents nor raised a jurisdictional issue. As to the second, the opinion in *Johnson* points out that *Payton* "did not announce an entirely new and unanticipated princi-

---

[40] *Id.* at 2591 n.17.

[41] *Id.* at 2587.

[42] *Ibid.*

[43] *Ibid.*

[44] *Ibid.*

ple of law."[45] Again picking up a phrase from a dissenting opinion, the Court continued:[46]

> In general, the Court has not subsequently read a decision to work a "sharp break in the web of the law," *Milton v. Wainwright*, 407 U.S. 371, 381, n. 2 (1972) (Stewart, J., dissenting), unless that doctrine caused "such an abrupt and fundamental shift in doctrine as to constitute an entirely new rule which in effect replaced an older one," *Hanover Shoe, Inc. v. United Shoe Machinery Corp.*, 392 U.S. 481, 498 (1968). Such a break has been recognized only when a decision explicitly overrules a past precedent of *this Court*, . . . or disapproves a practice *this Court* arguably has sanctioned in prior cases, . . . or overturns a long-standing and widespread practice to which *this Court* has not spoken, but which a near-unanimous body of lower court authority has expressly approved.

The critical portion of the categories established in *Johnson* is the requirement of the overturning of "a longstanding and widespread practice . . . which a near-unanimous body of lower court authority has expressly approved." That requirement of "near unanimity" is new, and the *Johnson* opinion offers no justification for its imposition. The opinion in *Johnson* adopts the "sharp break in the web of the law" phrase taken from Justice Stewart's dissent in *Milton v. Wainwright*, but it disregards his definition of such a break: "The issue [of retroactivity] is presented only when the decision overrules clear past precedent, . . . or disrupts a practice long accepted and widely relied upon."[47] Under the standard stated by Justice Stewart, Johnson's conviction would have been affirmed. His arrest, and the questionable search on May 5, 1977, preceded the Supreme Court's decision in *Payton* by more than two years. Payton's arrest was valid under the statutes and decisions of a majority of the states at the time it was made, as the Court pointed out in its decision in *Payton*.[48] In fact the Ninth Circuit Court of Appeals had

---

[45] *Id.* at 2588.

[46] *Ibid.* (emphasis added).

[47] *Ibid.*

[48] The Court's opinion in *Payton* described state of the law in 1980 with respect to warrantless felony arrests based upon probable cause: twenty-four states authorized the practice by statute. The question of the constitutionality of such searches had been before twelve state courts of last resort. Two of them had rejected the constitutional attack. One was the New York Court of Appeals in the *Payton* case itself. The other was the Supreme Court of Florida, and in that case the Supreme Court of the United States had denied *certiorari* in 1973. None of the ten cases that held the arrests invalid had been decided before

adopted an opinion affirming Johnson's conviction before *Payton* was decided by the Supreme Court. That opinion was then withdrawn, and the conviction was reversed on the authority of *Payton*.[49] While the decision in *Payton* unquestionably "disrupted a practice long accepted and widely relied upon," and so qualified as a "sharp break" under Justice Stewart's standard, it did not meet *Johnson's* newly invented requirement of "near unanimity."

The self-centered quality of the Court's concern permeates the entire opinion. The goal sought by the Court is summarized in these terms: "An approach that resolved all nonfinal convictions under the same rule of law would lessen the possibility that *this Court* might mete out different constitutional protection to defendants simultaneously subjected to identical police conduct."[50] Apparently the virtue of the *Linkletter* approach lies in the fact that the "different constitutional protection" which it causes will be meted out by other courts—not by "this Court." But the goal of similar constitutional protection "to defendants simultaneously subjected to identical police conduct" can be achieved only by focusing steadily on the time of the police conduct, without regard to the irrelevant rate of progress of cases through our judicial systems.

The emphasis upon "this court" as the source of reliable law is apparently a response to what was said in the Court's opinion in *United States v. Peltier*.[51] There the Court was considering the retroactivity of *Almeida-Sanchez v. United States*,[52] which had for the first time held border searches invalid when conducted without a warrant and without probable cause. In *Peltier*, the Court pointed out that a clear majority of the Courts of Appeal that had passed upon the question had sustained the validity of such searches. The Court therefore applied the traditional *Stovall* test, and concluded:[53]

January 14, 1970, when the arrest in *Payton* took place; only one of those ten decisions had come down before 1975. Seven United States Courts of Appeals had considered the question. Five had expressed the opinion that such arrests were unconstitutional, but all of those five decisions were rendered after the search in *Payton*. In 1970, the Supreme Court of the United States had denied *certiorari* in one of the two cases that sustained the constitutionality of such arrests. See 445 U.S. at 598–600.

[49] 102 S. Ct. at 2582.

[50] *Id.* at 2590–91.

[51] 422 U.S. 531 (1975).

[52] 413 U.S. 266 (1973).

[53] 422 U.S. at 541, 542.

Since the parties acknowledge that *Almeida-Sanchez* was the first roving Border Patrol case to be decided by this Court, unless we are to hold that parties may not reasonably rely upon any legal pronouncement emanating from sources other than this Court, we cannot regard as blameworthy those parties who conform their conduct to the prevailing statutory or constitutional norm. . . . If the purpose of the exclusionary rule is to deter unlawful police conduct, then evidence obtained from a search should be suppressed only if it can be said that the law enforcement officer had knowledge, or may properly be charged with knowledge that the search was unconstitutional under the Fourth Amendment.

The *Johnson* opinion's attempt to distinguish *Peltier* contains a surprising misstatement:[54]

Upon examination, however, the retroactivity question posed here differs from that presented in *Peltier*. As the Government concedes, *Payton* overturned neither a statute nor any consistent judicial history approving nonconsensual warrantless home entries. *See* Brief for United States 30, n. 18.

But the Government made no such concession in its brief, and the first sentence of the opinion of the Court in *Payton* stated: "These appeals challenge the constitutionality of New York statutes that authorize police officers to enter a private residence without a warrant and with force, if necessary, to make a routine felony arrest."[55]

After deciding that *Payton* did not fit within any of its three categories, the Court went on to consider whether the question of retroactivity "would be fairly resolved by applying the rule in *Payton* to all cases still pending on direct appeal at the time when *Payton* was decided. "Answering that question affirmatively," the Court continued, "would satisfy each of the three concerns stated in Justice Harlan's opinions in *Desist* and *Mackey*."[56] The Court first stated that such a determination would conform to the original understanding of retroactivity expressed in *Linkletter* and *Shott* and then continued:[57]

Moreover, such a principle would be one capable of general applicability, satisfying Justice Harlan's central concern: "Re-

---

[54] 102 S. Ct. at 2592.

[55] 445 U.S. at 574.

[56] 102 S. Ct. at 2590.

[57] *Ibid.*

fusal to apply new constitutional rules to all cases arising on direct review . . . tends to cut this Court loose from the force of precedent, allowing us to restructure artificially those expectations legitimately created by extant law and thereby mitigate the practical force of stare decisis . . . a force which ought properly to bear on the judicial resolution of any legal problem." *Mackey* v. *United States*, 401 U.S. at 680–81 (separate opinion).

Second, the Court pointed out that such a decision would comport with the Court's judicial responsibilities " 'to do justice to each litigant on the merits of his own case,' *Desist* v. *United States*, 394 U.S. at 259 (Harlan, J., dissenting)," and " 'to resolve all cases *before us* on direct review in light of our best understanding of governing constitutional principles.' *Mackey* v. *United States*, 401 U.S. at 679 (separate opinion of Harlan, J.)"[58]

The Court then observed that "application of the Harlan approach to respondent's case would further the goal of treating similarly situated defendants similarly."[59] And finally, the Court noted, "Applying *Payton* to convictions that were not yet final when *Payton* issued would accomplish the first step toward 'turning our backs on the *ad hoc* approach that has so far characterized our decisions in the retroactivity field and proceeding to administer the doctrine on principle.' *Jenkins* v. *Delaware*, 395 U.S. 213, 224 (1969) (Harlan, J., dissenting)."[60]

Justice Brennan concurred in the *Johnson* opinion with the cryptic comment: "I join the Court's opinion on my understanding that the decision leaves undisturbed our retroactivity precedents as applied to convictions final at the time of the decision. See, *e.g.*, *Stovall* v. *Denno*, 388 U.S. 293 (1967)."[61] It is hard to know just what this means, for the *Linkletter* "final judgment" rule was precisely designed to cut off cases on collateral attack. And it is the *ad hoc* "balancing approach" of *Stovall* v. *Denno* that was so bitterly attacked throughout the *Johnson* opinion.

In any event, the concluding portion of the *Johnson* opinion seems to reduce the end result of its proclaimed "rethinking of retroactivity" to a rule applicable only to the case in which it was announced.

---

[58] *Ibid.* (emphasis added).

[59] *Ibid.*

[60] *Id.* at 2594.

[61] *Id.* at 2595.

The statement, "To the extent necessary to decide today's case, we embrace Justice Harlan's views in *Desist* and *Mackey*," sounds like Mr. Justice Roberts's railroad ticket dictum—"good for this day and train only."[62] And the balance of the *Johnson* opinion seems to consist of disclaimers of all that has gone before:[63]

> We therefore hold that, subject to the exceptions stated below, a decision of this Court construing the Fourth Amendment is to be applied retroactively to all convictions that were not yet final at the time the decision was rendered.
>
> By so holding, however, we leave undisturbed our precedents in other areas. First, our decision today does not affect those cases that would be clearly controlled by our existing retroactivity precedents. Second, because respondent's case arises on direct review, we need not address the retroactive reach of our Fourth Amendment decisions to those cases that still may raise Fourth Amendment issues on collateral attack. . . . Third, we express no view on the retroactive application of decisions construing any constitutional provision other than the Fourth Amendment. Finally, all questions of civil retroactivity continue to be governed by the standard enunciated in *Chevron Oil Co. v. Huson*, 404 US 97, 106–7, (1971).

The first of the enumerated exceptions, coupled with Justice Brennan's limited concurrence, which provided the fifth vote for the *Johnson* opinion, seems to contradict all that has been said by way of criticism of "our existing retroactivity precedents." The second exception is even more surprising than the first, for the entire purpose of the *Linkletter* direct appeal approach was to exclude cases coming before the court on collateral attack. In a footnote the Court points out that it has very sharply limited the possibility of collateral attack in Fourth Amendment cases.[64] The third exception limits the effect of the *Johnson* opinion to Fourth Amendment cases, and thus destroys the stated objective of a principle "capable of general applicability." And the final exception states that all questions "of civil retroactivity" will continue to be governed by the standard in *Chevron Oil*. That case, of course, adapted and applied the standard of *Stovall v. Denno*.

---

[62] Smith v. Allwright, 321 U.S. 649, 669 (1944) (Roberts, J.).

[63] 102 S. Ct. at 2594–95.

[64] *Id.* at 2594 n.20.

IV

One week after the release of the *Johnson* opinion, the Court decided *Northern Pipeline Construction Co. v. Marathon Pipe Line Company*.[65] The Bankruptcy Act of 1978 had established a bankruptcy court in each judicial district and authorized those courts to exercise jurisdiction over all "civil proceedings arising under Title XI [the Bankruptcy Title] or arising in or related to cases under Title XI."[66] A plurality of four justices held this broad grant of jurisdiction invalid on the ground that the judicial power of the United States can be exercised only by judges who have the life tenure and protection against salary diminution provided by Article III of the Constitution. Under the Act, bankruptcy judges were appointed for fourteen-year terms and were subject to removal by the judicial council of the circuit in which they served. Their salaries were subject to adjustment. A footnote rejected the possibility of severing the excessive grant of jurisdiction and allowing the remainder of the Act to stand. In the concluding section of its opinion, the plurality turned to the question of the retroactive effect of its decision, and said:[67]

> Our decision in *Chevron Oil Co* v. *Huson*, 404 U.S. 97 (1971), sets forth the three considerations recognized by our precedents as properly bearing upon the issue of retroactivity. They are, first, whether the holding in question "decid[ed] an issue of first impression whose resolution was not clearly foreshadowed" by earlier cases, *id.*, at 106; second "whether retrospective operation will further or retard [the] operation" of the holding in question, *id.*, at 107; and third, whether retroactive application "could produce substantial inequitable results" in individual cases, *ibid.* In the present case, all of these considerations militate against the retroactive application of our holding today. It is plain that Congress' broad grant of judicial power to non–Art. III bankruptcy judges presents an unprecedented question of interpretation of Art. III. It is equally plain that retroactive application would not further the operation of our holding, and would surely visit substantial injustice and hardship upon those litigants who relied upon the Act's vesting of jurisdiction in the

---

[65] 102 S. Ct. 2858 (1982).

[66] *Id.* at 2862.

[67] *Id.* at 2880.

bankruptcy courts. We hold, therefore, that our decision today shall apply only prospectively.

The judgment was stayed, however, until October 4, 1982, to "afford Congress an opportunity to reconstitute the bankruptcy courts or to adopt other valid means of adjudication, without impairing the interim administration of the bankruptcy laws."[68]

Justices Rehnquist and O'Connor concurred in the result on the narrower ground that the Act was invalid insofar as it authorized a bankruptcy court to exercise jurisdiction over the common law claim of a debtor against a third party, which was the question immediately involved in the *Northern Pipeline* case. And because they agreed that the grant of this jurisdiction was not severable from the rest of the Act, they concurred in the judgment. They also agreed with the plurality's discussion of retroactivity and with the stay of the judgment.[69]

Chevron Oil Co. v. Huson,[70] on which the plurality primarily relied for its conclusion of nonretroactivity, involved no problems of jurisdiction or judicial competence. A "see also" footnote[71] cited *Buckley v. Valeo*, 424 U.S., at 142; *Chicot County Drainage District v. Baxter State Bank*, 308 U.S. 371, 376–77 (1940); and *Insurance Corporation of Ireland, Ltd. v. Compagnie Des Bauxites De Guinea* [102 S. Ct. 2099, 2104, n. 9] (1982). The cited portion of *Buckley v. Valeo* expressed the view that *de facto* validity should be accorded to the past actions of the Federal Election Commission, even though the method of appointment of the members of the Commission was invalid because it violated the principle of separation of powers. And in *Buckley* the Court pointed out that it had similarly accorded *de facto* validity to legislative acts performed by legislators held to have been elected in accordance with an unconstitutional apportionment plan. The reference to *Chicot County Drainage District* is to that portion of the opinion which held that courts, including courts of limited jurisdiction, have jurisdiction to determine questions affecting their jurisdiction. In *The Insurance Corporation* case, decided earlier in June of 1982, the Court held that jurisdiction over

---

[68] *Ibid.*

[69] *Id.* at 2880–82.

[70] 404 U.S. 97.

[71] 102 S. Ct. at 2880 n.41.

the person can be treated as established for purposes of a sanction imposed under Rule 37 of the Federal Rules of Civil Procedure for failure to comply with orders seeking discovery of facts relating to the jurisdiction of the court.

None of these authorities expressed a view as to the retroactivity of a decision that denied the competence of the tribunal to adjudicate. Views on that issue had, however, been expressed by some Justices and implied by others, with respect to courts martial, described by the plurality as one of the "three narrow situations" not subject to the constitutional command that the judicial power of the United States must be vested in Article III courts. In *Gosa v. Mayden*,[72] in 1973, the Court had considered the retroactive effect of its decision in *O'Callahan v. Parker*,[73] four years earlier, which had held that a serviceman charged with a crime not connected with his military service was entitled to be indicted by a grand jury and to be tried by jury in a civilian court, rather than by a court martial. A plurality of four Justices applied the *Stovall-Denno* test[74] and held that *O'Callahan* was not to be applied retroactively. Justice Douglas was of the opinion that *Gosa* should be set for reargument on the question of whether or not the question of jurisdiction was *res judicata*. He expressed no opinion on retroactivity. Justice Rehnquist concurred in the judgment because he believed that *O'Callahan* had been wrongly decided and would prefer to overrule it. He also observed:[75]

> I do not believe that decisions of this Court would support a holding that the rule announced in *O'Callahan v. Parker*, 395 U.S. 258 (1969), should not be applied retroactively to court-martial convictions entered before the decision in that case. In *O'Callahan*, the Court clearly held that courts-martial did not have jurisdiction to try servicemen for "non–service connected" crimes. For substantially the reasons stated by my Brother Marshall, I believe that *Robinson v. Neil*, 409 U.S. 505 (1973), and prior decisions mandate that O'Callahan be applied retroactively.

Mr. Justice Stewart dissented, saying:[76]

---

[72] 413 U.S. 665 (1973).

[73] 395 U.S. 258 (1969).

[74] 413 U.S. at 685.

[75] *Id.* at 692.

[76] *Id.* at 693.

I dissented in *O'Callahan* v. *Parker*, 395 U.S. 258, 274 (1969), and continue to believe that that case was wrongly decided. Until or unless *O'Callahan* is overruled, however, I think it must be given fully retroactive application for the reasons stated in my Brother Marshall's persuasive dissenting opinion, *post*, this page. Accordingly, I join his dissenting opinion as it applies to No. 71-6314, *Gosa* v. *Mayden*.

Justice Marshall's dissent in *Gosa*, in which Justices Brennan and Stewart joined, pointed out that in *O'Callahan* "the Court was concerned with the fact that the presiding officers at courts-martial do not enjoy the independence that is thought to flow from life tenure and undiminishable salary."[77] His dissent also stated:[78]

> Mr. Justice Blackmun's plurality opinion, by its efforts to establish that *O'Callahan* v. *Parker*, 395 U.S. 258 (1969), was not a decision dealing with jurisdiction in its classic form, implicitly acknowledges that if O'Callahan were in fact concerned with the adjudicatory power—that is, the jurisdictional competency—of military tribunals, its holding would necessarily be fully retroactive in effect.
>
> *   *   *
>
> I am unable to agree with the plurality's characterization of *O'Callahan*. In my view, it can only be understood as a decision dealing with the constitutional limits of the military's adjudicatory power over offenses committed by servicemen. No decision could more plainly involve the limits of a tribunal's power to exercise jurisdiction over particular offenses and thus more clearly demand retroactive application.

Surely, the decision in *Northern Pipeline* was similarly concerned with the adjudicatory power—the jurisdictional competence of bankruptcy judges under the 1978 Act. Again, in *Waller v. Florida*,[79] the Court held that successive municipal and state prosecutions for the same offense constituted double jeopardy, and that decision was given retroactive effect because it eliminated the judicial power to conduct a second trial.

V

Although the effort of the Court in *Johnson* was not productive, "rethinking retroactivity" may still have value.

---

[77] *Id.* at 697.

[78] *Id.* at 693–94.

[79] 397 U.S. 387 (1970).

One way to begin is by examining the value of *Linkletter v. Walker*[80] as a retroactivity precedent. The Court's consideration of retroactivity in that case was seriously inhibited by the fact that it had already retroactively applied its ruling in *Mapp v. Ohio*[81] in earlier cases. What was needed, therefore, was a formula to accommodate those earlier decisions, while still limiting the retroactive reach of *Mapp*. The Court found that formula in the language of Chief Justice Marshall in *The Schooner Peggy*.[82] In that case, the ship *Trumbull* had been commissioned by the President of the United States to capture any armed French vessel found on the high seas. The *Peggy* was captured pursuant to that authority and a proceeding was instituted to condemn the ship and its cargo as forfeited "to the use of the United States, and of the officers and men of the Trumbull," one-half to the United States and the other half to the officers and men.

The district court was of the opinion that the *Peggy* was not on the high seas at the time she was captured and therefore ordered that the schooner and her cargo be restored to her French owners. The circuit court reversed, and determined that the *Peggy* and her cargo were a lawful prize. The decree of the circuit court was entered September 23, 1800. While the case was pending on further review in the Supreme Court, the Treaty with France was ratified by the President. The Treaty provided: "Property captured, and not yet definitely condemned," shall be mutually restored.

Chief Justice Marshall first pointed out that "[t]he Constitution of the United States declares a treaty to be the supreme law of the land," and that "to condemn a vessel, the restoration of which is directed by the law of the land, would be a direct infraction of that law, and, of consequence, improper."[83] His opinion then continued:[84]

> It is, in the general, true, that the province of an appellate court is only to inquire whether a judgment when rendered, was erroneous or not. But if, subsequent to the judgment, and before the decision of the appellate court, a law intervenes and posi-

---

[80] 381 U.S. 618 (1965).

[81] 367 U.S. 643 (1961).

[82] 1 Cranch 103 (1801).

[83] *Id*. at 110.

[84] *Ibid*.

tively changes the rule which governs, the law must be obeyed, or its obligation denied. If the law be constitutional, and of that no doubt, in the present case, has been expressed, I know of no court which can contest its obligation. It is true that in mere private cases between individuals, a court will and ought to struggle hard against a construction which will, by a retrospective operation, affect the rights of parties, but in great national concerns, where individual rights, acquired by war, are sacrificed for national purposes, the contract making the sacrifice ought always to receive a construction conforming to its manifest import; and if the nation has given up the vested rights of its citizens, it is not for the court, but for the government, to consider whether it be a case proper for compensation.

In *The American Judicial Tradition*, Professor G. Edward White describes the rhetorical pattern of Chief Justice Marshall's opinions as generally containing a "broad formulation of an abstract and seemingly innocuous general principle of law and government, with little effort to tie the principle in a precise way to the case before him."[85]

That pattern was followed in *The Schooner Peggy*, which did not involve an ordinary change in the applicable law during the pendency of an appeal. Nor did *The Schooner Peggy* involve any issue as to retroactive application of a statute or decision. The Treaty with France was expressly retroactive, and as it bore upon the case before the Supreme Court, the Treaty limited the power of the Court to a determination of whether or not the decision of the Circuit Court was "definitely final." If it was, the case was beyond the reach of the appellate jurisdiction of the Supreme Court. And if it was not, the Treaty deprived the Court of the power to do anything other than to return the vessel to its former owners. No question of the retroactive effect of a statute or judicial decision was before the Court.

Nevertheless, there has been extensive exegesis of the supposed holding of *The Schooner Peggy*, in addition to *Linkletter v. Walker*. For example, in *Bradley v. Richmond School Board* the opinion states:[86] "The concerns expressed by the Court in *The Schooner Peggy* and in *Thorpe* relative to the possible working of an injustice center upon (*a*) the nature and identity of the parties, (*b*) the nature of their

---

[85] WHITE, THE AMERICAN JUDICIAL TRADITION 25 (1976).

[86] 416 U.S. 696, 717 (1974).

rights, and (c) the nature of the impact of the change in law upon those rights." Each of these "aspects" is then examined at length. The contrast with *The Schooner Peggy* is sharp. All that was there said about the potential injustice to the commander and crew of the *Trumbull* was that the Supreme Court could do nothing about it.

The second stage of a "rethinking" process would emphasize the critical importance of recognizing the retroactivity problem in the law-changing decision itself. The problem that the Court faced in *Linkletter* in 1965 was obvious in 1961, when *Mapp v. Ohio* was decided, and it should have been faced then, just as the problem that the Court faced in *Johnson* in 1982 was obvious and should have been faced in 1980, when *Payton* was decided.

The suggestion is not new. In 1934 a law review note described an early Pennsylvania case that gave judgment for the plaintiff "not because he had the law but because he was entitled to believe he had it when he took the mortgage," and commented:[87]

> Inconsistency between an overruling decision and subsequent cases may be eliminated if the problem is faced when the overruling case is before the court. At that time the court must consider whether the reasons in favor of overruling justify whatever confusion and hardship may be expected to result in future cases from reliance on the precedents. If the seriousness of the error is deemed to warrant an overruling notwithstanding probable hardship to present and future litigants, the overruling decision should become law for any future case. The argument that one party to the later case was "entitled to believe that he had [the law]" will have been anticipated and answered in the overruling case.

Professor Beytagh has pointed out that if the question of retroactivity is not faced initially, it is "likely to fester in the lower courts for a few years and then return to the Court for final resolution."[88] And former Chief Justice Roger J. Traynor recently said that he perceived nonretroactive rulings as presenting "two concomitant but distinct issues. First, should there be a new rule? If so, a second issue would be whether to apply the new rule retroactively. Since the issue of retroactivity turns on reliance, a party who may have significantly relied on the overruled precedent is very differently

---

[87] Note, *The Effect of Overruled and Overruling Decisions on Intervening Transactions*, 47 HARV. L. REV. 1403, 1413 (footnotes omitted) (1934).

[88] Beytagh, note 18 *supra*, at 1588.

situated from parties in the future who will have no comparable basis for reliance."[89]

A third approach to "rethinking" would consider again the desirability of adopting a method that would eliminate the inequalities that are inherent under *Linkletter* and *Stovall-Denno*. The law-changing decision could apply the existing rule to the case before it, but the opinion could also announce a new rule which would govern all future events and transactions. This technique is known as "purely prospective" ruling; it has also been termed "prospective-prospective."

Because the predictive portion of such an opinion has no binding force, it has been considered subject to the objection that it is an advisory opinion and so beyond the capacity of courts whose jurisdiction is limited to cases or controversies. But the purely prospective judicial opinion does not have all the objectionable characteristics of an advisory opinion. In his analysis of advisory opinions, then Professor Felix Frankfurter pointed out: "Advisory opinions are bound to move in an unreal atmosphere. The impact of actuality and the intensities of immediacy are wanting. . . . Advisory opinions are rendered upon sterilized and mutilated issues."[90] Those characteristics are not present in the purely prospective ruling. The issue that the court decides has not been sent to it by a doubting legislature, perhaps seeking to avoid its own responsibilities. It has arisen in an actual case, brought before the court by adversary parties in the ordinary course of litigation.

A purely prospective ruling is, however, subject to other objections. Since the new rule it announces has no effect whatsoever upon the parties to the case, it is technically dictum and so, theoretically at least, it is not binding upon other courts or even, in future cases, upon the court that announces it. Indeed, there have been instances in which courts have walked away from previous purely prospective rulings, but they are isolated.[91] The practical criticism that litigants will not urge the overruling of undesirable precedents if their success will bring no tangible reward is important. It is by

---

[89] Traynor, *Essay in Law*, 1980 UTAH L. REV. 255, 269.

[90] Frankfurter, *A Note on Advisory Opinions*, 37 HARV. L. REV. 1002, 1006 (1924).

[91] See, *e.g.*, Scheele v. City of Anchorage, 385 P.2d 582 (Alaska 1963); City of Fairbanks v. Schaible, 375 P.2d 201 (Alaska 1962); Naftalin v. King, 257 Minn. 498, 102 N.W.2d 301 (1960); Naftalin v. King, 252 Minn. 381, 90 N.W.2d 185 (1958).

no means a complete answer to point to the institutional litigant in civil cases. And in criminal cases a public defender represents an individual defendant and can hardly ethically advocate a result that will not benefit his client.

The purely prospective law-changing decision would give full scope to the reliance factor. It would, however, disregard completely the purpose of the change in the law—a factor that has been heavily emphasized by the Court. Another difficulty with a purely prospective overruling has not been recognized in judicial opinions, but I suspect that it weighs at least as heavily with reviewing courts as those that have been mentioned. It is the psychological fact that the dissatisfaction with the existing rule that is strong enough to produce an overruling decision is usually also strong enough to produce a tangible result in the case at hand.

Rethinking retroactivity should result also in abandonment of the quest for an overriding general principle that will govern all cases. The retroactive impact of an overruling judicial decision is the same as the impact of a judicial determination of statutory invalidity, and what was said by Chief Justice Hughes in *Chicot County Drainage District v. Baxter State Bank* is equally applicable to overruling decisions:[92]

> The actual existence of a statute, prior to such a determination, is an operative fact and may have consequences which cannot justly be ignored. The past cannot always be erased by a new judicial declaration. The effect of the subsequent ruling as to invalidity may have to be considered in various aspects,—with respect to particular relations, individual and corporate and particular conduct, private and official. Questions of rights claimed to have become vested, of status, of prior determinations deemed to have finality and acted upon accordingly, of public policy in the light of the nature both of the statute and of its previous application, demand examination. These questions are among the most difficult of those which have engaged the attention of courts, state and federal, and it is manifest from numerous decisions that an all inclusive statement of a principle of absolute retroactive invalidity cannot be justified.

A final significant benefit that could result from a rethinking of retroactivity would be an express or tacit recognition that any change in the law is not just a change in an abstract doctrine, that it

---

[92] 308 U.S. 371, 374 (1940).

has an impact on the events and transactions in the lives of real people. Recognition of that fact was responsible for the rules of construction that militate against retroactive legislation as well as the constitutional provisions relating to *ex post facto* laws and the impairment of contracts. A conscious awareness of that fact by judges who are considering the effect to be given a law-changing judicial decision might reduce the strident pitch of the judicial decisions on the question and produce less rhetoric and more reasoning.

DOUGLAS G. BAIRD

BANKRUPTCY PROCEDURE AND STATE-CREATED RIGHTS: THE LESSONS OF GIBBONS AND MARATHON

During the 1981 Term, the Supreme Court found two federal bankruptcy laws unconstitutional. Neither case raised much notice initially. The *Wall Street Journal* mentioned neither in an article that purported to summarize the important business opinions of the Term. One of the first hints in the press that either case might have a noticeable impact on the day-to-day workings of the federal judiciary appeared in an advertisement in late summer that explained why the Manville Corporation had filed a Chapter 11 petition. In this advertisement, the president of Manville stated, almost as an afterthought, that Congress needed to straighten out "an important technical point of bankruptcy court jurisdiction." His concern arose from one of the bankruptcy cases in which the Supreme Court struck down all the jurisdictional provisions of the Bankruptcy Reform Act of 1978. The "technical point" about the jurisdiction of the bankruptcy courts was that, in the absence of congressional action, they would have none.

Bankruptcy law, both in its historical antecedents and in its day-to-day workings, is concerned with sorting out the claims of com-

Douglas G. Baird is Assistant Professor of Law, The University of Chicago.
AUTHOR'S NOTE: I thank Albert Alschuler, Walter Blum, David Currie, Frank Easterbrook, Thomas Jackson, Richard Posner, and Cass Sunstein for their helpful comments.

peting creditors and with ensuring that valid claims against the debtor are paid to the greatest extent possible.[1] The needs of creditors shape the structure of bankruptcy law and bankruptcy proceedings. As important as a discharge in bankruptcy may be for individuals as a matter of policy, the presence or absence of a right to discharge has little effect on the way the Bankruptcy Code is structured. The debtor's right to discharge could be removed from the Bankruptcy Code without greatly affecting most of its other provisions.[2] This observation about bankruptcy law—that it has been and remains largely a federal forum in which the state-created rights of competing creditors are sorted out—helps to illuminate the two bankruptcy cases the Court decided this Term.

I

Railway Labor Executives' Association v. Gibbons[3] was the first of the two bankruptcy cases. In 1975, the Rock Island Railroad filed a petition for reorganization under the 1898 Bankruptcy Act. It continued to operate until 1979, when a labor strike halted its operations. Nine months later the district court directed the total abandonment of the railroad system. All the assets of the railroad were to be liquidated and divided among its creditors. The railroads that acquired some of Rock Island's trackage hired some of its former employees. Many of the employees, however, remained out

---

[1] See Jackson, *Bankruptcy, Non-Bankruptcy Entitlements, and the Creditors' Bargain*, 91 YALE L.J. 857 (1982). As part of providing individual debtors with a fresh start, the Code does, however, allow individuals to exempt some property, such as the tools of their trade, from the claims of creditors. A state's own exemptions for debtors, however, can override federal exemptions. See 11 U.S.C. § 522 (Supp. III 1979). The Seventh Circuit has rejected the argument that the provisions of the Bankruptcy Code that allow states to opt out of the federal exemptions violate the uniformity requirement of the Bankruptcy Clause. See *In re Sullivan*, 680 F.2d 1131 (7th Cir. 1982).

[2] Many of the hundreds of thousands of bankruptcy disputes heard every year are brought by individual debtors. If a discharge of past indebtedness were made unavailable (or less freely available), one might expect the number of filings to drop. See S. Rep. No. 446, 97th Cong., 2d Sess. 2–3 (1982). Whether an individual debtor has a right to discharge or whether a particular debt is dischargeable are questions that can and do generate litigation. The existence of a discharge right, therefore, may have a profound effect on the docket of the bankruptcy judge. My point, however, goes to the many other issues that a bankruptcy judge must face. The presence or absence of a discharge right has only a small effect on such issues as rights of secured creditors in bankruptcy, priorities among unsecured creditors, voidable preferences, fraudulent conveyances, automatic stay, adequate protection, and rejection of executory contracts.

[3] 102 S. Ct. 1169 (1982).

of work and they had no claim against the railroad. They were not owed back wages, and the district court found that a federal statute that required a railroad to compensate employees who lost their jobs as a result of a reorganization did not apply when a railroad liquidated and ceased operation.[4]

Congress responded by passing the Rock Island Transition and Employee Assistance Act, which granted displaced employees of Rock Island Railroad a claim against the railroad to compensate them for their lost jobs for a four-year period.[5] Congress also directed that the employees' claims be honored before those of any general creditors. In the event that the assets of the railroad could not satisfy the claims of the workers, Congress directed the Secretary of Transportation to guarantee the claims up to $75 million.

The effect of this legislation was to transfer millions of dollars from those who had lent money to the railroad to former employees, who, before the legislation, had no cognizable legal claim against the railroad. Congress stated in the legislation that uninterrupted service over Rock Island lines depended upon adequate employee protection and that a cessation of services would seriously affect the public. The legislation, however, came months after the Rock Island Railroad had ceased operating and after the district court had decided to liquidate the railroad. Although other railroads might function more smoothly if their employees were protected, by its terms the legislation applied only to the Rock Island Railroad.

The district court struck down the statute as an unconstitutional taking of property without just compensation. When Congress protects displaced employees, taxpayers—rather than investors in a particular enterprise—typically bear the cost. Yet the investors in this case were general creditors; they did not have a security interest in specific assets of their debtor as did the secured creditors who successfully challenged the constitutionality of the Frazier-Lemke Act during the 1930s.[6] In the Bankruptcy Code itself, Congress readjusts the rights of general creditors and subordinates their interests, for example, to the claims of workers earned ninety days

---

[4] *Id.* at 1172. The district court was construing the Milwaukee Railroad Restructuring Act, § 17(a), 45 U.S.C. § 915(a) (Supp. III 1979).

[5] 45 U.S.C. § 1001 *et seq.* (Supp. IV 1980).

[6] Louisville Joint Stock Land Bank v. Radford, 295 U.S. 555 (1935).

before the date of the petition[7] and the claims of individuals for the purchase of consumer goods.[8] The statute at issue in *Gibbons* was arguably a taking of property, however, not only because employees were granted special rights but also because the investors in this railroad were being forced to bear burdens that others similarly situated (such as investors in other insolvent railroads) were not.

Congress responded to the district court's invalidation of the statute by providing, in a piece of amending legislation, that if the statute did constitute a taking, the general creditors could bring an action against the United States under the Tucker Act. The district court nonetheless declined to reconsider its original decision that the statute was unconstitutional.

The Supreme Court never reached the Fifth Amendment question. It held that Congress lacked the power to pass the legislation regardless of whether the investors were compensated. Writing for the Court, Justice Rehnquist found that the Constitution limited the Congress to passing uniform laws on the subject of bankruptcies. Because the legislation in *Gibbons* responded to the problems of a single bankrupt railroad, it was not uniform. The decision was the first to strike down bankruptcy legislation on the ground that it was not uniform,[9] and it was only the third time that the Court found a bankruptcy statute constitutionally defective on any ground.[10]

To invalidate the legislation, Justice Rehnquist had to show that the uniformity provision of the Bankruptcy Clause limited Congress's ability to enact the same legislation under another one of its enumerated powers, such as its power to regulate commerce among the several states. In recent years, Congress's power to regulate interstate commerce has been virtually limitless. If Congress can use its power to regulate interstate commerce to reach Ollie's Bar-

---

[7] 11 U.S.C. § 507(a)(3) (Supp. III 1979) (limited to $2,000).

[8] 11 U.S.C. § 507(a)(5) (Supp. III 1979) (limited to $900).

[9] Hanover Nat'l Bank v. Moyses, 186 U.S. 181 (1902); Stellwagen v. Clum, 245 U.S. 605 (1918); Vanston Bondholders Protective Comm. v. Green, 329 U.S. 156, 172–73 (1946) (Frankfurter, J., dissenting); Blanchette v. Connecticut Gen. Ins. Corp. (The Regional Railroad Reorganization Act Cases), 419 U.S. 102 (1974).

[10] Louisville Joint Stock Land Bank v. Radford, 295 U.S. 555 (1935) (Frazier-Lemke Act invalidated on Fifth Amendment grounds); Ashton v. Cameron County Water Improvement Dist. No. 1, 298 U.S. 513 (1936) (municipal bankruptcy law held an unconstitutional encroachment on state powers).

becue in Birmingham, Alabama,[11] it would not seem to require a great leap of imagination to conclude that the same clause gave it the power to control the dismantling of a railroad that extended over several states. In neither case, one might argue, must one ask if Congress also could have passed the same law under another enumerated power.

Justice Rehnquist, however, reasoned that the Bankruptcy Clause requires that all federal bankruptcy legislation must be uniform regardless of whether another clause of the Constitution might have empowered Congress to enact such legislation in the absence of the Bankruptcy Clause. This more specific clause contains both a grant of power and a limitation upon it: The Clause provides both that Congress may enact bankruptcy laws and that Congress may not enact bankruptcy laws that are not uniform.[12]

In *Gibbons*, Justice Rehnquist assumed that each grant of power affects the scope of other grants. The Framers would not have written both a broad Commerce Clause that appears to comprehend bankruptcy laws and a limited Bankruptcy Clause, unless they intended the Bankruptcy Clause to limit the otherwise broad commerce power. The importance of Justice Rehnquist's method of using one clause of the Constitution to limit another may lie in its effect in areas other than bankruptcy law. For example, Congress has some powers under the Fourteenth Amendment it does not have under the Commerce Clause and vice versa. The interaction between these two provisions has yet to be fully explored.[13]

The general problem of the construction of section 8 of Article I of the Constitution is not often addressed squarely. In his discussion of section 8, William Winslow Crosskey, who read the Com-

---

[11] Katzenbach v. McClung, 379 U.S. 294 (1964).

[12] The Constitution gives Congress the power "To establish an uniform Rule of Naturalization, and uniform Laws on the subject of Bankruptcies throughout the United States." U.S. Const. Art. I, § 8, cl. 4. For Justice Rehnquist's analysis, see 102 S. Ct. at 1176 ("Unlike the Commerce Clause, the Bankruptcy Clause itself contains an affirmative limitation or restriction upon Congress' power: bankruptcy laws must be uniform throughout the United States. Such uniformity in the applicability of legislation is not required by the Commerce Clause. . . . Thus, if we were to hold that Congress had the power to enact nonuniform bankruptcy laws pursuant to the Commerce Clause, we would eradicate from the Constitution a limitation on the power of Congress to enact bankruptcy laws").

[13] See, *e.g.*, EEOC v. Wyoming, 514 F. Supp. 595 (D. Wyo. 1981), *prob. juris. noted*, 102 S. Ct. 996 (1982).

merce Clause expansively, found the technique of "enumerating of particular governmental powers *in order* to express limitations upon them . . . a favorite device of the Federal Convention."[14] Crosskey believed that only by interpreting a limited enumeration of one power as creating a correlative limitation on other powers could meaning be given to every part of the Constitution.

There are several responses to Justice Rehnquist and Professor Crosskey's position. First, the drafters of the Constitution knew that circumstances would change over time and that others would be the arbiters of the meaning of the document. The Framers might have wanted to ensure that Congress could enact uniform laws on the subject of bankruptcies, regardless of how the Commerce Clause came to be construed. Although the canon of interpretation that clauses of a constitution should not be redundant is useful, it is not absolute. The Framers might well have accepted some redundancy as a cost of being clear. Second, even if one wanted to avoid redundancy, one is not compelled to construe words of grant as both a grant of power and a limitation of power. One can also interpret each grant narrowly. The presence of a clause granting one power may be evidence that the power granted by another is narrow. This second rejoinder, of course, is not available to those who have already concluded, as did Crosskey, that the Commerce Clause must be interpreted broadly.[15]

But even if the Bankruptcy Clause limits Congress's power, one must still determine what limitations the requirement that bankruptcy laws be uniform imposes. Justice Rehnquist reasoned that a bankruptcy law was "uniform" only if it applied generally. Congress is forbidden to pass private bankruptcy bills. A bankruptcy law is not uniform if it applies to only the division of the assets of a

---

[14] 1 CROSSKEY, POLITICS AND THE CONSTITUTION IN THE HISTORY OF THE UNITED STATES 486 (1953).

[15] One might argue that Congress lacked the power to enact the statute under either its bankruptcy power or its commerce power. These powers allow Congress to pass legislation that promotes commerce among the several states or helps to sort out rights among creditors and between creditors and their debtor, and the statute involved here, being the narrowest kind of special interest legislation, arguably does neither. It does not affect commerce because the railroad is defunct, and it is not a bankruptcy law because the ex-workers are not creditors. The weakness of this argument is that the commerce power has been interpreted expansively and embraces employer-employee relations and the rights of the unemployed. In these areas, as in others, Congress has broad powers to create causes of action and establish claims where none existed before. See, *e.g.*, Turner Elkhorn Mining Co. v. Usery, 428 U.S. 1 (1976).

single debtor, such as the Rock Island Railroad. Justice Rehnquist rested his conclusion in part on his interpretation of the Clause's drafting history. At the time of the Constitutional Convention, several states had no general insolvency law and debtors had to petition their state legislatures to be discharged from their debts or to be protected from imprisonment.[16] This feature of debtor relief law seems to have brought the attention of the Convention to the subject of bankruptcy.

On August 29, 1787, the Convention considered Article XVI of the draft Constitution reported by the Committee of Detail on August 6. This Article largely repeated the full faith and credit clause of the Articles of Confederation, but added a requirement that full faith be given to the acts of state legislatures as well as to the records and judicial proceedings of state courts. A delegate from the floor asked why the change had been made. He was told that some acts of a legislature—such as acts of insolvency—served the same purpose as judgments of a court and ought therefore to be treated the same way. Charles Pinckney then proposed to give to Congress the power to establish uniform laws upon the subject of bankruptcies.[17] Thus, the Framers considered giving Congress the power to enact bankruptcy laws immediately after a discussion of private acts of insolvency. This sequence of events, however, does not explain why Pinckney proposed that Congress's power to enact bankruptcy laws be limited to enacting laws that were "uniform." Possibly Pinckney feared that Congress would abuse its power if it could pass special legislation that, like some state insolvency acts, applied only to the affairs of an individual debtor.[18] It follows from this interpretation that the statute in *Gibbons* is suspect, because it applied only to the Rock Island Railroad.

This historical interpretation, however, assumes a connection between state insolvency law and bankruptcy law that the Framers may not have made. In the *Federalist Papers*, James Madison talked about the Bankruptcy Clause just before talking about the full faith and credit clause:[19]

---

[16] See Nadelmann, *On the Origin of the Bankruptcy Clause*, 1 AM. J. LEGAL HIST. 215, 221 (1957). Nadelmann provides a comprehensive review of the drafting of the Bankruptcy Clause.

[17] 2 FARRAND, THE RECORDS OF THE FEDERAL CONVENTION OF 1787, at 447 (1911).

[18] Crosskey draws this inference. See 1 CROSSKEY, note 14 *supra*, at 491–92.

[19] FEDERALIST PAPERS, No. 42 at 277–78.

> The power of establishing uniform laws of bankruptcy is so intimately connected with the regulation of commerce, and will prevent so many frauds where the parties or their property may lie or be removed into different States, that the expediency of it seems not likely to be drawn into question.

Madison talks about the Bankruptcy Clause not as if it were for the protection of debtors but rather as if it were for the protection of creditors. In any event, his attention focused on disputes that cross jurisdictions. The Framers may have wanted bankruptcy laws because a federal cause of action would provide a federal forum for resolving debtor-creditor disputes, which often involved the conflicting laws of several jurisdictions.

From this perspective, the "uniformity" requirement takes on a different meaning. Rather than preventing Congress from passing private bills, the uniformity requirement was intended to ensure that Congress enacted laws that were applicable across jurisdictions. (If they were not, the point of creating federal laws on bankruptcy—facilitating the resolution of disputes across several jurisdictions—would be lost.) In other words, the final phrase of the Bankruptcy Clause describes the respect in which the bankruptcy laws must be "uniform": They must be "uniform" "throughout the United States."

This interpretation of the uniformity requirement seems plausible for a number of reasons. First, while no evidence suggests that state legislatures abused their power to pass private acts of insolvency, multijurisdictional disputes involving insolvent debtors and their creditors were actively litigated at the time of the Convention. Indeed, one of the delegates, Jared Ingersoll, appeared in two of them. The state courts that heard such cases had to choose between refusing to recognize as binding a discharge granted in another jurisdiction[20] and recognizing the discharge as binding upon a creditor who had not been to the other jurisdiction and who had no actual notice of the insolvency proceeding and no opportunity to collect his pro rata share of the debtor's assets.[21]

Moreover, this interpretation is consistent with the general

---

[20] James v. Allen, 1 Dallas 188 (Pa. C.P. 1786).

[21] Miller v. Hall, 1 Dallas 229 (Pa. 1788). *Miller* was pending at the time of the Convention. Ingersoll represented the creditor in the first case and the debtor in the second. He prevailed in both. James v. Allen and Miller v. Hall are discussed in Nadelmann, note 16 *supra*, at 224–25.

understanding of the Congress's power to pass a uniform rule on the subject of naturalization, which is granted in the same clause of the Constitution. Just before he talked about the Bankruptcy Clause in the *Federalist Papers*, Madison discussed the naturalization clause, and emphasized that the need for a uniform naturalization rule stemmed from the disparities in the rules of naturalization in the several states.[22] In another number of the *Federalist Papers*, Hamilton explicitly recognized that a uniform federal rule was the only alternative to distinct rules in each of the states.[23] Madison and Hamilton were concerned that citizens of one jurisdiction might not be citizens in another. They did not suggest that Congress was forbidden to pass special private bills that naturalize a particular person.[24] Rather, Congress was simply forbidden to pass a bill that, for example, made someone a citizen of Virginia, but not of Pennsylvania.[25]

Finally, this interpretation of the uniformity provision is consistent with the eighteenth-century distinction between "bankruptcy" and "insolvency" laws. The former emphasized the rights of merchants and traders and enabled them to force an insolvent debtor to gather his assets and distribute them to his creditors. A debtor could not initiate bankruptcy proceedings until well into the nineteenth century. Special acts that ailing debtors could call upon were "insolvency acts," not "bankruptcy laws."[26] If the Framers

---

[22] FEDERALIST PAPERS, No. 42 at 276–77.

[23] *Ibid.*, No. 32 at 195.

[24] Indeed, Congress has, from time to time, passed special private bills that naturalized particular individuals. *E.g.*, Nellie Grant Sartoris, 30 Stat. 1496 (1898); Eugene Prince, 37 Stat. 1346 (1912); George Edward Lerrigo, 38 Stat. 1476 (1915); Augusta Louise de Haven-Alten, 41 Stat. 1463 (1920); Mary Cohen Bienvenu, 53 Stat. 1533 (1939); see Hazard, *The Immigration and Nationality Systems of the United States of America*, 14 F.R.D. 105, 126 n.90 (1954). More recently, Congress has passed private bills that direct the INS to issue an individual a visa for permanent residence. *E.g.*, Dr. Toomas Eisler & Carmen Elizabeth Eisler, 94 Stat. 3623 (1980).

[25] One should not press the analogy between a rule on naturalization and laws on the subject of bankruptcies too far. The former refers to a single uniform rule, the latter to multiple uniform laws. The two clauses were joined late in the Convention. See Nadelmann, note 16 *supra*, at 217 n.10. Moreover, while bankruptcy law by its nature affects state-created rights (the creditor's claim), the law governing naturalizations is exclusively federal. See Nemetz v. INS, 647 F.2d 432 (4th Cir. 1981) (INS cannot defer to state law prohibition of homosexuality to determine whether alien has good moral character).

[26] John C. Calhoun railed against the obliteration of the Framer's distinction in congressional debates in the 1840s. See WARREN, BANKRUPTCY IN UNITED STATES HISTORY 61–62 (1930).

intended to empower Congress to pass laws that aided insolvent debtors, but to forbid Congress to pass private laws that freed particular debtors from past debt or imprisonment, they would likely have used the word "insolvencies" instead of "bankruptcies" in the Constitution.

The lone vote cast against the Bankruptcy Clause was based on grounds that had little to do with insolvency statutes—the dissenter feared that giving Congress the power to pass bankruptcy laws would permit Congress to punish bankruptcies by death, as had been done in England. The response to this objection was not that bankruptcy laws were debtor-protection measures, but rather that there was little danger of abuse.[27]

This interpretation of "uniformity" might lead to a different result in *Gibbons*, because the statute in issue, though it applied only to the Rock Island Railroad, applied uniformly to all its assets regardless of the jurisdiction in which they were located. This view of uniformity would have been consistent with earlier litigation over the uniformity requirement, which focused not on the problem of private legislation, but on the extent to which a bankruptcy law could adopt substantive rules of different states and still remain uniform in the constitutional sense. In *Hanover National Bank v. Moyses*,[28] the Court upheld a provision of the 1898 Act incorporating state statutes that exempted some of a debtor's property (such as his clothes and tools of trade) from execution. The amount of these exemptions and the property they covered varied from state to state. The creditor argued that the 1898 Bankruptcy Act was not uniform, because the size of a creditor's recovery against a debtor in a bankruptcy proceeding depended upon the state in which the debtor lived. The Court rejected this argument. The effect of a bankruptcy law was the same as a general levy upon all of a debtor's property for the benefit of all the creditors. A bankruptcy law was uniform, in the constitutional sense, when the property that was available to the creditors was the same property that would have been subject to levy had the bankruptcy law not been passed.[29]

In *Hanover National Bank*, the Court explicitly recognized that federal bankruptcy law is largely procedural, rather than substan-

---

[27] 2 FARRAND, note 17 *supra*, at 489.

[28] 186 U.S. 181 (1902).

[29] *Id.* at 189–90.

tive, as far as the creditors are concerned. Of course, various provisions of the bankruptcy law work substantive changes on creditor's claims, but the claims themselves exist independently of federal bankruptcy law. A bankruptcy proceeding is principally a forum in which all of a debtor's creditors can gather, assemble the debtor's assets, and divide them among themselves, according to the rights that state law gives them.[30] Creditors value bankruptcy laws because in their absence each creditor would have to resort to separate proceedings in state court. Each could vindicate his rights by levying on property of the debtor, but rights to the debtor's property would be determined by whoever levied first. Creditors collectively benefit more from having a single proceeding in which the debtor's assets can be assembled and divided up in an efficient and orderly way than from racing each other to the courthouse to divide the debtor's assets piecemeal. Federal bankruptcy law provides a single forum and procedures that are directed specifically at the problem of identifying claims and gathering assets. Moreover, federal bankruptcy law reduces the debtor's chance of defrauding his creditors by hiding his assets or by playing one creditor off against another.

In short, the crucial battle over the central meaning of the uniformity requirement was fought at the beginning of this century. The Bankruptcy Clause does not require a federal definition of substantive rights that remains constant across jurisdictions. Because federal bankruptcy law is in the first instance procedural, the Bankruptcy Clause simply requires that the basic federal bankruptcy procedure does not vary significantly from one state to another. Congress cannot enact bankruptcy laws that apply only in South Dakota and leave creditors in every other jurisdiction with recourse only to state law.

Justice Rehnquist did not recognize that the uniformity requirement reconciles the constitutional requirement of consistency across jurisdictions with the need to recognize the different state substantive rights that underlie all bankruptcy adjudication. If he had, *Gibbons* might have been decided differently. To adopt his

---

[30] See Butner v. United States, 440 U.S. 48, 54–55 (1979) ("Apart from [provisions governing fraudulent conveyances and voidable preferences], Congress has generally left the determination of property rights in the assets of a bankrupt's estate to state law. Property interests are created and defined by state law. Unless some federal interest requires a different result, there is no reason why such interests should be analyzed differently simply because an interested party is involved in a bankruptcy proceeding").

view of uniformity as a ban on private bankruptcy bills, Justice Rehnquist had to overcome a number of difficult problems. He had to reconcile different and apparently overlapping grants of power in the Constitution; he had to infer a distaste for private bills from ambiguous historical evidence; and he had to distinguish this case from one the Court heard only six years earlier, in which it rejected out of hand the argument that a statute was invalid because it applied to a single insolvency proceeding.[31] These difficulties, however, pale beside those the Court faced in the second bankruptcy case it decided last Term.

II

Northern Pipeline Construction Corp. v. Marathon Pipe Line Co.[32] was, like *Gibbons*, a bankruptcy dispute fought on constitutional terrain. Northern brought a contract action against Marathon about a year before Northern filed a petition in bankruptcy court. Northern's suit against Marathon (its possibility of recovering a money judgment) was an asset of the estate that could help to satisfy the claims of Northern's creditors. Northern removed the action to the bankruptcy court so that this question could be adjudicated along with the others that concerned Northern. Marathon, however, claimed that the bankruptcy court had no jurisdiction over the dispute, because resolving such a dispute was inherently an exercise of the "judicial power," which Article III entrusts to judges who, unlike bankruptcy judges, enjoy life tenure and an undiminishable salary.

The Supreme Court held that the bankruptcy judge lacked jurisdiction over the dispute between Northern and Marathon because he was not an Article III judge. Moreover, because the provision of the Bankruptcy Reform Act of 1978 that granted the bankruptcy judge jurisdiction over this dispute was inextricably linked with the remaining jurisdictional provisions, the Court struck them all down. The Court stayed its judgment until October 4 to give Congress time to enact appropriate legislation. It later extended the stay. Justice Brennan wrote the plurality opinion, in which Justices

---

[31] Blanchette v. Connecticut Gen. Ins. Corp. (The Regional Railroad Reorganization Act Cases), 419 U.S. 102 (1974).

[32] 102 S. Ct. 2858 (1982).

Blackmun, Stevens, and Marshall joined. Justice Rehnquist, joined by Justice O'Connor, tipped the balance against the statute in a concurring opinion.

Article III requires that the "judicial power" be vested in courts whose judges enjoy life tenure and an undiminishable salary, and bankruptcy judges under the Bankruptcy Reform Act of 1978 enjoy neither. Thus, if the question were approached on a blank slate, it would not seem to be difficult. Bankruptcy judges do seem to exercise a power that might fairly be called judicial. The differences between the powers of a district judge and those of a bankruptcy judge do not seem relevant for purposes of Article III.

Under the 1978 Code, bankruptcy judges have jurisdiction over all civil proceedings arising in or related to bankruptcy proceedings. If a debtor in a bankruptcy proceeding is enmeshed in an antitrust dispute, the bankruptcy judge has jurisdiction over the case.[33] A bankruptcy judge may have jurisdiction over a property dispute between spouses that turns on state divorce law.[34] There are few civil proceedings over which a bankruptcy judge will not have jurisdiction as long as a plausible connection between the civil proceeding and the Bankruptcy Code can be drawn.

Moreover, the bankruptcy judge can issue writs of habeas corpus.[35] He can conduct jury trials[36] and hold individuals in contempt.[37] Appeal from a bankruptcy court lies either in the district court or the court of appeals. A bankruptcy judge's findings of fact, like the findings of fact of a district judge, are subject only to appellate review. A bankruptcy judge's powers differ from a district judge's in only three respects: (1) his jurisdiction extends only to civil proceedings that are related in some way to Title 11 of the United States Code;[38] (2) he cannot enjoin other courts;[39] and (3) he can hold individuals in criminal contempt only for acts committed in his presence and he cannot punish these contempts with impris-

---

[33] *E.g.*, *In re* Repair & Maintenance Parts Corp., 19 Bankr. 575 (Bankr. N.D. Ill. 1982).

[34] *In re* Heslar, 16 Bankr. 329 (Bankr. W.D. Mich. 1981). In this case, as in several others, the bankruptcy judge, after he decided he had jurisdiction, abstained and left the resolution of the issue to the state courts.

[35] 28 U.S.C. § 2256 (Supp. III 1979).

[36] *Id.* § 1480.

[37] *Id.* § 1481.

[38] *Id.* § 1471.

[39] *Id.* § 1481.

onment.[40] None of these limitations on the bankruptcy judge's power seem to transform the power from one that is essentially "judicial" into something else.

The Supreme Court did not face a blank slate. Chief Justice Marshall recognized that Congress had the power to create tribunals that would act as courts in territories.[41] Subsequent interpretations by the Supreme Court of the mandates of Article III have for the most part recognized Congress's power to carve out one exception after another. Congress has the power to create courts martial.[42] Moreover, Congress can create Article I tribunals to adjudicate some rights between the government and individuals, provided that the rights are not inherently judicial.[43] Finally, Congress can create administrative agencies that can decide disputes between private individuals, such as those between employer and employee, that concern "public rights."[44] The Supreme Court summarized these exceptions in *Palmore v. United States*:[45]

> [T]he requirements of Art. III, which are applicable where laws of national applicability and affairs of national concern are at stake, must in proper circumstances give way to accommodate plenary grants of power to Congress to legislate with respect to specialized areas having particularized needs and warranting distinctive treatment.

It is difficult to place the bankruptcy courts into one of the exceptions. It is also difficult to argue that bankruptcy is a specialized area that falls within Congress's power to create Article I tribunals. The clause that gives Congress the power to enact laws on the subject of bankruptcies is no different from clauses in Article I and constitutional amendments that give Congress the power to enact laws on other subjects. If Congress can create lower federal tribunals under Article I to govern bankrupty disputes, it follows that Congress can create lower federal tribunals to govern copyright disputes, commerce disputes, and, for that matter, civil rights

---

[40] *Ibid.*

[41] American Ins. Co. v. Canter, 26 U.S. (1 Pet.) 511 (1828).

[42] Dynes v. Hoover, 61 U.S. (20 How.) 65 (1858).

[43] Murray's Lessee v. Hoboken Land & Improvement Co., 59 U.S. (18 How.) 272 (1856).

[44] Crowell v. Benson, 285 U.S. 22, 51 (1932) (dictum).

[45] 411 U.S. 389, 407–8 (1973).

disputes. Limiting the subject matter over which a tribunal could act should not enable Congress to escape the dictates of Article III.

But even if Congress could create Article I bankruptcy tribunals by restricting the jurisdiction of the tribunal, it did not do so in the 1978 Code. The jurisdiction of the bankruptcy courts is not "specialized" in the sense that only a narrow class of disputes can come before them. No Article III judge exercises jurisdiction over a wider range of disputes. Perhaps Article III of the Constitution might be satisfied if an Article III court could review the decisions of judges who lack life tenure and undiminishable salaries, but this conclusion does not follow naturally from language that vests the judicial power "in one supreme Court, and in such inferior Courts as the Congress may from time to time ordain and establish."[46]

Finally, the rights a bankruptcy judge adjudicates do not seem to be "public rights" that an Article I administrative tribunal is competent to decide. Many, such as the breach of contract action at issue in *Marathon*, arise under state common law. If such rights are "public," then so are all other rights that are subject to litigation.[47]

In *Marathon*, the Court embarked on a long dissertation on the history of Article III cases. Inevitably, it tried to reconcile its decision with as many earlier ones as possible. But no amount of historical exegesis could save the Court from deciding between two unpleasant alternatives: either Article III does not apply to lower federal trial tribunals, or it does. The first alternative would have been unpalatable, because it would render illusory the apparent requirement that those exercising the judicial power have life tenure. Why would the Framers empower Congress to create inferior federal courts whose judges must have tenure for life and an undiminishable salary and also tribunals that do exactly the same thing but whose judges need to have neither tenure for life nor an undiminishable salary? The argument Justice Rehnquist used in *Gibbons*, that one constitutional provision implicitly limits another, operates with greater force here, because an essential part of the balance between the legislature and the judiciary is at stake.

---

[46] U.S. Const. Art. III, § 1.

[47] David Currie has carefully placed *Marathon* against the background of a century and a half of Article III litigation in *Bankruptcy Judges and the Independent Judiciary*, 16 CREIGHTON L. REV.———(1982).

The second alternative would have been unpalatable because of its costs. Finding that courts that hear over half a million disputes a year lack jurisdiction has practical consequences. The simplest course available to Congress is to make bankruptcy judges Article III judges, but appointing and confirming them would take time. In the 1978 Code, Congress allowed six years for the bankruptcy judges to be chosen and provided that the referees under the old Act (called bankruptcy judges since 1973) sit as temporary bankruptcy judges until the new judges took office in 1984. Congress expected the President, with the help of the Judicial Conference in each circuit, to find qualified individuals who wanted to be bankruptcy judges with fourteen-year terms. It would be odd to have Congress, in response to *Marathon*, establish an appointment process for Article III bankruptcy judges that was more casual, yet the Court should be reluctant to permit a stay until 1984. Such a stay would allow bankruptcy judges to exercise jurisdiction for years after the Court had ruled that such an exercise was unconstitutional.

Can bankruptcy judges be given little enough power so that they do not have to be Article III judges and yet enough power so that district courts do not become swamped and bankruptcy proceedings remain a useful forum in which creditors can sort out rights among themselves? A difficulty with this inquiry is that distinctions between Article III courts whose judges must have life tenure and Article I tribunals whose judges need not are difficult to find.

In his concurring opinion, Justice Rehnquist argued that the Court needed to decide only whether the bankruptcy courts could exercise jurisdiction over Marathon. This question he found straightforward:[48]

> From the record before us, the lawsuit in which Marathon was named defendant seeks damages for breach of contract, misrepresentation, and other counts which are the stuff of the traditional actions at common law tried by the courts at Westminster in 1789. There is apparently no federal rule of decision provided for any of the issues in the lawsuit; the claims of Northern arise entirely under state law. No method of adjudication is hinted, other than the traditional common law mode of judge and jury.

---

[48] 102 S. Ct. at 2881.

The lawsuit is before the Bankruptcy Court only because the plaintiff has previously filed a petition for reorganization in that Court.

Justice Rehnquist reasoned that because the dispute involved in *Marathon* had been regarded as judicial since time immemorial it could only be heard by an Article III judge. Justice Rehnquist reasoned further that he need not (and indeed should not) say more. Justice Rehnquist's position would have been more understandable if he had stated simply that a bankruptcy judge could not hear a dispute like the one in *Marathon* and that determining the exact contours of a bankruptcy judge's powers should await further litigation. Justice Rehnquist also agreed, however, with the plurality that the provision of the Bankruptcy Code giving the bankruptcy judge jurisdiction over this dispute was hopelessly entwined with all the other provisions giving the bankruptcy judge jurisdiction. *Marathon* did not merely adjudicate a dispute between two private parties; it forced Congress to rethink the relationship between bankruptcy jurisdiction and Article III. Given that Congress had to begin this inquiry quickly, Justice Rehnquist might well have explained his decision at greater length. Because his vote and Justice O'Connor's were the crucial ones, Congress must try to divine from Justice Rehnquist's opinion a sense of what would pass constitutional muster and what would not. It would have violated no deeply seated notion of jurisprudence for Justice Rehnquist to have ensured that he was not misunderstood.

The first person to interpret Justice Rehnquist's opinion and to advise Congress how to draft an appropriate statute was the Chief Justice. In his one-page dissenting opinion, he noted:[49]

> [T]he Court's holding is limited to the proposition stated by Justice Rehnquist in his concurrence in the judgment—that a "traditional" state common-law action, not made subject to a federal rule of decision, and related only peripherally to an adjudication of bankruptcy under federal law must, absent the consent of the litigants, be heard by an "Article III court" if it is to be heard by any court or agency of the United States. . . .
>
> It will not be necessary for Congress, in order to meet the requirements of the Court's holding, to undertake a radical restructuring of the present system of bankruptcy adjudication.

---

[49] *Id.* at 2882.

> The problems arising from today's judgment can be resolved
> simply by providing that ancillary common-law actions, such as
> the one involved in this case, be routed to the United States
> district court of which the bankruptcy court is an adjunct.

The Chief Justice's characterization of Justice Rehnquist's opinion
is somewhat puzzling. Nowhere in his opinion does Justice Rehnquist say that Marathon's state law claim must be heard by an
Article III court because it is "ancillary" or "peripheral" to a bankruptcy proceeding. Nor does Justice Rehnquist suggest that, had
the parties consented to the jurisdiction of the bankruptcy court,
the bankruptcy court would have had the power to hear the case.

The Chief Justice may have focused on the fact that the parties in
Marathon did not consent and on the fact that the dispute was
"ancillary" to the bankruptcy proceeding because these features
made *Marathon* a case that a bankruptcy referee could not have
heard under the 1898 Bankruptcy Act. One of the options for
Congress to consider in revising the Bankruptcy Code was a return
to the division of authority between district courts, the state courts,
and bankruptcy referees that was in effect under the old Act.

The jurisdictional provisions of the 1898 Act might seem to be a
safe harbor. But the referee system grew gradually over time, and
referees did not initially exercise the power that they ultimately
exercised under the 1973 Bankruptcy Rules. Although the Supreme Court promulgated these Rules, the Court's work merely
endorsed the efforts of an advisory committee that included referees and scholars. More important, none of the opinions explain how
the 1898 Act could be upheld in the wake of *Marathon*. In his
plurality opinion, Justice Brennan makes several distinctions between the old Act and the new Code, emphasizing in particular the
control of a district judge over the bankruptcy referee under the old
Act that did not exist under the new Code. But Justice Brennan
does not endorse the old Act, and explicitly notes that before
Marathon, the Court had not done so either.[50] In his dissent, Justice
White, joined by Justice Powell and the Chief Justice, insists that
the plurality never explains why the differences between the old
Act and the new Code are relevant for purposes of Article III.

Before the 1978 Code, bankruptcy law distinguished between

---

[50] *Id.* at 2876 n.31.

bankruptcy proceedings proper and other legal disputes in which a debtor who had filed a bankruptcy petition could be a party. Bankruptcy proceedings over which the referee presided were *in rem* actions. The referee supervised the gathering of property that was in the debtor's actual or constructive possession and then divided it among the creditors after he evaluated each of their claims. The referee had no jurisdiction over a dispute between a debtor and someone who owed the debtor money or refused to hand over the debtor's property, unless the person actually or constructively consented. The representative of the general creditors in the bankruptcy proceeding, the trustee in bankruptcy, had to pursue the party in state court or, if it had jurisdiction, in district court.

The law that preceded the 1898 Act was different. The Bankruptcy Act of 1867 provided for federal jurisdiction over both bankruptcy disputes and disputes between the representative of the general creditors and anyone who owed the estate money or held its property. The 1898 Act removed this second branch of jurisdiction from the federal courts, unless the parties consented. The trustee had to pursue those who did not themselves have claims against the bankruptcy estate in other forums. In other words, a distinction was made between state law actions brought against the estate and state law actions brought by the estate.

Just as the trustee may run the debtor's business and may enter into various transactions in order to preserve and enhance the value of the estate, so too can the trustee preserve and enhance the value of the estate by bringing a law suit. These actions merely increase the value of the assets that are available to satisfy the claims of the creditors. When these increases come only after years of litigation in another forum, they may make it hard to administer a bankruptcy proceeding, especially if a reorganization is involved and creditors are to be paid not in cash but in shares in the reorganized company. But the cost may not be so large that it interferes with the essential purpose of bankruptcy law, which is to provide a forum to sort out the rights of competing creditors.

The drafters of the 1898 Act decided that the federal judiciary should not control actions against third parties, unless an independent basis for federal jurisdiction existed or unless the parties consented. They thought these disputes were properly left to the state courts and that under the 1867 Act federal courts had taken away too many disputes from the state courts. But it does not follow that the accommodation struck between bankruptcy concerns and federal-state concerns in 1898 should also be the boundary between Article I tribunals and Article III courts in 1982. The 1898 Act balanced state and federal power, while the dispute in *Marathon* concerned separation of powers at the federal level.

One can argue that the distinction between a summary bankruptcy proceeding and a plenary one is coincidentally one of constitutional dimension, because the summary bankruptcy proceeding is a specialized area of the law "having particularized needs and warranting distinctive treatment," and that a plenary action is not. But the special characteristics of a summary bankruptcy proceeding arise largely from the need to coordinate the claims of many creditors. The procedural rules needed to resolve a dispute among many parties should not obscure the commonplace character of the rights being adjudicated.

One party to a bankruptcy proceeding may claim that it lent money and that the debtor never repaid it. Another may claim that the debtor committed a tort against it. Identifying such claims and the appropriate measure of damages is the stuff of which every law suit is made. In all of the previous cases in which Article I tribunals have been upheld as constitutional, something special about the claim itself or the place where it arose warranted a decision by an Article I tribunal. Disputes in a summary bankruptcy proceeding lack this characteristic.

Justice Brennan suggests at one point that summary bankruptcy proceedings differ from the dispute at issue in *Marathon* because, in a summary bankruptcy proceeding, rights between creditors and debtor are readjusted. Bankruptcy law, however, does not involve, at its core, a restructuring of debtor-creditor relations, at least not when the debtor is a corporation. Even if it did, Justice Brennan does not explain why that should matter. He seems to suggest that the individual debtor's right to a discharge is a "public right" and therefore may be adjudicated by an Article I tribunal. But why does a statute that readjusts rights between debtor and creditor confer a "public right" on the debtor and transform the remaining state-created rights of the creditor into rights that an Article I tribunal can adjudicate? Indeed, all statutory rights are "public rights" in Justice Brennan's sense. In any event, such a "public

right" seems irrelevant when the debtor, like Northern, is a corporation and has no Chapter 7 discharge right.[51]

The requirements of Article III, like the uniformity requirement
of the Bankruptcy Clause, are best understood if the fundamentally
procedural nature of federal bankruptcy law is kept in mind. Justice
Rehnquist's opinion emphasizes this point. He noted that the action by Northern against Marathon was a traditional action at common law. In all likelihood, so too were most of the existing claims
against Northern. Justice Rehnquist also noted that no federal rule
of decision would guide a court in deciding Northern's dispute
against Marathon. Similarly, most of the claims creditors have
against Northern probably raise only state law questions.[52]

The only difference that one can draw from Justice Rehnquist's
opinion between Northern's claim against Marathon and the claims
others have against Northern is that the former will be resolved by
a jury and the latter would, under the old Act, be resolved by the
referee. Jury trials never arose in bankruptcy proceedings because
they developed out of the chancery courts. For centuries, bankruptcy proceedings have been proceedings over which the chancery
courts exercised control.[53] The equitable, rather than legal, nature
of bankruptcy proceedings makes them no less an exercise of the
judicial power. Indeed, Article III states explicitly that the judicial
power extends to several types of disputes (such as those arising in
admiralty) that were heard in equity courts. The distinctions between bankruptcy disputes that Article I tribunals can hear and
those that only Article III courts can hear are obscure.

Once one establishes that an Article III court must hear some
kinds of disputes involving a debtor who has filed a petition in
bankruptcy, one cannot draw a safe distinction between Article III
issues and non–Article III issues. Article III does not necessarily
require all issues of fact and law to be decided by an Article III

---

[51] See 11 U.S.C. § 727(a)(1) (Supp. III 1979). In Chapter 11, Northern's rights are no
greater, in theory, than under Chapter 7. Every creditor whose rights have been impaired
can insist upon getting at least as much in a Chapter 11 reorganization as it would have gotten
in a liquidation under Chapter 7. 11 U.S.C. § 1129(a)(7) (Supp. III 1979).

[52] As an example of actions against another debtor, consider most of the creditors of
Manville Corporation, who, in the absence of the bankruptcy petition, would maintain
conventional tort actions in the state courts.

[53] See Jones, *The Foundations of English Bankruptcy: Statutes and Commissions in the Early
Modern Period*, 69 TRANSACTIONS AM. PHIL. SOC'Y, pt. 3, at 40–51 (1979).

judge. Such a proposition is inconsistent with the tradition of special masters in equity. District courts, or indeed any Article III courts, may have adjuncts to assist them in bankruptcy disputes, as long as they are adjuncts in fact as well as in name.

Only two terms ago, in *United States v. Raddatz*,[54] the Court found the Federal Magistrates Act to be consistent with the mandates of Article III. That Act provided that magistrates could hear and decide suppression motions, but that the district court had to make a de novo determination of any portion of the magistrate's report to which objection was made. The issue in *Raddatz* was whether the district judge was required to conduct an evidentiary hearing when the disputed issue was one of credibility. In other words, the Court decided whether the district judge could forgo an evidentiary hearing, even if the gist of the magistrate's report was, "I deny the motion to suppress because, on the basis of their demeanor on the witness stand, I am more inclined to believe the policeman than the defendant," and the district court had no way of confirming the magistrate's judgment.

The Court found that because district courts retained ultimate authority over the case, Article III was not violated. The district judge could decline to refer the question to the magistrate in the first instance and, when objection was made to it, he could reject it in whole or in part. That the district judge must rely on judgments the magistrate made did not alter the fact that he retained complete control over the magistrate's activities. The control the district judge exercises over magistrates is, in fact, similar to the control that district courts exercised over bankruptcy referees before the 1973 Bankruptcy Rules. The 1978 Code is not consistent with *Raddatz*, because it attempted to accommodate the mandates of Article III with labels. Bankruptcy judges are not "adjuncts" of the district courts if they have complete control over their dockets and their factual findings are subject only to appellate review.

III

The Bankruptcy Reform Act of 1978 provided one forum in which all disputes affecting a bankruptcy estate could be decided. Of course, not every aspect of a bankruptcy dispute needs to be

---

[54] 447 U.S. 667 (1980).

resolved in one forum. The 1898 Act did not provide such a forum. But the absence of such a forum brings costs. The bankruptcy proceeding of a large corporation can involve thousands of creditors and billions of dollars of claims. It is a procedural nightmare even when only one judge is making the decisions. The more judges there are, the more difficult it is to resolve conflicting rights.

The 1978 Code, like any other piece of legislation, has flaws.[55] For the most part, however, it remained true to the basic principles of bankruptcy and it provides a forum in which the affairs of wage earners and of Fortune 500 companies can be sorted out after the fall. For too long, bankruptcy law has remained the domain of a small part of the bar and has seemed arcane, even to lawyers who were masters of other major areas of the law. Most of bankruptcy law, however, is neither mysterious nor controversial. Its greatest concern is that the procedure by which state-created rights are recognized is fair.

Gibbons was brought about because Congress, responding to special interests, used its power to enact bankruptcy laws to create substantive rights. Although the creation of some substantive rights may be within the scope of Congress's power, they turn away from the central purpose of bankruptcy law, a purpose that is served, in the first instance, by creating procedural rules rather than substantive rights. Amending legislation—such as that the Court required in *Marathon*—invites special interest lobbying and political compromise. Ill-conceived and inappropriate substantive rights are a frequent by-product, as are awkward and inefficient procedures. It would be unfortunate, as a matter of bankruptcy policy, if the ultimate legacy of *Marathon* was an inferior bankruptcy law.

---

[55] Many of the flaws are merely technical. For example, 11 U.S.C. § 109(d) (Supp. III 1979) declares "stockholders" ineligible for Chapter 11. This is nonsense. (The word "stockbroker" was intended.)

WALTER BERNS

JUDICIAL REVIEW
AND THE RIGHTS AND
LAWS OF NATURE

I

The current controversy over the proper role of the judiciary can be said to have begun twenty years ago with Herbert Wechsler's appeal for Supreme Court decisions resting on "neutral principles of constitutional law."[1] More recently, Alexander Bickel and Philip Kurland charged that the Court had become brazenly political yet lacked political competence.[2] This provoked one well-known federal judge not only to defend the Court but contemptuously to dismiss its critics—Wechsler as well as Bickel and Kurland—as "self-appointed scholastic mandarins."[3] Since then there has been a further "explosion of judicial power."[4]

The controversy provoked by this explosion is over the proper role of the judiciary in constitutional cases. In a recent paper, Judge (then Professor) Ralph Winter, while acknowledging the differ-

Walter Berns is a Resident Scholar, American Enterprise Institute for Public Policy Research.

[1] Wechsler, *Toward Neutral Principles of Constitutional Law*, 73 HARV. L. REV. 1, 15 (1959).

[2] BICKEL, THE SUPREME COURT AND THE IDEA OF PROGRESS 175 and passim (1970); KURLAND, POLITICS, THE CONSTITUTION, AND THE WARREN COURT esp. xx ff. (1970).

[3] Wright, *Professor Bickel, the Scholarly Tradition, and the Supreme Court*, 84 HARV. L. REV. 769, 777 (1971).

[4] Winter, *The Growth of Judicial Power*, in THE JUDICIARY IN A DEMOCRATIC SOCIETY 29 (Theberge ed. 1979).

ences within each of the two schools, divided the profession of constitutional lawyers into those who argued that the judges are limited to finding the law in the constitutional text and those who argued that they are empowered to go beyond the text and make constitutional law out of history or natural law or fundamental "values." He referred to these as the "interpretive" and "judicial power" models of judicial review, and, although treating them as if they were equal contenders for acceptance by courts and commentators, he had to concede that the judicial power model had become the dominant.[5]

The critics of the courts are faced with a difficult task. To make the case that judges are misusing judicial power and to urge a return to the "interpretive model," or "pure interpretive model," has implications that not many critics and probably no judges would be willing to accept. Professor Thomas C. Grey has provided a list of examples of judicial creativity, and, with some exceptions that I think could be shown not to be exceptions, they all involve Fourteenth Amendment adjudication—for example, state cases involving freedom of speech and religion or cruel and unusual punishment.[6] This list is instructive because it indicates the extent to which the growth of judicial power is related to—or even limited to—this one Amendment, an Amendment seemingly worded in so general a fashion that the judges are invited to provide it with a substance fashioned from their own "values."

It is of little use to complain that the alleged vagueness of the Amendment is, in fact, a product or a consequence of judicial misinterpretation of its terms.[7] There is no feasible way open to us now to restore its intended meaning. Yet, it deserves mention that fidelity to the original text would have avoided the era of "substantive due process" and its progeny, "substantive equal protection." It would have spared us the embarrassments of Raoul Berger's disclosure of the cat that many of us wanted, for political reasons, to keep in the bag of our history, namely, that the Equal Protection Clause was not intended to forbid segregated schooling or require

---

[5] *Id.* at 49 and *passim.*

[6] Grey, *Do We Have an Unwritten Constitution?* 27 STAN. L. REV. 703, 710–14 (1975).

[7] The case has been made by Professor Michael Zuckert of Carleton College in two as yet unpublished papers (one of them coauthored by Marshall McDonald) that, rather than being vaguely written, the three troublesome clauses of the Fourteenth Amendment are precisely drafted. Each one is addressed, as it were, to a different branch of the state governments.

public busing to effect desegregated schooling.[8] It would have spared us a generation of constitutional lawyers who feel obligated to spin out elegant (but obviously absurd) theories in the vain attempt to provide some valid textual basis for the Court's Fourteenth Amendment decisions.[9] Best of all, it would have made it easier to preserve the public's esteem for the Constitution as fundamental law.

As Dean John Hart Ely has recently demonstrated, the friends of judicial power are faced with an equally difficult task when they attempt to justify what the Court is doing.[10] Some of them do not even make the attempt. Here are the words of Lynn D. Compton, a California appeals court judge:[11]

> Let's be honest with the public. Those courts are policymaking bodies. The policies they set have the effect of law because of the power those courts are given by the Constitution. The so-called "landmark decisions" of both the U.S. Supreme Court and the California Supreme Court were not compelled by legal precedent. Those decisions are the law and are considered "right" simply because the court had the power to decree the result. The result in any of those cases could have been exactly the opposite and by the same criteria been correct and binding precedent.
>
> In short, these precedent-setting policy decisions were the product of the social, economic and political philosophy of the majority of the justices who made up the court at a given time in history. . . .

This means that the Constitution cannot be misinterpreted; that it is a thing without form or substance, except that it authorizes the judges to give it substance. In providing that substance, the judges need consult only their own "social, economic and political philosophy."

---

[8] BERGER, GOVERNMENT BY JUDICIARY: THE TRANSFORMATION OF THE FOURTEENTH AMENDMENT, ch. 7 (1977).

[9] One example of such absurdities: aliens, according to Kenneth L. Karst, are covered by the "principle of equal citizenship," even though they "lack citizenship in the narrow sense." Karst, *The Supreme Court, 1976 Term—Foreword: Equal Citizenship under the Fourteenth Amendment*, 91 HARV. L. REV. 1, 45 (1977). This is like saying a definition of cat that excludes dog is a narrow definition of cat.

[10] Ely, *The Supreme Court, 1977 Term—Foreword: On Discovering Fundamental Values*, 92 HARV. L. REV. 5–55 (1978).

[11] Compton, LOS ANGELES TIMES, February 20, 1977. As quoted in Pritchett, *Living with a Living Constitution: 200 Minus 10 and Counting*, a paper prepared for delivery at the 1977 Annual Meeting of the American Political Science Association, p. 13.

Such candor on the part of judges is unusual, and, despite this desire to "be honest with the public," it may be doubted that we shall ever encounter it in the official reports. Even Justice Douglas, who earned the praise of Professor Kenneth L. Karst for his unsurpassed willingness to ask what is best for the country and to "translate his answers to that question into constitutional law,"[12] always claimed to be expounding the Constitution, if not its explicit provisions then, at least, its emanations, penumbras, or lacunae.

Some friends of judicial power attempt to justify it by claiming the authority of the most venerable of our judges, John Marshall. To live under a constitution, the argument goes, means to live under a living constitution, and this, of necessity, requires the judges to adapt it to the times and circumstances. C. Herman Pritchett argued that this idea of a " 'living Constitution' . . . can trace its lineage back to John Marshall's celebrated advice in *McCulloch v. Maryland* (1819): 'We must never forget that it is a Constitution we are expounding . . . intended to endure for ages to come, and consequently to be adapted to the various crises of human affairs.' "[13] The opinion attributed here to Marshall is at odds with his well-known statements that, for example, the "principles" of the Constitution "are deemed fundamental [and] permanent" and, except by means of formal amendment, "unchangeable."[14] But the discrepancy is not Marshall's; it is largely the consequence of the manner in which Pritchett renders Marshall's opinion in *McCulloch*: Pritchett employs ellipses to join two statements separated by some eight pages in the original. Marshall's meaning is not that the Constitution may be adapted to "the various crises of human affairs," but that the legislative powers granted by the Constitution are adaptable to meet these crises. The first statement, in which Marshall admonishes us to remember that we are expounding a constitution, is part of his argument that a constitution cannot specify "all the subdivisions of which its great powers will admit"; if it attempted to do that it would "partake of the prolixity of a legal code."[15] In the second statement, Marshall's subject is the neces-

---

[12] Karst, *Invidious Discrimination: Justice Douglas and the Return of the "Natural-Law-Due-Process Formula,"* 16 U.C.L.A. L. REV. 716, 720 (1969).

[13] Pritchett, *Living with a Living Constitution*, note 11 *supra*, at 1.

[14] Marbury v. Madison, 1 Cranch 137, 176, 177 (1803).

[15] McCulloch v. Maryland, 4 Wheat. 316, 407 (1819).

sary and proper provision which, he says, "is made in a constitution intended to endure for ages to come, and consequently, to be adapted to the various crises of human affairs."[16] The immediate sequel makes it even clearer that he is talking of legislative powers, not the Constitution itself: "To have prescribed the means by which the government should, in all future time, execute its powers, would have been to change, entirely, the character of the instrument, and give it the properties of a legal code." His meaning is put beyond any doubt in an essay he published in the *Alexandria Gazette* in which, with specific reference to his *McCulloch* statement concerning adaptation, Marshall says this: "Its [the statement's] sole object is to remind us that a constitution cannot possibly enumerate the means by which the powers of government are to be carried into execution."[17] It was not Marshall's view that the Constitution must be kept in tune with the times; on the contrary, his view was that the times, to the extent possible, must be kept in tune with the Constitution. Marshall cannot be counted among the friends of judicial power as that term is currently understood.

The difficulties of reconciling an expansive judicial power—indeed, judicial review itself—with majoritarian democracy are explored in two recent and important books. If, as Jesse H. Choper says in the first of these, "majority rule has been considered [by Madison, Jefferson, and Lincoln, as well as in "this nation's constitutional development"] the keystone of a democratic political system in both theory and practice,"[18] then, of course, judicial review has no place whatever. But, to say nothing here of Madison and Jefferson, Lincoln led this nation into the Civil War rather than submit to the proposition, known as popular sovereignty, that the issue of slavery in the territories ought to be determined by majority vote of the people in the territories. Fortunately, this initial misstatement plays no part in Choper's subsequent analysis of the issue. The Supreme Court is not democratic, but, as he proceeds to show in detail, neither are the political branches simply majoritarian. They were not intended to be, as any reader of *Federalist* No.

---

[16] *Id.* at 415.

[17] Marshall, *A Friend of the Constitution*, in JOHN MARSHALL'S DEFENSE OF MCCULLOCH V. MARYLAND 185 (Gunther ed. 1969).

[18] CHOPER, JUDICIAL REVIEW AND THE NATIONAL POLITICAL PROCESS: A FUNCTIONAL RECONSIDERATION OF THE ROLE OF THE SUPREME COURT 4 (1980).

10 alone must know. Simple majoritarianism was likely to lead to rule by majority faction, and, as Publius shows, the Constitution's elaborate and complex structure was designed to prevent such majorities. "In the extent and proper structure of the Union," he concludes, "we behold a republican remedy for the diseases most incident to republican government."[19]

As I shall shortly argue at some length, the Constitution was intended "to secure these rights" (not to enable a majority of the people to rule), so the question becomes whether the judiciary has a legitimate role to play in the securing of rights, either by protecting the structure or by intervening when, through some structural or systemic failure, rights have been violated by or in the political branches. Since the victims of such violations are more likely to be members of minority groups, it is, Choper argues, primarily on their behalf that the judiciary should exercise its powers.[20] But which minorities? And, in addition to those "specifically designated" in the constitutional text, which rights? Choper recognizes the problem—". . . each time any group loses any political battle . . . it may lay claim to the label of . . . 'submerged and beaten minority,'"[21]—but he has no principled way to resolve it. Like John Hart Ely, he says the critical question facing constitutional scholarship is the development of a principled approach to judicial enforcement of the Constitution's open-ended provisions that secure individual rights; unlike Ely, however, Choper "does not attempt to resolve [it]."[22]

Like Choper, Ely is no friend of unguided or unprincipled judicial power, largely because he denies that the Constitution, on the whole, embodies the "substantive values" on the basis of which the courts may invalidate the actions of the other branches of government. In his view, the Constitution as written is "overwhelmingly concerned, on the one hand, with procedural fairness in the resolution of individual disputes (process writ small), and on the other, with what might capaciously be designated process writ large, with ensuring broad participation in the processes and distributions of

---

[19] THE FEDERALIST PAPERS, No. 10 at 84 (Mentor ed. 1961).

[20] CHOPER, note 18 *supra*, at 64.

[21] *Id.* at 76.

[22] *Id.* at 79.

government."[23] There is more truth in this statement than some of his critics have allowed. Ely, of course, recognizes that the Constitution embodies some "substantive values"; for example, the government it establishes is popular in form (not monarchic or aristocratic), and that form will affect the way justice is distributed (or, in Harold Lasswell's phrase, who gets what) in the political process. It obviously promotes a commercial society, which will affect how we live and, indeed, what we are; and, as Laurence Tribe points out, "in many of its parts, the Constitution also evinces a substantive commitment to the institution of private property and to the contractual expectations that surround it."[24] Nevertheless, the Constitution as it came from the Philadelphia convention was, as Ely says, mainly concerned with "process writ large." What he fails to appreciate, however, is that the process—or, as I should prefer to say, the structure governing the process—was designed with a view to a particular and substantive end. It was designed to secure the rights with which all men by nature are equally endowed.

Ely cannot acknowledge this "substantive value" because he denies the existence of natural rights and natural law. What was self-evident to the authors of the Declaration of Independence is not at all evident to Ely. Jefferson and his colleagues may have appealed to "the Laws of Nature and of Nature's God," but Ely cannot credit them with being serious. The Declaration is a mere lawyer's brief, he maintains ("with certain features of an indictment"), and like those who write briefs, the authors of the Declaration threw in "arguments of every hue." Some "broadly accepted natural law philosophy surely could have found a place within [the Constitution], presumably in the Bill of Rights [but] such philosophies were not that broadly accepted."[25]

Because he cannot take seriously the idea that the Founders were persuaded of the fact of natural rights, he does not recognize that the gravest fault in our history as a people was a fault precisely because it was a violation of natural right. By natural right no man may be governed without his consent, yet black Americans (or the

---

[23] ELY, DEMOCRACY AND DISTRUST: A THEORY OF JUDICIAL REVIEW 87 (1980).

[24] Tribe, *The Puzzling Persistence of Process-based Constitutional Theories*, 89 Yale L.J. 1063, 1065 (1980).

[25] ELY, note 23 *supra*, at 49.

overwhelming majority of them) were denied the opportunity to vote for or against the Constitution. Denied that fundamental right, they were also denied the constitutional right to be represented in the majorities assembled in the legislative process, the majorities that made the laws.

The Founders recognized their treatment of blacks to be contrary to natural right.[26] Ely, however, even though he justifies judicial review on behalf of those groups that are not represented in the governing process, or do not fare well in it, has no principled basis on which to distinguish groups that are mistreated from those that are not mistreated, or those deserving of judicial solicitude from those not deserving of it.[27] He cannot provide a principled basis for judicial review, and he cannot do so because he does not recognize that the Constitution was and is designed to secure rights and, in that respect, is informed by moral principle.[28]

Thomas C. Grey's work, still in progress, promises to provide the judicial power school with what it has always lacked, a sound theoretical and historical basis. For him, the issue whether the judiciary should exercise a sweeping policymaking power does not turn mainly on "how one evaluates the practical results" of the decisions—whether, for example, one favors or opposes a liberal abortion policy—but on the legitimacy of what the judiciary is doing. As he states it, the decisive question is whether in writing the Constitution we left "in the hands of [the] judges the considerable power to define and enforce fundamental human rights without substantial guidance from constitutional text and history."[29] His answer is yes.[30]

> For the generation that framed the Constitution, the concept of a "higher law," protecting "natural rights," and taking precedence over ordinary positive law as a matter of political obligation, was widely shared and deeply felt. An essential element of American constitutionalism was the reduction to written form— and hence to positive law—of some of the principles of natural

---

[26] See, e.g., Berns, *The Constitution as Bill of Rights*, in HOW DOES THE CONSTITUTION SECURE RIGHTS? (Goldwin & Schambra eds. forthcoming 1982).

[27] Tribe, note 24 *supra*, at 1072–77.

[28] For a more extensive critique of the Ely book, see Barber, *The Constitutionalism of John Hart Ely*, a paper prepared for delivery at the 1981 Annual Meeting of the American Political Science Association.

[29] Grey, note 6 *supra*, at 714.

[30] *Id.* at 715–16.

rights. But at the same time, it was generally recognized that written constitutions could not completely codify the higher law. Thus in the framing of the original American constitutions it was widely accepted that there remained unwritten but still binding principles of higher law. The [N]inth Amendment is the textual expression of this idea in the federal Constitution.

As it came to be accepted that the judiciary had the power to enforce the commands of the written Constitution when these conflicted with ordinary law, it was also widely assumed that judges would enforce as constitutional restraints the unwritten natural rights as well.

The issues he raises in this essay, and which he begins to answer in a subsequent essay,[31] are of the first importance and their resolution does indeed require "lengthy and detailed historical documentation." It also requires an inquiry—more extensive than I can hope to provide here[32]—into the doctrine of modern natural right and its connection to American constitutionalism. Grey does not essay such an inquiry here because, although he recognizes the role of modern natural rights in the revolutionary break with England, he denies their role "in the disputes that led up to the break."[33] His argument is that Americans clung to the traditional understanding of natural law, the natural law (perhaps) first taught by Cicero, put into Christian terms by Thomas Aquinas, and made known to Americans in the opinions of a famous English judge, Sir Edward Coke. Here are Coke's words in *Calvin's Case* (1609):[34]

> The law of nature is that which God at the time of creation of the nature of man infused into his heart, for his preservation and direction; and this is *Lex aeterna*, the moral law, called also the law of nature. And by this law, written with the finger of God in the heart of man, were the people of god a long time governed before the law was written by Moses, who was the first reporter or writer of law in the world. . . .

---

[31] Grey, *Origins of the Unwritten Constitution: Fundamental Law in American Revolutionary Thought*, 30 STAN. L. REV. 843–93 (1978).

[32] For a comprehensive treatment of modern natural right, see STRAUSS, NATURAL RIGHT AND HISTORY, ch. 5 (1953).

[33] Grey, *Origins of the Unwritten Constitution*, note 31 *supra*, at 891.

[34] Calvin's Case, 77 Eng. Rep. 377, 392 (K.B. 1609). As quoted in CORWIN, THE "HIGHER LAW" BACKGROUND OF AMERICAN CONSTITUTIONAL LAW 45–46 (1955). First published in 42 HARV. L. REV. 149–85; 365–409 (1928–29).

This, Grey argues, was "the dominant view of natural or fundamental law among revolutionary Americans."[35] But with due respect for his scholarship, which is formidable, I must say that in the
essential respects he is mistaken. Like every American constitutional lawyer and judge who has written on this subject and whose
work I have read, from Corwin[36]—considered the authority by
several generations of Americans—to Justice Black and others still
living and writing, Grey does not understand the doctrine of modern natural rights and natural law from which, as I hope to show,
we derive our understanding of constitutionalism.

II

The modern natural rights teaching begins with the assertion, which its authors regarded as no more than a recognition of
the fact, that men are by nature adversaries. Being hostile one to
another, and living naturally without government, their lives were,
in Hobbes's famous formulation, "solitary, poor, nasty, brutish,
and short,"[37] and even under government their lives too frequently
resembled this natural condition. The problem thus posed was to
find a way that these naturally hostile men could live, or could be
made to live, in peace. The solution to this problem consisted in
organizing politics on the basis of something as to which all men
can agree, and, second, excluding from politics those subjects that
traditionally give rise to strife and disorder. One can say that nature
is the problem, or the cause of the problem, and the escape from
nature the solution. This means, stated here only provisionally,
that the laws of nature, instead of constituting a body of "higher
law" as Grey uses the term—meaning, a model or a set of principles by which one judges the goodness of the positive law—are a
set of directions enabling men to escape from their natural condition, which is unbearable.

They are, these laws of nature in the modern sense, all derivative
from and, as it were, made necessary by, the rights of nature, or,
man's natural rights, the rights that all men possess equally. Nature
is the problem precisely because all men possess natural rights, the

---

[35] Grey, *Origins of the Unwritten Constitution*, note 31 *supra*, at 892.

[36] CORWIN, note 34 *supra*.

[37] HOBBES, LEVIATHAN, ch. 13.

right to self-preservation and the right to use whatever means are required, or are thought by each man to be required, to preserve himself. As Hobbes makes explicit, if his own preservation requires it, or is thought to require it, every man has a natural right not only to take from another but to kill the other.[38] Locke, whom we are more inclined to acknowledge as a founder of our modern politics, taught the same lesson but less explicitly.[39] Again, the fact that, according to nature, "every man has a right to everything,"[40] is that which gives rise to the problem. It is because men have natural rights of this description and are only too inclined to exercise them that the state of nature is a state of war "of every man, against every man."[41] The rights of nature give rise to war; the laws of nature point the way to peace. As Hobbes puts it, "as long as this natural right of every man to every thing endureth, there can be no security to any man. . . . [C]onsequently, it is a precept, or general rule of reason, *that every man, ought to endeavour peace. . . .*" The first branch of which rule "containeth the first, and fundamental law of nature; which is, *to seek peace, and follow it.*" The second is derived from the first: *"that a man be willing, when others are so too, as far-forth, as for peace, and defence of himself he shall think it necessary, to lay down this right to all things; and be contented with so much liberty against other men, as he would allow other men against himself."*[42] Except that no man can give up the right to resist them "that assault him by force, or take away his life," the laws of nature require men mutually to lay down their natural rights by entering into a covenant one with another. By the third of these natural laws, men are enjoined to perform this covenant, this mutual divesting of rights, but Hobbes knew that men, tempted by "avarice, ambition, lust, or other strong desire," cannot be held to performance by mere words; they must be made to fear the consequences of breaking their word. ("The passion to be reckoned upon is fear.") Hence, if the first aspect of the covenant, or social contract, is the agreement to lay down their natural rights, the second aspect is the agreement to recognize the sovereign, to whom these rights are transferred, and, by means of this

---

[38] *Id.*, ch. 14.

[39] LOCKE, TREATISES I, secs. 86, 88; TREATISES II, secs. 12, 13, 87.

[40] HOBBES, LEVIATHAN, ch. 14.

[41] *Id.*, ch. 13.

[42] *Id.*, ch. 14.

transfer, to endow him (or it) with an absolute power to require performance. The threat or terror of punishment must overcome the temptation to break the covenant;[43] and the covenant is the foundation of peace and of all justice. (There is no justice in the state of nature.) The sovereign preserves the peace among beings who are by nature enemies.

Hobbes's political science is built on these propositions: that there is no basis in nature for opinions of good and bad, that men are certain to disagree about good and bad, but that men can agree on the need for peace.[44] It is the only thing they can agree on, but, precisely because of that, civil society is possible. The peace of this civil society would be jeopardized, however, if men were permitted to dispute questions of good and bad, or, to say the same thing, if men in their capacity as citizens were permitted to raise questions concerning the end or ends of civil society. Such questions must be suppressed in the modern liberal state. (Whether they can be suppressed is another matter.) In principle, by contracting with each other to yield their rights to the sovereign in exchange for the peace which will provide the only real security for their rights, men agree not to raise such questions. Each man agrees that his opinions of good and bad, right and wrong, justice and injustice are just that—private opinions—and the principle of equality requires him to acknowledge that other opinions, even if they are contrary to his own, have as much (or as little) dignity as his own. What this means is that each man agrees to forgo his private judgment of the goodness or badness of the sovereign's laws; he agrees to obey the sovereign in exchange for similar promises on the part of his co-covenantors. The sovereign enforces those promises. Hobbes summarizes all this, or encapsulates it, in his famous revision of the Golden Rule: *"Do not that to another, which thou wouldest not have done to thyself."*[45] Not: *do* unto others, for to do means to act on the basis of some idea of the good, and every idea of the good is mere opinion, without foundation; so to act implies a right to impose one's own idea of the good on others and this gives rise to dispute. Hence, the revised rule: do *not* do as you would *not* have done to you. Leave other men alone in exchange for their promise, which

---

[43] *Id.*, ch. 15.

[44] HOBBES, DE CIVE, ch. III, §32 (Lamprecht ed. 1949) 58.

[45] HOBBES, LEVIATHAN, ch. 15.

the sovereign will enforce, to leave you alone. The happy consequence of this sovereign's peace is liberty, which is why some have given the name liberalism to this kind of politics.

Harvey C. Mansfield, Jr., whose formulations I have adopted, provides a convenient statement of the conclusion to be drawn from much of what I have said thus far about the origin of modern natural right:[46]

> If men could stop disputing the ends of politics and agree on the condition of all ends, they could follow privately those ends whose pursuit is consistent with the same allowance to other ends. Under Hobbes's golden rule, the universe of tolerated ends is defined by the condition of all ends, including the intolerable, and that is civil peace. The end of government thus becomes security for those ends that can be represented.

To recapitulate: men are created equal in the sense that everyone by nature has a right to rule himself, which means that no one by nature has a right to rule anyone other than himself. Hobbes's sovereign is an artificial ruler because no real person is a ruler of anyone but himself. This artificial ruler represents all the real persons insofar as he is the representative of all the private rights that had to be renounced to make civil society (and peace) possible. He is an absolute ruler because he represents all the absolute rulers who entered into the covenant and because only an absolute ruler can guarantee the achievement of the end of sovereign power, peace.[47] It may seem paradoxical, but Hobbes, whose reputation is simply that of a teacher of absolutism, is the founder of self-government in the modern sense. We govern ourselves through the sovereign who is ourselves, and, in Hobbes's scheme, this government is made possible only because we renounce our natural rights. With the exception of the right to defend ourselves against physical attack, we transfer our rights to the sovereign; it is our rights that he exercises. It goes without saying that this doctrine of natural rights has no room for judicial review.

In fact, judicial review is likely to prove a threat to the civil society built on natural rights, for, as Hobbes makes clear in a number of places in his writings, the greatest threat to civil peace

---

[46] Mansfield, *Hobbes and the Science of Indirect Government*, 65 AM. POL. SCI. REV. 107 (1971).

[47] *Id.* at 102.

comes from men who, in violation of the covenant and moved by their vanity, claim the right to pass judgment—which necessarily means "private judgment"—on the laws or the sovereign's commands. "[H]ow many rebellions hath this opinion been the cause of, which teacheth that the knowledge whether the commands of kings be just or unjust, belongs to private men, and that before they yield obedience, they not only may, but ought to dispute them."[48] He was concerned mostly with priests because in his day—and our own time is not without its examples of this class of potentially dangerous men[49]—it was primarily the various denominations of priests who taught the right of private judgment and, by so doing, represented a constant threat to the civil peace. But next on his list of potential public enemies were the lawyers.[50] Lawyers cannot claim to be "the Lord's anointed," but their possession of the Latin and the other strange tongues of the law feeds their vanity until it becomes overweening. As Mansfield says, by way of explaining Hobbes's attitude toward lawyers, "expertise in law implies a standard of law external to the will of the sovereign, such as the common law or the traditional natural law of 'right reason.' "[51] It is not judicial review but rather Justice Black's complaints of his "natural-law-due-process" colleagues that find their origin in Hobbes's natural right teaching. Hobbes could have predicted that, unless we take steps to protect ourselves, the day would come in which lawyers, when "called" to the bench, will decide what is best for the country and then "translate [their] answers to that question into constitutional law."[52]

I indicated above that Hobbes the absolutist is the founder of self-government in the modern sense and acknowledged that this would be seen as a paradox. This is so because his teaching has come down to us—in the sense of being installed among us—in a form that is, outwardly at least, much more benign, and therefore more acceptable to us, and in one important respect is in fact more benign. We know it, and Grey knows it, in the form it assumes in

---

[48] HOBBES, DE CIVE, Preface to the Reader.

[49] The Ayatollah Khomeini is a perfect example of the sort of man Hobbes had in mind.

[50] HOBBES, A DIALOGUE BETWEEN A PHILOSOPHER AND A STUDENT OF THE COMMON LAWS OF ENGLAND (Cropsey ed. 1971).

[51] Mansfield, note 46 *supra*, at 108.

[52] Karst, INVIDIOUS DISCRIMINATION, note 12 *supra*, at 720.

the teaching of John Locke, "America's philosopher," as someone
called him. Locke made two significant changes that greatly con-
tributed to the practical success of the new natural rights teaching:
he found a way to conceal the absolutist character of sovereignty
and he discovered the principles of the modern commercial society
which we call capitalism.

Locke's civil society is a Hobbesian society with a difference, but
not so great a difference as is sometimes thought. Corwin, for
example, says that where "Hobbes and Locke part company is in
their view of the state of nature, that is to say, in their view of
human nature when not subjected to political control." Locke, he
says, in contrast to Hobbes, "depicts the state of nature as in the
main an era of 'peace, goodwill, mutual assistance, and preservation'. . . . "[53] Corwin is mistaken. Locke, in the section from which
Corwin quotes, does not say that the state of nature is peaceful, or
even in the main peaceful. What he says is that the state of nature
and the state of war are distinguishable; they are "as far distant . . .
one from another" as are a state of peace and a state of enmity, or as
are a state of "good will" and a state of "malice."[54] Well, what is the
distance between the state of peace and the state of enmity and,
therefore, the state of nature and the state of war? Locke's answer is
given almost immediately in the beginning sentence of section 21:
"To avoid this state of war . . . is one great reason of men's putting
themselves into society, and quitting the state of nature." Men quit
the state of nature in order to avoid the state of war. Thus, for
Locke too, civil society comes into being with a contract made by
self-interested men who, if not enemies to the extent of Hobbesian
men, are nevertheless compelled by the conditions of nature to be
adversaries.[55] He, too, requires men to renounce their natural
rights (except, again, what he calls the natural power to preserve
themselves) and specifically the right of "private judgment
[respecting] any matter of right."[56] And he, too, faces the problem
of how to ensure that men will perform the terms of the contract.
He does not, however, follow Hobbes to the extent of endowing a

---

[53] CORWIN, note 34 *supra*, at 66.

[54] LOCKE, TREATISES II, sec. 19.

[55] Goldwin, *John Locke*, in HISTORY OF POLITICAL PHILOSOPHY 453–60 (Strauss & Cropsey eds. 1972).

[56] LOCKE, TREATISES II, sec. 87.

person with sovereignty and teaching that that person must rely on fear as a means of controlling men. In his teaching no person is the embodiment or representative of the people. Instead, "political power" is first of all the "right of making laws."[57] It follows that sovereignty, or as he puts it, the supreme power, is in the hands of those who share in the legislative power.[58] Locke succeeds in institutionalizing sovereignty, which is to have great consequences in and for America. His sovereign speaks not in commands but in laws, and the laws apply to everyone, even to those who share in the making of them.[59] In this way Locke makes it less likely that absolute rule would be arbitrary or tyrannical rule. But this rule by law or by means of law is not the rule by lawyers. There is no room for judicial review in Locke's system. Locke, who emphasizes the legislative power and, however reluctantly, concedes the need of what we call the executive power,[60] makes no provision for—he does not even recognize—the judicial power. Thus, while it remains to be seen whether Grey is correct in saying that Americans "assumed that judges would enforce as constitutional restraints the unwritten natural rights,"[61] it is absolutely clear that this view of the role of the judiciary was not shared by Locke or Hobbes, the first philosophers of natural rights.

Locke's second contribution to the success of the new natural rights teaching was his discovery of the principles of the new commercial society. With these principles Locke could promise not merely self-preservation but comfortable preservation, in fact, a very commodious life. The "wise" and "godlike" prince who establishes laws of liberty respecting the acquisition, use, and disposition of property, and by doing so promotes "the honest industry of mankind," is the greatest of mankind's benefactors. Under his laws, Locke predicts the wealth with which nature endowed mankind will increase a thousandfold. Indeed, compared with what is possible under this new—that is, capitalist—prince, nature's providence

---

[57] *Id.*, sec. 3.

[58] *Id.*, secs. 134, 151.

[59] *Id.*, sec. 143.

[60] *Id.*, ch. 14 ("Of Prerogative").

[61] Grey, *Do We Have an Unwritten Constitution?* note 6 *supra*, at 716.

is "almost worthless."[62] Men will perform the terms of the contract—which is to say, they will obey this sovereign's laws and forgo the right they had in the state of nature to pass private judgment "concerning any matter of right"—because it will be so profitable for them to perform and obey. The new commercial society promises a larger and ever larger gross national product, and this product can be shared more readily than the scarce wealth of the past. There will be a steady improvement in the material conditions of all men. As a consequence, the passions of men will be redirected from great causes to the small, from the poetic to the prosaic, from dreams of heaven and glory to dreams of money, from the subjects as to which they disagree to the one subject as to which they can agree. In Mansfield's terms, Locke found a better way to achieve the Hobbesian end. In the new commercial society men would "stop disputing the ends of politics and agree on the condition of all ends"—civil peace—because they would devote themselves to making money and they would succeed. They would become tolerant, being content to live and let live, because they would cease to care about the things that men tend to be intolerant about. Hobbes promised peace if men would transfer their rights to a heavily armed policeman. Locke promised peace if men would pursue wealth, in exchange for which Locke promised to conceal the policeman. In the Lockean regime, men are still adversaries, but their hostility is channeled into the safest of all forms, that of free economic competition. This competition is safe because it is productive of the things Lockean men want: material goods. James Madison, America's Founder, revealed his debt to Locke when, in the famous *Federalist* No. 10, he said that "the chief object of government [is] the protection of different and unequal faculties of acquiring property. . . ." The government's duty to protect unequal faculties (or talents) derives from its duty to secure equal rights.

According to a most authoritative statement on the subject, governments are instituted to secure the rights with which all men are naturally endowed. America's Founders learned from Hobbes and Locke, and others, that these rights cannot be secured except under govenment, which is why the Constitution they wrote in Philadel-

---

[62] LOCKE, TREATISES II, secs. 37–43. See Goldwin, note 55 *supra*, at 451–86.

phia was essentially one of powers. It did not even contain a bill of rights because, as Hamilton said, "the Constitution is itself, in every rational sense, and to every useful purpose, A BILL OF RIGHTS."[63] They also learned that to secure these rights the power of government must be limited, and that the most efficient way to limit power was not to withhold powers—although they did that too—but to organize power in a particular way.

In sum, the doctrine of natural rights as expounded by Hobbes and Locke, and the natural laws to which the rights give rise, is not a "higher law" doctrine as understood by Grey. He means by it what Coke meant in *Calvin's Case*, a law that was part of the law of England and, as Grey puts it, taking precedence over earthly law because "it was of Divine origin, eternal and unchanging."[64] This understanding of natural law derives from the Stoics and Thomas Aquinas. But the new natural law merely commanded men to seek peace, in Hobbes's case, or, in Locke's, to find the arrangement under which men might preserve both themselves and others. Natural law in this modern sense is not a legal discipline. Lawyers, simply as lawyers or even as judges, have no competence in it, and courts have no jurisdiction over it. As for natural rights themselves, or the powers that men enjoyed in the state of nature, with the exception of the right of self-defense, they had to be renounced or transferred to the sovereign.

III

The issue is whether the Founders endowed judges with the authority to "define and enforce fundamental human rights without substantial guidance from constitutional text and history."[65] Grey contends that they did, but he implies that he can find no support for his answer in the writings of Hobbes and Locke when he says

---

[63] THE FEDERALIST PAPERS No. 84, note 19 *supra*, at 515. My colleague Robert A. Goldwin has pointed out that in the unamended Constitution the word "right" or "rights" appears only once, namely, in the Article I, sec. 8, clause 8 provision respecting the "exclusive right [of authors and inventors] to their respective writings and dfiscoveries," and even here the "right" is seen as a means of enabling Congress to exercise its "power . . . to promote the progress of science and useful arts."

[64] Grey, *Origins of the Unwritten Constitution*, note 31 *supra*, at 853.

[65] Grey, *Do We Have an Unwritten Constitution?* note 6 *supra*, at 714.

he can find none in Locke and Blackstone. Natural rights "rhetoric" played a role in the break with England, he concedes, and is embodied in the Declaration of Independence and in Tom Paine's *Common Sense*, but the "dominant view of natural or fundamental law among revolutionary Americans" derived from a different source.[66] "While Americans drew on the natural rights rhetoric of Locke and Blackstone, they found the best contemporary support for their own more traditional constitutional views in those curious products of the Age of Reason, the systematic treatises on the law of nature and nations [written by Pufendorf, Burlamaqui, Vattel, and Rutherforth]."[67] But, even assuming that revolutionary Americans continued to understand natural law in the old sense, a subject the investigation of which would be an enterprise in itself, they could not have found support for this understanding in these treatises—unless, of course, they misread them—because these treatises propound a natural law teaching that is Hobbesian in every essential respect.

That these treatise writers sought to conceal their indebtedness to Hobbes can, I think, be demonstrated, especially in Pufendorf's case, and that they would have reason to want to do so is known to students of the history of political philosophy. Hobbes's name was, as Locke said, "justly decried," and a writer's reputation—in those circles where it was decried—depended in part on the distance, or the seeming distance, he put between himself and Thomas Hobbes. (Locke owed his popular success to his seeming distance from Hobbes.) Thus, we find in Pufendorf[68] countless references to the Bible and the other approved books, and to God as "the author of natural law," from which it is easy to conclude that we are in the presence of a writer steeped in the Christian tradition and propounding a Christian natural law teaching. That God is the author of natural law, he says, is a "fact which no sane man can question." He then goes on to say, however, that it is "uncertain *how* the divine will can be discovered, and on what evidence we can

---

[66] Grey, *Origins of the Unwritten Constitution*, note 31 *supra*, at 892.

[67] *Id.* at 860.

[68] Considerations of space require me to limit my discussion to Pufendorf's DE JURE NATURAE ET GENTIUM, first published in 1672 and first translated into English in 1703. I shall refer to the 1934 translation used by Grey.

be certain that God wished to include this thing or that under the natural law."[69] This, he admits, is an "inconvenience," a problem. What is instructive is how he solves that problem. He solves it by following Hobbes's method of examining man's natural condition and propensities, discovering that man is most of all consumed by love for himself and the "desire to preserve himself by any and all means," that man is weak and therefore unable to "live and enjoy the good things that in this world attend his condition," and that the reasonable thing for men to do—the dictate of right reason working from the new premises—is to seek peace by becoming sociable and to become sociable by entering into a covenant one with another to form civil society. This Pufendorf describes as the fundamental law of nature. And this Hobbesian method is, he says, patently the "way of eliciting the law of nature."[70]

There are, as I said, numerous passages in which Pufendorf seems to refer to the "natural and divine laws" in a traditional sense. These, he says, are of universal obligation, and those who transgress against these laws can expect to be punished. But punished by whom? Not, it turns out, by any civil authority, unless natural offenses have been made civil crimes. And what is the principle to be followed by the civil authority in deciding what offenses against "natural and divine laws" should be made civil offenses and which should "be left to the vengeance of God"? Pufendorf's answer is taken straight from Hobbes: "[T]he force of civil law [will be accorded to] those precepts of nature, the observance of which is *absolutely* necessary for the continuance of internal peace."[71]

He appears to differ from Hobbes, who argues[72] that whereas murder, for example, is contrary to natural law, there is no way of knowing what murder is until the civil law defines it. Pufendorf replies that "we who venerate Sacred Scripture" can know what murder is from "the laws which God gave the Jews, and from other revelations."[73] But he had earlier said that it was "uncertain . . . on what evidence we can be certain that God wished to include this

[69] PUFENDORF, OF THE LAW OF NATURE AND NATIONS, Book II, ch. 3, #5 at 185 (Oldfather & Oldfather trans. 1934).

[70] *Id.*, Book II, ch. 3, #13–15 at 202–8.

[71] *Id.*, Book VIII, ch. 1, #1 at 1131 (emphasis added).

[72] HOBBES, DE CIVE, ch. VI, sec. 16; ch. XIV, secs. 9–10.

[73] PUFENDORF, note 69 *supra*, Book VIII, ch. 1, #3 at 1134.

thing or that under the natural law."[74] The careful reader is obliged
to wonder, therefore, whether Pufendorf included himself among
those who "venerate Sacred Scripture."[75] (The following passage is
instructive on this issue. The context is his "method of deducing
the natural law," and he is responding to the objection that given
this method, there can be no demonstration of the validity of the
precepts it yields, that, on the contrary, the virtuousness of what is
called virtue can be proved only by assuming divine punishment
which, in turn, depends on the soul being immortal. Pufendorf
says, "the view of a certain scholar, that upon our principle the
virtue of fortitude [for example] cannot be proved unless a basis is
laid for it in the immortality of the soul, since otherwise no reward
could fall to the lot of the man who sacrifices his life for a worthy
cause, his view, I say, offers little difficulty. Although it is impious
to deny or to cast doubt upon such a belief, still it is possible to
show that even without it a soldier can be commanded to do battle
to the death for his country. For . . . it is certainly agreed that it lies
within the power of the supreme authority to arm citizens, and to
proclaim upon pain of death that no one flee from his appointed
place. Now of two evils a man cannot avoid choosing the lesser. But
it is the lesser evil to fight with peril to one's life, and even to one's
last breath, than to face certain death."[76]

Various conclusions can be drawn from this interesting passage,
one of them being—although it may be "impious" to say so—men
can be made to do what they should do without any catechism from
the churches and without any instruction in, or guidance by, the
traditional law of nature. Fear, as Hobbes also pointed out, is the
passion to be reckoned on, fear not of eternal damnation but of a
sovereign armed with a "sting."[77])

Despite these pieties, anyone who reads him with a modicum of
care should be able to recognize his disagreements with the tradition and his agreement with Hobbes on the essential issues. Like
Hobbes, he argues that sociality is not natural, but that men can be
forced to be social, or forced to observe the rights of others, and
that by nature man is the fiercest and most uncontrolled of beings

---

[74] *Id.*, Book II, ch. 3, #5 at 185.

[75] *Id.*, Book I, ch. 2, #6 at 27; Book II, ch. 3, #4 at 184.

[76] *Id.*, Book II, ch. 3, #19 at 216.

[77] *Id.*, Book VII, ch. 2, #4 at 971.

whose situation makes peaceful coexistence impossible in the state of nature. Man is totally dependent on his own strength and judgment as to when, and by what means, it is necessary to defend himself. Thus, when "sane reason suggests that he is threatened" by another man, he may kill him, and do so without violating any of nature's laws. This, Pufendorf boldly says, is Hobbes's meaning too. Sociality comes with civil society, and civil society is founded when men, anxious to escape "the infinite miseries of a state of nature"—strong Hobbesian language that—covenant one with another to transfer their natural powers to a sovereign. Civil society arises out of fear and it is ultimately fear that the sovereign relies on to get men to obey the terms of the covenant: "divine vengeance moves with slow foot and often unfolds itself in hidden ways."[78]

His differences with Hobbes are, however, significant. To a greater extent than did Locke, Pufendorf delineates an institutional arrangement designed to deal with the problem that Hobbes acknowledged but left unsolved, that of a tyrannical sovereign. Men are "endowed with natural liberty and equality" and when they covenant to enter civil society they may do so either absolutely or, unlike Hobbes's men, conditionally. The agreement is absolute if they agree to remain subject to the sovereign authority no matter what form of government the majority of them subsequently decide on, or conditional on the part of a man who "stipulates that the form of government be such as he approves of." What is more important, and was to prove decisive to the future of constitutional government, Pufendorf requires another covenant, this one between the members of the civil society so formed and the sovereign, or "rulers," a covenant by which the former agree to obey and the latter agree to care for "the common security and safety."[79] On the basis of Hobbes's principles, Pufendorf moves beyond Hobbes to state the necessity of a written constitution. The supreme sovereign is not "accountable." In fact, he (or it) is "superior" to the civil laws and "to raise any question regarding divine and natural laws would be folly."[80] But he is bound by the "express convention" he made with the people. The limits to the sovereign's powers, like the

[78] *Id.*, Book VII, ch. 1, #4, 7, 10, 11; ch. 8, #1 at 1103; see also Book VII, ch. 3, #1 and ch. 4, #3.

[79] *Id.*, Book VII, ch. 2, #6, 7, 8 at 974–77.

[80] *Id.*, Book VII, ch. 6, #2, 3 at 1055, 1056.

powers themselves, derive from the will of the people and not from God or the laws that, according to Coke and others of his time and before, God wrote in the heart of man. Because the people transfer to him their natural rights, they may themselves, at the time of the transfer, limit sovereignty. Specifically, they may prescribe "certain institutions and a particular manner of conducting affairs."[81] Here is one of the sources in modern political philosophy of the idea of a written constitution; but there is nothing here to support Grey's suggestion that Pufendorf endowed judges with the authority to enforce the terms of this constitution, to say nothing of an "unwritten" constitution.

Pufendorf, he writes, "made clear that acts by a ruler violating either natural law or the constitution were not merely wrongful or unjust but were void—without legal effect."[82] The passage he cites in support of this statement, and the only passage he cites, is as follows:[83]

> The sovereignty of a king is more strictly limited, if, at its transfer, an *express* convention is entered into between king and citizens that he will exercise it in accordance with certain basic laws, and on affairs, over the disposal of which he has not been accorded absolute power, he will consult with an assembly of the people or council of nobles, and that without the consent of one of the last two he will make no decision; and if he does otherwise, the citizens will not be bound by his commands on such affairs. The people that has set a king over them in this way is not understood to have promised to obey him absolutely and in all things, but in so far as his sovereignty accords with their bargain and the fundamental laws, while whatever acts of his deviate from them, are thereby void and without force to obligate citizens.

This is his authority for saying that Pufendorf supports those revolutionary Americans who (he says) insisted that judges have the power to enforce fundamental human rights or an unwritten constitution. But the passage says no such thing. It says nothing about a judiciary, nothing about natural law, and the context makes it clear that by "fundamental laws" Pufendorf is referring to the terms of the "express convention."

---

[81] *Id.*, Book VII, ch. 6, #9 at 1066.

[82] Grey, *Origins of the Unwritten Constitution*, note 31 *supra*, at 861.

[83] PUFENDORF, note 69 *supra*, Book VII, ch. 6, #10 at 1070 (emphasis added).

Because men are anxious to escape the "infinite miseries of a state of nature," they are willing to give up a portion of their natural liberty and powers to the sovereign whom they endow by their convenant. They will do so because they think their condition will be improved in civil society. To make it more certain that it will be improved, they will transfer to the sovereign "no more power . . . than what a man of reason may judge" to be necessary to "the common peace and defence." The next question is obvious: Who decides whether the sovereign has violated the covenant by exceeding the limits of his lawful powers? Pufendorf answers this question in the sentence last quoted: "What may at any particular moment work to that end [that is, will conduce to the common peace and defense] is a matter for decision, not by those who do the transferring, but by him on whom that power was transferred."[84] If, despite the institutional checks that are written in the "express covenant," the sovereign abuses his power, Pufendorf, like Hobbes, can only counsel the people to endure these crimes with the same patience with which they endure "drought, floods, and all other acts of nature."[85] If the crimes become unendurable, they can exercise their natural right to rebel.

Pufendorf might have advocated judicial review—that is, he might have constituted a body of judicial guardians of the "express convention"—but his principles would not permit judicial enforcement of the terms of an unwritten constitution. This can be demonstrated by reflecting on what it means to say that the decisive political fact is that all men are by nature free and equal.

To hold this view is to hold that there are no natural differences among men that qualify anyone to rule anyone other than himself: no right by grace of God and no entitlement by virtue of a quality possessed unequally. If the decisive political fact is that men are naturally free and equal, then no one possesses a valid claim to rule, whether he be wise, good, godly, beautiful, strong, experienced, or whatever. In Mansfield's terms, the only legitimate ruler is an artificial ruler. Stated otherwise, the only legitimate government is man-made, an artifact fashioned out of the wills of men anxious to escape their natural condition, which is characterized by the ab-

---

[84] *Id.*, Book VII, ch. 6, #13 at 1077.

[85] *Id.*, Book VII, ch. 2, #14 at 985.

sence of rule and unendurable. "We the people" make government. Pufendorf's view is wholly in accord with this:[86]

> Now a union of wills cannot possibly be encompassed by the wills of all being naturally lumped into one, or by only one person willing, and all the rest ceasing to do so, or by removing in some way the natural variation of wills and their tendency to oppose each other, and combining them into an abiding harmony. But the only final way in which many wills are understood to be united is for every individual to subordinate his will to that of one man, or of a single council, so that whatever that man or council shall decree on matters necessary to the common security, must be regarded as the will of each and every person.

According to the traditional natural law teaching, however, men are not equal in every relevant respect. In principle, the illuminations of reason are available to all men, but they are clearer to virtuous men and, because they are clearer to them, these men can acquire an expertise in the natural law and may rightly claim political authority. Men in general can have only a "superficial" knowledge of this law of nature, said one English authority. Even the king's knowledge is, compared with that of his judges, "superficial."[87] Indeed, the esteemed Sir Edward Coke dared to make this very point in his famous confrontation with King James at Hampton Court in 1608.[88] Thus, if it were the case that Pufendorf held to this older understanding of natural law, he would have had to recognize that it was a legal discipline and that those who were schooled in that discipline would be entitled to exercise authority—even if only a judicial authority—over other men. But he did not do this. He could not consistently do this so long as he subscribed to the principles of the new natural law with respect to which no one can claim to be an expert or so long as he held to the view that all men are, in decisive respects, naturally free and equal.

On the basis of these new principles, legitimate government can arise only from a "union of wills," all wills being equal. For every man to "subordinate his will to that of another, or of a single council," requires him to acknowledge that his opinions of good

---

[86] *Id.*, Book VII, ch. 2, #5 at 972.

[87] FORTESCUE, DE LAUDIBUS LEGUM ANGLIAE, ch. 8. As quoted in CORWIN, note 34 *supra*, at 37.

[88] *Id.* at 38.

and bad or justice and injustice have no status in this process, that they are merely private opinions. He will acknowledge this only when other men, his co-covenantors, also acknowledge it, which is to say that everyone must agree that nobody is wise, good, or otherwise naturally qualified to rule. It is consistent with Pufendorf's principles if men, upon entering civil society, agree to withhold certain powers from the sovereign they "will" into being, and to do so in an "express convention." It would not be inconsistent if he were to counsel them to take the next step and endow a body of judicial guardians with the authority to represent their collective will and enforce it against the sovereign. But it would be inconsistent if Pufendorf were to permit men to endow anyone with the authority to enforce the terms of an unexpressed convention or an "unwritten constitution." Government built on the principle of the natural freedom and equality of all men is absolute government except—Pufendorf's contribution—insofar as certain powers are withheld. But when government is built entirely out of materials supplied by the will—or a union of wills—that will must be expressed. In a world where all opinions of justice and injustice are understood to be merely private opinions, no man can rationally agree to an arrangement where another man is authorized to convert his opinion into fundamental law.

Contrary, then, to what is said by Grey, Pufendorf lends no support for the view that the judiciary should enjoy a jurisdiction over an "unwritten constitution." There can only be private opinions of what is unwritten. This is also true of the treatises of Burlamaqui, Vattel, and Rutherforth.[89]

---

[89] Burlamaqui agrees that the sovereign authority may be limited by "fundamental laws" and that these laws are set down in a "formal engagement." They are, he says, "nothing else but the means" by which powers are limited. Examples are the requirements that the sovereign "consult the people themselves or their representatives" or that there be a formal separation of powers. BURLAMAQUI, THE PRINCIPLES OF NATURAL AND POLITICAL LAWS (trans. Nugent), Part I, ch. 1, secs. xlvi, xlii, xlvii, at 48–49 and *passim*. This is the chapter cited by Grey, but clearly it does not support his point about unwritten fundamental laws.

Grey is of course correct in saying that Vattel teaches that the sovereign is limited by fundamental laws, but he is, again, incorrect with respect to the source of these laws. Vattel says the people "ought to determine them and make them known with plainness and precision." VATTEL, THE LAW OF NATIONS, OR PRINCIPLES OF THE LAW OF NATURE (trans. Chitty), Book I, ch. 3, at 9. This is the chapter cited by Grey.

Rutherford's work is interesting only insofar as it demonstrates the extent to which, within a century, even Protestant "Divines" were speaking the language of Thomas Hobbes. Man lives originally in a "state of nature," which has a law of nature that forbids injury to others but of which each man is himself the executor: he has the right to use force against anyone

IV

One would have had reason to believe that the successful outcome of the Civil War would set to rest all doubt concerning the principles on the basis of which our country was founded. Chief Justice Taney's depreciation of the Declaration of Independence in his *Dred Scott* opinion was answered not only on the battlefield of Gettysburg but, a few months later, by Lincoln's address on the site of that battlefield. Lincoln insisted there, as he had in many other places and on many other occasions, that the nation was born in 1776 when the men in Philadelphia set it down as a self-evident truth that all men are created equal and are endowed by their Creator with certain unalienable rights, and that government is instituted to secure these rights. Taney, and the South in general, had denied this—John C. Calhoun and Alexander Stephens said it was a self-evident lie and went so far as to denounce Jefferson for asserting it—but what the South then lost to the arbitrament of battle it seems now to have won back in the groves of contemporary journalism and academe. Garry Wills, for example, has recently been praised in many important places for telling us that Lincoln was wrong about the Declaration of Independence,[90] and many a scholar has asserted that it was mere propaganda, a convenient weapon to use against the British and no more. Americans may have said that "the laws of nature and of Nature's God" entitled them to rebel against one government and to found a new one, but, we are now solemnly told, they did not mean it. They "never intended" that the "natural law" be used as a measure of "the rights and wrongs of colonial life."[91] As for self-evident truths, "our society does not, rightly does not, accept the notion of a discoverable and objectively valid set of moral principles."[92] So say some schol-

---

who puts him "in danger of suffering an injury." Because of the miseries of the state of nature men contract to form "civil society," agreeing to give up their natural rights. Grey notes that Rutherford teaches that men are not obliged always to obey the sovereign, but fails to note that this disobedience takes the form of rebellion. He also notes that Rutherford speaks of "unwritten laws," but fails to note that these laws may be repealed by simple legislation. In short, Rutherford offers no support to Grey's thesis. RUTHERFORD, INSTITUTES OF NATURAL LAW 255, 257, 396–97, 453–55 (2d American ed. Baltimore 1832).

[90] WILLS, INVENTING AMERICA: JEFFERSON'S DECLARATION OF INDEPENDENCE, esp. xxiii–xxvi (1978).

[91] POLE, THE PURSUIT OF EQUALITY IN AMERICAN HISTORY 11 (1978), as quoted in Ely, note 10 *supra*, at 24.

[92] *Id.* at 31–32.

ars. In our official documents, however, now as in the past, in what are described as "The Organic Laws of the United States," the Declaration of Independence occupies first place: in the Statutes at Large, in the Revised Statutes, in the United States Code, and in a volume entitled, *The Federal and State Constitutions, Colonial Charters, and Other Organic Laws of the United States.*[93] Whatever place it holds in the hearts and minds of today's scholars, in the Organic Law it is first and it is listed first. First, the Declaration of Independence; second, the Articles of Confederation; third, the Northwest Ordinance of 1787; and fourth, the Constitution and its amendments. And there, one should like to think, it will continue to be, an obstacle, as Lincoln rightly said, to anyone who "might seek to turn a free people back into the hateful paths of despotism." Its authors knew "the proneness of prosperity to breed tyrants, and they meant when such should re-appear in this fair land and commence their vocation they should find left for them at least one hard nut to crack."[94]

Of course, there was in the beginning, as there is now and, as Ely shows,[95] as there has been throughout the course of our history, a good deal of confusion as to what is meant by natural right and natural law. But what matters is the Founders' understanding and not that of Thomas Hutchinson, John C. Calhoun, or the host of modern writers quoted by Ely. And the Founders were not confused.

They referred to man's natural condition as a "state of nature."[96] They said that men were created free and equal, and that government was instituted by men to secure their equal rights—it was even proposed in the first Congress that the Bill of Rights contain as its first provision one stating not that power derives from God, but "that all power is originally vested in, and consequently derives

---

[93] I The Public Statutes at Large of the United States of America 1–3 (1854); Revised Statutes of the United States 3–6 (1878); I United States Code xix–xxi; (1940); I The Federal and State Constitutions, Colonial Charters, and Other Organic Laws of the United States 3–6 (1877). I am indebted for this information to an unpublished paper, Jaffa, *Inventing the Past: Garry Wills's Inventing America, and the Pathology of Ideological Scholarship.*

[94] Lincoln, speech at Springfield, Ill., June 26, 1857, in II The Collected Works of Abraham Lincoln 406 (Basler ed. 1953).

[95] Ely, note 10 *supra*, at 22–32.

[96] I Annals of Congress 421–22. See Berns, The First Amendment and the Future of American Democracy 16–18 (1976).

from the people," which was rejected only on the grounds of its redundancy (the Constitution's Preamble already made that point when it began with the words, "We the People").[97] In declaring their *right* to self-government, they invoked not the God of the Old and New Testaments (who, of course, says nothing about that right and whose grace—*Dei gratia rex* or *Dei gratia regina*—has traditionally been claimed by kings and queens), but "Nature's God"; and not the laws of nature that a providential God writes in the hearts of men and which only the judges can read, but the self-evident "laws of nature" that direct men to seek peace and security for their rights by contracting one with another to form society. They then, being authorized by those natural laws, ordained and established a Constitution in which they granted power, divided power, and, especially in the ninth and tenth sections of the first article, withheld powers. Modern natural law culminates in a government of powers. Anyone who argues that the Founders intended the courts to exercise a natural rights–natural laws jurisdiction must come to terms with the fact that the original and unamended Constitution contains precious few provisions for such courts to work with. Among the powers granted, however, was the "judicial power of the United States," which was vested in an independent judiciary. The importance of this cannot be exaggerated.

The idea of a constitutionally independent judiciary did not make its appearance in modern natural rights theory until the publication in 1748 of Montesquieu's *Spirit of the Laws*, a work that had an enormous influence in America.[98] To the Founders, Montesquieu—the "celebrated Montesquieu"[99]—was the man who, more than anyone else, showed them how to solve what they understood to be the problem of modern republican government. If Locke and Pufendorf feared a tyrannical monarch, the Founders had greater reason to fear a tyrannical people who would rule by right and misrule by inclination unless somehow prevented from doing so.

---

[97] I ANNALS OF CONGRESS 451, 790.

[98] The English judiciary described by Montesquieu had achieved a good deal of independence by the Act of Settlement of 1701. By this Act, the tenure of judges was made independent of the monarch. According to Hamilton, the independent judiciary is one of the discoveries of the new "science of politics." See THE FEDERALIST PAPERS No. 9, note 19 *supra*, at 72.

[99] THE FEDERALIST PAPERS, Nos. 47, 78, note 19 *supra*, at 301 and 466.

Montesquieu's system of separated powers provided the key to the solution of this problem. There is, however, a significant difference between his system and the American, and that difference has to do with the role of the judiciary. The American situation required a more powerful judiciary; unlike Montesquieu's judiciary, the American must have the power of judicial review.

Montesquieu presented his teaching respecting the separation of powers in the context of a discussion of what he saw, or pretended to see, as the English constitution. I recently explained this as follows:[100]

> In England not only was the legislative power separated from and thereby independent of the executive, and the judiciary separated from each of the other branches, but the legislative—in modern times the most dangerous branch—was itself divided into two houses, one popular and the other representing the hereditary nobility. Thus, the separation of the legislative power corresponded to a division of power between the traditional factions, the rich and the poor, or the few and the many. It would be an unstable balance . . . were it not for the fortuitous presence of the hereditary monarch who belonged to neither faction and whose interests could be said to correspond more or less to those of the country as a whole. The monarch used his absolute veto to maintain this balance between the factions and, thereby, to prevent each from oppressing the other. The judiciary was not involved in this balancing of factions; its role was to enforce the rule of law. What emerges from the legislature takes the form of law applicable to everyone, and the balance achieved in its formation guarantees its nonoppressive character. It is the function of the executive, separated from the legislature, to apply this law to everyone; and it is the function of the independent judiciary to see to it that it is the law, and only the law, that is being applied. . . . The *balance* of power, in which the judiciary plays no role, prevents class oppression; the *separation* of powers, in which the judiciary plays the indispensable role, prevents the oppression of any individual. This is how the separation of powers preserves liberty understood as security under the rule of law.

This was the judicial power described by Montesquieu as "in some measure next to nothing,"[101] and to which Hamilton referred in *Federalist* No. 78 as "next to nothing." It was not, and of course is not, the judicial power of the United States. In addition to the

---

[100] Berns, note 4 *supra*, at 5.

[101] MONTESQUIEU, THE SPIRIT OF THE LAWS, Book XI, ch. 6 at 156 (Nugent trans. 1949).

powers described by Montesquieu, the American judiciary was intended to exercise powers accorded by Montesquieu to the English monarch and the English House of Lords. The existence in England of these two institutions made possible the separation of powers in England. "If these hereditary institutions had not existed in England," I wrote, "it would have been necessary for [Montesquieu] to invent them; their absence in America made it necessary for the Founders to invent a substitute for them."[102] What they invented was a written constitution and judicial review, an approximation of the English monarch's absolute veto and the House of Lords's power to mitigate the severity of the laws.[103]

> What Montesquieu sought to accomplish by dividing the legislative power between two factions—the people and the nobility—the American Constitution seeks to accomplish by means of a written document that limits the legislative power by specifying "exceptions to the legislative authority; such, for instance, as that it shall pass no bills of attainder, no *ex post facto* laws, and the like." By enforcing these limitations, the Supreme Court will, in its way, maintain a balance between the factions that will arise in America, not between nobles and the people, but between few and many or creditors and debtors. What we have in America is a constitutional balance in the form of a limited Constitution, and the Court is very much a part of that balance.

In principle, either faction—the few or the many—might threaten the constitutional balance by seeking to promote its interests at the expense of the interests of others, but, clearly, the Founders expected the many to pose the greater danger.[104] They invented judicial review in order to preserve the written Constitution and its balance of power. The judges were to be, Hamilton said, "faithful guardians of the Constitution." Hence, when the Court first declared an act of Congress unconstitutional, Marshall justified this action, in part, by pointing to the requirement that public officials take an oath to support the Constitution and said that this applies "in an especial manner" to the judges.[105] What he meant is that their relation to the Constitution is unique. Unlike

---

[102] Berns, note 4 *supra*, at 6.

[103] *Id*. at 8. The quoted statement is from THE FEDERALIST PAPERS, No. 78, note 19 *supra*, at 466.

[104] THE FEDERALIST PAPERS, No. 78, note 19 *supra*, at 470.

[105] Marbury v. Madison, note 14 *supra*, at 180.

other officials, the judges have no constituents in the usual sense of
that term, and, this being so, they represent the Constitution and
derive all their authority from it. And by preserving the Constitution, the judges will secure rights, for the Constitution was adopted
"to secure these [natural] rights."

V

More, of course, than the principles of modern natural right
and law went into the founding of the United States. In theory, the
country was founded by men claiming rights against each other; in
fact, they were men closely associated in families, churches, and a
host of other institutions. In their books, government is created by
men living in a state of nature and seeking to escape its miseries; in
fact, the American government was created by men whose charac-
ters had been formed under the laws of an older and civilized
politics.

Moreover, although they knew that their principles forbade the
use of the laws directly to generate virtuous habits—the First
Amendment, which embodies those principles, forbids religion to
be established—they understood the need to preserve such habits,
and they did not regard it as improper for the laws to support the
private institutions (for example, the churches) in which they were
generated and were to be generated.[106] And they apparently took it
for granted that the laws would support the institution of the family; even the Supreme Court recognized its political importance.
Here is John Marshall writing for the Court in 1823:[107]

> All know and feel . . . the sacredness of the connection between
> husband and wife. All know that the sweetness of social inter-
> course, the harmony of society, the happiness of families, de-
> pend on that mutual partiality which they feel, or that delicate
> forbearance which they manifest towards each other.

The family may have had no place in liberal theory, or the theory
of modern natural rights,[108] but it was indispensable to the perpetu-

---

[106] BERNS, note 95 supra, ch. 1.

[107] Sexton v. Wheaton, 8 Wheat, 229, 239 (1823). Cf. Roe v. Wade, 410 U.S. 113 (1973),
and Planned Parenthood of Central Missouri v. Danforth, 428 U.S. 52 (1976).

[108] LOCKE, TREATISES II, ch. 6.

ation of the liberal state. So said Tocqueville,[109] and the Founders would surely have agreed.

It is not sufficient to say that the Founders looked only to the principles of modern natural right and law when they established and empowered the major political institutions. More than the teachings of Locke, Pufendorf, and Montesquieu went into their design for the Senate, for instance. This can be understood, I think, by asking what Hamilton meant when, in *Federalist* No. 9, he described representation as one of the "wholly new discoveries [made by] the science of politics." There had been representative bodies for thousands of years, so one must wonder what is new about American representation. Madison provides a clue to the answer in *Federalist* No. 63 when he says that in America there is no representation of the people *"in their collective capacity."* Whereas previously representation was used as a means of drawing people into government and administration, now, as Herbert Storing used to point out, it is meant to exclude the people as such from direct participation in government and administration. The Senate best illustrates representation in this modern sense. There was no noble class in America, and the Founders did not expect one, or want one, to develop. Thus, unlike in Montesquieu's system, there would be no noble class to balance against the people, and the separation of the legislative power would not in itself produce a balance of power. Furthermore, Madison, unlike John Adams, had no confidence that the American society would in time produce a natural aristocracy. Time, he anticipated, would produce distinctions in the society, but these would be along the lines of rich and poor, and the rich, merely as rich, would bring nothing of value to the Senate. But what Senators did not themselves bring into the Senate, they might nevertheless acquire in the Senate by being given long tenure, special powers, and being restricted in number. Combined, these constitutional elements might produce a substitute for a natural aristocracy. Madison's words in the Constitutional Convention are instructive on this point (he is speaking against the proposal to enlarge the number of Senators):[110]

---

[109] TOCQUEVILLE, II DEMOCRACY IN AMERICA, Book III, chs. 8–11.

[110] I THE RECORDS OF THE FEDERAL CONVENTION of 1787, 152 (Farrand ed. 1937) (emphasis added).

> The more the representatives of the people [are] multiplied, the more they [partake] of the infirmities of their constituents, the more liable they [become] to be divided among themselves either from their own indiscretions or the artifices of the opposite factions, and of course the less capable of fulfilling their trust. *When the weight of a set of men depends merely on their personal characters; the greater the number the greater the weight. When it depends on the degree of political authority lodged in them the smaller the number the greater the weight.*

Thus, with the institutions they devised, as well as with those private institutions they inherited from a preliberal past, the Founders sought to ensure the success of a country founded on the new principles of natural right and law. A country so founded —which is to say, a country founded on the principle of self-interest—could not be expected to flourish if it consisted only, or mainly, of self-interested men.

Nowhere is this better recognized than in the case of the federal judiciary. Only a few men, said Hamilton, "will have sufficient skill in the laws to qualify them for the stations of judges," and, even more to be regretted, fewer still who will unite "the requisite integrity with the requisite knowledge." It was, therefore, essential that these few be persuaded to forgo self-interest in favor of public service, or, as Hamilton puts it, to quit "a lucrative line of practice to accept a seat on the bench."[111] They must be promised life tenure and, if not a high salary, then at least one that may not be diminished during their continuance in office; this will guarantee their independence of the electors as well as of the persons they elect. Beyond that, the judges can expect to be honored for their services as "faithful guardians of the Constitution."[112]

This is the source of the problem of our time. Recipients of honors are not independent; they are dependent on those who bestow the honors. Hamilton does not acknowledge this problem, but he must have known that this method of perpetuating constitutional government will depend ultimately on the continued presence of a disposition among the Court's most attentive public—in our day, the legal profession and especially the professors of law— to honor judges who do indeed "guard the Constitution"[113] and its

---

[111] THE FEDERALIST PAPERS, No. 78, note 19 *supra*, at 471.

[112] *Id.* at 470.

[113] *Id.*

"fundamental [and] permanent" principles.[114] Instead of being dependent on the electors, either directly or indirectly, there is always the possibility that the judges will seek the approval of the law professors who, like Kenneth Karst, tell them to translate their ideas of what is good for the country into constitutional law.[115] But, as we know from Ronald Dworkin,[116] what the professors hold to be good for the country, or even what they hold to be fundamental rights, will be indistinguishable from what Hobbes and Locke called "private judgment." Modern constitutionalism began when, for very good reasons indeed, they sought a way to deny private judgment any role in politics.

---

[114] See note 14 *supra.*

[115] See note 12 *supra.*

[116] DWORKIN, TAKING RIGHTS SERIOUSLY (1977). As one critic says, "Dworkin seems to provide no way of arguing that judicial opinions (at least in regard to 'fundamental personal or political rights') have greater legitimacy than our own, assuming that we too have sincerely weighed the relevant materials." Levinson, *Taking Law Seriously: Reflections on "Thinking Like a Lawyer,"* 30 STAN. L. REV. 1071, 1106–7 (1978). Another reviewer points out that when "he is being most candid, Dworkin shows that what he aims at is no more than a systematic account of his personal conception of fairness and his own policy preferences as a conforming liberal professor of the 1970s. [He] surely has as much right as anyone else to offer the public his own opinions on these important matters. One might expect, however, that he would not so cavalierly dress up his own opinions as 'natural rights,' or call the culture-bound process by which he arrives at them 'philosophy.' " Pangle, *Rediscovering Rights,* 50 PUB. INTEREST 157, 160 (1978).

FRANK H. EASTERBROOK

SUBSTANCE AND DUE PROCESS

The Supreme Court keeps saying that it is entitled under the Due Process Clauses of the Constitution to determine what process is "due" when governmental action affects a liberty or property interest. Although the Court gives legislatures the utmost deference in specifying the particulars of a substantive right, it retains the privilege of determining what procedures must be used to evaluate claims of entitlement arising under the substantive rule.

I propose to examine the rationale of the peculiar constitutional dichotomy between substance and process in cases in which legislatures are given free rein in defining substance. It is peculiar, not only because there is no immediately apparent warrant for the distinction in the structure or history of the Constitution, but also because substance and process are two aspects of the same phenomenon. The process a legislature describes for vindicating the entitlements that it creates is a way of indicating how effective its plan should be. The more process it affords, the more the legislature values the entitlements and thus is willing to sacrifice to avoid mistakes. A court that protects the legislative power to define substantive entitlements ought to give it control of process as well.

Frank H. Easterbrook is Professor of Law, The University of Chicago.

AUTHOR'S NOTE: This paper extends an argument made in brief compass in Easterbrook, *Due Process and Parole Decision-making*, in PAROLE IN THE 1980's 77, 81–83, 88–94 (U.S. Parole Comm'n 1981). I thank Douglas G. Baird, Lea Brilmayer, Richard A. Epstein, Douglas Laycock, and Henry P. Monaghan for helpful comments on that paper, pointing the way to what some of them will see as improvements in this effort. I also thank Cass R. Sunstein for helpful discussions on the topic, and Albert W. Alschuler, Baird, Mary E. Becker, David P. Currie, Bruce E. Fein, Daniel R. Fischel, Dennis J. Hutchinson, Laycock, Richard A. Posner, Geoffrey R. Stone, and Sunstein for their comments on an earlier draft.

I. Introduction: The Substance-Process Dichotomy

A recent case illustrates the Court's treatment of the roles of the political and judicial branches. In *Logan v. Zimmerman Brush Co.*[1] the Court held that an Illinois statute prohibiting discrimination in employment because of handicap gave the employee a property interest in the opportunity to have a discrimination claim resolved by a court. Under state law, when the State's Fair Employment Practices Commission failed to convene a hearing within the allotted 120 days after Logan's complaint, the statute automatically let the employer off the hook, ending all proceedings.[2] The Supreme Court held that this statutory extinguishment of the statutory entitlement to a determination whether the employer had transgressed the prohibition of discrimination was a violation of the Due Process Clause of the Fourteenth Amendment. The State was not permitted to allow the Commission's neglect to obliterate Logan's rights without an opportunity for a hearing on the subject.

Logan is one of a number of similar recent cases. In *Arnett v. Kennedy*[3] the Court considered civil service laws that limited removal to "cause" but allowed an employee to be fired without a prior hearing. Three Justices argued that the procedural rules give meaning (or lack of meaning) to the "cause" rule, that employees must take the bitter with the sweet, and that there was no entitlement to any hearing other than the postdischarge process provided by statute. Six Justices concluded that the "cause" rule creates a property interest, and therefore the Due Process Clause creates an entitlement to notice and opportunity for hearing.[4] The Court up-

---

[1] 455 U.S. 422 (1982).

[2] Or so the Supreme Court of Illinois held, 411 N.E.2d 277, and the Supreme Court of the United States did not say that the state's court was mistaken in its construction of the statute, or that the construction was itself a violation of the Constitution.

The statute did not necessarily let the *state* off the hook; there was a decent argument that the Commission's gaffe left it open to damages. The Supreme Court of the United States saw this as an immaterial sidelight because there had been no hearing before the Commission blundered. 455 U.S. at 435–37. This is a mysterious treatment, because the Court did not say that a state statute causing the public to pay for private misdeeds would in any way violate the rights of the wronged person.

[3] 416 U.S. 134 (1974).

[4] See 416 U.S. at 164–67 (Powell & Blackmun, JJ., concurring in the judgment), *id.* at 177–86 (White, J., dissenting in part), *id.* at 206–11 (Douglas, Brennan, & Marshall, JJ., dissenting).

held the statute only because three of these six also concluded that a postdischarge hearing is adequate process.

The disparate positions of the Justices in *Arnett* were transmuted into a majority opinion in *Vitek v. Jones*,[5] a case invalidating a state statute permitting a prisoner to be sent to a mental hospital. The Court held that the statutory requirement for a psychiatrist to render an opinion that the prisoner "suffers a mental disease or defect" created a liberty interest in not being transferred to a mental hospital unless he so suffered. This liberty interest could be extinguished only after an opportunity for a hearing. The Court brushed aside the State's argument that, under the statute, the prisoner's entitlement was to a finding by the psychiatrist after procedures the psychiatrist deemed sufficient for an informed medical judgment, not that the finding be correct.[6] The Court concluded that once the state had granted the prisoner the expectation that transfer depended on some cause, it could not disappoint that expectation without a hearing.

Under these holdings due process analysis is a two-step routine. First the Court determines whether by statute or regulation the State has created an entitlement ("liberty or property") the existence or extent of which turns on some determinable facts. It also is enough that there is an antecedent interest in personal liberty, one the government may not extinguish except for cause.[7] (I call such antecedent interests "natural liberty," for reasons I shall explain in Part II.) Many cases stop here with a finding that the claim involves neither liberty nor property.[8] If nothing turns on determinable facts, there is no need for a hearing, because the state's officer need not pay attention to the claimant's demands; the state may do what

---

[5] 445 U.S. 480 (1980).

[6] 445 U.S. at 490–91.

[7] *Vitek* probably was such a case, for its judgment rested on alternative holdings, and Youngberg v. Romeo, 102 S. Ct. 2452 (1982), certainly was. *Cf.* Connecticut Board of Pardons v. Dumschat, 452 U.S. 458, 467–68 (1981) (White, J., concurring); Jago v. Van Curen, 454 U.S. 14 (1981).

[8] *E.g.*, Board of Regents v. Roth, 408 U.S. 564 (1972); Paul v. Davis, 424 U.S. 693 (1976); Bishop v. Wood, 426 U.S. 341 (1976); Meachum v. Fano, 427 U.S. 215 (1976); Moody v. Daggett, 429 U.S. 78 (1976); Leis v. Flynt, 439 U.S. 438 (1979); O'Bannon v. Town Court Nursing Center, 447 U.S. 773 (1980); Connecticut Board of Pardons v. Dumschat, 452 U.S. 458 (1981); Jago v. Van Curen, 454 U.S. 14 (1981). Compare Wakinekona v. Olim, 664 F.2d 708 (9th Cir. 1981) (state procedural rules create a property interest even if there is no substantive entitlement), cert. granted, 102 S. Ct. 2294 (1982), with Shango v. Jurich, 681 F.2d 1091 (7th Cir. 1982) (procedural rules do not create liberty or property interests).

it pleases. A claimant turned away without either hearing or substance has lost nothing to which his claim was better than anyone else's.

Except in the case of natural liberty (or the rare case in which the Court finds the substantive rules unconstitutional), the definition of the entitlement is a question wholly within the power of the political branches to answer.[9] Any political unit dissatisfied with the Court's resolution of entitlement questions may amend its statutes or regulations so that the decision no longer is controlled by determinable facts. No entitlement, no process. And the Supreme Court reviews substantive law under the most lenient standards. Legislation affecting economic interests, and most other interests as well, will be sustained as long as the Court can conceive of a set of facts under which the legislation would be rational.[10] If, however, the constitution, statute, or regulation creates a liberty or property interest, then the second step—determining "what process is due"—comes into play. At this step the legislative disposition gets some, but not very much, deference.

The most important of the recent cases in this line is *Mathews v. Eldridge*.[11] The Court explained that[12]

> identification of the specific dictates of due process generally requires consideration of three distinct factors: First, the private interest that will be affected by the official action; second, the risk of an erroneous deprivation of such interest through the procedures used, and the probable value, if any, of additional or substitute procedural safeguards; and finally, the Government's interest, including the function involved and the fiscal or administrative burdens that the additional or substitute procedural requirement would entail.

---

[9] Cases such as *Leis* and *Dumschat* hold that there is no constitutional requirement that states have substantive rules. They may use a subjective or even a random process for determining both entitlement to benefits and exposure to detriments. Although many people find subjective or random, and thus often arbitrary, decisionmaking objectionable, there is no way around arbitrariness: the use of rules may yield results equally arbitrary.

[10] Schweiker v. Hogan, 102 S. Ct. 2597 (1982); Railroad Retirement Board v. Fritz, 449 U.S. 166 (1980); Vance v. Bradley, 440 U.S. 93 (1979); Usery v. Turner Elkhorn Mining Co., 428 U.S. 1 (1976). Often the conceived-of rationale is of transparent thinness, *e.g.*, Williamson v. Lee Optical Co., 348 U.S. 483 (1955); Kotch v. Board of River Port Pilot Commissioners, 330 U.S. 552 (1947), and in many cases, such as those using the step-at-a-time doctrine, there is no conceived-of rationale at all, e.g., Clements v. Fashing, 102 S. Ct. 2836, 2847 (plurality opinion), 2850 (Stevens, J., concurring) (1982).

[11] 424 U.S. 319 (1976).

[12] *Id.* at 335.

The Court made it clear that it would conduct the balancing itself, assigning its own weights and assessing the probabilities and interests. To be sure, it would listen to the legislature's views on these subjects, embodied in the statutes, with interest and respect, but with no need to accept the views as binding.

In cases since *Eldridge* the Court has conducted an essentially unrestrained interest balancing. In two cases it has held that judicial damages remedies for administrative error were sufficient process,[13] but in the others it has insisted on hearings, more or less elaborate, as part of an administrative procedure. The administrative procedure itself must afford an opportunity for a hearing "at a meaningful time and in a meaningful manner,"[14] which sometimes varies with the identity of the affected party and the nature of his problem.[15]

In many of the cases the amount of process that was due varied directly with the Court's assessment of the weight of the interest at stake. The greater the interest, the more errors matter to the affected people; the more errors matter, the more society should be willing to spend to prevent errors; the more it should be willing to spend, the more the Constitution requires it to spend. So, for example, when the case involves termination of a parent's rights in his children, only the most elaborate process, including counsel and an elevated burden of proof, will do.[16] But when a prisoner seeks release on parole only a cursory review is necessary. Because he has already been convicted after a trial, his interest in freedom is largely gone anyway.[17]

---

[13] Ingraham v. Wright, 430 U.S. 651 (1977); Parratt v. Taylor, 451 U.S. 527 (1981).

[14] Armstrong v. Manzo, 380 U.S. 545, 552 (1965), a question-begging formula quoted most recently in Logan v. Zimmerman Brush Co., 455 U.S. 422, 437 (1982).

[15] Lassiter v. Department of Social Services, 452 U.S. 18 (1981) (due process entitlement to counsel in parental rights termination matters must be evaluated case by case); Greene v. Lindsey, 102 S. Ct. 1874, 1879 (1982) (in circumstances of a particular case, notice of eviction by posting on a tenant's door is unconstitutional). More commonly, however, "procedural due process rules are shaped by the risk of error inherent in the truthfinding process as applied to the generality of cases, not the rare exceptions." Mathews v. Eldridge, 424 U.S. 319, 344 (1976). See also Santosky v. Kramer, 102 S. Ct. 1388, 1396 (1982); Bishop v. Wood, 426 U.S. 341, 349–50 (1976). *Cf.* Vermont Yankee Nuclear Power Corp. v. Natural Resources Defense Council, Inc., 435 U.S. 519, 546–47 (1978) (procedural rules always should be determined before the proceeding starts).

[16] Santosky v. Kramer, 102 S. Ct. 1388 (1982). But see Vance v. Terrazas, 444 U.S. 252 (1980) (Due Process Clause does not bar Congress from selecting preponderance of the evidence standard for denationalization proceedings). Grandchildren may be another matter. Ellis v. Hamilton, 669 F.2d 510 (7th Cir. 1982).

[17] Greenholtz v. Inmates, 442 U.S. 1 (1979).

The Court approaches its due process question much as an ideal legislature would, asking statute by statute, and sometimes case by case, what is the optimal amount of process. The Court does not treat substantive entitlements in anything like that manner.

II. CONSTITUTIONAL HISTORY

One possible reason for the difference could be that the language of the Constitution requires it. This is not a very good reason, though. The language of the provisions—"No person shall . . . be deprived of life, liberty, or property, without due process of law"—could mean just about anything. To one steeped in the decisions of the last twenty years, it seems quite natural to read the words as a general grant of power to courts to ensure that all procedures are "due," or fair.[18] But this is hardly the only possible reading. "Process" could be a term of art, as in service of process. Then the Clause requires service in every case, ensuring that judicial proceedings are not carried out ex parte. Or perhaps "law" is a term of art, referring to statutes, so that the Clause requires courts to comply with procedures laid down in law but does not authorize judicial revision of law. One cannot choose among these readings without an understanding of what the words meant in 1791.

An increasing number of scholars maintain that history is no sure guide—indeed no guide at all—to constitutional interpretation. Three overlapping arguments are available to this end. One is that the meaning of the words in 1791 is not controlling and that each generation must invent its own constitution.[19] Another is that his-

---

[18] A (partial) list of those who take such a position reads like a list of constitutional all-stars. *E.g.*, ELY, DEMOCRACY AND DISTRUST: A THEORY OF JUDICIAL REVIEW 19 (1980); TRIBE, AMERICAN CONSTITUTIONAL LAW 501–62 (1978); Dworkin, *The Forum of Principle*, 56 N.Y.U.L. REV. 469 (1981); Mashaw, *Administrative Due Process: The Quest for a Dignitary Theory*, 61 B.U.L. REV. 885 (1981); Michelman, *Formal and Associational Aims in Procedural Due Process*, in NOMOS XVIII: DUE PROCESS 126 (Pennock & Chapman eds. 1977); Monaghan, *Of "Liberty" and "Property,"* 62 CORNELL L. REV. 405 (1977); Van Alstyne, *Cracks in "The New Property": Adjudicative Due Process in the Administrative State*, 62 CORNELL L. REV. 445 (1977). The views of these scholars concerning the "right" treatment of due process claims are as widely divergent as may be, but all treat the due process clauses as authorization for courts to identify and set in place those procedures courts judge to be fair and appropriate. (The groupings of scholars in subsequent notes also bring together people with divergent views, and that qualification should be taken as implicit in them.)

[19] *E.g.*, PERRY, THE CONSTITUTION, THE COURTS, AND HUMAN RIGHTS: AN INQUIRY INTO THE LEGITIMACY OF CONSTITUTIONAL POLICYMAKING BY THE JUDICIARY (1982); Parker, *The Past of Constitutional Theory—and Its Future*, 42 OHIO ST. L.J. 223 (1981).

tory is vague and manipulable and, worse, that there is no historical guide to the appropriate level of generality at which to read history.[20] Finally, it is argued that the Framers put open-ended clauses into the Constitution so that the judiciary could revise the rules to meet the needs of each new age.[21] The third, the "living constitution" approach, is the only one judges will confess to taking seriously.[22]

One branch of the living constitution approach rests on the language and history of particular constitutional provisions. One could prove or disprove it clause by clause. Another branch, perhaps the dominant one today, simply asserts that the Constitution as an entity should be construed with great flexibility, perhaps because of a meta-intent of the Framers, perhaps because there are a few clauses so elastic that the strictures of others are unimportant, perhaps just because the absence of such flexibility produces undesirable consequences. To the extent this second branch prevails, the history of each clause is less important, and the three positions are barely distinguishable in practice. Any of them allows courts to proceed in accordance with the judges' own notions of justice.

It is easy to become mired in a discussion of these approaches to constitutional construction. Scholars who spend too much time debating how to conduct a discourse may never be able to say anything. I therefore reject all three approaches without extended discussion here. It is enough for now to say that I agree with Justice Holmes, Judges Bork and Hand, Professors Black and Monaghan, and many others, that language and structure, informed by constitutional history, are the proper basis of interpretation and that, perhaps, they are all that count.[23]

---

[20] *E.g.*, Brest, *The Misconceived Quest for the Original Understanding*, 60 B.U.L. REV. 204 (1980); Dworkin, note 18 *supra*.

[21] *E.g.*, Grey, *Do We Have an Unwritten Constitution?* 27 STAN. L. REV. 703 (1975); Grey, *Origins of the Unwritten Constitution: Fundamental Law in American Revolutionary Thought*, 30 STAN. L. REV. 843 (1978); Laycock, *Taking Constitutions Seriously: A Theory of Judicial Review*, 59 TEX. L. REV. 343 (1981).

[22] *E.g.*, Trop v. Dulles, 356 U.S. 86, 101 (1958); Olmstead v. United States, 277 U.S. 438, 472–73 (1928) (Brandeis, J., dissenting); Weems v. United States, 217 U.S. 349, 373 (1910).

[23] Easterbrook, *Ways of Criticizing the Court*, 95 HARV. L. REV. 802, 828–29 & n.57 (1982). See BLACK, STRUCTURE AND RELATIONSHIP IN CONSTITUTIONAL LAW (1969); HAND, THE BILL OF RIGHTS 56–77 (1958); HOLMES, COLLECTED LEGAL PAPERS 295 (1920); Bork, *The Impossibility of Finding Welfare Rights in the Constitution*, 1979 WASH. U.L.Q. 695; Bork, *Neutral Principles and Some First Amendment Problems*, 47 IND. L.J. 1 (1971); Monaghan, *Our*

To the extent we wish to make propositions about the constitution we have, rather than about the one we wish we had, we must start with language, structure, and history even if we do not end there. That these tools of interpretation do not answer all questions does not mean they are useless. History lays down the baseline against which other arguments are measured; it also lays down the principles by which we can elaborate further from the historical experience.

The three methods of evading history that I sketched above are—at least if the second meaning is given to the living constitution argument—a method of constituting the courts a council of revision. Yet the Framers considered and rejected a council of revision. They provided an amending clause to permit accommodation of changed circumstances but to make that accommodation difficult. Nothing else would assure the initial support by extraordinary majorities that characterizes constitutional structure. An easy process of alteration produces instability in the nation's fundamental institutions, an instability that becomes more pronounced as time passes, if only because the chance of error increases as the years separate us from 1789. The whole idea of having a written constitution is inconsistent with constant revisions in interpretation, and there is no good evidence that the Framers designed such flexibility into the document. Words are designed to control. We have a text and must make sense of it even at some cost to today's notions of moral philosophy.

It is hard, moreover, to take the position that judges have great flexibility without saying that the rest of the actors in the government have similar flexibility, unbounded by either language or the commands of courts. Consider, for example, why we adhere to the notion of judicial review, to the principle that the legislative and

---

Perfect Constitution, 56 N.Y.U.L. Rev. 353 (1981); Rehnquist, *The Notion of a Living Constitution*, 54 Tex. L. Rev. 693 (1976); Lochner v. New York, 198 U.S. 45, 75–76 (1905) (Holmes, J., dissenting). See also the statements of Thomas Jefferson, reproduced in Haskins & Johnson, II History of the Supreme Court of the United States, Foundations of Power: John Marshall 1801–15, at 66 (1981). Compare Frankfurter & Corcoran, *Petty Federal Offenses and the Constitutional Guaranty of Trial by Jury*, 39 Harv. L. Rev. 917 (1927) (using historical approach to discover the meaning of the Sixth Amendment). Strangely enough, one of the strongest proponents of judicial revisionism concedes that Judge Bork's arguments are unanswerable. Perry, *Interpretivism, Freedom of Expression, and Equal Protection*, 42 Ohio St. L.J. 261, 266–84 (1981).

executive branches are bound by the judiciary's pronouncements. Judicial review, at least as Marshall proclaimed it, rests on the belief that the Constitution has an ascertainable meaning and, as the document granting power to Congress and the Court alike, limits what each may do.

When the Court states a judgment of unconstitutionality, it cannot just say why it finds its disposition a just result. It must also state a good reason why the other branches are required to pay attention. If the Court does not accept Congress's treatment of Congress's powers, why should Congress accept the Court's? When the Court claims a power of constitutional review, it must give a compelling reason why Congress and the President should follow the Court's view of Congress's power and of the Court's power too. The reason the Court states will usually take the form of an appeal to jointly held principles. It will assert, at a level of generality capable of generating belief:[24] "Someone else decided this question, at an earlier time, in a way that you will agree binds all institutions of government." Such a claim to prior decision forecloses a claim to substantial powers of judicial revision. A Court that finds in the Constitution limits on the power of Congress and the states has found the limits on its own power.

Surely it cannot avoid these limits by saying that it may update constitutional rules because the enunciation and application of principles is a function at which courts have become skilled, or because courts administer general principles better than any other institution. An argument based on experience begs the question whether the Court legitimately obtained (or maintains) this relative expertise. Moreover, the argument that power flows from aptitude is identical to the President's argument that he could seize and run the steel mills without Congress's authorization because Executives are good at such things, and to Congress's argument that Congress may appoint members to the Federal Election Commission because Members of Congress have special skills in election matters. The

---

[24] This is a variant of the neutral principles argument. The level of generality is important because there is a limit to the number of separate legal commands the Court can find in our rather short Constitution without giving rise to laughter by its listeners. *Miranda*, the abortion cases, and other statute-like decisions offend in this way by announcing that the Constitution contains a level of detail that is plainly missing.

reasons the Court gave for rejecting the President's and Congress's arguments apply to it too.[25]

This takes us back to the fundamental question: Did the Due Process Clause authorize courts in 1791 to write the procedural rules whenever Congress established a substantive entitlement by statute? I examine this by looking at the structure of the Bill of Rights, at the history of the due process language, and at the early judicial treatment of that language.

A. STRUCTURE

The Constitution of 1787 contains many specific procedural guarantees. There shall be no ex post facto legislation and no bills of attainder; the writ of habeas corpus is preserved; judgments are to receive full faith and credit. The Bill of Rights contains many more procedural guarantees: jury trial in civil cases; juries, bail, counsel, indictment, compulsory process, speedy and public trial, and the privileges against double jeopardy and self-incrimination in criminal cases. In the midst of these rules sits the Due Process Clause. It is inconceivable that such a clause could have been designed as a general authorization to courts to find and enforce whatever procedures judges thought important when the government threatened the people with loss. The rules specifically listed in 1787 and 1791 were the procedures then thought important to just adjudication. It is hard to name any procedural right that was left out, and the Framers carefully distinguished between criminal and civil suits in listing what was to be protected.

Now, there is nothing structural that forecloses the possibility that the Due Process Clause authorizes judges to add to the list of necessary procedures. Neither, however, is there support for such an interpretation, and the genesis of the Bill of Rights as a whole suggests how implausible it would be. The Bill of Rights was a palliative grudgingly added to the Constitution by Federalists convinced that it was unnecessary but who were nonetheless willing to assure doubters that the new central government would not snatch

---

[25] Buckley v. Valeo, 424 U.S. 1, 118–43 (1976) (only the President may appoint Officers of the United States under Article II); Youngstown Sheet & Tube Co. v. Sawyer, 343 U.S. 579 (1952) (even in national emergency, only Congress may authorize the seizure of steel mills).

back the freedoms so recently won in the Revolutionary War.[26] Those who opposed the Constitution argued that a tyrannical legislature would sweep away the rights hard won, and that a faithless Executive, like the King of England, would disregard the rules laid down by the people's representatives. The Bill of Rights was designed to allay these fears. It was a promise that the known rights would not be lost. Its provisions were drawn from state constitutions and declarations of rights with antecedents in England; almost all had understood meanings in the colonies. The Bill of Rights should be understood, like some environmental legislation, as containing a nondegradation principle. Things were not supposed to get worse.

B. ANTECEDENTS OF DUE PROCESS

The inferences from structure are confirmed by the history of the due process language inserted in the Fifth Amendment. Due process is not a new phrase but one borrowed from England with an established meaning—or, rather, two established meanings.[27] One of the sources of the due process language is the Magna Carta, in which the King promised to conduct certain matters "per legem terrae," or "by the law of the land." This had, at least initially, a plain enough meaning. The King's hands were tied when it came to criminal procedure, because he could not arbitrarily declare the law of the land without consulting his barons. The law was customary law, but the emerging Parliament came to have a hand in its creation. The other source is a statute enacted in 1354 which used the magic words "due process." The statute provided that no person could be evicted from lands or leases, disinherited, imprisoned, or

---

[26] For brief histories of the development of the Bill of Rights from two perspectives, see GOEBEL, I HISTORY OF THE SUPREME COURT OF THE UNITED STATES: ANTECEDENTS AND BEGINNINGS TO 1801, at 431–56 (1971); STORING, WHAT THE ANTI-FEDERALISTS WERE FOR (1981).

[27] The history has been covered repeatedly. The following references to secondary sources support the assertions in the text and reduce the number of footnotes. BERGER, GOVERNMENT BY JUDICIARY 193–200 (1977); II CROSSKEY, POLITICS AND THE CONSTITUTION IN THE HISTORY OF THE UNITED STATES 1102–16 (1953); McKECHNIE, MAGNA CARTA: A COMMENTARY ON THE GREAT CHARTER OF KING JOHN (2d ed. 1914); Corwin, *The Doctrine of Due Process of Law before the Civil War*, 24 HARV. L. REV. 366–85, 460–79 (1911); Jurow, *Untimely Thoughts: A Reconsideration of the Origins of Due Process of Law*, 19 AM. J. LEGAL HIST. 265 (1975); McIlwan, *Due Process of Law in Magna Carta*, 14 COLUM. L. REV. 27 (1914).

executed, "without being brought in answer by due process of law."[28] This, too, had a plain enough meaning. The courts could not proceed in any important civil or criminal case without "process," that is, without service of a writ on the defendant giving him an opportunity to appear in answer to the charges. The statute forbids ex parte procedures in important judicial matters. The Magna Carta bound the King and the 1354 statute the judges. Parliament was unfettered. Procedures named in statutes were due process of law.

Although Parliament continued to create new procedures as it went, without hindrance by the courts (on this score at least), Lord Coke insisted, both in his *Institutes* and in *Dr. Bonham's Case*, that "per legem terrae" also included some component of natural law that Parliament could not evade.[29] Coke was a solitary voice in English law. His natural law utterances were uninfluential with other English judges and other commentators. Blackstone simply recites that the language "protected every individual in the nation in the free enjoyment of his life, his liberty, and his property, unless declared to be forfeited by the judgment of his peers or the law of the land."[30] It is necessary to pay attention to Coke, not because he was right in describing the law of England, but because the Framers may have thought Coke right and incorporated his error into our fundamental law.

Both the Magna Carta language and the 1354 statute were known in the colonies. Blackstone, for example, mentions the statute and again uses the magic words.[31] Coke's *Institutes* were well read in the colonies, too, so that his interpretation of "per legem terrae" was available. Eight of the original states had constitutional provisions that employed "law of the land" language, implying the Magna Carta as a source and, perhaps, implying adoption of Coke's view that some principles of natural law restricted the power of the legislature to change established judicial practices. None of the states had a "due process" clause in its constitution.

The language of the Fifth Amendment is a mixture of the two English provisions. The horticulturalist for this hybrid was an un-

---

[28] 28 Edw. III ch. 3 (1354).

[29] II COKE, INSTITUTES 50 (4th ed. 1671); Bonham's Case, 8 Rep. 118a.

[30] 4 BLACKSTONE, COMMENTARIES ON THE LAWS OF ENGLAND 417 (1st ed. 1769).

[31] *Id.* at 313.

known member of the legislature of New York, which adopted it as part of a statutory guarantee of liberties on January 17, 1787.[32] The bill went through the state's legislature without debate and then was mined by John Lansing for tidbits to be included in New York's list of recommendations for the Bill of Rights. Once again it passed without debate. And when it was presented to Congress, it was included in the Bill of Rights and passed without (recorded) debate still a third time. Whether no one noticed the hybridization—or whether no one cared, because all assumed that it had one or both of the traditional meanings—is now unknowable.

All of this makes the history of the language in New York of some interest, and the legislators in New York were aware of Coke's views. To the extent they discussed English commentators, they mentioned Coke but not Blackstone. Thus one would like to know what Coke's position entailed. As it turns out, not much. Coke did not maintain that natural law supplied judges with roving commissions. Coke's natural law was a rather tame creature, satisfied with the inalienable rights to indictment and jury trial.[33] Coke's natural law dealt only with judicial proceedings, and it did not have much to say about them. He would have required that Parliament adhere to certain procedural rights established fom the time of Magna Carta, but he never asserted that judges could add to the stock of procedural rules.

Moreover, Coke's approach applied only to life, liberty, or property. Those words then described a small collection of rights. Life referred to capital punishment; liberty to freedom from physical custody; property to estates in fee and to a motley collection of additional interests (leases, estates) that made up the bulk of private wealth.[34] These were largely the rights then thought to exist by

---

[32] 2 Laws of the State of New York 344.

[33] Coke's presentation of his position on the meaning of the law of the land is too rambling to present here, but the following quotation gives the flavor, II INSTITUTES 47 (4th ed. 1671): "No man shall be . . . dispossessed of his Freehold (that is) lands, or livelihood, or of his liberties, or free customes, as belong to him by his free birthright, unlesse it be by the lawfull judgment, that is, verdict of his equals (that is, of men of his own condition) or by the Law of the Land (that is, to speak it once for all) by the due course and processe of the Law."

[34] Compare COKE, note 33 *supra*, Curtis, *Review and Majority Rule*, in SUPREME COURT AND SUPREME LAW 177 (Cahn ed. 1954), Pound, *Liberty of Contract*, 18 YALE L.J. 454 (1909); and Shattuck, *The True Meaning of the Term "Liberty" in Those Clauses in the Federal and State Constitutions Which Protect "Life, Liberty, and Property,"* 4 HARV. L. REV. 365 (1891) (collecting earlier sources), with Board of Regents v. Roth, 408 U.S. 564, 572 (1972).

virtue of natural law and not from the intervention of government. They were the basic rights that a Hobbesian man could assert even against Leviathan. Additional entitlements, such as the dole, were not part of the list; Coke's procedural guarantees did not apply. In this paper I use "natural liberty" to refer to the kind of entitlements that Coke or the Framers would have seen as part of "life, liberty, or property." Although the Court has added a detailed gloss to the words since 1791, there is no support in either the structure or history of the Constitution for a conclusion that Coke's natural law procedural rights should be applied to every subsequent addition to "life, liberty, or property."

Once again, I have not tried to offer a definitive reading of due process, both because Coke's views are not wholly clear and because the extent to which the Framers adopted Coke is not certain. Moreover, there are doubtless cases in which the difference between the Magna Carta reading and the 1354 statute reading of the language would affect the outcome. All of these matters of potential dispute are of little moment to the broad outlines. It may be assumed that the Due Process Clause embodies Coke's views at their broadest. This would not affect very many cases. Whatever reading holds, the Due Process Clause places little or no legitimate restraint on the contents of legislation. Judges and Presidents must follow rules laid down in "law"; judges may not act ex parte in important matters; but Congress may establish as law such procedures as it pleases, subject only to the constraint that it not abrogate certain long-recognized judicial procedures when fundamental natural liberties are at stake.[35] Because Coke's fundamental procedures

---

[35] This may have been what Alexander Hamilton had in mind in a speech made to the legislature of New York on February 6, 1787, one of the few extant treatments of due process by one of the Framers. Hamilton protested that the Act of January 26, 1787, which disqualified privateers from public office, acted directly on particular people's property without due process: "Some gentlemen will hold that the law of the land will include an act of the legislature. But Lord Coke . . . in his comment upon a similar clause in Magna Charta, interprets the law of the land to mean presentment and indictment. . . . But if there were any doubt upon the constitution, the bill of rights enacted in this very session removes it. It is there declared that, no man shall be disfranchised or deprived of any right, but by 'due process of law,' or the judgment of his peers. The words 'due process' have a precise technical import, and are only applicable to the proceedings of the courts of justice; they can never be referred to an act of the legislature. Are we willing then to endure the inconsistency of passing a bill of rights, and committing a direct violation of it in the same session?" 4 WORKS OF ALEXANDER HAMILTON 35 (Syrett & Cooke eds. 1962). Hamilton's view was that although legislatures may well commit wrongs—as by taking property directly without compensation or passing bills of attainder or ex post facto laws, other provisions of the Bill of

were secured by other provisions of the Bill of Rights, this branch
of the language's ancestry drops out. All that is left are prohibitions
designed to compel other departments of government to follow the
legislature's plan.

A provision so limited would do little service unless, contrary to
the expectations of the Federalists, the Executive began to behave
in a monarchical fashion. (Congress was not worried in 1791 about
judicial tyranny.) But monarchy and tyranny did not appear in the
United States under the Constitution. Laws were passed and (usually) obeyed in the ordinary course. The Due Process Clause accordingly was largely irrelevant. The Clause that entered the Constitution without debate, indeed almost without notice, fell into
desuetude. The Supreme Court was not even to mention it for
sixty-five years, although in the interim it handed down hundreds
of cases interpreting other provisions of the Constitution.[36] The
Due Process Clause escaped the Court's notice for the same reason
it escaped the Framers': it stated an uncontroversial principle that
was expected to be trivial.

Early commentators took what was, if possible, an even narrower reading of the clause than the one I have offered. They saw it
as limited to criminal cases. Chancellor Kent remarked that due
process meant only "law in its regular course of administration
through courts of justice" in criminal cases.[37] Justice Story agreed,

---

Rights to which he referred—the "due process" language describes the business of courts.
Legislatures may not justify their own appropriations by calling legislative hearings "due
process." Hamilton's speech both supports the proposition that the Due Process Clause
derived from Magna Carta and establishes its nature as a source of procedural rules for
courts. Professor Laycock's assertion that Hamilton was maintaining that New York's law
violated due process, as opposed to other notions of just government, is groundless. See
Laycock, *Due Process and Separation of Powers: The Effort to Make the Due Process Clauses Nonjus-
ticiable*, 60 TEX. L. REV. ——— (1982).

[36] Most state courts during these years also concluded that the clause places no limits on
legislation. Meanwhile, however, a few of them were experimenting with the natural law
overtones of Coke's approach. Corwin, note 27 *supra*. These experiments were to turn into
the doctrine of substantive due process, which found its first expression on the Supreme
Court in Chief Justice Taney's opinion for three Justices in Scott v. Sandford, 60 U.S. (19
How.) 393, 450 (1857): "And an act of Congress which deprives a citizen of his liberty or
property, merely because he came himself or brought his property into a particular Territory
of the United States, and who had committed no offence against the laws, could hardly be
dignified with the name of due process of law." Acting in a disgraceful cause, Taney invoked
due process in the only way he could: without citation of authority or any semblance of
reasons.

[37] 2 KENT, COMMENTARIES ON AMERICAN LAW 13 (1st ed. 1827); see also *id.* at 9–10; and
see the 9th ed., 1853, at 608–9, 620–21.

treating the due process language as limited to criminal trials and then assuring only indictment and proceedings in conformity with the prevailing modes.[38] Kent and Story thought that mere conformity to prevailing procedures, plus adherence to Coke's fundamental rights of indictment and jury, always would satisfy the constitutional demand. The Clause had no application at all to civil cases, and both Kent and Story would have found incoherent an assertion that the Clause had something to say about the procedures Congress could specify for poor relief, public employment, or the disposition of other new substantive entitlements.

C. THE EARLY CASES

The use of due process to revise procedures laid down in statutes for the disposition of statutory entitlements is a recent invention. The Supreme Court first addressed the meaning of the Due Process Clause in 1856. The long delay has significance of its own, because Congress got in the habit, right from the start, of passing statutes that specified few procedures. The First Congress, for example, enacted in 1789 a law requiring coasting vessels of specified weights to obtain licenses and limiting issuance to vessels owned by citizens. The statute did not specify any procedures for use in determining the weight of the vessels or the nationality of their owners.[39] The first patent law, enacted a few months later, allowed patents for "useful and important" inventions but neither defined the term nor specified procedures for use in making the determination.[40] Like the license statute, it committed these things to the discretion of civil servants. If people at the time thought such procedure-free statutes questionable, they did not want for opportunities to test them.

The first case, *Murray's Lessee v. Hoboken Land & Improvement Co.*,[41] was a suit brought by the transferees of a collector of customs who, according to the Treasury Department, was some $1.3 million in arrears in turning over the proceeds. The Solicitor of the Treasury, acting pursuant to statute, issued a distress warrant and seized the collector's property. The collector received no opportu-

---

[38] 3 STORY, COMMENTARIES ON THE CONSTITUTION 652–61 (1833).

[39] Act of Sept. 1, 1789, 1 Stat. 55.

[40] Act of April 10, 1790, 1 Stat. 109.

[41] 59 U.S. (18 How.) 272 (1856).

nity for a hearing; the Solicitor just engaged in self-help, and the distress warrant gave the collector notice of the purpose of the invasion. The Court held, unanimously, that this governmental action did not violate the Due Process Clause.

Justice Curtis's scholarly opinion traced the origin of the Clause from Magna Carta, explaining that the words due process "were undoubtedly intended to convey the same meaning as the words 'by the law of the land.' "[42] He also referred to Coke, and, drawing on Coke's natural law precepts—no longer natural law if they had been embodied in the Fifth Amendment—concluded that "it was not left to the legislature to enact any process which might be devised,"[43] apparently because free rein for Congress would enable it to destroy every person's natural liberties. But then what would guide the Court in devising these constraints on legislation? Justice Curtis thought that this called for a two-step inquiry: first reference to specific constitutional provisions and then inspection of "those settled usages and modes of proceeding existing in the common and statute law of England."[44]

The problem with this inquiry, of course, is that settled modes of proceeding call for pleas, answers, and trials before people may be deprived of property, as the collector had been. So Curtis took two more steps. He observed that distress collections of debts due the crown had been exceptions to the usual proceedings in England, and he noticed that the collector took his job knowing of this method of distress collection.[45]

There was, finally, a complication. The distress collection statute waived the sovereign immunity of the United States by permitting the collector to bring suit to recover his property if he could show that he had not withheld sums from the Treasury. The collector argued that this made the proceeding a judicial matter. As a result, he maintained, due process required notice and trial before the deprivation. In modern terminology, he argued, as did the employee in *Arnett*, that his right to sue meant that he could be deprived of his property only for judicially ascertainable "cause";

---

[42] *Id.* at 276.

[43] *Ibid.*

[44] *Id.* at 277.

[45] The statute had been passed in 1820, and the Court thought there was common knowledge of it and other distress collection devices. *Id.* at 278, 281–82.

therefore the judges must decide what process is due and should not honor the statute. But this argument got him nowhere. The Court dismissed it by saying that the involvement of the judiciary in one part did not make of the whole a judicial proceeding. Because Congress was free to grant the collector nothing, it could grant half a loaf also.[46]

In the first due process case the Court adopted the historical method of construction yet sustained a procedure that gave the complainant less than the process usually available. He got less because, under historical precedents, this was the kind of dispute that Congress could remove from courts altogether, so that the usual judicial procedures fell away. He also got less because less was part of the bargain he struck, albeit implicitly, on becoming a collector of customs. One could almost call *Murray's Lessee* the first of the new property cases, in which the Court holds that a legislature with power to control substantive entitlements also may control procedure.

There are no other important procedural due process cases until *Hurtado v. California*[47] was decided in 1884. *Hurtado* involved the Due Process Clause of the Fourteenth Amendment, which, the Court held, meant the same as the Due Process Clause of the Fifth.[48] The defendant argued that due process in a criminal case required the state to obtain an indictment to commence any criminal proceeding. The case put a delicate question to the Court because the indictment requirement did not appear in the Fourteenth Amendment. To find an indictment requirement in due process is thus to accuse the Framers of some shockingly poor drafting. But not to find an indictment requirement in due process is to turn one's back on Coke, for indictment and jury trial were the two pillars of Coke's natural law addition to "per legem terrae," and *Murray's Lessee* had purported to follow Coke.

The Court got out of this difficulty by minimizing the role of natural rights in Coke's work. According to the opinion by Justice Matthews, Coke never meant that "per legem terrae" included par-

---

[46] *Id.* at 282–86.

[47] 110 U.S. 516 (1884).

[48] *Id.* at 534–35. The "incorporation" debate to one side, there is no serious argument that Congress intended the Due Process Clause to secure against the states rights more extensive than those secured by the Bill of Rights against the federal government.

ticular customary procedures; it included only the essential ones, suited to the matter at hand. Indictment was a requirement only in private prosecutions; public prosecutions often began by information.[49] Thus, the Court inferred, states may change their procedures: "a process of law, which is not otherwise forbidden, must be taken to be due process of law, if it can show the sanction of settled usage both in England and in this country; but it by no means follows that nothing else can be due process of law."[50] The Due Process Clause does not freeze existing procedures because that would "deny every quality of the law but its age, and . . . render it incapable of progress or improvement."[51]

It would have been neater had the Court recognized that the existence of prosecutions by information in England simply meant that Coke had been wrong—as he surely was—about the natural law content of "per legem terrae," or held that his views had not been adopted by the Framers. But the Court got to the same end by noticing how little Coke really had claimed for natural law. As a result, legislatures were substantially free to control the process to be used in courts, and any plausible legislative decision would be honored. It wound up by saying that due process "refers to that law of the land which derives its authority from the legislative powers . . . exercised within the limits" of the explicit constitutional rules.[52]

The Court nonetheless planted the seeds of subsequent revision. About to embark on an orgy of substantive due process, it baldly stated that arbitrary acts are not "law" and so cannot satisfy due process.[53] And Justice Matthews dropped into the opinion one passage that has been taken as an assertion that the demands of due process grow with time: "It is more consonant to the true philosophy of our historical legal institutions to say that the spirit of personal liberty and individual right . . . was preserved and developed by a progressive growth and wise adaptation to new circumstances."[54] Although this was inserted to show why legislatures

---

[49] *Id.* at 524–26.

[50] *Id.* at 528.

[51] *Id.* at 529.

[52] *Id.* at 535.

[53] *Ibid.* See Mugler v. Kansas, 123 U.S. 623, 661 (1887).

[54] *Id.* at 530.

could provide less process than everyone had thought necessary, it has been used since as an argument that courts may require legislatures to supply more process.

By the time of *Twining v. New Jersey*,[55] holding that due process does not require the states to implement any privilege against self-incrimination in criminal cases, there had been an outburst of due process decisions, most of them of the substantive variety.[56] The rules of procedural due process nonetheless were still simple. Legislative decisions were honored, and only two kinds of things had been found to violate the clause—ex parte judicial proceedings and judicial decisions in excess of statutory jurisdiction.[57] Subject to these requirements, the Court "has up to this time sustained all state laws . . . regulating procedure, evidence, and methods of trial."[58]

Justice Moody's opinion for the Court discussed *Murray's Lessee* with approval, but he had a familiar problem. Under the approach of *Murray's Lessee* the state law was of questionable constitutionality because the privilege was an inveterate part of English procedure.[59] If the law were to be sustained, the Court would have to elaborate on the *Hurtado* approach. Elaborate it did. States could omit any historical procedural step unless that step was "a fundamental principle of liberty and justice which inheres in the very idea of free government and is the inalienable right of a citizen of such a government."[60] As in *Hurtado* this was to be a modest inquiry, for Justice Moody cautioned that "we must take care that we do not import into the decision our own personal views of what would be wise, just and fitting rules of government to be adopted by a free people and confound them with constitutional limitations."[61] After all, the inquiry was designed to control omission of historically recognized steps in criminal prosecutions, which involved natural liberty. Certainly the Court was not so much as hinting that its

---

[55] 211 U.S. 78 (1908).

[56] *E.g.*, Lochner v. New York, 198 U.S. 45 (1905); Allguyer v. Louisiana, 165 U.S. 578 (1897).

[57] 211 U.S. at 110–12 (collecting cases).

[58] *Id.* at 111.

[59] *Id.* at 103–6.

[60] *Id.* at 106.

[61] *Id.* at 106–7.

"fundamental principle" approach could justify additions to the historical list, or any process at all in cases involving statutory entitlements: it forswore any such intention in the passages quoted above. Nonetheless, it was only a matter of time before the language of *Twining* would be turned against the purpose of its drafters.

Twining was decided in 1908. The transformation was not completed until *Goldberg v. Kelly* in 1970.[62] The movement was almost imperceptibly slow, but it is worth mentioning a few of the milestones.

Procedures honored only as shams are worthless. A phony trial violates due process because the defendant does not receive the benefits of the statutory procedures. In *Moore v. Dempsey*[63] the Court held that kangaroo courts are unconstitutional. There could have been no serious dispute about this outcome: the defendant received neither the (statutory) law of the land nor Coke's minima. The case is significant because of the way it reached the result: the opinion is reasoned wholly as a matter of natural law, with no reference to statutes, historically recognized procedures, or any of the earlier due process decisions. It is the first departure from the Court's assertion in *Twining* that only ex parte decisions or those without jurisdiction had been found unconstitutional.

The honor of being the first case to declare a state law unconstitutional for want of adequate procedures (other than for use of ex parte procedures) belongs to *Tumey v. Ohio* in 1927.[64] The statute gave the judge an allowance out of the fines in certain criminal cases but nothing otherwise, so that he was paid only if he convicted. The Court applied what it took to be the approach of *Murray's Lessee*, searching English precedents for any similar procedure in criminal cases.[65] It found only a general rule against excessive bias, and it concluded that the statute was invalid. One may quarrel with the application of Coke's method here, but the decision was rooted in a historical view of the Clause, and it plainly involved natural liberty.

---

[62] 397 U.S. 254 (1970).

[63] 261 U.S. 86 (1923).

[64] 273 U.S. 510.

[65] *Id.* at 522–26.

Powell v. Alabama,[66] the case of the Scottsboro boys, is an application of "per legem terrae" in a different style. An Alabama statute gave the defendants in this murder case the right to counsel, but in a racially charged atmosphere the judge manipulated counsel so that the defendants would not enjoy independent advice or assistance. A right present in the law was withheld in practice, albeit cleverly. The Court enforced the state-created right to counsel, but the approach of *Murray's Lessee* was nowhere in sight. It was unimportant, Justice Sutherland's opinion said, that English and colonial law would not have recognized a right to counsel at public expense; it was enough that Alabama's law did (as did the law of every state in capital cases). But there was more. The Court broadly hinted that on the facts before it, with uneducated defendants in a hostile community, due process required counsel no matter the contents of any law. Counsel in such cases may be "fundamental." For this it cited *Murray's Lessee*, *Hurtado*, and *Twining* without recognizing that those cases give no support to judicial augmentation of historically recognized procedures.

The kangaroo court holding in *Moore* supplied the basis of the decision in *Brown v. Mississippi*[67] that states could not extract confessions by torture. Torture was banned by law in England and every state. The Court thus could have distinguished *Twining* with no difficulty: in *Brown* it needed only to enforce rules that were universally recognized, not to question any law. Nonetheless it said more. Whether or not Brown's trial was conducted "per legem terrae" need not be answered because torture is "revolting to the sense of justice."[68] The Court would follow current ideas of justice, not hoary statutes and rules. It dealt with *Murray's Lessee* and *Hurtado* in the only way it could. It ignored them.

Still, the Court had yet to hold a statute unconstitutional for failing to provide procedures that could not be found in English law. This it did for the first time in 1943, holding in *Tot v. United States*[69] that Congress violated the Due Process Clause by making possession of a firearm by a felon presumptive evidence that the firearm had been shipped in violation of the statute. Congress may

---

[66] 287 U.S. 45 (1932).

[67] 297 U.S. 278 (1936).

[68] *Id.* at 286.

[69] 319 U.S. 463 (1943).

be free to define the substantive elements of the offense, the Court said, but it is not free to create an irrational presumption easing the prosecution's job in proving one of them.

Tot is the direct ancestor of *Arnett* and other cases holding that although legislators control substance, judges control procedure, but it is not four-square on point. The Court, rightly or wrongly, has tended to put questions of burdens of proof and persuasion in criminal cases in a separate category.[70] The opinion did not grapple with the problems discussed so far, because the Court saw the case as presenting distinct issues. It cited instead a long line of presumption cases, each upholding a statute, that had to do with whether the substantive rule of decision was rational enough to pass muster under the Equal Protection Clause. In *Tot* that was an important inquiry, for the presumption went to the jurisdictional element, a matter of Congress's power to act. At all events *Tot* involved natural liberty, not an entitlement created by the statute along with the procedures for its enforcement.

After *Tot*, *Adamson v. California*[71] reexamined the self-incrimination problem in *Twining* but followed only the holding of the earlier case. In place of *Twining*'s historically founded analysis *Adamson* substituted a rather freewheeling search for procedures seen as fundamental by modern judges. This inquiry soon led to holdings that state procedures were not fundamentally fair. For example, in *Griffin v. Illinois*,[72] a case that rests uneasily between due process and equal protection analysis, the Court held that although a state may decline to allow appeals in criminal cases, if it permits appeals it must provide free transcripts to indigent defendants. The Court did not say that transcripts were required "per legem terrae" here or in England; it did not think the matter pertinent. And although *Griffin* involved natural liberty, the decision the same Term in *Slochower v. Board of Higher Education*,[73] in which the Court held that a teacher could not be fired for asserting the

---

[70] See, most recently, Engel v. Isaac, 102 S. Ct. 1558, 1567–68 (1982). I agree with Professors Jeffries and Stephan that the Court's pretense that criminal presumption cases are some unique species is indefensible and that legislative control of substance should imply control of presumptions as well. *Defenses, Presumptions, and Burdens of Proof in the Criminal Law*, 88 YALE L.J. 1325 (1979). Nonetheless, the Court's pea-shell game makes it difficult to connect *Tot* with *Arnett* as neatly as I would like.

[71] 332 U.S. 46 (1947).

[72] 351 U.S. 12 (1956).

[73] 350 U.S. 551 (1956).

privilege against self-incrimination, did not. *Slochower*, though, had overtones of First Amendment analysis and substantive due process; we still had not arrived at the basis of *Arnett*.

The Court's first serious attempt to promulgate a code of procedure for a particular kind of decision probably was *Willner v. Committee of Character and Fitness*,[74] which involved admission to the bar. Once more, the desire of a person to engage in a legitimate private occupation probably is an aspect of natural liberty, preventing *Willner* from being the first of the *Arnett* cases. The Court was concerned in *Willner* that rules had been concocted to implement some substantively forbidden objective. In other cases the Court found several creative ways to avoid deciding whether Congress could create such procedures as it pleased for its substantive inventions.[75] But in *Willner*, as in the other cases of this era, *Murray's Lessee*, *Hurtado*, and *Twining* lie forgotten. The Court's opinion cited no history.

Goldberg v. Kelly[76] is the first unmistakable assertion by the Court of a general power to establish procedures once legislation specifies substance. The case involved welfare benefits; there could be no question of abridgements of natural liberty. The Court accepted the substantive rules of decision as plainly within the legislature's power. Yet by 1970 the Court was treating any case decided before 1954 as important only when it contained useful language.[77] Once more it ignored *Murray's Lessee*, *Hurtado*, and *Twining*. All that was left of history was a requirement that every deprivation be accompanied by a meaningful hearing, and the Court would be the judge of what was meaningful.

Nowhere in the transition from 1908 to 1970 did the Court supply an argument why it was entitled to disregard the history and early construction of the Due Process Clause. The Court never

---

[74] 373 U.S. 96 (1963).

[75] *E.g.*, Vitarelli v. Seaton, 359 U.S. 535 (1958) (finding a violation of regulations and therefore avoiding constitutional question); Greene v. McElroy, 360 U.S. 474 (1959) (finding want of statutory authorization for summary action and therefore avoiding constitutional question).

[76] 397 U.S. 254 (1970).

[77] The Court relied heavily on Goldsmith v. Board of Tax Appeals, 270 U.S. 117, 123 (1926), which contains a paean to hearings in administrative matters and suggests that the denial of a hearing has due process implications. The Court did not mention that *Goldsmith* involved only the construction of a statute and that the language was dictum because Goldsmith has not sought a hearing. He lost the case.

overruled *Murray's Lessee* or reexamined the history. The transition was accomplished by a series of small accretions, each a reasonable step from what had gone before if one views "reasonable" as "not far removed." But the effect of a series of small steps over a long time was to sever the Court from all restraints save those imposed by the Justices' consciences. The result is far removed from the beginning. It therefore could be justified only by one of the three arguments, discussed above, that history does not bind the Court. These arguments are not persuasive, and the current approach to due process is unsupportable unless there is another argument.

One possible candidate for the missing argument is stare decisis. The law of due process, like a riverbed, has moved slowly by accretion, and because it has been revising the law for so long the Court has acquired an easement of sorts to continue on course. This approach draws on both the common law method and on the first (semihistorical) branch of the living constitution argument.[78] I have expressed elsewhere great doubt that stare decisis is a useful tool of constitutional interpretation,[79] but I am willing to put these doubts to one side for now.

III. Modern Justifications of the Substance-Process Dichotomy

There are two modern justifications of the substance-process dichotomy, one that the Court offers for its decisions and one that scholars offer. The Court's justification is largely instrumental, the scholars' justification largely noninstrumental.

A. THE INSTRUMENTAL JUSTIFICATION

The Court's justification for specifying process once the statute has specified substance is that "any other conclusion would allow the State to destroy at will virtually any state-created property interest."[80] This would be a good argument if the Court could explain why a state may not destroy the interests it creates, at least

---

[78] *E.g.*, Monaghan, note 23 *supra* at 387–91; Monaghan, *Taking Supreme Court Opinions Seriously*, 39 Md. L. Rev. 1 (1979).

[79] Easterbrook, note 23 *supra*. See also Blume & Rubinfeld, *The Dynamics of the Legal Process*, 11 J. Legal Stud. 405 (1982), for a perspective on the costs of stare decisis.

[80] Logan v. Zimmerman Brush Co., 455 U.S. 422, 432 (1982).

prospectively. But the Court has never so argued. Under the Court's decisions legislatures are free to enact precatory statutes, statues that contain no rules of decision, retroactive statutes, statutes that lack any methods of enforcement, statutes creating absolute immunities, and otherwise to have vacuous "entitlements."[81] To use some invented numbers, If states may elect ten percent reliability in enforcement (the amount of adherence to a precatory statute), why can they not elect ninety percent (the amount obtainable from rudimentary procedures)? Why, in other words, is the expedient of enfeebling a statutory entitlement by providing "deficient" procedures out of bounds? The Court's cases contain no answers to this question because they are not consistent. There is no single view that could be respected in the name of stare decisis.

To the extent the Court supplies any explanation, it lies in the formula from the *Eldridge* decision. The formula exalts instrumental objectives. The goal of due process is to hold as low as possible the sum of two costs: the costs created by erroneous decisions, including false positives and false negatives, and the costs of administering the procedures. Holding this sum to a minimum maximizes society's wealth, and the gains may be shared among all affected persons. This, however, produces a puzzle. If the goal of the *Eldridge* formula is the maximization of society's wealth, why did the legislature not enact the preferable procedures in the first place? The legislative and executive branches have access to information about the costs and error rates produced by particular procedures. They are well aware that the accuracy of decisions may be improved by adopting more elaborate procedures. That they choose not to use these procedures is strong evidence that their costs outweigh their benefits.

Some might object that the legislative and executive branches do not make impartial decisions in this respect—that is, they are not well-motivated. Given interest group politics, their choices about the types of procedures to employ in decisions might be the result of political compromise rather than any desire to maximize society's well-being. This surely is true for many, perhaps most, statutes,

---

[81] Pennhurst State School and Hospital v. Halderman, 451 U.S. 1 (1981) (precatory statute); Usery v. Turner Elkhorn Mining Co., 428 U.S. 1 (1976) (retroactive statutes); note 8 *supra* (statutes without rules). In the paragraph immediately following the sentence quoted in the text, the Court said in *Logan* that states may make their statutes unenforceable by creating defenses and immunities. In the private right of action cases, the Court has held that legislatures may create phantom "rights" by withholding remedies.

but so what? The observation is equally true for substantive rules. The statute books are full of rules having little purpose other than to transfer wealth from one group to another. The regulation of taxicabs and the subsidy to tobacco farmers and northeast railroads are the rule, not the exception. Even statutes with some essential purpose other than wealth transfers will be influenced in some fashion by interest group politics.

The role of interest groups does not make legislators ill-motivated in a constitutional sense. It does not involve race, sex, or another forbidden ground of decision. Interest group statutes are upheld all the time, on the flimsiest of pretexts. And if the Constitution permits interest group politics to sway decisions and influence the goals of legislation, what principled objection can there be to legislators' achieving part of the preference for an interest group through choice of procedural rules? (One answer, that procedural rules are less visible, will not do; there are lots of poorly perceived substantive rules.)

This discussion overstates the importance of interest group politics in the choice of procedures. Even when the statute affects "weak" groups, there is little reason to think that the procedural rules will be selected on the basis of some animus against those groups that distorts the legislature's ability to make choices that enhance social well-being. Welfare benefits provide an example. Poor people have shown sufficient political power to obtain a welfare system. We know from the existence of the benefits that they have overcome whatever reticence or hostility exists, and they have obtained transfers in their favor. If they (and their altruistic allies) use their power to obtain $X in money transfers and no elaborate procedures, why should anyone be entitled to complain? A claimant disappointed at the outcome of his own application would have a legitimate gripe only if due process created a personal right not to be the victim of a mistake. But the Court's recent cases are clear that due process does not create any personal right to escape the consequences of blunders. The *Eldridge* criteria focus on the welfare of the statutory beneficiaries as a group, and the Court treats errors in individual cases as a cost but not as an independent violation of the guarantee.[82]

---

[82] See note 15 *supra*. "We must accept the harsh fact that numerous individual mistakes are inevitable in the day-to-day administration of our affairs." Bishop v. Wood, 426 U.S. 341, 349 (1976). Mistakes do not impair the equity of the procedure because they do not alter ex

There will be terms of trade between process and procedure for almost any statute. Trade need not involve money. Take parole. Prisoners and their allies have obtained parole release systems. The allies of prisoners in this respect include all segments of society. Anyone, even the president of a large corporation, is a potential prisoner, and anyone is a potential victim of crime. Everyone thus has an interest in optimal rules that release prisoners at the "right" time and after procedures that do not leave them frustrated, vindictive, and disposed to commit more crimes. Even legislators implacably hostile to crooks would have no extraordinary hostility to procedural rights; their hostility would infect the substance of the rules for release on parole. Legislators without sympathy to criminals nonetheless worry that mistakes would hurt "us" as well as "them," a concern equally important for other entitlements.

Whether new and costly procedures are worthwhile depends on the costs of an erroneous denial of parole. But the costs of erroneous denials depend in turn on why we have parole, what the release decision is designed to achieve. Perhaps the function of parole is not to set a "just" time of release for each prisoner but to reduce a little the consequences of sentencing disparity by judges. That objective may be obtained by the most rudimentary procedures, involving mechanical application of guidelines, without regard to the treatment of particular parole cases. A high "error" rate—if such a thing could be defined at all—would be unimportant to the legislative plan.

If the nature of the statutory plan makes errors undesirable, it would be possible to trade some additional jail time for more extensive procedures. That legislators and prisoners have not done so suggests that procedures beyond those found in the statutes and rules are not worth the cost, or, indeed, that "errors" are irrelevant. There is thus every reason to think that a judicial rebalancing of costs and benefits under the banner of due process would reduce society's welfare.

Substance and process are intimately related. The procedures one uses determine how much substance is achieved, and by

---

ante prospects. On the use of ex ante analysis to identify "fair" procedures, see Easterbrook, Landes, & Posner, *Contribution among Antitrust Defendants: A Legal and Economic Analysis*, 23 J.L. & ECON. 331, 337–44 (1980); Easterbrook & Fischel, *Corporate Control Transactions*, 91 YALE L.J. 698 (1982).

whom. Procedural rules usually are just a measure of how much the substantive entitlements are worth, of what we are willing to sacrifice to see a given goal attained. The body that creates a substantive rule is the logical judge of how much should be spent to avoid errors in the process of disposing of claims to that right.[83] The substantive rule itself is best seen as a promised benefit coupled with a promised rate of mistake: the legislature sets up an $X\%$ probability that a person will receive a certain boon. The Court cannot logically be reticent about revising the substantive rules but unabashed about rewriting the procedures to be followed in administering those rules. These propositions are not new. Scholars examining the due process decisions have made several of them before and remarked that the Court's substance-process dichotomy is illogical.[84] More to the point, the Court recognized this before the scholars did, although the Court's recognition took a slightly different form.

Some statutes contain rules written in such a way as to obviate the need for process. In repudiating its late, unlamented flurry of irrebuttable presumption cases, the Court recognized that the procedures one uses (or does not use) determine the substantive result one gets.[85] Other statutes contain only the most general standards, calling for careful case-by-case adjudication. In declining to call one such standard unconstitutionally vague, the Court pointed out that

---

[83] This treatment does not transgress the unconstitutional conditions line of argument, for reasons I have explained elsewhere. Easterbrook, *Insider Trading, Secret Agents, Evidentiary Privileges, and the Production of Information*, 1981 SUPREME COURT REVIEW 309, 347–49.

[84] *E.g.*, TRIBE, note 18 *supra*, at 536; Brest, *The Substance of Process*, 42 OHIO ST. L.J. 131 (1981); Mashaw, note 18 *supra*; Tushnet, *The Newer Property: Suggestion for the Revival of Substantive Due Process*, 1975 SUPREME COURT REVIEW 261. The most perceptive analysis along these lines is provided by Professor Grey, who lays out with some care why the Court's purportedly process-based decisions make sense only if the Court is in fact withdrawing the substance of the programs from legislative control. *Procedural Fairness and Substantive Rights*, NOMOS XVIII: DUE PROCESS 182, 190–201 (Pennock & Chapman eds. 1977).

[85] *E.g.*, Weinberger v. Salfi, 422 U.S. 651 (1976) (a rule requiring nine months' marriage denies benefits to some bona fide spouses, but case-by-case determinations would grant benefits to bogus ones); Usery v. Turner Elkhorn Mining Co., 428 U.S. 1 (1977) (a rule granting benefits to certain miners "irrebuttably presumed" to be disabled is just a roundabout way of granting benefits to those with the condition triggering the presumption; unless a direct grant would be unconstitutional, there is no objection to the method Congress used to achieve its objective); Califano v. Boles, 443 U.S. 282, 284–85 (1979) (all social welfare statutes face a categorization problem, requiring drafters to choose between rigid rules and flexible standards to achieve an objective; a "process of case-by-case adjudication that would provide a 'perfect fit' in theory would increase administrative expenses to a degree that benefit levels would probably be reduced, precluding a perfect fit in fact").

rules of greater specificity would change the substantive content of the law[86]—a proposition well known to tax lawyers. In still other statutes, the substantive meaning explicitly depends on procedural rules. This is so in statutes that govern presumptions and burdens of proof, and again the Court (occasionally) has recognized the identity of substance and process.[87]

The close relation between process and substance parallels the better-recognized relation between rights and remedies. By the reasoning that the Court has used in due process cases, legislatures would be forbidden to enact rights without remedies; the lack of remedy would dilute the right. Yet the private right of action cases permit Congress to enact rights without private remedies. Similarly, when an agency promulgates a regulation, it may choose the procedures and remedies for enforcing its rules.[88] Only when the underlying substantive right is beyond legislative control does the Court reserve to itself the right to create or supervise remedies. Thus damages actions for violations of the Constitution, the exclusionary rule for violations of the Fourth Amendment, and transportation of students for the purpose of desegregating the schools are judicially controlled remedies, but only because the legislature may not manipulate remedies to alter the substantive entitlements.[89] When the legislature controls the entitlement, it may control the remedy.

---

[86] United States v. Powell, 423 U.S. 87, 93–94 (1975). The statute banned the mailing of firearms capable of being concealed on the person. "Had Congress chosen to delimit the size of the firearms intended to be declared unmailable, it would have written a different statute and in some respects a narrower one than it actually wrote."

[87] See text and notes at notes 67–68 *supra*.

[88] *E.g.*, United States v. Caceres, 440 U.S. 741 (1979) (holding that courts may not suppress evidence obtained in violation of IRS rules; the IRS may specify its own enforcement devices, and judicial creation of remedies unwanted by the IRS might simply lead the executive branch to change the substantive rules).

[89] North Carolina Board of Education v. Swann, 402 U.S. 36 (1970). The Court draws the distinction between remedies for constitutional violations and remedies for the violation of legislatively created rights quite frequently. *E.g.*, Crawford v. Los Angeles Board of Education, 102 S. Ct. 3211, 3221–22 (1982). See also Texaco, Inc. v. Short, 454 U.S. 516, 528 (1982) ("We have . . . made clear . . . that, when the practical consequences of extinguishing a right are identical to the consequences of eliminating a remedy, the constitutional analysis is the same"); Davis v. Passman, 442 U.S. 228, 241–42 (1979) (Court creates remedy for constitutional violation while acknowledging right of Congress to have no remedy for Title VII violation); Bronson v. McKinzie, 42 U.S. (1 How.) 311, 317 (1843) ("no one, we presume, would say that there is any substantial difference between a retrospective law declaring a particular contract or class of contracts to be abrogated and void, and one that took away all remedy to enforce them, or encumbered it with conditions that rendered it useless or impractical to pursue it"); Green v. Biddle, 21 U.S. (8 Wheat.) 1, *75–*76 (1823).

All of this means that the Court's due process cases are incoherent unless the Court has its own view of substance. The Court must be devising procedures that vindicate the Justices' views of the relative importance of different substantive entitlements, rather than legislators' views. Substantive and procedural due process turn out not to be so different.[90] Yet the Justices leave loopholes for legislators: by abolishing private remedies or substantive standards altogether, they may escape the implications of the Justices' substantive preferences.

B. THE NONINSTRUMENTAL JUSTIFICATIONS

Scholars have suggested noninstrumental justifications for the Court's decisions. They suggest that process may be valuable in itself, and not for the benefits it bestows indirectly. There are two lines of noninstrumental justification, dignitary justifications and governmental structure justifications.

1. *Dignity.* Several have argued that process is valuable in itself because it treats each person as an equal, entitled to respect and autonomy, rather than as an object.[91] Such dignitary considerations are exceptionally important to many people. Nonetheless, an argument about the value of process for its own sake is not substantially different from an argument about the value of property, another kind of personal interest. Property in law is the right, within defined limits, to dominion over things and therefore to structure one's relation with others. Without property there is no autonomy and little dignity; property is thus an aspect of personal liberty.[92] Yet the Court permits the legislature the broadest possible scope in the regulation of property and, derivatively, of dignity. The argument linking due process with dignity thus carries no force unless

---

[90] Equal protection analysis, too, turns out to be concerned almost wholly with substance. Westen, *The Empty Idea of Equality*, 95 HARV. L. REV. 537 (1982). See also Clements v. Fashing, 102 S. Ct. 2836, 2849–50 (Stevens, J., concurring). It should thus be no surprise when an upsurge in due process reasoning is accompanied by the use of the Equal Protection Clause to hold economic statutes unconstitutional. *E.g.*, Zobel v. Williams, 102 S. Ct. 2309 (1982), and Schweiker v. Wilson, 450 U.S. 221 (1981) (dissenting opinion).

[91] *E.g.*, TRIBE, note 18 *supra* at 538–41; Laycock, note 35 *supra;* Mashaw, note 18 *supra;* Michelman, note 18 *supra*. But see Grey, note 84 *supra*, at 204–5 n.17. The usual caveat applies; see note 18 *supra*.

[92] Lynch v. Household Finance Corp., 405 U.S. 538, 550–52 (1972); McCloskey, *Economic Due Process and the Supreme Court: An Exhumation and Reburial*, 1962 SUPREME COURT REVIEW 34; Stigler, *Wealth, and Possibly Liberty*, 7 J. LEGAL STUD. 213 (1978).

its proponent can show why the Constitution removes decisions about the appropriate level of dignity from the legislature only when claims to hearings are involved but otherwise allows the legislature full control.

Surely that task cannot be accomplished with the tools of historical analysis. It cannot be accomplished by reading the Clause or analyzing its structure, either, for an argument that the Clause commits process decisions to courts once the statute creates liberty or property[93] begs the question. If "due process of law" means "process according to law," as history indicates, the fact that courts enforce the clause does not entitle them to add dignitary considerations that legislatures left out.

Stare decisis also does not do the trick. The Court's decisions require no process at all unless the decision involves liberty or property, which means that by fuzzing up the substantive grant the legislature may dispense with process entirely, no matter how important the decision to the person affected.[94] No one could argue that the Court's cases actually reflect the dignitary argument, given the ability of legislatures to require important decisions to be made without substantive rules or process. The argument for "dialogue" with decisionmakers as a basis of dignity is strongest when the rules are most uncertain; what plagued K in *The Trial* was essentially the absence of known substantive standards, not the mystery surrounding the procedure. Yet under the cases ambulatory substantive standards allow the legislature to dispense with process.

Moreover, when liberty or property is at stake, *Eldridge* calls for a utilitarian calculus in determining appropriate process. Process is designed to avoid errors, and when the likelihood of error, or the stakes, decreases, so does the need for process. Dignitary considerations are omitted, as a subsequent case shows in holding that an employee fired without a hearing did not state a prima facie case of a constitutional violation because he did not argue that a hearing would have made a difference in the outcome of the decision.[95]

---

[93] *E.g.*, Laycock, note 35 *supra*. Professor Laycock also makes a structural argument that process decisions in general are committed to courts in light of the extensive list of procedural rules laid out in the Constitution. This argument is not compelling, though, because it does not supply the connection between the explicit rules (for example, jury trial in civil cases exceeding $20) and the Due Process Clause. One might as easily infer that the Framers' special procedural rules were expressly listed, leaving the legislature with control over all procedures not listed. It requires historical analysis to determine which inference is accurate.

[94] See pages 87–88, *supra*.

[95] Codd v. Velger, 429 U.S. 624 (1977). But *cf.* Carey v. Piphus, 435 U.S. 247 (1978)

All that is left—save the forbidden revisionist arguments—is a play on the analysis of *Carolene Products*.[96] It may be possible to depict dignitary considerations as fundamental values slighted by majoritarian processes. I agree with Dean Ely that it is unwarranted for Justices to make up fundamental values,[97] but one can reject a fundamental values treatment of dignity even if one disagrees with Ely's view. There is simply no reason to suppose that process values are slighted by legislatures.

There is no logical reason why legislatures would underestimate the value of process. Process and substance are of a piece. Legislators frequently are lawyers or other specialists in process, not quick to forget their training (or the interests of their friends, also process providers). Process is not historically disfavored. Statutes overflow with process, sometimes to the point of choking the ability of executives to act. Consider for a moment the difficulty a supervisor faces in firing a secretary under the civil service laws. And there is no apparent relationship between the amount of process provided by law and the favor (or disfavor) legislators show for the affected people. Murderers are not an especially favored class, yet statutes provided elaborate procedural protections for murder cases long before the Court entered the due process fray. It can take a decade or more to deport an illegal alien, all because of procedural rules, created by statute, exceeding constitutional requirements.[98] On the other hand, summary procedures under the Social Security Act principally affect lifetime wage earners, not the poor.

Hearings for claimants are a form of in-kind benefit. It is a commonplace observation that in-kind benefits (including food, housing, and other nonmoney transfers, as well as hearings) are worth less to the recipients than it costs society to provide them. Some of the difference between the cost of the benefits and their value to the recipients is simply lost to society; some of the difference is captured by those who render the benefits. It is not irrational for those

---

(awarding $1 damages for denial of hearing even in absence of allegation that hearing would have altered the decision; the case apparently recognizes a dignitary function of hearings but concludes that dignity is not worth very much); Marshall v. Jerrico, Inc., 446 U.S. 238, 242 (1980) (stating in dictum that "the promotion of participation and dialogue by affected individuals in the decisionmaking process" is one of the "central concerns of procedural due process").

[96] United States v. Carolene Products Co., 304 U.S. 144, 152–53 n.4 (1938).

[97] Ely, *Foreword: On Discovering Fundamental Values*, 92 HARV. L. REV. 5 (1978).

[98] *E.g.*, INS v. Jong Ha Wang, 450 U.S. 139 (1981); Agosto v. INS, 436 U.S. 748 (1978).

affected by a program to spurn elaborate hearings and demand more concrete benefits instead. They may prefer money, which can be turned into other things, to dignity, which cannot be. The important consideration is that if people potentially eligible under the substantive terms of a statute value hearings at more than the cost of providing them, they will clamor for hearings even at the cost of lower money benefits. The contents of the legislation are the best available evidence about the value the affected people place on hearings. Surely it should come as no surprise that the usual proponents of hearings in welfare cases are middle- and upper-class lawyers, professors, and judges—the class from which bureaucrats, administrative law judges, and other process providers come.

2. *Governmental structure.* Professors Stewart and Sunstein have identified another constellation of functions served by hearings.[99] Judicial insistence on procedures might, for example, compel Congress to be more candid in identifying all dimensions of the entitlements it creates, or to deliver on its promises, or to reduce the extent of delegation to agencies. In other words, it would promote the Rule of Law, in which determinate standards rather than potentially capricious bureaucrats establish entitlements. Although these functions have instrumental overtones—less delegation might be thought "better" legislation—they are usually seen as valuable in themselves.[100]

These are weak arguments, as Stewart and Sunstein concede. The objective of "honest" legislation is more threatened by precatory laws, by "rights" without remedies, than by deficient procedures. The objection to delegation is much more forceful when the legislature passes statutes containing no substantive rules than when it enacts rules but does not provide for particularly accurate administration. These laws most subject their beneficiaries to the whims of ill-motivated bureaucrats.

The Stewart and Sunstein arguments sound odd as matters of due process. Governmental structure for the federal branches was settled by Articles I and II, not by the Bill of Rights. The nondele-

---

[99] Stewart & Sunstein, *Public Programs and Private Rights*, 95 HARV. L. REV. 1193, 1258–63 (1982).

[100] Because legislatures are our society's instruments for identifying "good" legislation, it is also hard to argue that forcing legislatures to establish procedures that they find undesirable would produce "better" laws. See also Michelman, *Politics and Values, or What's Really Wrong with Rationality Review*, 13 CREIGHTON L. REV. 487 (1980).

gation doctrine is a name without a doctrine. Improperly motivated decisions are controlled by doctrines other than due process.[101] There is no general rule that Congress must legislate so clearly that people with grade school educations can follow; if it wants to use roundabout methods of stating its purpose, so be it.[102] And states may delegate as they please; administrative agencies or judges may enact state laws.

Stewart and Sunstein maintain that the Court's control over process is justified only when (*a*) necessary to force Congress to make a clear statement of its aims or (*b*) necessary to enforce favored substantive rights, among which they would include welfare. Part *a* of the test is unsupportable for state governments, and even for Congress it puts the Court in the position of holding a very clear law (say, one providing that there shall be no process for firing a federal employee) unconstitutional because Congress has not been clear enough in its total package. A rule of this sort, unjustified by history or precedent, also gives the Court almost unlimited power. Any law, taken in its entirety, is unclear in some respect. Part *b* of the test, however, just returns us to a proposition presented several times before: there is not much difference between substance and process, and therefore the Court's substance-process dichotomy is unsupportable.

IV. THE 1981 TERM'S CASES

The Court's 1981 Term was rich in due process cases.[103] *Logan v. Zimmerman Brush Co.*,[104] with which this article began, is

---

[101] See note 9 *supra*. Compare Meachum v. Fano, 427 U.S. 215 (1976) (no procedures necessary when statute supplies no standards), with Montanye v. Haymes, 547 F.2d 188 (2d Cir. 1976) (lack of procedure not pertinent to inmate's claim that transfer was in retaliation for his speech), on remand from 427 U.S. 236 (1976).

[102] Usery v. Turner Elkhorn Mining Co., 428 U.S. 1, 20–24 (1976). One portion of the social security statute, discussed in Califano v. Boles, 443 U.S. 282 (1979), grants benefits to a covered person's mother, but it promptly defines his spouse to be his mother. This statutory incest does not prevent the payment of benefits.

[103] I do not discuss any criminal due process matters. I also omit four civil cases: Jago v. Van Curen, 454 U.S. 14 (1981) (the setting of a tentative parole release date does not create a liberty or property interest); Texaco, Inc. v. Short, 454 U.S. 516, 532–37 (due process does not require a state to give each potentially affected party notice of a new state law; the state may require owners of mineral rights to register or forfeit them); Schweiker v. McClure, 102 S. Ct. 1665 (1982) (hearing examiners for Medicare program are adequate, neutral umpires for due process purposes); Kremer v. Chemical Construction Corp., 102 S. Ct. 1833 (1982) (the administrative and judicial process available in employment discrimination cases in New York is sufficient to afford binding quality to the judgments of New York's courts).

[104] 455 U.S. 457 (1982).

the most at odds with the historical approach. The State need not have created any right to be free of discrimination because of handicap or given the right any particular dimensions. That being so, the State also should have been allowed to employ such procedures as it pleased for adjudicating (or not adjudicating) Logan's claim.[105]

The Court did not find anything suspect in the State's substantive rules concerning remedies. The opinion rests on a disguised proposition about the nature of permissible entitlements. The Court seemed most concerned that the Illinois system allowed claims to be extinguished by mistake; the Court saw this as the next best thing to allowing claims to be extinguished by chance, which (the Court assumed) would not be permissible. Why not? The Court's many cases upholding statutes and rules that contain no criteria at all must stand for the included proposition that states may decide by lot. If people may be sent to one prison rather than another for no reason,[106] they may be assigned prisons by lot. Selective service drafted people by lot. Why not a lottery to weed out excessive cases that delay relief for others? Indeed, any system constructed under the *Eldridge* criteria is a lottery because it permits incorrect decisions. The rules are crafted not to eliminate errors but to set tolerable rates of error, even though there is no reason at all to deny benefits to the unlucky victims of the anticipated errors. The federal courts use a system of rules that has the potential for cutting off the rights of unsuspecting litigants. For example, a party who loses in the district court must appeal within thirty days, even if he lacks notice of the adverse judgment.[107] If he fails to do so, through no fault of his own, his rights are nonetheless forfeit. It is thought better to extinguish some claims, at some expense to personal rights, than to try to construct a foolproof system. The Illinois system, like the federal one, balanced the chance of disregarding some potentially legitimate claims against the costs to employers of

---

[105] This is true even within the Court's two-stage approach. As the Supreme Court of Illinois saw things, the statute (effectively) allowed Logan's claim to be extinguished for no reason at all. Thus the statute gave Logan no property right. Bishop v. Wood, 426 U.S. 341 (1976). The Court never told us why it was disregarding the state court's construction of the state's statute. See also note 2 *supra*.

[106] Meachum v. Fano, 427 U.S. 215 (1976).

[107] See National Coalition for Public Education and Religious Liberty v. Hufstedler, 449 U.S. 808 (1980), dismissing for want of jurisdiction appeal from 489 F. Supp. 1248 (S.D.N.Y.); Rogers v. Watt, 680 F.2d 1295 (9th Cir. 1982); Fed. R. Civ. P. 77(d) and the Advisory Committee's commentary. But see James v. U.S., 103 S. Ct. 465 (1982) (Brennan, J., on denial of certiorari).

protracted proceedings. It is hard to see much difference, yet the Court surely would uphold the federal rule.

Santosky v. Kramer[108] held that a State may end parents' rights in their natural children only by establishing the facts necessary to support that decision by "clear and convincing evidence." The state statute, which made a "fair preponderance of the evidence" sufficient, was held unconstitutional. Although *Santosky* involved a parental interest predating any statute, the case is easy under the historical approach. No rule in England or the United States in 1791 called for extraordinary burdens of proof as part of the law of the land, when legislation employed the ordinary burdens. Coke's natural law arguments, taken at their extreme, would not have raised any question concerning New York's process, which contained wave after wave of notices and hearings. *Santosky* also turns out to be as unsupportable under the Court's usual due process analysis as under the historical approach.[109]

Once more, though, the interesting feature of the case is the Court's barely concealed review of the substance of New York's legislation. The Court recited that the burden of proof embodies "a social judgment" about how to distribute the costs of mistake or reflects the value "society" places on the substantive right.[110] Indeed it does, but "society" usually speaks through its elected representatives. Federal judges have life tenure precisely to insulate them from the ebb and flow of society's views. The Court used "society" in *Santosky* as a euphemism for "the Court." The opinion makes sense only if read as holding that the parents' interest in retaining at least nominal[111] custody of their children is a great deal

---

[108] 102 S. Ct. 1388 (1982).

[109] In civil cases the Court has treated the allocation of burdens of proof as a matter of substance more than as a matter of procedure, deferring to the legislature unless, as in Addington v. Texas, 441 U.S. 418 (1979), the matter involved physical confinement. For example, in Vance v. Terrazas, 444 U.S. 252 (1980), the Court held that an act of Congress establishing the preponderance of the evidence standard to determine whether someone committed a denationalizing act is constitutional. Incredibly, the Court did not cite *Terrazas* in *Santosky*, and the Court asserted three times in *Santosky* that some earlier cases required a clear and convincing evidence standard for denationalization matters and established the primacy of the Court in setting burdens. See 102 S. Ct. at 1395, 1396, 1397. As the Court explained in *Terrazas*, however, each of the cases on which the Court relied in *Santosky* had been decided as a matter of statutory construction, not of constitutional law. 444 U.S. at 264–67.

[110] 102 S. Ct. at 1395 (three times), 1400.

[111] The parents in *Santosky* had long been separated from their children; even if the state

more substantial than New York's legislature thought, and there-fore could not be terminated at all unless certain facts were estab-lished.

The Court used its decision on the burden of proof to revise the substantive rule. It did not create a new procedural hoop; it instead set up a procedural rule that makes termination impossible in cer-tain circumstances in which it had been possible under New York law (e.g., when the testimony supports conflicting inferences). The decision embodies a view of family values obtained via substantive due process. It is therefore not surprising that the five Justices who joined the opinion in *Santosky* were the same five who formed the majority in *Moore v. City of East Cleveland*,[112] where an explicit substantive due-process/family-values approach accounts for the decision.

A third case of the Term is *Greene v. Lindsey*.[113] A Kentucky statute permitted the landlord to serve process on his tenants in eviction actions by attempting service in hand and, if that failed, by posting the eviction notice on the apartment door. The Court held this statute unconstitutional, at least as applied to apartment build-ings with unruly children, because of the risk that someone would tear the notice off the door and prevent the tenant from learning of the proceedings. The Court suggested that notice by mail would be adequate; the dissenting Justices thought the mails risky too and argued that the Court acted without evidence that service-by-posting was ineffective in more than a handful of cases.

The empirical thrust and parry among the Justices is unimpor-tant here. The disagreement among the Justices went only to the details of the *Eldridge* utilitarian calculus, not to the appropriateness of such an inquiry. There is a more interesting problem in *Greene*. At first glance the historical approach supports the Court's deci-sion. To the extent it can be traced to the statute of 1354, the Due Process Clause is directed against ex parte judicial proceedings end-

---

court had refused to enter a decree terminating their parental rights, the children would have continued to reside in foster homes.

[112] 431 U.S. 494 (1977). The five are Justices Brennan, Marshall, Blackmun, Powell, and Stevens. Justice Powell wrote an explicit substantive due process opinion in *Moore;* Justice Stevens concurred only in the result, but on a rationale that was even more startling than that of Justice Powell and would have made almost all zoning laws unconstitutional. Justice Blackmun wrote for the five in *Santosky*. In each case the other four dissented.

[113] 102 S. Ct. 1874 (1982).

ing in deprivations of property; Kentucky's statute allowed just such proceedings. Moreover, the tenant's interest in his apartment is not a creature of statute. The legislature had not purported to control the substantive terms of leases or to allocate apartments to particular people, and thus its argument for controlling process is weaker. All that is left, apparently, is the historical argument that Coke's views must be disregarded, so that any procedure the legislature names is enough, a position rejected in passing in *Murray's Lessee*.

There is, nonetheless, a good argument that *Greene* is not significantly different from *Murray's Lessee*, in which the Court sustained summary distraint of the collector's money and goods. *Murray's Lessee* was based, as I have recounted, on two things: the support in English procedure for summary collection of revenues by the sovereign, and the relationship between the Treasury and the collector that made a bargained adjustment of risks possible. The parallel to *Greene* is striking. There is a long history of summary eviction proceedings, often by landlords' self-help. Moreover, the lessor and lessee have an agreement allocating rights between themselves. The terms for service of process, provided by statute, could be characterized as an implicit term of the lease.[114] If the rules for service sometimes lead to wrongful eviction, landlords must expect to pay their tenants back through an *ex ante* adjustment in rentals. An insecure tenancy is worth less than a secure one. If tenants want better notice than posting, lessors who offer leases with superior notice provisions would in the long run prosper relative to others. Over time—and most lease provisions have evolved over a *long* time—leases would come to contain the clauses tenants valued at more than the increase in the rental necessary to compensate the landlords. (They need compensation because legal rules that make it harder to evict nonpaying tenants reduce the average rate of paying occupancy.) Yet to the extent leases deal explicitly with the problem, they commonly do so by specifying less process than the statutory, implicit terms.

This analysis suggests that landlords and tenants, pursuing their own interests, have made a utilitarian calculus more exacting and

---

[114] It would clearly be constitutional as an explicit term in the lease. See Swarb v. Lennox, 405 U.S. 191 (1972) (states are not forbidden by the Due Process Clause to enforce confession of judgment clauses in consumer notes).

more enduring than the Court's. The Court's balancing is at least presumptively mistaken. *Greene* thus must depend either on a belief that implicit bargains between landlord and tenant do not occur or on a suppressed assumption that they are substantively forbidden, perhaps because the analysis of tenants' risks must be conducted *ex post* rather than *ex ante*.[115] Although the Court did not explore these matters, the case illustrates once more the inseparable nature of substance and process.

The last case of the Term to be discussed is *Youngberg v. Romeo*,[116] which involved the rights of retarded people committed to institutions in Pennsylvania. These state institutions often shackled their charges for long periods to prevent them from harming other people, including the staff. At other times the staff left the institutions' residents where they could be harmed—perhaps because other residents were not shackled.

The Court first held that the residents have natural liberty interests, not extinguished by the orders committing them, in their personal safety and freedom from physical restraint. Yet because many patients were large and violent, securing the interest in safety would mean sacrificing the interest in restraint unless some way could be found to reduce the level of violence. This was the genesis of the Court's holding that the residents had an interest in training to ensure some degree of both safety and freedom from restraint. This newly minted substantive interest dominates the case, yet the Court did not make it absolute. It could be abridged or qualified, and that implies process. In two cursory paragraphs, the Court stated that the process due is consideration of training needs by a medical professional, according to accepted professional judgment. The process is what the professional decides it should be. He would, apparently, perform the *Eldridge* calculus in deciding on a quantum of process. Any law to the contrary is unconstitutional.

---

[115] Neither of the two possible grounds is strong. All available evidence suggests that prices adjust to implicit terms of trade, so the first assumption would be questionable. See Hirsch, *Landlord-Tenant Relations Law*, in THE ECONOMIC APPROACH TO LAW 277 (Burrows & Veljanovski eds. 1981) (collecting evidence). Even if one assumes that very few tenants do comparative shopping for prices and terms of leases, a few may be quite sufficient, when the process continues for many decades and everyone searches for housing at one time or another. See Schwartz & Wilde, *Intervening in Markets on the Basis of Imperfect Information: A Legal and Economic Analysis*, 127 U. PA. L. REV. 630 (1979). The other ground implies a judicial preference for ex post analysis, which would be inconsistent with the principles of the *Eldridge* calculus itself.

[116] 102 S. Ct. 2452 (1982).

Why is the Court unwilling to allow a legislature, with due deliberation, to define the appropriate process for dispensation of entitlements created by the legislature, while it is willing to permit scattered physicians and psychologists to exercise ad hoc judgment in cases involving liberties that stem from no legislature? Once more, the only plausible answer has to do with the Court's view of the substantive entitlements. In *Youngberg* the Court synthesized a liberty interest in treatment. Having specified the interest, one that depended as a matter of substance on an obligation to supply a medical response, it tried to match the procedure to what it had created. In private life, someone with a medical problem consults a physician and follows his advice; the Court apparently had the same sequence in mind for the residents of Pennsylvania's institutions. But because the Court did not know the appropriate solution to the medical problem, there was no way in which it could have defined an "error" by the physician, and therefore no way to specify any procedures at all. The decision to abdicate on matters of process flowed from the (non)definition of the right. The Court constructed the same sort of fuzzy-right/limited-process sequence that it has held unconstitutional when constructed by legislatures.[117]

V. CONCLUSION

We have come a long way from 1791. This Term's cases have no roots in history and few roots in any decision older than twenty years. The opinions do not cite older cases. *Murray's Lessee* and *Hurtado* vanished long ago. The cases the Court does cite are descendants not of *Murray's Lessee* but of the substantive due process opinions that it was issuing at the same time *Moore, Powell*, and *Brown*, initiating the modern round of procedural due process decisions, cut all ties to the eighteenth and nineteenth centuries. Neither history nor stare decisis explains the doctrines. Today the Court makes no pretense that its judgments have any basis other than the Justices' view of desirable policy. This is fundamentally the method of substantive due process. Giving judges this power of revision may be wise or not. The Court may design its procedures well or poorly. But there is no sound argument that this is a legitimate power or function of the Court.

---

[117] See Vitek v. Jones, 445 U.S. 480 (1980), discussed at page 87, *supra*.

CASS R. SUNSTEIN

PUBLIC VALUES, PRIVATE INTERESTS, AND THE EQUAL PROTECTION CLAUSE

The Equal Protection Clause is directed at the legality of classifications. When a classification is challenged, the first question is whether it is drawn on the basis of race or some other characteristic thought to call for "heightened" scrutiny.[1] That question is usually an easy one; it can be reframed as an inquiry into whether the statute classifies "on its face" in terms of the forbidden characteristic. If there is such a classification, the statute must be invalidated unless it survives heightened scrutiny, either strict or intermediate.

If no such classification is involved, a second inquiry becomes necessary. Was the classification motivated by an "intention" to treat some class differently on the basis of race or, again, any other

---

Cass R. Sunstein is Assistant Professor of Law, University of Chicago.

AUTHOR'S NOTE: I would like to thank Albert W. Alschuler, Douglas G. Baird, Mary E. Becker, David P. Currie, Charles G. Curtis, Jr., Frank H. Easterbrook, Richard A. Epstein, Daniel R. Fischel, J. David Greenstone, Geoffrey R. Miller, Richard A. Posner, Paul Shechtman, David A. Strauss, Geoffrey R. Stone, James B. White, and Hans Zeisel for their helpful comments. Roy B. Underhill provided valued critical and research assistance. I am also grateful to participants in the Law and Social Theory workshop series of the University of Southern California—and especially to Scott H. Bice, Margaret Jane Radin, Larry G. Simon, and Christopher R. Stone—for valuable help. For financial support I am indebted to a grant from the Lilly Foundation to the Law and Economics Program, University of Chicago, for research in law and government.

[1] I do not consider whether and when classifications merit heightened scrutiny under the equal protection clause because they interfere with a "fundamental right." See, *e.g.*, Plyler v. Doe, 102 S. Ct. 2382 (1982); Shapiro v. Thompson, 394 U.S. 618 (1969); Zablocki v. Redhail, 434 U.S. 374 (1978).

characteristic said to call for heightened scrutiny? If the answer is affirmative, heightened scrutiny must be applied; if negative, the statute must be upheld unless it is not rationally related to a legitimate state interest.

That is the current law of equal protection in a nutshell. It is frequently characterized as a self-contradictory melange of "rules" supported by no plausible source of constitutional doctrine. The framework has been severely tested by the Supreme Court's recent decisions in the *Seattle School District*[2] and *Crawford*[3] cases. In those cases, the Court was confronted with classifications that did not distinguish between whites and blacks but that singled out a racial problem—in particular, the problem of pupil transportation, or "busing"—for special treatment. The challenged classifications were in this sense race-specific. In *Seattle*, the Court invalidated an enactment that barred local school boards from requiring students to be assigned to distant schools for purposes of desegregation. In *Crawford*, the Court upheld an enactment that imposed a similar prohibition on the state courts.

To attempt to understand the two decisions, it is necessary to have some notion of the evil at which the Equal Protection Clause is aimed and of the purpose of the various devices the Court has developed to stifle that evil. As I read it, the function of the Clause is to prohibit unprincipled distributions of resources and opportunities. Distributions are unprincipled when they are not an effort to serve a public value, but reflect the view that it is intrinsically desirable to treat one person better than another. Such an understanding as this focuses on the reasons or motives that underlie classifications. It serves to explain cases involving classifications that are facially neutral, facially discriminatory, and, most important for present purposes, race-specific. In applying this concept to *Seattle* and *Crawford*, my ultimate purpose here is to suggest that the current law of equal protection is not self-contradictory, but a more or less principled response to a more or less unitary understanding of what the Equal Protection Clause is about.

---

[2] Washington v. Seattle School District No. 1, 102 S. Ct. 3187 (1982).

[3] Crawford v. Los Angeles Bd. of Educ., 102 S. Ct. 3211 (1982).

I. The Framework

What is the evil at which the Equal Protection Clause is aimed? Surprisingly little attention has been devoted to the question.[4] On occasion it is suggested that the framers' sole concern was discrimination on the basis of race and perhaps nationality, and that any effort to go further is doomed to arbitrariness and subjectivity.[5] This view is, however, hard to reconcile with the language of the Clause,[6] and in any event it has been repudiated so decisively and for so long a period of time that it is probably no longer worth taking seriously.[7]

Nonhistorical efforts to give content to the Equal Protection Clause, however, have not fared well. Too often the question is simply begged, or it is believed sufficient to note that the Clause prohibits classifications based on "prejudice," or whim, or "irrationality."[8] The confusion reflects the elasticity of the notion of equality itself. The notion is subject to multiple meanings which derive from sharply divergent conceptions of the correct understanding of the term.[9] To require equality is in essence to require that those similarly situated be treated similarly. But classifications are the stuff of legislation; and legislation that classifies does not, solely by virtue of that fact, offend any sense of "equality." To find inequality, one has to know when people are similarly situated. And to know that, some substantive value—and not the formal

---

[4] For some of the more important historical efforts, see Bickel, *The Original Understanding and the Segregation Decision*, 69 Harv. L. Rev. 1 (1955); tenBroek, Equal under Law (1951); Frank & Munro, *The Original Understanding of "Equal Protection of the Laws,"* 50 Colum. L. Rev. 131 (1950). For a general but nonhistorical treatment, see Perry, *Modern Equal Protection: A Conceptualization and Appraisal*, 79 Colum. L. Rev. 1023 (1979).

[5] See Trimble v. Gordon, 430 U.S. 762, 777–79 (1977) (Rehnquist, J., dissenting); Berger, Government by Judiciary: The Transformation of the Fourteenth Amendment (1977); Bork, *Neutral Principles and Some First Amendment Problems*, 41 Ind. L. J. 1 (1971).

[6] See Ely, Democracy and Distrust 30–32 (1980).

[7] This is not to say that it would not have been possible to adopt such a narrow interpretation in the first instance, as the Court suggested it would do in The Slaughterhouse Cases, 16 Wall. 36 (1873), but that it is too late in the day to confine the Clause to racial discrimination.

[8] A notable exception is the classic piece by Tussman & tenBroek, *The Equal Protection of the Laws*, 37 Cal. L. Rev. 341, 350–51 (1949).

[9] See, *e.g.*, Rae, Equalities (1981).

notion of equality—is necessary.[10] That substantive value must in turn identify, and limit, the category of reasons for which it is permissible to treat one group or person differently from another. The Equal Protection Clause is an empty vessel insofar as it is understood merely to suggest that the similarly situated must not be treated differently.

All this seems quite obvious. But the Supreme Court persists in invoking the Equal Protection Clause to invalidate legislation. Some have charged that the Court's approach amounts to an endless tinkering with legislative judgments supported by no underlying substantive value.[11] But it is possible to sketch a principle[12] that captures the evil at which the Court thinks the Equal Protection Clause is aimed, and to tie that general principle to the subsidiary doctrines the Court has developed to ensure that the evil does not occur. My analysis is primarily descriptive, not a justification for the Court's approach.

I begin with a familiar point.[13] The basic requirement of the Equal Protection Clause is that statutory classifications must be rationally related to valid statutory purposes. But every statutory classification is, by definition, rationally related to its purposes; it is intended to do what it in fact does.[14] Rationality review therefore makes sense only if it is accompanied by a willingness to close off the universe of permissible statutory purposes—to limit the reasons for which one person can be treated differently from another, and to require that the applicable reasons be stated at an intermediate

---

[10] GUTMANN, LIBERAL EQUALITY 10 (1980); Flathman, *Equality and Generalization: A Formal Analysis*, in IX NOMOS: EQUALITY 38 (Pennock & Chapman eds. 1967); Weston, *The Empty Idea of Equality*, 95 HARV. L. REV. 537 (1982); Lucas, *Against Equality*, 40 PHILOSOPHY 296 (1965). See also TRIBE, AMERICAN CONSTITUTIONAL LAW 991 (1978); Sandalow, *Racial Preferences in Higher Education: Political Responsibility and the Judicial Role*, 42 U. CHI. L. REV. 653, 654–63 (1975).

[11] Posner, *The DeFunis Case and the Constitutionality of Preferential Treatment of Racial Minorities*, 1974 SUPREME COURT REVIEW 1; Linde, *Due Process of Lawmaking*, 55 NEB. L. REV. 197 (1976); Bork, note 5 *supra*; Trimble v. Gordon, 430 U.S. 762, 777 (1977) (Rehnquist, J., dissenting).

[12] It would be foolhardy to suggest that a single principle can explain all of the Court's decisions in this complex area. See Easterbrook, *Ways of Criticizing the Court*, 95 HARV. L. REV. 802 (1982).

[13] See Note, *Legislative Purpose, Rationality, and Equal Protection*, 82 YALE L.J. 123 (1972); Linde, note 11 *supra*.

[14] With the trivial exception of inadvertencies, which are rarely the subject of equal protection challenge. But see United States Railroad Retirement Board v. Fritz, 449 U.S. 166, 187–93 (1980) (Brennan, J., dissenting).

level of generality. If certain purposes are impermissible bases for classifications, judicial inspection of whether there is a rational relation between a challenged classification and a legitimate purpose can be understood as a means of ensuring that unconstitutional motivations do not in fact account for statutory classifications.[15] If there is no such relation, the legitimate purpose does not explain the classification; if there is such a relation, a court has at least some assurance that the legitimate purpose is at work.

To say this much is to suggest that the function of the Equal Protection Clause is to limit the class of reasons for which one person may be treated differently from another. Scrutiny of the relationship between permissible ends and statutory means serves to "flush out" impermissible ends, albeit imperfectly when the most deferential forms of rational basis review are employed. Modern equal protection jurisprudence thus operates as a limitation on the reasons—sometimes treated as "motives"[16]—that are permitted to underlie statutory classifications. That limitation is, I believe, a means of understanding not only the race cases and others involving "heightened" scrutiny, but the rationality decisions as well. Indeed, the limitation derives from the same basic principle in a wide range of equal protection cases. It is in this sense that equal protection jurisprudence can be understood as reflecting a unitary understanding of the central meaning of the Clause.

What does the Court treat as an illegitimate reason for treating one person differently from another? In brief, the Court requires differential treatment to be justified by reference to some public value. A justification that rests on the intrinsic value of treating one person differently from another is prohibited. The basic principle comes through clearly in the rationality cases, and it is the dominant theme in cases involving heightened scrutiny as well.

---

[15] The argument is elegantly made in ELY, DEMOCRACY AND DISTRUST 145–48 (1980). See also Brest, *Palmer v. Thompson: An Approach to the Problem of Unconstitutional Legislative Motive*, 1971 SUPREME COURT REVIEW 95; and Simon, *Racially Prejudiced Governmental Actions: A Motivational Theory of the Constitutional Ban against Racial Discrimination*, 15 S.D. L. REV. 1041 (1978).

[16] The Court was originally unwilling to review the motives of legislatures. See Fletcher v. Peck, 6 Cranch 87 (1810); Ex parte McCardle, 7 Wall. 506 (1869). For a long time, however—indeed, from the beginning—it has been clear that the Equal Protection Clause requires consideration of the reasons underlying statutory classifications. Consideration of reasons leads naturally, if not inevitably, to consideration of motives. *Cf.* Ely, *Legislative and Administrative Motivation in Constitutional Law*, 79 YALE L.J. 1205 (1970).

A. RATIONALITY

In *Daniel v. Family Security Life Ins. Co.*,[17] the Court upheld a South Carolina statute that prohibited life insurance companies and their agents from operating an undertaking business and that barred undertakers from serving as agents for insurance companies. Most of the plaintiff insurance company's employees were undertakers. The lower court invalidated the statute, noting that there was only one insurance company in South Carolina—the plaintiff—that was adversely affected by the statute, and concluding that the statute was designed to destroy that company in order to allow existing insurance companies to eliminate the plaintiff as a competitor. The Court's opinion implies that if that was in fact the purpose of the statute, and if it was a mere bow to the "insurance lobby," it would be unconstitutional.[18] The Court upheld the statute on the ground that there was a possibility of abuse and overreaching in funeral insurance and that the classification could be understood as a response to that possibility.[19]

In *New Orleans v. Dukes*,[20] the Court sustained a New Orleans statute which prohibited pushcart vendors from operating in the French Quarter but exempted from the prohibition those who had "continually operated the same business for eight years prior to January 1, 1972." The exemption may have been a response to political pressure from pushcart vendors who had been in the business a long time; it may have resulted from a sense on the part of the legislature that long-established vendors have a special claim of equity to continued operation. The Court did not refer to either possibility. It found that the classification could be justified as a means of preserving local appearance and custom and thus of promoting tourism. The Court ignored the possibility that the exemption was a response to political pressures, and the opinion implies that such a justification would be impermissible.

In *Minnesota v. Clover Leaf Creamery Co.*,[21] the Court upheld a Minnesota statute that banned the retail sale of milk in plastic nonreturnable, nonrefillable containers but permitted such sale in

---

[17] 336 U.S. 220 (1949).

[18] *Id.* at 224.

[19] *Id.* at 222–23.

[20] 427 U.S. 297 (1976).

[21] 449 U.S. 456 (1981).

other nonreturnable, nonrefillable containers, such as paperboard milk cartons. The statutorily stated purpose was to promote environmental goals.[22] The Minnesota trial court found that the classification would not in fact serve those goals and that its real purpose "was to promote the economic interests of certain segments of the local dairy and pulpwood industries at the expense of the economic interests of other segments of the dairy industry and the plastics industry."[23] The trial court thought that this purpose rendered the statute unconstitutional. The Minnesota Supreme Court concluded that the stated purposes were the real ones, but that the discrimination was not rationally related to those purposes because the Minnesota legislature had misconceived the facts.

The Supreme Court reversed. What was relevant was not whether the Minnesota legislature was right but whether its motives were legitimate, and whether the means of fulfilling those purposes were "rational."[24] As to the trial court's finding, the Court stated that a state statute would not be invalidated "merely because some legislators sought to obtain votes for the measure on the basis of its beneficial side effects on state industry."[25] If those side effects had been the actual purpose of the legislation, however, it would fall: "If a state law purporting to promote [legitimate] purposes is in reality 'simple economic protectionism,' we have applied a 'virtually per se rule of invalidity.' "[26] This is also a central lesson of the celebrated decision in *Williamson v. Lee Optical*.[27]

There is a common theme in these cases, decided over a period of almost fifty years. In all of them, and in many others as well,[28] the

---

[22] "The legislature finds that the use of nonreturnable, nonrefillable containers for the packaging of milk and other milk products presents a solid waste management problem for the state, promotes energy waste, and depletes natural resources." Minn. Laws 1977, ch. 268, section 1, codified as Minn. Stat., §116 F.21 (1978).

[23] 449 U.S. at 460.

[24] *Id.* at 466.

[25] *Id.* at 463 n.7.

[26] *Id.* at 471, quoting Philadelphia v. New Jersey, 437 U.S. 617 (1978); see also Hunt v. Wash. State Apple Advertising Comm'n, 432 U.S. 333 (1977). The cases relied on by the Court were decided under the Commerce Clause, but the *Clover Leaf* principle is explicitly derived from the Equal Protection Clause.

[27] 348 U.S. 483 (1955). There, the Court upheld a statute that made it unlawful for opticians to fit lenses or to duplicate or replace lenses, except with the written permission of an optometrist or an ophthalmologist. The Court upheld that statute, not on the ground that an effort at monopoly by optometrists or ophthalmologists would be permissible, but on the ground that the statute could be understood as a means of protecting consumers.

[28] See, *e.g.*, Goesaert v. Cleary, 335 U.S. 464, 466–67 (1948); Railway Express Agency, Inc. v. New York, 336 U.S. 106, 110 (1949). See also notes 33–37 *infra*.

Court has ruled out of bounds certain justifications for statutory classifications and stretched far to find a justification that does not fall out of those bounds. The out-of-bounds justifications have a common characteristic. When the government operates to benefit A and burden B, it may do so only if it is prepared to justify its decision by reference to a public value. A bare decision to prefer A to B, because the comparative disadvantage is intrinsically desirable, is not sufficient. If A is to be preferred, it must not be because the preference is an end in itself, but because it is a means to some public end. Legislation may not be merely the adjustment of private interests or the transfer of wealth or opportunity from one person to another; it must be in some sense public-serving.[29] B can be disadvantaged if the disadvantage is an incidental consequence of a decision that is based on other grounds; if the differential treatment is not incidental, but is the basic purpose of the classification, it is invalid.[30]

Nor is political strength a legitimate justification. Preferential distribution of wealth or opportunities cannot be supported on the sole ground that the eventual winners exerted considerable pressure on legislators. The institution that made the discrimination must be attempting to remedy a perceived public evil, and must not be responding only to the interests or preferences of some of its constituents. The category of forbidden justifications thus includes, but is not limited to, discriminations made on the basis of some desire to "harm" the groups burdened by the classification. The category also includes something arguably less invidious: discriminations made because of a belief that those benefited merit by their very nature preferential treatment—are to be preferred, that is, not

---

[29] See Bennett, *"Mere" Rationality in Constitutional Law: Judicial Review and Democratic Theory*, 67 CAL. L. REV. 1049, 1077–88 (1979); Bice, *Rationality Analysis in Constitutional Law*, 65 MINN. L. REV. 1 (1980). *Cf.* Mashaw, *Constitutional Deregulation: Notes toward a Public, Public Law*, 54 TULANE L. REV. 849 (1980).

[30] Compare Ronald Dworkin's sketch of a governmental obligation to treat people "with equal concern and respect," an obligation that bars unequal distribution of "goods or opportunities . . . on the ground that some citizens are entitled to more because they are worthy of more concern." DWORKIN, TAKING RIGHTS SERIOUSLY 273 (1977). See also ACKERMAN, SOCIAL JUSTICE IN THE LIBERAL STATE 11 (1980).

The notion that unequal distribution of resources and opportunities is permissible only as a means of promoting the common good has a long pedigree. For recent discussion, see Benn, *Egalitarianism and the Equal Consideration of Interests*, in PENNOCK & CHAPMAN, note 10 *supra*; SINGER, PRACTICAL ETHICS 19 (1979); Laski, *A Plea for Equality*, in THE DANGERS OF DISOBEDIENCE 232 (1930).

because some public value will be served but because they are in some sense "better" than those burdened. Under the Court's approach, some adequate articulation is required to explain why it is that one person or group is favored over another.

This is the essence of the equality principle that underlies the Court's equal protection jurisprudence. Discrimination that is inconsistent with that principle receives the appellation "invidious," an often puzzling term that has played a prominent role in equal protection jurisprudence over the past hundred years. In this respect, the requirement of equal protection is one aspect of the general constitutional effort to prevent the capture of governmental authority by powerful private factions.[31] The Equal Protection Clause, as usually interpreted, operates to ensure that factions are not permitted to obtain legislation merely because it is in their favor.

In the rationality cases, of course, the principle is not enforced with much vigor; the Court is willing to uphold a classification on the basis of the most attenuated relationship between a public value and the classification under review. To say that is not, however, to weaken the force of the general point, which is that some such justification must be offered. The basic proposition can be found in an enormous number of cases.[32] In its first decision invalidating a classification for irrationality, the Court stated that the "equal protection of the laws . . . forbids that one class should by law be compelled to suffer loss that others may make gain."[33] Twenty years later, the Court invalidated a law containing a facial discrimination against aliens on the ground that the "discrimination . . . in

---

[31] See Stewart & Sunstein, *Public Programs and Private Rights*, 95 HARV. L. REV. 1193, 1232–33, 1278–79 (1982).

[32] See, *e.g.*, Engel v. O'Malley, 219 U.S. 128 (1911); Tigner v. Texas, 310 U.S. 141 (1940); Heath & Milligan Mfg. Co. v. Worst, 207 U.S. 338 (1907); Butcher's Union Co. v. Cresent City Co., 111 U.S. 746, 765–66 (1884) (concurring opinion); Rosenthal v. New York, 226 U.S. 260 (1912); Central Lumber Co. v. South Dakota, 226 U.S. 157 (1912); Lindsley v. Natural Carbonic Gas Co., 220 U.S. 61 (1911). See further Tussman & tenBroek, note 8 *supra*, at 361–65.
The cases do not form an unbroken line. Holmes, for example, believed that the sort of redistribution of which I am speaking is an ordinary and permissible aspect of government. See Quong Wing v. Kirkendall, 223 U.S. 59 (1912). And Justice Black sometimes appeared of the same view. See Ferguson v. Skrupa, 372 U.S. 726 (1963). *Cf.* SPRAGENS, THE IRONY OF LIBERAL REASON (1981).

[33] Reagan v. Farmers' Loan & Trust Co., 154 U.S. 362, 410 (1894). *Reagan* was argued on eminent domain grounds but decided under the Equal Protection Clause.

the wide range of employments to which the act relates is made an end in itself."[34] In invalidating a New York statute that limited a one cent per quart differential to milk dealers who had been in business since a certain date, the Court stated that the provision "is not a regulation of a business or activity in the interest of, or for the protection of, the public, but an attempt to give an economic advantage to those engaged in a given business at an arbitrary date as against all those who enter the industry after that date."[35] And in striking down a provision of the food stamp act that limited assistance to households consisting of groups of "related persons," the Court rejected the idea that it was permissible to attempt to exclude "hippie communes" from the statutory program.[36] According to the Court, "a bare congressional desire to harm a politically unpopular group cannot constitute a *legitimate* governmental interest."[37]

There is, of course, vagueness in any formulation that makes the constitutionality of a classification turn on the existence of a "public" justification. What sorts of justifications count as "public," or "general," in such a way as to furnish a permissible basis for a classification? To answer that question, one needs a background theory that will identify prohibited and permissible justifications in more particular terms. A large number of justifications accepted by the Court consist of legislative efforts to furnish collective goods— those that cannot be provided to one person without simultaneously being provided to all or many.[38] Thus, for example, promotion of traffic safety and environmental welfare count as sufficient justifications for differential treatment.

But justifications based on the presence of collective goods do not

---

[34] Truax v. Raich, 239 U.S. 33, 41 (1915). See also Korematsu v. United States, 323 U.S. 214, 216 (1944), noting that the exclusion order was based not on a perception that discrimination was desirable for its own sake but on a legitimate effort to respond to a public emergency; Yick Wo v. Hopkins, 118 U.S. 356, 374 (1886), noting that discrimination was impermissible because based on hostility to Chinese.

[35] Mayflower Farms, Inc. v. Ten Eyck, 297 U.S. 266, 274 (1936). The Court added: "The appellees do not intimate that the classification bears any relation to the public health or welfare generally; that the provision will discourage monopoly; or that it was aimed at any abuse, cognizable by law, in the milk business." See also Quaker City Cab Co. v. Pennsylvania, 277 U.S. 389, 402 (1928); cf. Borden's Farm Products Co. v. Ten Eyck, 297 U.S. 251, 263 (1936).

[36] United States Dept. of Agriculture v. Moreno, 413 U.S. 528 (1973).

[37] Id. at 534.

[38] See OLSON, THE LOGIC OF COLLECTIVE ACTION (1971); HARDIN, COLLECTIVE ACTION (1982).

exhaust the field. Other sorts of redistribution are permissible if they can be said to serve some widely shared social norm. Thus, there can be no doubt that an effort to give favorable treatment to a particular industry, or group of persons, is permissible if the discrimination is meant to serve some public value. The distinction between pulpwood and other industries in *Clover Leaf* would be unlikely to count as mere economic protectionism if the favorable treatment of pulpwood industries was offered as a means of aiding a sagging business or of promoting employment in a sector of the economy that was particularly in need of help. The critical point is that some such justification must be offered.

Similarly, discriminations that operate to redress individual suffering or perceived inequalities arising out of the marketplace—such as the progressive income tax or welfare statutes—are constitutionally unobjectionable. Such statutes do not discriminate against the relatively richer because it is inherently desirable to do so or is an end in itself; the underlying notion is that the discrimination serves to promote a more equitable distribution of wealth. In such cases, and in cases in which government attempts to supply a collective good, the relevant classification is justified by reference to some generally shared public value. Among the values that have been prominent in the cases are environmental protection, national defense, traffic safety, and fair distribution of wealth or opportunities.[39] The question is not whether a large number of persons are benefited by a classification but whether it is possible to invoke a public value that the classification can be said to serve.

What I have said thus far should be sufficient to suggest what counts as a permissible justification for a classification. The class of prohibited justifications consists of what might be termed naked preferences—preferences based on a perception that one person is in some sense "better" than another, or to be preferred simply because of who he or she is. (It is of course irrelevant that such a preference may also be characterized as in some sense a "public value.") When government has responded to political pressure in

---

[39] It is a critical assumption of this approach that there exists a category of commonly held, or public, values—an assumption that I find plausible, at least if the relevant values are described at a sufficiently high level of generality, but that is of course subject to question. See Freeman, *Truth and Mystification in Legal Scholarship*, 90 YALE L.J. 1229 (1981); Hand, *Is There a Common Will?* (1929), in THE SPIRIT OF LIBERTY (Phoenix ed. 1977). Under the Court's approach, such values may change over time, see note 59 *infra*. How a particular value becomes public is something of a mystery. See VINING, LEGAL IDENTITY 171 (1978).

order to aid politically powerful groups simply by virtue of their political power, the redistribution is merely ad hoc, and no proper justification is furnished;[40] the satisfaction of individual tastes is not a permissible basis for the disposition of social force in favor of one individual or group at the expense of another.[41] Under the Court's approach, differential treatment cannot be justified on the sole ground that it maximizes aggregate social utility, or wealth; one must explain in other terms why one person is being treated differently from another.

It is not difficult to see that this principle is not process based.[42] It is frankly substantive, for it grows out of a particular perception of the substantive evil forbidden by the Clause. That perception serves, moreover, as a quite general explanation of decisions in numerous areas of equal protection jurisprudence. Indeed, it is possible to describe each of the requirements of modern equal protection doctrine as an effort to implement this understanding of the central meaning of the Clause.

B. DISCRIMINATORY PURPOSE

In the last few years the Supreme Court has made clear that the Equal Protection Clause is not violated in the absence of a showing

---

[40] Thus the "economic protectionism" condemned in *Clover Leaf* does not serve a public value in the same sense as, for example, a welfare statute or even a statute redistributing resources to the wealthy on the ground that such redistribution will aid the economy as a whole. On public values, see Greenstone, *The Transient and the Permanent in American Politics: Standards, Interests, and the Concept of Public*, in PUBLIC VALUES & PRIVATE POWER IN AMERICAN POLITICS 3, 12–13 (Greenstone ed. 1982).

There is, of course, a sense in which it is misleading to suggest that some classifications are adopted because it is intrinsically desirable to differentiate between two groups. For example, when a legislature prefers one set of industries to another in order to promote "economic protectionism" of the sort forbidden in *Clover Leaf*, it does so not because the preference is in itself desirable but in order to benefit the preferred group and perhaps to prolong the political careers of incumbent legislators. To make this observation is not, however, to diminish the force of the general point: that certain kinds of justifications for differential treatment are forbidden under the Equal Protection Clause. A classification that aids one group at the expense of another is instrumental in that it is a means to a goal; but the goal—aiding the preferred group for no reason other than its political power—is forbidden by the Clause.

[41] For similar reasons, the Court's approach suggests that otherwise unprincipled redistributions cannot be justified as a means of channeling private desires into peaceful avenues; some justification at a lower level of generality is required.

[42] See Tribe, *The Puzzling Persistence of Process-based Constitutional Theories*, 89 YALE L.J. 1063 (1980). The approach does, however, make relative burdens of proof dependent on the likely functioning of the political process.

that the relevant decisionmaker acted for an impermissible reason.[43] This requirement has encountered skepticism,[44] largely because it is so difficult to prove subjective motivations, especially those of institutional decisionmakers.[45] But a focus on purpose rather than on effect is consistent with the Court's general view of the function of the Equal Protection Clause. For constitutional purposes, a person is treated unequally if he is purposely denied a benefit or confronted with a burden; he is not so treated if he faces a detriment as an incidental consequence of a decision that was intended to do something other than to discriminate.

A good illustration is *Personnel Administrator of Massachusetts v. Feeney.*[46] The issue there was the constitutionality of Massachusetts's veterans preference statute. The statute operated to the detriment of a class of whom a disproportionately large number were women. Its purpose, however, was not to disadvantage women but to advantage veterans. The disadvantage caused by the classification was in this respect an incidental consequence of the legislative intention—not the legislative intention or an end in itself. As the Court suggested, it was necessary to show that the legislation was passed "at least in part 'because of,' not merely 'in spite of,' its adverse effects upon an identifiable group."[47] Because no such showing was made, there was no violation of the Equal Protection Clause.

Similarly, in *Fullilove v. Klutznick,*[48] the Court upheld an affirmative action plan with a suggestion that the disadvantage to the white plaintiffs was an "incidental" consequence of the program; it was not its purpose. "Failure of nonminority firms to receive certain contracts is, of course, an incidental consequence of the program, not part of its objective."[49] *Feeney* and *Fullilove* share the same perception that underlies the rationality cases: that the

---

[43] See, *e.g.*, Washington v. Davis, 426 U.S. 229 (1976); Personnel Administrator of Mass. v. Feeney, 442 U.S. 256 (1979).

[44] See, *e.g.*, TRIBE, AMERICAN CONSTITUTIONAL LAW 1032 (1978).

[45] See Note, *Reading the Mind of the School Board: Segregative Intent and the De Facto/De Jure Restriction*, 86 YALE L.J. 317 (1976); Brest, note 15 *supra; cf.* Easterbrook, note 12 *supra*, at 828.

[46] 442 U.S. 256 (1979).

[47] *Id.* at 279.

[48] 448 U.S. 448 (1980).

[49] *Id.* at 484 (Burger, C.J., joined by Powell and White, JJ.).

Equal Protection Clause prohibits government from treating one person differently from another unless the differential treatment is in the service of a public value.

C. HEIGHTENED SCRUTINY

It is now a commonplace that the purpose of heightened scrutiny is to filter out illegitimate motives in cases in which such motives are especially likely to be at work.[50] Heightened scrutiny is therefore applied when there is a basis for fear that the government is acting in response to a perception that it is intrinsically desirable to treat A better than B. When a classification is drawn against blacks, for example, history suggests that the forbidden sort of discrimination is likely. The same might be said of discrimination against aliens, women, and illegitimates, three other groups sometimes treated as partially "suspect" classes.[51] In such cases, there is an unusual likelihood that the classification will not be an attempt to promote a public value, but instead the product of the capture of government processes by powerful private groups.

The device of heightened scrutiny thus serves to dispense with the need for individualized proof of impermissible purpose by providing a presumption that such a purpose is at work. The presumption, however, can be overcome by a showing that legitimate purposes in fact support the classification—as the Court thought that it was in the *Korematsu*[52] case, on the theory that the singling out of Japanese-Americans resulted not from a perception that persons of Japanese ancestry were worse than anyone else, but instead from a neutral desire to provide a classic public good, national security.[53] The *Korematsu* case is thus another illustration of the understanding that the Equal Protection Clause is a means of ensuring that one person can be treated differently from another only in the service of some public value.

---

[50] ELY, note 15 *supra*, at 145–48 (1980); Brest, *Foreword: In Defense of the Antidiscrimination Principle*, 90 HARV. L. REV. 1 (1976).

[51] For discussion of what classes ought to be treated as "suspect," see ELY, note 15 *supra*, at 160–70.

[52] Korematsu v. United States, 323 U.S. 214, 216 (1944).

[53] *Id.* at 223.

D. FACIAL CLASSIFICATIONS

Statutes that classify on their face according to race are presumptively unconstitutional. How is this conventional principle to be explained? It is far too easy to say that statutes that classify on their face according to race are inevitably based on some malevolent motive. Statutes that authorize segregation may, for example, be based on a good faith belief that segregated education is best for all concerned. Moreover, the Court has not required proof of bad motive at all in cases in which there is a facial racial classification; the very fact that the statute is drawn on the basis of a racial characteristic is sufficient to trigger heightened scrutiny.[54] The fact that the intention to classify is "benign" plays a part at other stages of the inquiry,[55] but not at the initial level.

The answer lies in a judgment that is similar to that underlying heightened scrutiny. When a legislative classification is drawn on the basis of race, it is peculiarly likely that there has been a violation of the constitutional principle of equality. The fact that a statute is drawn in terms that single out blacks for disadvantageous treatment alerts the judge that the prohibited motive may well account for the legislation. A very heavy burden of justification is placed on the state to show otherwise; the ordinary requirement of individualized proof of improper motive is eliminated.

E. RATIONALITY REVISITED

How, then, are we to explain the fact that in most cases the state is confronted with the minimal burden of showing that its classification is "rational"? This result is reached even when statutes have a disproportionately severe impact on members of racial minority groups.[56] Some have argued that courts should closely scrutinize the relationship between legitimate ends and statutory means in order to assure that illicit transfers are in fact "flushed out."[57]

---

[54] As the Court explicitly recognized in *Seattle School District No. 1*, 102 S. Ct. 3187.

[55] See Fullilove v. Klutznick, 448 U.S. 448 (1980); Regents of the Univ. of Cal. v. Bakke, 438 U.S. 265 (1978).

[56] See, *e.g.*, Washington v. Davis, 426 U.S. 229 (1976).

[57] See Gunther, *Foreword: In Search of Evolving Doctrine on a Changing Court: A Model for a Newer Equal Protection*, 86 HARV. L. REV. 1 (1972). A problem with this approach is the

The answer—at least that provided by current equal protection doctrine—should be fairly simple in the light of the foregoing discussion. When the government enacts a classification that does not single out a particular disadvantaged group, it is appropriate to adopt a strong presumption that the reason discrimination has occurred is not that discrimination is good for its own sake, but that it is a means to some public end. The fact that the Court has adopted this strong presumption does not diminish the descriptive force of the account suggested here, for the Court's perception of the evil at which the Equal Protection Clause is aimed is accompanied by a reluctance, rooted in separation of powers concerns, to conclude too readily that the evil is in fact taking place. It is for this reason that the Court has generally been willing to hypothesize permissible legislative purposes in the absence of actual articulation by the legislature and to demand only the loosest fit between a public value and a statutory classification.[58] Constant judicial vigilance to ensure that legislation consists of more than an unprincipled redistribution of resources or opportunities might well be inconsistent with the basic constitutional premise of representative democracy.[59]

---

familiar phenomenon of "logrolling"—a problem with which the Court has yet to come to terms.

[58] See United States R.R. Bd. v. Fritz, 449 U.S. 166 (1980). Proposals to demand actual articulation and "tighter fit" should therefore be understood as intended to promote vigilance in ensuring that unprincipled redistributions do not take place. The Court's general rejection of those proposals, but see Zobel v. Williams, 102 S. Ct. 2309 (1982), should not be taken as an implicit acceptance of the constitutionality of such redistributions. The rhetoric of the decisions, which provides important data, see Fried, *The Laws of Change: The Cunning of Reason in Moral and Legal History*, 9 J. LEGAL STUD. 335 (1980), reveals that the Court believes that unprincipled redistributions are prohibited. The same principle underlies the results in the area of "suspect" classes. The fact that almost all legislation survives rationality review is thus a product of institutional constraints on the judiciary and does not affect the general portrait presented here of the sort of classification forbidden by the Equal Protection Clause.

[59] The constitutional principle of equality, as I have defined it, bears close resemblance to notions of substantive due process at work in the *Lochner* era. See JACOBS, LAW WRITERS AND THE COURTS 98–159 (1954). The downfall of *Lochner* was in large part a product of an increasing recognition that the market status quo was neither "natural" nor inviolate, and that, as a result, the redistribution of resources to relieve poverty was a legitimate effort to promote the public good. See Kennedy, *Form and Substance in Private Law Adjudication*, 89 HARV. L. REV. 1685, 1746–51 (1976); TRIBE, note 44 *supra*, at 438–55; West Coast Hotel Co. v. Parrish, 300 U.S. 379 (1937). In part, however, it was also the result of the notion that it would be intolerable, in a representative democracy, for courts closely to scrutinize legislation for public purposes. See Mashaw, note 30 *supra*. There are also close affiliations between the substantive guarantee of equal protection, as described in the text, and the Fifth Amendment's prohibition against uncompensated takings. Both principles are directed at a similar evil: the capture of governmental power by private groups seeking to redistribute wealth or opportunities in their favor. See Calder v. Bull, 3 Dall. 385, 388 (1798) (Chase, J.).

It is important to acknowledge that almost all classifications, indeed almost all government decisions, are justifiable and often justified by reference to a public value.[60] Legislatures almost always act on the basis of mixed motives. Indeed, even those who make the most invidious decisions generally invoke the common good, and frequently they do so sincerely. The problem of characterization is therefore a critical one: When does the Court accept a public-serving justification, and when does it treat such a justification as a fraud?

The doctrinal framework just described supplies a substantial answer. In the rationality cases, the Court is willing to adopt a nearly irrebuttable presumption that statutory classifications have been made in the service of a public value, but it still demands that some such justification be made. In contrast, the device of heightened scrutiny reflects skepticism that a public value is in fact being served and represents a presumption that the public justification is a facade, serving to conceal the actual basis for the classification.

In sum, the Court's decisions in the equal protection area respond to an identifiable but quite general understanding of the evil at which the Clause is directed. That evil consists of an effort to treat one person differently from another because it is intrinsically desirable to do so—because, to use currently fashionable terminology, the disadvantaged person is not entitled to "equal concern and respect"[61] or because that person is not "as good as" the benefited one.[62] In this respect, the prevailing understanding of equal protection is classically liberal, indeed a reflection of one of the central tenets of liberalism.[63]

Recent attacks on rationality review have, however, given reason for modesty in any attempt to suggest that unprincipled distribu-

---

Some have argued that such judicial supervision would also be unnecessary, because legislation is simply not that sort of redistribution. See Michelman, *Politics and Values or What's Really Wrong with Rationality Review*, 13 CREIGHTON L. REV. 487 (1980). Others disagree. See Posner, *Economics, Politics, and the Reading of Statutes and the Constitution*, 49 U. CHI. L. REV. 263, 285–86 (1982).

[60] See, *e.g.*, POSNER, THE ECONOMICS OF JUSTICE 376–77 (1981).

[61] See DWORKIN, note 30 *supra*, at 273. I do not mean to suggest, however, that Dworkin's phrase perfectly captures the notion used here.

[62] See ACKERMAN, note 30 *supra*, at 17; UNGER, KNOWLEDGE AND POLITICS 42–46 (1975).

[63] See ACKERMAN, note 30 *supra*, at 11–12, 15–16, 356–71; SPRAGENS, THE IRONY OF LIBERAL REASON 280–81, 383–85 (1981). Rawls's difference principle may be understood as a more rigorous version of the same notion. See RAWLS, A THEORY OF JUSTICE 75–83 (1971).

tion is prohibited. Those attacks, echoing the largely discredited[64] pluralist political science of the late 1950s and early 1960s, purport to show that unprincipled redistribution is the foundation underlying statutory enactments.[65] The interest-group theory of legislation is based on a notion that the political process consists of an effort by various well-organized factions, armed with conflicting preferences, to impose their will on the rest of us. With that understanding, review of legislation for rationality is incoherent. It either results in hypocrisy about the reasons for statutory enactments or threatens judicial tyranny in the form of invalidation of an enormous number of statutory classifications.

The rationality requirement, as understood by the Court, represents a rejection of this characterization of politics. The Court's approach assumes that it is plausible to treat the political process not as a struggle among interest groups equipped with preexisting preferences, but instead as an effort to develop and select those preferences in the form of shared public values. In other words, preferences are not necessarily filtered into the democratic process as exogenous variables; they are developed and shaped, indeed defined, during the political process.[66] Under this characterization, legislation is forbidden if it does not represent an effort at such a definition, but is instead the essentially private redistribution of wealth or opportunities to politically powerful groups, or factions. I do not venture an evaluation of the Court's characterization here, but it may be suggested that the characterization does conform to common conceptions of what the political process ought to be and

---

[64] See RAWLS, note 63 *supra*, at 360–61; DAHL, DILEMMAS OF AMERICAN PLURALISM (1982); KARIEL, THE DECLINE OF AMERICAN PLURALISM (1961); WOOLF, THE POVERTY OF LIBERALISM (1968); LOWI, THE END OF LIBERALISM (1969). For a positive and normative critique, see SPRAGENS, note 63 *supra*, at 301–10.

[65] There is an extensive literature on the subject, much of it economic in origin. See, *e.g.*, Posner, note 59 *supra*; Peltzman, *Toward a More General Theory of Regulation*, 19 J.L. & ECON. 211 (1976); Jordan, *Producer Protection, Prior Market Structure and the Effects of Government Regulation*, 15 J.L. & ECON. 151 (1972). Although this characterization of the political process has been pressed vigorously by conservatives, it is shared by some commentators on the left, see, *e.g.*, Parker, *The Past of Constitutional Law—and Its Future*, 42 OHIO ST. L.J. 223 (1981). See also BICKEL, THE LEAST DANGEROUS BRANCH 35–46 (1962). One major difficulty with the Court's approach is the assumption that it is plausible in a large, industrialized society composed in part of competing, well-organized groups, to reject this characterization of the political process. See MANSBRIDGE, BEYOND ADVERSARY DEMOCRACY (1980).

[66] ARENDT, ON REVOLUTION (1965); Michelman, note 59 *supra*; Kennedy, note 59 *supra*, at 1771–74; *cf*. Stewart & Sunstein, note 31 *supra*, at 1242–43 & n.191, 1279–80 & n.360.

at least sometimes is.[67] In a society composed of diverse groups with competing interests, the notion of shared public values may sometimes seem untenable, but the persistence of the requirement attests to the hardiness of the notion that the political process is not properly regarded as a Hobbesian struggle among interest groups.[68]

II. RACE-SPECIFIC CLASSIFICATIONS: THE PRECEDENTS

Thus far, I have outlined a principle that has informed the Court's interpretation of the Equal Protection Clause and have suggested the ways in which that principle helps simultaneously to explain rationality review, heightened scrutiny, and the requirement of a showing of impermissible motive. The resulting framework is designed largely for two polar cases: those in which a statute is drawn on its face according to race (or something like it[69]) and those in which a statute is facially neutral and not apparently motivated by a discriminatory purpose. There is, however, a category of intermediate cases. In such cases, the government does not distinguish between whites and blacks, but instead singles out a racial problem—for example, the problem of fair housing legislation—for special treatment. Cases falling within this category involve what might be termed race-specific classifications. The difficulty the Court has faced with such classifications is a natural product of the approach outlined above, and is in this sense a testimonial to the explanatory power of the approach. At the same time, the problems posed by race-specific classifications suggest the limitations of the approach.

Hunter v. Erickson[70] is the first example. The Akron City Council had enacted a fair housing ordinance and created a Commission on Equal Opportunity in Housing to enforce the antidiscrimination

---

[67] The same conception was at least a prominent strain in the framing of the Constitution. See MADISON, FEDERALIST NOS. 10, 51. See also Michelman, note 59 *supra*; Sagoff, *At the Shrine of Our Lady of Fatima or Why Political Questions Are Not All Economic*, 23 ARIZ. L. REV. 1283 (1981); Mashaw, note 29 *supra*. For discussion of an analogous conception in the context of adjudication, see VINING, note 39 *supra*; Kennedy, note 39 *supra*, at 1771–74; Sunstein, *Participation, Public Law, and Venue Reform*, 50 U. CHI. L. REV. 976 (1982).

[68] *Cf.* MANSBRIDGE, note 65 *supra*; Sunstein, *Cost-Benefit Analysis and the Separation of Powers*, 23 ARIZ. L. REV. 1267 (1981).

[69] Such as gender, see Craig v. Boren, 429 U.S. 190 (1976), or illegitimacy, see Trimble v. Gordon, 430 U.S. 762 (1977), or alienage, see Sugarman v. Dougall, 413 U.S. 634 (1973).

[70] 393 U.S. 385 (1969).

provisions of the ordinance. Hunter sought to avail herself of the enforcement machinery, but she was confronted with an amendment to the city charter that barred the City Council from implementing any ordinance dealing with discrimination in housing without the approval of the majority of Akron voters.

The Supreme Court held that the amendment was unconstitutional on the ground that it discriminated on its face according to race.[71] Groups seeking protection against discrimination were required to obtain not merely approval from the City Council but also ratification from the voters at a general or regular election. Groups seeking to regulate real property transactions for other reasons faced no such obstacles. This "explicitly racial classification treating racial housing matters differently from other racial and housing matters"[72] was sufficient to doom the charter amendment.

Now there is an obvious response to this reasoning: on its face, the charter amendment was not drawn in racial terms at all. The classification distinguished between those seeking discrimination-related legislation and those seeking other sorts of legislation. It did not distinguish blacks from whites. The Court was not entirely insensitive to this point.[73] It responded in two ways. First, it stated that, despite its failure to refer to race, the statute distinguished between those who sought antidiscrimination legislation and those who sought other sorts of enactments. This distinction, the Court suggested, was in principle no different from a genuine racial classification. Second, the Court indicated that "the law's impact falls on the minority."[74] The differential impact, the Court said, was enough to justify careful scrutiny of the asserted justifications. The ordinance, of course, failed such scrutiny: the amendment was not necessary in order to implement a decision to proceed slowly or to allow public participation in controversial decisions. Under

---

[71] Thus, the Court was not required to decide whether the decision in Reitman v. Mulkey, 387 U.S. 369 (1967), was applicable in this setting. See Karst & Horowitz, *Reitman v. Mulkey: A Telophase of Substantive Equal Protection*, 1967 SUPREME COURT REVIEW 39.

[72] *Id.* at 389.

[73] See *id.* at 390.

[74] According to the Court, this "is no more permissible than denying them the vote, on an equal basis with others." The Court cited Reynolds v. Sims, 377 U.S. 533 (1964), as support. *Id.* at 391. The analogy to *Reynolds* was unsuccessful, for in the absence of a violation of the one-person, one-vote principle, there is no right to be free of discriminatory effects in the political process. See Rogers v. Lodge, 102 S. Ct. 3272 (1982).

preexisting Akron law, a petition with ten percent of the voters' signatures would have required a general referendum.

Justice Harlan, joined by Justice Stewart, wrote a separate concurring opinion using a different rationale. In his view, a statute intended to disadvantage racial minorities faces heightened scrutiny, "[l]ike any other statute which is discriminatory on its face."[75] The provision at issue here, he suggested, "has the clear purpose of making it more difficult for certain racial and religious minorities to achieve legislation that is in their interest," and is therefore "discriminatory on its face."[76] Facially discriminatory legislation, according to Justice Harlan, is indistinguishable from legislation which has the kind of purpose at issue in *Hunter*.

Hunter was, of course, decided before the Court had made it clear that a showing of discriminatory purpose is required to make out a violation of the Equal Protection Clause, and the difficulty now of understanding the Court's opinion stems largely from that subsequent development. Are the opinions in *Hunter* reconcilable with the more recent decisions? As to the Court's approach, it is hardly obvious that the amendment discriminated on its face on the basis of race. The law is now clear that a statute will not be so found if two conditions hold: (1) if some persons in the group placed in one category by the statute are non–minority group members and (2) some in the other category are minority group members.[77] Thus a statute does not classify on the basis of sex if it classifies on the basis of status as a veteran: some women are veterans, and most men are not veterans.[78] Note that the test is not whether the groups "disadvantaged" and "benefited" by a statute contain members of both majority and minority groups, but whether a statutory classification treats one group differently from another or, in other words, whether it classifies on the basis of race.[79]

---

[75] *Id.* at 393.

[76] *Id.* at 395.

[77] See Schweicker v. Wilson, 450 U.S. 221 (1981); but *cf.* Geduldig v. Aiello, 417 U.S. 484 (1974).

[78] Personnel Administrator of Mass. v. Feeney, 442 U.S. 256 (1979).

[79] The Supreme Court appeared to recognize the point in the *Seattle* case. See 102 S. Ct. at 3195. See also Schweicker v. Wilson, 450 U.S. 221, 233–34, noting that relevant intent, in assessing whether there is a facial racial classification, is intent to classify. Similarly, the intent that is relevant for purposes of determining whether there is "discriminatory intent" is not intent to harm but intent to treat differently on the basis of race. *Id.*

The Akron ordinance did no such thing. It singled out for special treatment those who sought to obtain ordinances dealing with racial discrimination. People of all races might seek or oppose such legislation. The classification, in short, was not "explicitly racial" at all. The Court thought the fact that it did not refer by its terms to race did not make it neutral; it was not necessary to go far below the surface to see that the classification was facially discriminatory— much as a provision that distinguished between those with sickle cell anemia and those with other illnesses might be. But the Akron enactment was not the same as such a classification, for it was not a mere guise or proxy for race.[80] Perhaps it seems odd to suggest that the Akron ordinance should be given as deferential treatment as any other enactment, but the Court was incorrect to conclude that the ordinance contained an "explicit racial classification."

Justice Harlan, by contrast, should be taken to suggest that the sort of singling out achieved by the Akron ordinance is unlikely to be supportable in noninvidious terms. When the government puts in a separate category legislation that protects minority group members and imposes a special disability on those who seek such legislation, it is a reasonable inference that invidious purposes are at work. But it is not necessarily the case that the Akron ordinance was motivated by an intention to make it harder for members of racial and religious minority groups to obtain legislation in their interest. At least in principle, the legislation could have been a neutral effort to ensure that a broad consensus supported potentially divisive enactments or those which interfered with certain sorts of liberties. To resolve the problem, it would be necessary to undertake a particularized inquiry into the history of the ordinance and the regularity with which controversial issues are subjected to the requirement of a special referendum.

Justice Harlan attempted to carry out such an inquiry, noting that the amendment was unnecessary if it was intended as a means of ensuring that sensitive issues are decided by the electorate. Akron already required a general referendum on any issue if ten percent of the voters so requested. In this sense, "the charter amendment will have its real impact only when fair housing does *not* arouse extraordinary controversy."[81] For this reason, it is hard to

---

[80] The Court has not always been willing to see through such guises. See Geduldig v. Aiello, 417 U.S. 484 (1974).

[81] 393 U.S. at 395–96.

believe that the asserted purpose was the actual basis for the special requirement.

Some more general conclusions may be drawn from this discussion. An illegitimate reason or motive is both necessary and sufficient to doom a classification under the Equal Protection Clause. The classification in *Hunter* was not quite a racial classification on its face; but, by its very nature, it gave rise to suspicion that an impermissible motive was at work. Although the Court has made clear that even classifications having a demonstrated and foreseeable discriminatory impact are subject to deferential scrutiny, the rule is different for the classification in *Hunter*, because of the nature of the line drawn in that case. In *Hunter*, it was clear from the face of the statute that the drafters and supporters were aware that a racial question was involved and that the effect of the enactment was to impose special barriers on those who sought legislation for protecting blacks.[82] The rationale for applying special scrutiny to such classifications is similar to that underlying hostile judicial treatment of facially racial classifications.[83] In both cases, there is a peculiar likelihood—though not a certainty—that the evil that the Equal Protection Clause is designed to prevent is in fact occurring. Both cases, moreover, form a relatively discrete class that can be given special treatment without requiring abandonment of the principle that a showing of discriminatory purpose is necessary to establish a violation of the Equal Protection Clause.

It is for this reason that the classification at issue in *Hunter*, though not a conventional racial classification, might be afforded similar treatment. Although it does not distinguish between blacks and whites, it targets a racial problem. A classification might therefore be termed race-specific if it singles out a racial problem for special and disadvantageous treatment.[84] Not all race-specific

---

[82] This may have been what Justice Harlan meant in suggesting that the law was discriminatory on its face. 377 U.S. at 395. Compare James v. Valtierra, 402 U.S. 137 (1971) and City of Eastlake v. Forest City Enterprises, 426 U.S. 668 (1976). See Sager, *Insular Majorities Unabated:* Warth v. Seldin *and* City of Eastlake v. Forest City Enterprises, Inc., 91 HARV. L. REV. 1373 (1978).

[83] The approach suggested here for special treatment of race-specific classifications is similar to the approach suggested by Professor Stone for what he calls "subject matter restrictions" in the First Amendment area. See Stone, *Restrictions of Speech because of Its Content: The Peculiar Case of Subject-Matter Restrictions*, 46 U. CHI. L. REV. 81 (1978).

[84] The next case involving a race-specific classification was Lee v. Nyquist, 318 F. Supp. 710 (W.D.N.Y. 1970), *aff'd*, 402 U.S. 935 (1971). At issue there was a New York statute that prohibited school assignment or attendance at any school "on account of race" unless there

classifications are unconstitutional; in some cases, a legislature may decide, for unobjectionable reasons, to single out racial problems for special treatment, even if the special treatment is disadvantageous in comparison with the treatment given to other measures. The true lesson of *Hunter* is that there is a category of classifications that qualify neither as facially neutral nor as facially discriminatory and that, while not as suspicious as the latter, ought not to receive the deference due to the former.

III. SEATTLE AND CRAWFORD

A. BACKGROUND

Seattle and *Crawford* involved state efforts to limit the use of busing for purposes of school desegregation. The *Seattle* case grew out of the long struggle of certain local school authorities to promote integrated education in Washington. Three school districts were involved. For the sake of illustration, it will be sufficient to discuss the Seattle experience.

From 1976 to 1977, the Seattle School District developed and publicized a magnet school system that permitted transfer to schools with special programs. Although the magnet plan at first increased integration to some degree, it did not bring about racial balance. As a result, the District decided to adopt an altogether different plan. The plan, apparently the product at least in part of fear of litigation and of a desire to prevent a threatened loss of federal funds, included an initial assignment of students to schools other than those geographically most proximate. The result of the first-year phase of the program was a substantial increase in the racial balance of the Seattle system. This, however, was not met with pleasure by the Washington electorate. A citizens' group, the Citizens for Voluntary Integration Committee, brought Initiative 350 before the voters. Patterned after certain federal legislation,[85] the Initiative was designed to bar school desegregation except where constitutionally required.

---

had been approval from the board of education. The district court found that the statute was facially discriminatory, since it treated educational matters involving racial criteria differently from all other matters. The Supreme Court summarily affirmed.

[85] See 20 U.S.C. 1714(a) (1976), 90 Stat. 1434, P.L. 95–205; see Brown v. Califano, 627 F.2d 1221 (D.C. Cir. 1980).

Initiative 350 prohibited any school district or school board from "directly or indirectly requir[ing] any student to attend a school other than the school which is geographically nearest or next nearest the student's place of residence within the school district . . . and which offers the course of study pursued by such student." There were three exceptions: (1) cases in which a student requires special education, care, or guidance available only at some other school; (2) cases in which there are hazards or physical barriers between the student's place of residence and the nearer schools; and (3) cases in which the nearer schools are unfit or inadequate because of overcrowding, unsafe conditions, or lack of physical facilities. In the light of the breadth of the exceptions, the only real effect of Initiative 350 was to ban local school boards from ordering transportation for purposes of school desegregation. If busing were to be used for those purposes, it would be necessary to receive authorization from the state legislature rather than from the local school boards that had formerly decided such questions.

The district court invalidated the initiative on the ground that it was not materially distinguishable from the antibusing statute at issue in *Lee v. Nyquist*[86] or the Akron referendum in *Hunter v. Erickson*.[87] The court of appeals affirmed on the *Hunter v. Erickson* ground.[88]

The California case followed a different route. In 1976, the California Supreme Court held that the equal protection clause of the state constitution required "state school boards . . . to take reasonable steps to alleviate segregation in the public schools, whether the segregation be de facto or de jure in origin."[89] This standard is different from that of the Equal Protection Clause, which does not bar de facto segregation.[90] The California court thus ordered desegregation of the Los Angeles schools regardless of whether de jure segregation had been practiced in those schools. A

---

[86] 473 F.Supp. 996, 1011 (W.D. Wash. 1979). It was found as well that the initiative was motivated by a discriminatory purpose, and that it was impermissibly broad because it prohibited school assignments even where necessary to remedy de jure segregation. *Id.* at 1011.

[87] 393 U.S. 385 (1969).

[88] 633 F.2d 1338, 1342 (9th Cir. 1980).

[89] Crawford v. Board of Education, 17 Cal.3d 280, 290 (1976).

[90] See, *e.g.*, Swann v. Charlotte-Mecklenburg Bd. of Educ., 402 U.S. 1 (1971); Dayton Bd. of Educ. v. Brinkman, 433 U.S. 406 (1977); *cf.* Keyes v. School District No. 1, 413 U.S. 189, 217 (1973) (Powell, J., dissenting).

plan including school reassignments and pupil transportation was put into effect in 1978.

In 1979, California voters approved Proposition I as an amendment to the due process and equal protection clauses of the state constitution. Proposition I barred any state court from imposing on the State of California or any of its subdivisions an obligation to assign or bus students, except to the extent that the obligation would be imposed under federal law by a federal court acting pursuant to the Equal Protection Clause.[91] The California Court of Appeal held that Proposition I rendered unlawful that part of the plan requiring student reassignment and transportation. Moreover, the court upheld the enactment on the ground that it was facially neutral and was not adopted with a discriminatory purpose.

B. THE DECISIONS

The Supreme Court affirmed the decision of the court of appeals in *Seattle* by a 5–4 vote. It also affirmed the lower court decision in *Crawford* by an 8–1 vote. It will be useful to examine precisely what the Court said in reaching these apparently disparate results.

Writing for the majority in *Seattle*, Justice Blackmun (joined by Justices Brennan, White, Marshall, and Stevens) placed primary reliance on *Hunter* and *Lee*. Those cases, he said, established a "simple but central principle" that governments may not restructure political processes "by explicitly using the *racial* nature of a decision to determine the decisionmaking process."[92] Neutral requirements, such as executive vetoes, are permissible even if they make it more difficult for certain groups to secure favorable legislation. Initiative 350, however, used the racial nature of the issue to define the governmental decisionmaking structure and thus fell within the principle of *Hunter* and *Lee*.

---

[91] The text of Proposition I reads, "[N]o court of this state may impose upon the State of California or any public entity, board, or official any obligation or responsibility with respect to the use of pupil school assignment or pupil transportation, (1) except to remedy a specific violation by such party that would also constitute a violation of the Equal Protection Clause of the 14th Amendment to the United States Constitution, and (2) unless a federal court would be permitted under federal decisional law to impose that obligation or responsibility upon such party to remedy the specific violation of the Equal Protection Clause. . . ."

Because both Initiative 350 and Proposition I allowed busing to remedy a constitutional violation, neither case raised the question of the constitutionality of state or federal efforts to eliminate transportation remedies entirely. See North Carolina Bd. of Educ. v. Swann, 402 U.S. 43 (1971); Swann v. Charlotte-Mecklenburg Bd. of Educ., 402 U.S. 1 (1971).

[92] 102 S. Ct. at 3195.

The Court acknowledged that Initiative 350 did not by its terms refer to race or distinguish between blacks and whites. But the Court found it critical that "despite its facial neutrality there is little doubt that the initiative was effectively drawn for racial purposes."[93] In this regard, the Court emphasized that Initiative 350 was designed to interfere only with busing for purposes of desegregation. All other busing was permitted. The fact that blacks and whites could be found on both sides of the busing controversy was irrelevant; the same could have been said of the fair housing ordinance in *Hunter*. And the Court emphasized that like antidiscrimination legislation, busing was designed to, and did, benefit blacks.

The Court concluded that the reallocation of government power, limited only to a racial problem, was more than a mere repeal of a desegregation law. Unlike such a repeal, Initiative 350 burdened all future attempts to integrate Washington schools in districts throughout the State, "by lodging decisionmaking authority over the question at a new and remote level of government" and thus "impos[ing] direct and undeniable burdens on minority interests."[94] In the Court's view, the decision to withdraw authority from the local school district was an extraordinary departure from the ordinary allocation of authority between the state and the local school boards; the extraordinary nature of the measure tended to suggest that an impermissible motive was at work.

Finally, the Court rejected the claim that *Hunter* had been overruled by decisions requiring a showing of discriminatory purpose. That requirement, according to the Court, is applicable only "when facially neutral legislation is subjected to equal protection attack."[95] When a racial classification is involved, there is no need for "a particularized inquiry into motivation."[96] Statutes "of the kind challenged in *Hunter* similarly fall into an inherently suspect category."[97]

There is an obvious weakness in the Court's reasoning. Initiative 350 does not distinguish whites from blacks: it differentiates between one type of busing and all other types. Indeed, at one point

---

[93] *Id.* at 3195.

[94] *Id.* at 3202.

[95] *Id.*

[96] *Id.*

[97] *Id.* at 3203.

the Court appeared to acknowledge this, referring to the "facial neutrality" of the initiative. Later in the opinion, however, the Court suggested that "facially neutral" statutes would be upheld unless there was a discriminatory purpose but said that the principle was inapplicable to legislation "of the kind" at issue *Seattle*, which must be struck down regardless of any such purpose. This is of course a self-contradiction: the initiative is either facially neutral or it is not. To compound the confusion, the Court acknowledged, but attempted to meet the point, that the initiative was facially neutral with the suggestion that it "was effectively drawn for racial purposes."[98] But the Court said a few pages later that the purposes of the statute are irrelevant, because it is not facially neutral.

Justice Powell's dissenting opinion does little to illuminate the problem. His primary objection is that states have broad latitude to allocate governmental power among different levels of government. But that truism is irrelevant to the *Seattle* case: surely it would be unconstitutional for a state to say that whites may obtain legislation through local units but that blacks must obtain approval from the state as well. The question is whether the decision to single out pupil transportation and assignment for state rather than local control represents an allocation of power that violates the Equal Protection Clause, not whether there is any general constitutional restriction on state decisions as to how much power to accord a local entity.

As to the *Hunter* problem, Justice Powell argued that "even could it be assumed that Initiative 350 imposed a burden on racial minorities, it simply does not place unique political obstacles in the way of racial minorities."[99] More generally, the dissenting opinion suggests that matters other than mandatory busing were addressed at the state level and that the decision to bar local school boards from ordering such busing therefore does not amount to special treatment. But that observation does not meet the point that, by distinguishing busing for racial purposes from busing for all other purposes, and by making those who seek such busing appeal to the state legislature, the initiative should be treated as a kind of racial classification. The dissenting opinion does not, in short, explain why one ought to look to the entire universe of decisions made at

---

[98] *Id.* at 3195.

[99] *Id.* at 3209.

the state level, rather than to the decisions relating to the particular subject at issue.

It is difficult to believe that *Crawford* was decided by the same Court as *Seattle*, much less that it was decided during the same Term and on the same day. The point of departure of Justice Powell's opinion for the Court in *Crawford* is that it "would be paradoxical to conclude that by adopting the Equal Protection Clause of the Fourteenth Amendment, the voters of the State thereby had violated it."[100] Moreover, the Court found that the California amendment contained no racial classification. "It neither says nor implies that persons are to be treated differently on account of their race."[101] According to the Court, "in view of the demographic mix of the District it is not clear which race or races would be affected the most or in what way."[102] The *Crawford* majority added that there is a distinction between "state action that discriminates on the basis of race and state action that addresses, in neutral fashion, race related matters."[103]

The Court attempted to distinguish *Hunter* in two ways. First, the Court said that that case involved an effort to single out persons seeking antidiscriminatory housing laws for special treatment, whereas Proposition I was merely a partial repeal of the California equal protection clause, and one which still imposed on local school boards a greater duty to desegregate than does the Fourteenth Amendment. Second, the Court suggested that the referendum did not distort the political process for racial reasons, or allocate governmental power on the basis of a discriminatory principle. "Remedies appropriate in one area of legislation may not be desirable in another."[104] It was not unconstitutional for the federal government to have one set of remedies for antitrust violations and another for civil rights violations. Similarly, in fashioning remedies for violations of state-created rights, it was permissible to adopt in part the requirements of the Equal Protection Clause.

There are several tensions between the majority opinions in the *Seattle* and *Crawford* cases. In *Seattle*, the Court read *Hunter* to

---

[100] 102 S. Ct. at 3211, 3217.

[101] *Id.* at 3217–18.

[102] *Id.* at 3218.

[103] *Id.*

[104] *Id.* at 3220.

suggest that race-specific classifications are to be treated like conventional racial classifications, at least if they impose a burden on
the interests of minority group members. In *Crawford*, the Court
indicated that decisions that single out racial problems are not to be
treated like racial classifications at all. In *Seattle*, the Court suggested that the requirement of discriminatory purpose did not affect the *Hunter* analysis. In *Crawford*, the Court emphasized that a
facially neutral law must be upheld absent a showing of discriminatory purpose. The *Crawford* Court stated that the benefits of neighborhood schooling are racially neutral; the *Seattle* Court said that
busing inures primarily to the benefit of blacks and that a law is not
racially neutral merely because both blacks and whites support it.

Justice Blackmun, concurring in *Crawford*, suggested that *Seattle*
could be distinguished from *Crawford* on the ground that the
classification in *Seattle* distorted the political process, whereas that
in *Crawford* did not work "a structural change in the political *process*
so much as . . . simply repeal the right to invoke a judicial busing
remedy."[105] According to Justice Blackmun, the California voters
in *Crawford*, who created the obligation to integrate in cases of de
facto segregation in the first instance, had simply decided that the
obligation should not be judicially enforceable. Political mechanisms used to address racially conscious legislation were not singled
out for special treatment. There was simply a repeal of a state-
created right.

Justice Marshall argued in dissent that a racially based removal of
authority from local school boards should not be treated differently
from a racially based limitation on the power of the courts. If, as
the *Seattle* Court believed, Initiative 350 was not facially neutral,
then the governmental unit at which it was directed is irrelevant.
According to Justice Marshall, Proposition I is the functional
equivalent of a facial racial classification in precisely the same way,
and for precisely the same reasons, as Initiative 350: it singles out
busing for desegregation purposes and imposes a special burden on
those who seek such busing. A facial racial classification is invalid
regardless of the benefit or burden that it implicates.

But Marshall's response to the suggestion that Proposition I is a
mere repeal is unpersuasive. He argues that a repeal is permissible
if undertaken by the same entity that originally enacted the prior

---

[105] *Id.* at 3223.

law or policy, but not if it is accomplished by some other entity. Why that distinction is decisive is unclear. In the absence of specific proof of an impermissible motivation, surely it would not be unconstitutional for a state legislature to repeal or nullify a local ordinance prohibiting private discrimination on the basis of race.

C. MERE REPEALS, FACIAL NEUTRALITY, AND RACE-SPECIFIC CLASSIFICATIONS

It may be useful to begin by asking whether it is possible to distinguish between *Seattle* and *Hunter*. The Court pretended that there was no such distinction, and Justice Powell's effort to suggest a distinction was at least incomplete. But there is one genuine, and potentially important, difference between the two cases. The *Hunter* Court thought that an effort to single out antidiscrimination legislation for special disability is functionally equivalent to an effort to single out members of minority groups for the same purpose. This approach is essentially correct. The reason is that race-specific legislation is peculiarly likely to be supported by invidious justifications. Like the heightened scrutiny applied to facial racial classifications, heightened scrutiny in *Hunter* is justified by a suspicion that improper justifications are at work.

Initiative 350 did not, of course, contain a facial racial classification. It did not distinguish between blacks and whites; instead it distinguished between those who sought busing for purposes of desegregation and those who sought other sorts of action from the local school board. But to say this much is not to decide that it is appropriate to apply rational basis scrutiny: *Hunter* demonstrates that race-specific classifications ought not to be treated like ones that are facially racial.

Race-specific classifications are not, however, all the same. Opposition to busing for purposes of racial balance is different from opposition to antidiscrimination legislation, because it is more easily supportable with noninvidious justifications. One need not believe that busing is necessarily counterproductive in order to recognize that the argument to that effect is well-developed and that it is accepted by both white and black people in good faith.[106] The polls suggest that numerous blacks oppose busing for purposes of de-

---

[106] See, *e.g.*, ARMOR, WHITE FLIGHT, DEMOGRAPHIC TRANSITION AND THE FUTURE OF SCHOOL DESEGREGATION (1978); Bell, Book Review, 92 HARV. L. REV. 1826 (1979).

segregation; and numerous whites are in favor of busing for those purposes. Opposition to busing is sometimes based on opposition to racial equality, but it may also be based on a notion, for example, that busing impairs the education of both whites and blacks and wastes social resources. In short, noninvidious justifications are more plausibly made in opposition to busing than in support of statutes that distinguish on their face between blacks and whites. Moreover, arguments against busing are less likely to be animated by racial bias than are arguments against legislation preventing discrimination in housing. *Seattle* might therefore have been treated differently from *Hunter* on the ground that invidious motives may well not have been at work.[107] It is largely this perception that, I believe, makes *Seattle* the more difficult case.

Do these considerations suggest that Initiative 350 ought to be treated like any other classification, and to be subjected to the most deferential kind of review? Ought an enactment that singles out busing for purposes of desegregation, and imposes special burdens on those who seek such busing, to be treated the same as any other enactment? While opposition to busing is supportable on neutral grounds, it would be unrealistic to suggest that invidious motives may not play a part in decisions as to how best, and how enthusiastically, to desegregate the public schools. In both *Hunter* and *Seattle*, governmental action that is ordinarily believed to be in the interests of blacks was singled out for a special disability. A selective effort to prevent enactment of measures designed to desegregate—in the form of an unusual and perhaps extraordinary limitation on the authority of the local school board—may well be not an effort to promote a public value, but the sort of simply unprincipled redistribution of wealth or opportunities that was the focus of Part I of this essay. Even if the Court were incorrect to characterize Initiative 350 as a conventional racial classification, then, it was right in approaching the initiative with more than usual suspicion[108] and in inspecting it with care for the presence of neutral

---

[107] In *Seattle* it was argued that the local school board had adopted a race-conscious policy, and that such policies were dangerous and merit special scrutiny by the state legislature. The Court avoided the issue with a suggestion that the constitutionality of race-conscious assignments in the absence of de jure segregation had not been challenged. 102 S. Ct. at 3196 n.15.

[108] The Court in *Seattle* stated that "singling out the political processes affecting racial issues for uniquely disadvantageous treatment inevitably raises dangers of impermissible motivation." *Id.* at 3203 n.30. It will be remembered that this was precisely the route taken by Justice Harlan in *Hunter*: in his view, the Akron ordinance spoke for itself.

justifications. The question whether it survives such scrutiny on the facts presented in *Seattle* is perhaps less important, but it would appear that the Court was correct on that score as well.

The problem lies in determining precisely why it was thought necessary, not to abolish the local busing plan, but instead to reallocate governmental power so as to erect a permanent barrier to local desegregation efforts of that sort. A justification might be available in the form of reasons for demanding state approval of certain categories of controversial issues. The Court's treatment of that question was perhaps too cavalier, but in view of its understanding of state law, its basic approach appears sound. In cases involving facial racial classifications, and those that are race-specific, a substantial burden is correctly placed on the classifier.

Thus far I have suggested that both *Hunter* and *Seattle* conformed to the Court's usual understanding of the evil at which the Equal Protection Clause is aimed and to the ordinary role of heightened scrutiny in ensuring that that evil does not occur. It remains whether *Seattle* can be distinguished from *Crawford*. I believe that it can be. Briefly, the distinction is this. Proposition I in *Crawford* closely resembles a mere repeal. It is possible to argue that even such repeals should be subject to special scrutiny, but the Court's unwillingness to apply such scrutiny is at least understandable. Initiative 350 in *Seattle* had a far broader effect than a mere repeal. It was a "repeal plus," a race-specific classification in the form of a special burden on those who sought certain sorts of actions from the local school board.

To illustrate, let us imagine two polar cases. In the first, a state initially adopts a provision to the effect that de facto discrimination in a school system is unlawful and that busing must be used to bring about racial balance. Five years later, the provision is repealed on the ground that busing has proved harmful to both minority and majority members. In my second hypothetical case, a state both repeals the provision and adopts a further measure to the effect that any legislation that is (*a*) supported by seventy percent of black citizens and (*b*) goes beyond the requirements of the Equal Protection Clause must receive approval of a majority of the voters in a referendum.

It is plain that the second statute is unconstitutional; it discriminates on its face on the basis of race. The fact that it leaves intact rights under the Equal Protection Clause is of course irrelevant.

The *Hunter* and *Seattle* Courts treated the respective enactments as if they fell within the same category as this second statute. The two enactments in those cases reallocated government power and were more than mere repeals: if the decisions were wrong, it is because race-specific classifications should be treated like facially neutral ones.

In *Crawford,* the Court treated Proposition I as if it were the equivalent of a mere repeal and assumed that, in the absence of specific proof of improper motivation, such a repeal would be constitutional. It is ordinarily thought that repeals of legislation that outlaws, or provides remedies for, discrimination are unobjectionable. There is no constitutional right to statutory safeguards of that sort, and if there is no such right, one might suggest that a state must be permitted to change its mind and withdraw the benefit it had previously conferred. Repeals impose no special burdens on minority group members; they contain no racial classification; they merely restore the status quo ante, which, by hypothesis, was itself constitutional.

It has been questioned whether states are in fact free not to furnish protection against private racial discrimination,[109] but one need not resolve that problem in order to dispute the suggestion that repeals of legislation prohibiting discrimination ought to be treated as deferentially as other legislation. The reason for heightened scrutiny of facial racial classifications is the peculiar likelihood that an impermissible motivation is at work. If so, one might be more than usually suspicious of repeals of legislation intended to protect minority group members as well. In the case of such repeals, it is also likely that the legislature is not motivated by a legitimate or neutral purpose but by an intention to advantage or to disadvantage a particular group as an end in itself.[110] The suggestion is not inconsistent with the decided cases: the Court has been quite skeptical of legislative efforts to repeal antidiscrimination stat-

---

[109] See Karst & Horowitz, note 71 *supra; cf.* Michelman, *Foreword: On Protecting the Poor through the Fourteenth Amendment,* 83 HARV. L. REV. 7 (1969); Stewart & Sunstein, note 31 *supra,* at 1308–15.

[110] The *Seattle* Court furnished the elements of the argument in noting that busing is generally perceived to be designed to aid blacks, and that an effort to single out the issue for disadvantageous treatment raises dangers of impermissible motivation. 102 S. Ct. at 3196, 3203.

utes and has treated such repeals more harshly than ordinary legislation.[111]

The *Crawford* Court attempted to explain that repeals were permissible because a contrary rule would impose a serious limit on
legislative flexibility, committing states "irrevocably to legislation
that has proved unsuccessful or even harmful in practice."[112] Such a
result, the Court suggested, might discourage legislatures from
enacting protective legislation in the first instance or from changing
such legislation even when it has impaired the interests of minority
group members. This is only a partial answer, but a different response is available. Repeals of regulatory legislation are commonplace. The legislative process is in large part one of trial and error,
of experiment, of the discarding of solutions that turn out to be
counterproductive. To impose a constraint on that process—even
in the context of attempted solutions to the problem of racial injustice—might be thought inconsistent with the expected workings of
the political process and indeed with the basic constitutional premise of representative democracy. In this respect, repeals may be an
important means of promoting public values. It is this perception, I
believe, that underlies the strong appeal of the idea that mere repeals offend no constitutional right.

The Court in *Crawford* treated Proposition I as if it were a repeal,
suggesting that the voters of California modified a state-created
right against de facto segregation by disabling courts from ordering
busing remedies. If it was proper to treat Proposition I as a repeal,
the ultimate holding is understandable, if not unassailable. But it is
not entirely correct to say that *Crawford* involved a mere repeal, for
in two respects Proposition I could be understood as a race-specific
classification:

1. Proposition I, it might be argued, produced a situation in
which busing was unavailable for purposes of remedying de facto
segregation but available for many other purposes. The *Seattle*
Court found this distinction critical. The resulting discrimination
might in this respect be thought indistinguishable from that in
Hunter and *Seattle*.

There are two answers. First, to conclude that Proposition I is

---

[111] See Reitman v. Mulkey, 387 U.S. 369 (1967); Hunter v. Erickson, 393 U.S. 385
(1969).

[112] 102 S. Ct. at 3219.

invalid for this reason alone is to suggest that any situation in which a state has created a right to busing for some purposes, but not for purposes of remedying de facto desegregation, may itself be unconstitutional. Is an ordinance that creates a right to busing for special educational needs unconstitutional because it fails to create such a right for purposes of desegregation? Such an ordinance would contain a race-specific classification—because it would single out a racial problem for special and disadvantageous treatment—but not all such classifications are unconstitutional.

The Court itself argued that the distinction between busing for purposes of desegregation and busing for other purposes was unobjectionable. According to the Court, remedies necessarily vary with context. It is hardly impermissible to distinguish between the remedies created for antitrust violations and those created for violations of the civil rights laws.[113] Because of the wholly disparate nature of the antitrust and civil rights laws, the example is not altogether fair, but one may sympathize with the Court's view that to treat such distinctions in the same way as facial racial classifications would impose undue burdens on legislative efforts to deal with the problem of racial injustice. Moreover, and perhaps more important, Proposition I did not on its face distinguish between kinds of busing at all. Although the enactment was undoubtedly rooted in opposition to busing for purposes of desegregation, it flatly and evenhandedly prohibited all judicially ordered transportation remedies. Initiative 350 did no such thing.

2. A separate response to the decision in *Crawford* might emphasize that the California voters purported not to affect the state-created right to freedom from de facto discrimination: that right was left inviolate. Instead, Proposition I barred state courts from ordering pupil assignment or transportation unless so required by the federal Constitution. After Proposition I, those seeking to vindicate their legal rights could normally invoke judicial processes in order to do so; only one category of persons—those seeking pupil assignments or transportation for purposes of desegregation—were barred from invoking the courts. This too is a kind of race-specific classification.

It is possible to see why the Court rejected this argument. After Proposition I was passed, blacks and whites in California were in

---

[113] 102 S. Ct. at 3220.

substantially the same position. Indeed, those who sought busing were in substantially the same position as all others who wanted a judicially enforceable right. Those on all sides had to convince the State to confer that right. Even if it would be proper to find a constitutional distinction between repealing a right and allowing the right to stand but repealing a judicially enforceable remedy, Proposition I can be understood as doing no such thing. Proposition I simply redefined the preexisting right in a way that amounted to something less than a total repeal. After Proposition I the right to freedom from de facto segregation fell into the same category as numerous other "rights" that receive constitutional recognition but that are not subject to judicial enforcement. The Court apparently reasoned that if the right itself may be eliminated entirely, it may be redefined so as to preclude judicial enforcement. Such a step does not distinguish between those who seek busing and all others who have legal rights, but instead between all those with and all those without judicially enforceable rights—hardly a race-specific classification. And if repeals are constitutional, it is possible to understand why the Court believed that Proposition I was constitutional as well.

These considerations suggest why the *Crawford* Court regarded Proposition I as a repeal, while in *Seattle* the Court treated Initiative 350 as a "repeal plus" that amounted to the same sort of race-specific classification condemned in *Hunter*.[114] This distinction might be challenged, however, on the ground that *Seattle*, too, involved the equivalent of a repeal. Indeed, the State went only half as far as it might have. Instead of repealing any right to be bused, or enacting a prohibition on busing, the State merely said that anyone who wants busing must persuade the State legislature to authorize it. From the State's standpoint, Initiative 350 was a far less intrusive measure than a repeal or prohibition, both of which would be constitutional under *Crawford*. After Initiative 350, those seeking busing were placed in the same category as numerous persons who must obtain enactments from the State rather than from local

---

[114] For example, if a local board enacted a right to freedom from de facto segregation, and later repealed the right, its decision would in all likelihood be unobjectionable. If, on the other hand, the school board enacted a right and then put into effect both a repeal and a further requirement that no such right may ever be established without the support of some supermajority, the further requirement would fall under *Hunter*. In treating *Crawford* and *Seattle* as distinguishable, the Court acted as if *Crawford* was the first case, and *Seattle* the second.

school boards. Unlike the enactment in *Hunter*, Initiative 350 did not make it harder to obtain laws protective of blacks than to obtain all sorts of other enactments. And in this respect, *Seattle* and *Crawford* are in essence the same case: in both of them, the State removed decisionmaking authority over a particular issue to another level of government, and forced all those seeking legislation on that issue to proceed to that level, that is, to the state legislature.

Whether this reasoning is correct depends largely on state law. If the Court's characterization of state law is correct, Initiative 350 was akin to the ordinance in *Hunter* in the critical sense that it placed those who sought busing for purposes of desegregation in a special category, and imposed on them a different burden from that imposed on most others who sought action on matters relating to educational policy. The majority's lengthy effort to show that such interference is extraordinary as a matter of Washington law derives from a belief that highly selective interference provides a substantial basis for fear that an impermissible motive is at work.

By contrast, if the distinction is drawn between racial busing and all other busing rather than between racial busing and all other matters relating to educational policy, there is less basis for suspicion, for the frequency of state intervention suggests that noninvidious purposes may well be at work. For this reason, the power to repeal a right to busing altogether does not necessarily include the arguably lesser power to say that those who seek busing must surmount the unusual barrier of having to go to the state legislature, where favorable action may be much more difficult to obtain.

In short, the *Crawford* decision might be supported on the ground that Proposition I was a nondiscriminatory repeal of a state-created right, whereas Initiative 350 represented both a repeal and the selective erection of a barrier to efforts to procure busing remedies—a barrier that necessarily operates to the peculiar disadvantage of blacks, and that is unusually likely to be motivated by invidious purposes. On the Court's understanding of state law, *Seattle* involved a race-specific classification; *Crawford* did not.

IV. Conclusion

I have attempted to identify a consistent theme that runs throughout the Court's equal protection jurisprudence and that suggests a particular view of the evil at which the Equal Protection

Clause is aimed. That evil consists of the unprincipled redistribution of resources or opportunities from one group of persons to another—unprincipled because it is not an effort to promote a public value, but instead is a product of the idea that it is intrinsically desirable to favor the benefited at the expense of the burdened group. It is classifications that rest on this perception—of the intrinsic worth of treating some better than others—that receive the appellations "invidious," or "irrational," or "arbitrary." This development can be traced to some of the earliest of the Court's equal protection cases. It represents a rejection of a pluralist or interest-group theory of legislation, in which statutory enactments are characterized as necessarily unprincipled outcomes of a battle between competing groups for scarce social resources.

Under this approach, the Equal Protection Clause is centrally concerned with the reasons—sometimes described as the motives—that underlie statutory classifications. This understanding of the function of the Clause is manifested in the basic elements of current equal protection doctrine. The requirement of proof of discriminatory motivation derives from a perception that the function of the Clause is to impose a limit on the reasons that may justify government classifications. Heightened scrutiny, and the special distrust of facial classifications, are intended for those cases in which such prohibited purposes are peculiarly likely to be at work; they serve to dispense with the usual need for specific proof of impermissible motivation.

Under this framework, the Court was incorrect in *Seattle* in concluding that Initiative 350 embodied a pure racial classification. At the same time, one ought not to pretend that the classification in *Seattle* is like any facially neutral statute: when government acts to single out a racial problem for special treatment, and when the special treatment operates to the peculiar disadvantage of racial minorities, there is reason for more than usual suspicion of the legislative judgment. In this respect, race-specific classifications like those in *Hunter* and *Seattle* do not fit within either of the customary "tiers" for treatment of statutory classifications, but form a new category in which there is also a basis for judicial suspicion that an impermissible motivation is at work.

In *Crawford*, by contrast, there was no race-specific classification—no effort to single out legislation ordinarily supported by, and ordinarily perceived to benefit, members of racial minority groups for a special disability. There was instead a partial repeal of a statute that was not itself constitutionally required, a repeal which did not impose an unusual burden on those who sought legislation protecting blacks. In order to conclude that Proposition I was unconstitutional, the Court would have had to hold either that repeals of discrimination intended to protect blacks are themselves constitutionally suspect or that if a state provides busing for some purposes, it must also allow busing for purposes of remedying a state-created right to freedom from de facto segregation. While those principles are not without appeal, the Court did not need to go so far in order to invalidate Initiative 350 and in order to remain true to the doctrinal framework that has grown out of the Court's understanding of the principle of constitutional equality.

DENNIS J. HUTCHINSON

MORE SUBSTANTIVE
EQUAL PROTECTION?
A NOTE ON PLYLER v. DOE

In *Plyler v. Doe*,[1] the Supreme Court held by a five-to-four vote that the Equal Protection Clause of the Fourteenth Amendment forbids the State of Texas to "deny to undocumented school-age children the free public education that it provides to children who are citizens of the United States or [who are] legally admitted aliens."[2] The decision may be the Court's most important and groundbreaking interpretation of the Equal Protection Clause in a decade or a limited and somewhat untidy response to a novel case. In either event, the decision raises more questions than it answers, and the questions are far from trivial: May Congress, contrary to the teachings of *Shapiro v. Thompson*,[3] now, in certain circumstances, authorize states to violate the Equal Protection Clause? Are state classifications based on alienage no longer "suspect," at least as a general rule? What is the relationship between federal preemption of state laws that classify on the basis of alienage and the Equal Protection Clause? What is left of *San Antonio Independent School District v. Rodriguez?*[4] And, most important, Has the Court finally

---

Dennis J. Hutchinson is Associate Professor in the New Collegiate Division of The College and Associate Professor of Law, The University of Chicago.

[1] 102 S. Ct. 2382 (1982).

[2] *Id.* at 2388.

[3] 394 U.S. 618 (1969).

[4] 411 U.S. 1 (1973).

adopted the "sliding scale" analysis of the Equal Protection Clause urged by Justice Marshall in *Rodriguez?*

Justice Brennan's opinion for the Court in *Plyler* barely admits that the questions are even present in the case and carries no hint that the decision is either a landmark or a sport. His opinion—joined by Justices Marshall, Blackmun, Powell, and Stevens—concluded matter-of-factly: "If the State is to deny a discrete group of innocent children the free public education that it offers to other children residing within its borders, the denial must be justified by a showing that it furthers some substantial state interest. No such showing was made here."[5]

Two of the three Justices who filed concurring opinions saw no doctrinal landmark in the Court's effort. Justice Blackmun noted that "the nature of the interest at stake is crucial to the proper resolution of this case,"[6] rehearsed the majority's analysis, and certified his agreement in the "Court's carefully worded analysis."[7] Justice Powell's concurrence emphasized "the unique character of the case before us."[8] The Chief Justice's dissent, the only opinion filed by the minority, attempted to condemn and confine the majority analysis in a breath: "[T]he Court's opinion rests on such a unique confluence of theories and rationales that it will likely stand for little beyond the results in these particular cases."[9] Only Justice Marshall, who filed the other concurring opinion, sought to suggest the sweeping effect of the Court's opinion, but he did so obliquely in one paragraph that quoted or referred to his dissents in *San Antonio Independent School District v. Rodriguez* and in *Dandridge v. Williams.*[10]

Justice Marshall's point, lightly made, was that in *Plyler* the Court had finally adopted the "sliding scale" test for unconstitutionality under the Equal Protection Clause that he had suggested without success not only in *Rodriguez*[11] and *Dandridge*[12] but persis-

---

[5] 102 S. Ct. at 2402.

[6] *Ibid.*

[7] *Id.* at 2405.

[8] *Ibid.*

[9] *Id.* at 2408–9.

[10] 397 U.S. 471 (1970).

[11] 411 U.S. at 98–110, 124–30.

[12] 397 U.S. at 519–21. See also Richardson v. Belcher, 404 U.S. 78, 90 (1971) (Marshall, J., dissenting).

tently in other cases since then. Marshall saw the Court's opinion as necessarily vindicating his views and as incapable of limitation *ipse dixit*.

It would have been easy enough for Justice Marshall to detail his case had he wished. In the usual taxonomy of the Court's cases, there are three levels or "tiers" of judicial scrutiny for classifications challenged under the Equal Protection Clause: (1) "strict scrutiny" (for suspect statutory classifications and state action burdening fundamental rights); (2) "heightened scrutiny" (for quasi-suspect state classifications); and (3) "rationality" (for all the rest). The Court in *Plyler* purported to apply the middle-tier test. I say "purported," because it did so in a way in which it had never been applied before. The reason for heightened scrutiny in *Plyler* was not only the nature of the classification, but also the interest affected by the classification. In *Craig v. Boren*,[13] which gave the heightened scrutiny test its birth and its content, the vice of the Oklahoma statute in question had not been the interest it affected (in men being able to drink 3.2 percent beer at age eighteen along with women of that age), but in the fact that it classified on the basis of gender. *Plyler* expanded the test to classifications not quite quasi-suspect due to the importance of the interest affected. No better summary of the new content of heightened scrutiny could have been found than that in Marshall's dissent in *Dandridge*, to which he referred only by citation in his *Plyler* concurrence:[14]

> [C]oncentration [for purposes of Equal Protection analysis] must be placed upon the character of the classification in question, the relative importance to individuals in the class discriminated against of the governmental benefits they do not receive, and the asserted state interests in support of the classification. As we said only recently, "In determining whether or not a state law violates the Equal Protection Clause, we must consider the facts and circumstances behind the law, the interests which the State claims to be protecting, and the interests of those who are disadvantaged by the classification." *Kramer* v. *Union School District*, 395 U.S. 621, 626 (1969), quoting *Williams* v. *Rhodes*, 393 U.S. 23, 30 (1968).

Once the argument elliptically sketched in Justice Marshall's

---

[13] 429 U.S. 190 (1976).
[14] 397 U.S. at 520–21. *Cf.* 102 S. Ct. at 2402 (Marshall, J., concurring).

concurring statement is unpacked, it is difficult to resist the suggestion that *Plyler* has implicitly effected a major change in equal protection doctrine. But the cautionary concurring opinions of Justices Blackmun and Powell counsel against such a broad reading of the decision, as a matter of fact if not as a matter of logic.

Even if one accepts Justice Marshall's premises, however, *Plyler* is hardly "an occasion for dancing in the streets."[15] The Court qualified its ruling by implying that the Texas statute could be constitutionalized if Congress so ordained, or explicitly approved, pursuant to its plenary power over immigration and the concomitant power to deter illegal immigration. The Court did not explain whether it meant to carve out an exception to the categorical imperative of *Shapiro v. Thompson* that "Congress may not authorize the States to violate the Equal Protection Clause."[16] Indeed, *Shapiro* was not even mentioned.

What the Court did not do in *Plyler* is as puzzling as what it did do. In addition to the silent gloss on *Shapiro v. Thompson*, the Court declined to follow the two analytical paths that it had previously found to be important in weighing classifications based on alienage used by a state. It held that undocumented aliens did not constitute a "suspect class," and it elected not to reach the question whether the Texas law was preempted by federal law or policy. Both questions had been addressed by the Court in 1971 in *Graham v. Richardson*,[17] in which the Court first held state classifications based upon alienage to be suspect. *Rodriguez*, on the other hand, was mentioned in each of the five opinions filed in *Plyler*, although everyone except Justice Marshall came to bury it, not to praise it.

On close analysis, the narrow scope of the majority opinion and the even more limited concurrences of Justices Blackmun and Powell make detailed doctrinal analysis of the Court's performance somewhat artificial at best. The exercise is hardly academic, however: already there are cases[18] in the lower federal courts challenging the constitutionality under the Fourteenth Amendment of state

---

[15] Kalven, *The New York Times Case: A Note on "The Central Meaning of the First Amendment*," 1964 SUPREME COURT REVIEW 191, 221 n.125.

[16] 394 U.S. at 641. *Cf.* Katzenbach v. Morgan, 384 U.S. 641, 651 n.10 (1966).

[17] 403 U.S. 365 (1971).

[18] See NEW YORK TIMES, June 17. 1982, at p. 17.

denials of welfare benefits and emergency medical services to indigent illegal aliens.[19]

I. THE OPINION OF THE COURT

Prior to 1975, Texas law provided for tuition-free public
education to all children of the appropriate age residing in local
school districts, without regard to citizenship or alienage status. In
May 1975, the Texas legislature enacted § 21.031 of its education
code to permit local school districts to deny enrollment in the
schools to alien children who were not "legally admitted" to the
United States or to charge tuition to such children.[20] Apparently as
an incentive to compliance, the law also provided that state funds
for the education of such children would be withheld from local
school districts. There is no evidence in the record that either the
State or local school districts took active steps to enforce the new
law for nearly two years.

In 1977, a class action was filed on behalf of children in the Tyler
Independent School District who were charged tuition (who could
not afford to pay it) because they could not prove that they had
been legally admitted to the United States. After extensive hearings
the United States District Court for the Eastern District of Texas
granted permanent injunctive relief from enforcement of the
amended statute.[21] The court held that the statute violated both the
Supremacy Clause (as inconsistent with the national regulatory
scheme of the Immigration and Nationality Act[22] and with federal
laws covering funding and discrimination in education) and the
Equal Protection Clause (because the law was not supported by a
rational basis). The Court of Appeals for the Fifth Circuit
affirmed.[23] Although it found that the statute was not preempted
by federal law, the Court of Appeals held that it was "constitution-

---

[19] See Note, *Equal Protection for Undocumented Aliens*, 5 CHICANO L. REV. 29, 38–43
(1982); Conard, *Health Care for Indigent Illegal Aliens: Whose Responsibility?* 8 U.C. DAVIS L.R.
107 (1975).

[20] Tex. Educ. Code Ann. § 21.031 (Vernon Cum. Supp. 1981).

[21] Doe v. Plyler, 458 F. Supp. 569 (E.D. Tex. 1978).

[22] 8 U.S.C. § 1251 *et seq.*

[23] 628 F.2d 448 (5th Cir. 1980).

ally infirm regardless of whether it was tested using the mere rational basis standard or some more stringent test."[24]

While the case was pending in the Court of Appeals, the United States District Court for the Southern District of Texas issued an order in consolidated suits from the Southern, Northern, and Western Districts of Texas enjoining enforcement of the statute and an opinion holding that it violated the Equal Protection Clause.[25] Three months later, the Court of Appeals rendered judgment in *Plyler v. Doe* and shortly thereafter summarily affirmed the Southern District order on the authority of its decision in *Plyler*.[26] The Supreme Court noted probable jurisdiction in both cases and consolidated them for oral argument.[27]

Justice Brennan's opinion for the Court began with a statement of what the Court apparently viewed to be the practical conundrum posed in the case:[28]

> Since the late nineteenth century, the United States has restricted immigration into this country. Unsanctioned entry into the United States is a crime, 8 U.S.C. § 1325, and those who have entered unlawfully are subject to deportation, 8 U.S.C. §§ 1251–1252. But despite the existence of these legal restrictions, a substantial number of persons have succeeded in unlawfully entering the United States, and now live within various States, including the State of Texas.

After setting out the procedural history of the case and summarizing the findings of the trial courts, Justice Brennan proceeded to the easiest question he faced: Are illegal aliens protected by the Equal Protection Clause of the Fourteenth Amendment? He spent one-third of the opinion disposing of the point, not because it was difficult but perhaps because the State of Texas had devoted half of its brief before the Court to showing that "[i]llegal aliens are not within the scope of the equal protection clause."[29] Justice Brennan dispatched the argument in three easy steps: (1) many of the Court's prior cases assumed that aliens—however they came into the

---

[24] 628 F.2d at 458.

[25] In Re: Alien Children Litigation, 501 F. Supp. 544 (S.D. Tex. 1980).

[26] Unpublished order, February 23, 1981. See also Boe v. Wright, 648 F.2d 432 (5th Cir. 1981).

[27] 452 U.S. 937 (1981).

[28] 102 S. Ct. at 2388–89.

[29] Brief for Appellants at 14–22.

State's jurisdiction—were protected, at least in some measure, by the Clause; (2) the Clause, by its terms and by repeated interpretations, speaks to physical presence within a state's jurisdiction; and (3) the legislative history of section one of the Fourteenth Amendment, although "limited," demonstrates unequivocally that "person" was used in the Clause "expressly to insure that the equal protection of the laws was provided to the alien population."[30] He might have added that some members of the Thirty-ninth Congress were motivated by practical politics as well as by principle: aliens were entitled to vote in several states at the time, and at least one member of Congress pointed out that the prospects for ratification of the Amendment might be enhanced if aliens benefited from its provisions.[31]

Having disposed of the first issue, Justice Brennan turned to the "more difficult question"[32] whether the 1975 amendment of the education code violated the Clause. He sketched the three levels of scrutiny dictated by the Court's cases, and "reject[ed] the claim that 'illegal aliens' are a 'suspect class' " in a footnote.[33]

> Unlike most of the classifications that we have recognized as suspect, entry into this class, by virtue of entry into this country, is the product of voluntary action. Indeed, entry into the class is itself a crime. In addition, it could hardly be suggested that undocumented status is a "constitutional irrelevancy." With respect to the actions of the federal government, alienage classifications may be intimately related to the conduct of foreign policy, to the federal prerogative to control access to the United States, and to the plenary federal power to determine who has sufficiently manifested his allegiance to become a citizen of the Nation. No State may independently exercise a like power. But if the Federal Government has by uniform rule prescribed what it believes to be appropriate standards for the treatment of an alien subclass, the States may, of course, follow the federal direction. See *DeCanas* v. *Bica*, 424 U.S. 351 (1976).

If illegal aliens are a "subclass" to the Federal Government, they also constitute, to the Court, a "permanent caste," socially and

---

[30] 102 S. Ct. at 2393.

[31] JAMES, THE FRAMING OF THE FOURTEENTH AMENDMENT 23 (1956); see also *id.* at 90, 159, 160, 179, 195–96.

[32] 102 S. Ct. at 2394.

[33] *Id.* at 2396 n.19.

politically, which is encouraged to stay, by the "sheer incapability or lax enforcement" of entry laws, but which "is denied the benefits that our society makes available to citizens and lawful residents."[34] Children are special members of this caste. "Persuasive arguments support the view that a State may withhold its beneficence from those whose very presence within the United States is a product of their own unlawful conduct, [but] [t]hese arguments do not apply with the same force to classifications imposing disabilities on the minor *children* of such illegal entrants."[35] Thus, to impose "disabilities" on illegal alien children would be, constitutionally, as inconsistent with "fundamental conceptions of justice" as to penalize illegitimate children for the sins of their parents.[36] Justice Brennan conceded that his analogy to the Court's cases invalidating classifications based on illegitimacy was somewhat imperfect: "undocumented status is not irrelevant to any proper legislative goal. Nor is undocumented status an absolutely immutable characteristic since it is the product of conscious, indeed unlawful action."[37] But distinctions are beside the point, the Court seemed to say, because the Texas law "imposes its discriminatory burden on the basis of a legal characteristic over which children can have little control."[38]

The Court's analysis to this point is curious to say the least. Having set up an imperfect, if evocative, analogy, Justice Brennan proceeded to distinguish it and then to say that the analogy really did not matter very much anyway. To make matters worse, the argument appears to prove too much. If the children had "little control" over their unlawful entry, it would seem to follow that the Federal Government should be barred from penalizing that illegal entry by deportation. The point did not escape the Chief Justice in dissent: "The Court does not presume to suggest that [the children's] purported lack of culpability for their illegal status prevents them from being deported or otherwise 'penalized' under federal

---

[34] *Id.* at 2395–96. Both the Court and the parties treated the tuition requirement, as applied to the indigent plaintiffs, as if it were an absolute bar to attending the public schools. Compare Harris v. McRae, 448 U.S. 448 (1980).

[35] *Id.* at 2396.

[36] *Ibid.*

[37] *Id.* at 2396–97.

[38] *Id.* at 2397.

law."[39] But that is precisely the logical implication of Justice Brennan's observation.

It is only an implication, because the analogy to illegitimacy is only one-half of the Court's analysis of the factors to be considered in identifying the level of scrutiny required under the Equal Protection Clause. The other half is the nature of the interest that the classification affects—education. The Court conceded that education was not a fundamental right, "[b]ut neither is it merely some governmental 'benefit' indistinguishable from other forms of social welfare legislation."[40] To establish the importance of education, Justice Brennan recalled familiar passages from earlier opinions,[41] including *Meyer v. Nebraska*,[42] *Abington School District v. Schempp*,[43] *Wisconsin v. Yoder*,[44] and, of course, *Brown v. Board of Education*.[45] The exercise has a bizarre ring to it, because the Court had canvassed and rejected the same authorities in *San Antonio Independent School District v. Rodriguez*,[46] which held that education was not a fundamental constitutional right despite its unquestioned importance. In addition to the replay of the *Rodriguez* debate, Justice Brennan provided a new, and apparently constitutional, factor: "[D]enial of education to some isolated group of children poses an affront to one of the goals of the Equal Protection Clause: the abolition of governmental barriers presenting unreasonable obstacles to the advancement on the basis of individual merit."[47]

Relying on the analogy he had himself undercut and on the argument that *Rodriguez* had held did not rise to a fundamental constitutional level, Justice Brennan nonetheless reported that "[t]hese well-settled principles allow us to determine the proper level of deference to be afforded"[48] the Texas statute.[49]

---

[39] *Id.* at 2410.

[40] *Id.* at 2397.

[41] *Ibid.*

[42] 262 U.S. 390 (1923).

[43] 374 U.S. 203 (1963).

[44] 406 U.S. 205 (1972).

[45] 347 U.S. 483 (1954).

[46] See 411 U.S. at 29–30; *cf. id.* at 110–17 (Marshall, J., dissenting).

[47] 102 S. Ct. at 2397.

[48] *Id.* at 2398.

[49] *Ibid.*

> [The Texas law] imposes a lifetime hardship on a discrete class of children not accountable for their disabling status. The stigma of illiteracy will mark them for the rest of their lives. By denying these children a basic education, we deny them the ability to live within the structure of our civic institutions, and foreclose any realistic possibility that they will contribute in even the smallest way to the progress of our Nation. In determining the rationality of § 21.031, we may appropriately take into account its costs to the Nation and to the innocent children who are its victims. In light of these countervailing costs, the discrimination contained in § 21.031 can hardly be considered rational unless it furthers some substantial goal of the State.

The tone of the quoted passage is impassioned, but the even more striking feature of the passage is, of course, its adoption of the formula announced by Justice Brennan in *Craig v. Boren* for testing the constitutionality of gender classifications—rational furtherance of a substantial state goal. Prior to *Plyler v. Doe*, this "middle tier" of scrutiny had been confined to classifications based on gender.[50] Even then, the test was confined to classifications only and did not reach a mixture of classification plus interest affected. Moreover, the stringency of the test could give way to overriding interests of the State—such as military preparedness, in *Rostker v. Goldberg*,[51] or other factors, as in *Michael M. v. Superior Court*.[52] None of these considerations was mentioned by the Court.

To determine whether the Texas law furthered a substantial goal of the state, the Court felt obliged to undertake a two-step analysis. First, did the Federally imposed undocumented status of the children, standing alone, supply a sufficient rational basis for the state classification? Second, if not, was the classification substantially and closely enough related to an important state goal to avoid invalidation?

The first inquiry looks and sounds in preemption, although the Court announced earlier in its opinion that it had no occasion to reach the children's preemption claim in the light of its disposition of the Fourteenth Amendment issue.[53] But the Court proceeded to

---

[50] *Cf.* the cases on illegitimacy, *e.g.*, Mathews v. Lucas, 427 U.S. 495 (1976); Trimble v. Gordon, 430 U.S. 762 (1977); Lalli v. Lalli, 439 U.S. 259 (1978); Mills v. Habluetzel, 102 S. Ct. 1549 (1982).

[51] 453 U.S. 57 (1981).

[52] 450 U.S. 464 (1981).

[53] 102 S. Ct. at 2391 n.8.

analyze the inquiry by referring to its recent decision in *DeCanas v. Bica*,[54] in which it held that a California statute prohibiting employers from hiring illegal aliens was not preempted by either federal law or policy in the field. "States do have some authority to act with respect to illegal aliens," Justice Brennan (who also authored *De-Canas*) said, "at least where such action mirrors federal objectives and furthers a legitimate state goal."[55] While the statute in *DeCanas* "reflected" Congress's "intention" to bar from employment all aliens except those holding a valid work permit, "there is no indication [here] that [the Texas statute] corresponds to any identifiable congressional policy."[56]

The validity of the Court's conclusion depends upon the level of generality at which the Congressional policy must be expressed in order to "mirror" federal objectives. Pursuant to what the Court viewed in *Mathews v. Diaz*[57] to be its legitimate and plenary power over immigration, Congress has denied welfare benefits to aliens who have not entered the country legally. Illegal aliens are thus ineligible for Medicare,[58] food stamps,[59] unemployment compensation,[60] and Supplemental Security Income.[61] In addition, regulations promulgated under other federal statutes deny to illegal aliens Medicaid[62] and various other benefits.[63] The purpose of the restrictions is twofold: (1) to discourage unlawful immigration, as the Court recognized and assumed to be constitutionally permissible in *Mathews v. Diaz*, and (2) to preserve state fiscal resources against drains by those whom Congress has decreed are not entitled to immigrate, as the history of the restrictions in the food stamp program demonstrates.[64] If Congress's objective or intention is to avoid

---

[54] 424 U.S. 351 (1976).

[55] 102 S. Ct. at 2399.

[56] *Ibid.*

[57] 426 U.S. 67 (1976).

[58] *Ibid.*

[59] 7 U.S.C. § 2015(f) (Supp. III).

[60] 26 U.S.C. § 3304(a)(14)(A) (& Supp. III).

[61] 42 U.S.C. § 1382c(a)(1)(B).

[62] 42 C.F.R. 435.402 (b).

[63] 45 C.F.R. 233.50 (Aid for Families with Dependent Children); 45 C.F.R. 644.4(b), 646.3(b), 690.4(a)(4) (various higher education programs).

[64] See House Report No. 95-464 (June 24, 1977) at p. 145 on Food and Agriculture Act of 1977, P.L. 95-113, 91 Stat. 913, 964, codified at 7 U.S.C. § 2015. See also 7 C.F.R. 273.4 (1982). See further Senate Report No. 95-180.

providing incentives to illegal immigration by denying illegal aliens eligibility to general public services, then the Texas statute in issue is at the very least not inconsistent with that policy. To ask for a more specific statement from Congress that education, too, should be off limits to illegal aliens would be to ask for a statement of policy in an area that Congress has virtually no occasion to address in the same way that it is obliged to do in defining eligibility requirements for federal grant-in-aid programs.

The Court nonetheless found Congress's silence telling but, more important, concluded that the Texas statute "does not operate harmoniously within the federal program."[65] The disharmony was not a function of facial inconsistencies between the state law and the immigration scheme, but between the state law and the discretionary enforcement provisions built into the federal immigration laws. While undocumented aliens, including the plaintiff children, are subject to deportation, "there is no assurance that a child subject to deportation will ever be deported."[66] The Court pointed out that federal law provides that illegal entrants may be granted permission to continue to reside in the country by the Federal Government and may even become eligible to be naturalized. The disharmony thus became manifest:[67]

> In light of the discretionary federal power to grant relief from deportation, a State cannot realistically determine that any particular undocumented child will in fact be deported until after deportation proceedings have been completed. It would of course be most difficult for the State to justify the denial of education to a child enjoying an inchoate federal permission to remain [in the Country].

To say that future prosecutorial discretion or executive clemency might one day extinguish present liability or its collateral consequences does not, needless to say, extinguish present liability. For example, if it did, ex-felons now debarred from voting in state elections would have a colorable claim to be reenfranchised in the light of the existence of the pardoning power.[68] Justice Brennan's analysis makes sense only if there is evidence that the Federal Gov-

---

[65] 102 S. Ct. at 2399.

[66] *Ibid.*

[67] *Ibid.*

[68] *Cf.* Richardson v. Ramirez, 418 U.S. 24 (1974).

ernment is actively planning some sort of amnesty program for illegal aliens, such as was suggested during the Carter and Reagan Administrations. But there is no evidence of that now, nor is there any evidence that the Federal Government views its discretionary powers as "inchoate" permission to violate the immigration laws. For the time being, the permission to stay is a function of prosecutorial paralysis and not of policy.

With the federal issue, whatever its relevance to the equal protection analysis, out of the way, Justice Brennan turned to the final question, whether the classification used by the State in § 21.031 was "reasonably adapted to 'the purposes for which the State desires to use it.' "[69] The State asserted in its brief that "[t]he preservation of the state's limited resources for education of its lawful residents is clearly a legitimate state interest,"[70] but the Court dismissed the argument on the ground that it simply begged the question. Instead, the Court discerned three colorable state interests "suggested" by the State that might support the statute: (1) to protect the State from an influx of illegal immigrants; (2) to avoid the special burdens that such aliens "impose on the State's ability to provide high quality public education";[71] and (3) to preserve the benefits of free public education to those who, unlike the plaintiff children, were most likely to remain within the State and to put their education to productive social or political use within the State.

The Court properly rejected the third interest as "most difficult to quantify"[72] and speculative at best. With respect to the second interest, Justice Brennan approved the trial courts' findings that the State had provided no "credible supporting evidence" that the proportion of funds devoted to educating the plaintiff children had a "grave impact on the quality of education" provided to others.[73] The first interest was clearly the most substantial and the most problematic. The Court conceded that the State had "an interest in mitigating potentially harsh economic effects of sudden shifts in population"[74] but concluded that the statute was infirm, under the

---

[69] 102 S. Ct. at 2400, quoting Oyama v. California, 332 U.S. 633, 664–65 (1948) (Murphy, J., concurring).

[70] Brief for Appellants at 26.

[71] 102 S. Ct. at 2401. But see Schweiker v. Hogan, 102 S. Ct. 2597 (1982).

[72] 102 S. Ct. at 2401.

[73] *Ibid.*, quoting 501 F. Supp. at 583.

[74] 102 S. Ct. at 2400.

circumstances, because it was ineffectual. Justice Brennan found that the record developed in the trial courts showed (1) no evidence that illegal aliens "impose any significant burden on the State's economy"; (2) indeed, that illegal aliens tend to "underutilize public services, while contributing their labor to the local economy and tax money to the State fisc"; and (3) that the dominant motive for illegal immigration was employment, not the availability of free public education.[75]

The Court's conclusions are sound, but only because they are dictated by their premises, which are not. Once a state is forced to show that its classification is efficacious, it is bound to be unable to do so, because no legislative measure that purports to deter is ever wholly effective. We accept this extraordinary degree of scrutiny (" 'strict' in theory and fatal in fact"[76]), if at all, because as a matter of constitutional interpretation we are convinced that the ground of classification is so offensive to the Equal Protection Clause (*e.g.*, race or national origin) that it must pass extraordinary hurdles to be upheld. Outside of the small handful of offensive classifications (race, national origin, and, more recently, illegitimacy and gender), the Court has permitted state classifications to be upheld if they simply bear an arguable relationship to a goal within the state's police power. This extremely deferential standard is a product of two determinations: that the ground of classification is not repugnant to the Equal Protection Clause, and that a higher standard of scrutiny will invalidate a judgment upon which reasonable people may reasonably differ (*i.e.*, that generally the legislature and not the courts is the appropriate constitutional organ to make the judgment in question). Once the Court in *Plyler v. Doe* concluded that a higher standard than "mere rationality" was required by § 21.031, the statute was virtually doomed.

If the mere rationality standard had been applied, the statute should have been upheld. The problem of illegal immigration is highly controversial. Even the most sustained studies of the economic impact of illegal immigration are strikingly inconclusive.[77]

---

[75] *Id.* at 2401.

[76] Gunther, *Foreword: In Search of Evolving Doctrine on a Changing Court: A Model for the Newer Equal Protection*, 86 HARV. L. REV. 1, 8 (1972).

[77] U.S. IMMIGRATION POLICY AND THE NATIONAL INTEREST: THE FINAL REPORT AND RECOMMENDATIONS OF THE SELECT COMMISSION ON IMMIGRATION AND REFUGEE POLICY 38–41 (1981); U.S. IMMIGRATION POLICY AND THE NATIONAL INTEREST: THE STAFF REPORT OF THE SELECT COMMISSION ON IMMIGRATION AND REFUGEE POLICY 506–33

The perceived cost is substantial, and, because of the lack of data about the problem, no deterrent measures adopted by the legislature can be predicted to be even substantially efficacious. Reasonable legislators could conclude that § 21.031 could deter some illegal immigration and that the savings to the State educational system could be significant. From a longer perspective, § 21.031 could be seen as supplying one more disincentive to illegal immigration whose absence would cost more cumulatively than its enactment could hope to provide.

The Court declined to apply this test to the classification employed in § 21.031. The reason was not that the classification was repugnant to the Equal Protection Clause, but that the combination of the classification and the subject matter it affected was repugnant. In essence, it was the net effect of the statute and not its classifying characteristic that condemned it. The Court underscored this in its peroration after its assessment of the validity of the State's interests:[78]

> It is difficult to understand precisely what the State hopes to achieve by promoting the creation and perpetuation of a subclass of illiterates within our boundaries, surely adding to the problems and costs of unemployment, welfare, and crime. It is thus clear that whatever savings might be achieved by denying these children an education, they are wholly insubstantial in light of the costs involved to these children, the State, and the Nation.

The Court's declamation should not be read as an implicit adoption of a constitutional cost-benefit analysis for the Equal Protection Clause. The statement, together with the classification-plus-interest analysis stitched together by Justice Brennan, tends to show instead that *Plyler v. Doe* is better understood as substantive due process (or substantive equal protection) rather than traditional equal protection.[79]

(1981); Chiswick, *Immigrants and Immigration Policy* 285, 320–21, in CONTEMPORARY ECONOMIC PROBLEMS 1978 (Fellner ed.); Reimers, *Recent Immigration Policy: An Analysis* 13, 45–48, in THE GATEWAY: U.S. IMMIGRATION ISSUES & POLICIES (Chiswick ed. 1982); U.S. DOMESTIC COUNCIL COMMITTEE ON ILLEGAL ALIENS: PRELIMINARY REPORT 185–87 (1976). See generally Teitelbaum, *Right v. Right: Immigration and Refugee Policy in the United States*, 59 FOREIGN AFFAIRS 21 (1980).

[78] 102 S. Ct. at 2402.

[79] See further, *e.g.*, Karst, *Invidious Discrimination: Justice Douglas and the Return to the "Natural-Law-Due-Process Formula,"* 16 U.C.L.A. L. REV. 716 (1969); KURLAND, POLITICS, THE CONSTITUTION, AND THE WARREN COURT 150, 167 (1970); *cf.* Karst & Horowitz, *Reitman v. Mulkey: A Telophase of Substantive Equal Protection*, 1967 SUPREME COURT REVIEW 39.

The Court refused to analyze the constitutionality of the statute on the basis of the classification alone, but it was also at pains to reaffirm the holding of *Rodriguez* that education is not a fundamental right. Unless the Court is repudiating a decade of refusals to adopt Justice Marshall's sliding-scale test[80]—and the concurring opinions of Justices Blackmun and Powell carry no such hint—*Plyler* stands for the substantive proposition that the penalty imposed by the State is simply too great for the crime.

The same substantive concern was evident in *Carey v. Population Services.*[81] In *Carey*, the Court held that a state statute prohibiting the sale or distribution of nonprescription contraceptives to minors (under age sixteen) violated the Due Process Clause of the Fourteenth Amendment. Justice Brennan's plurality opinion was "reluctant" to conclude that the statute " 'prescribed pregnancy and birth of an unwanted child . . . as punishment for fornication,' "[82] but the Court's actual analysis of the constitutional vice of the statute is much less cogent. In *Plyler v. Doe*, the Court explicitly condemned illiteracy as simply too severe a punishment for illegal immigration, especially where those punished "have little control" over their crime. As substantive due process, *Plyler* is of a piece with *Carey;* as equal protection, *Plyler* is simply a *tour de force.*

Had the Court turned to analogous equal protection case law to test the Texas statute, § 21.031 should not have been held unconstitutional. The statutory classification turns on the lawfulness of residence within the State and nation. For a decade, the Court has expressly upheld the constitutionality of residence requirements that distinguish between "bona fide" in-state resident and out-of-state residents for purposes of charging differential tuition at state colleges and universities. In *Vlandis v. Kline,*[83] the Court held unconstitutional a Connecticut residence requirement because it

---

[80] In addition to *Rodriguez* and Dandridge v. Williams, see, *e.g.*, Harris v. McRae, 448 U.S. 297, 341–42 (1980) (Marshall, J., dissenting); Vance v. Bradley, 440 U.S. 93, 113–15 (1979) (Marshall, J., dissenting); Massachusetts Bd. of Retirement v. Murgia, 427 U.S. 307, 318–21 (1976) (Marshall, J., dissenting). Other members of the Court have expressed their impatience with the two-tiered approach. See, *e.g.*, Clements v. Fashing, 102 S. Ct. 2836, 2848–50 (1982) (opinion of Stevens, J.); Vlandis v. Kline, 412 U.S. 441, 456–59 (1973) (opinion of White, J.); Harris v. McRae, 448 U.S. at 342 n.3 and examples cited there (Marshall, J., dissenting).

[81] 431 U.S. 678 (1977).

[82] *Id.* at 695–97.

[83] 412 U.S. 441 (1973).

created an "irrebuttable presumption" that prevented "new" residents from showing that they had become bona fide in-state residents so as to enjoy lower tuition charges. But the Court "fully recognize[d] that a State has a legitimate interest in protecting and preserving the quality of its colleges and universities and the right of its own bona fide resident to attend such institutions on a preferential tuition basis."[84] The Court added: "The State can establish such reasonable criteria for in-state status as to make virtually certain that students who are not, in fact, bona fide residents of the State, but who have come there solely for educational purposes, cannot take advantage of the in-state rates."[85] Section 21.031 appears on its face to be addressed to the same concerns: lawful residents (regardless of citizenship, nationality, alienage or other status) are entitled to tuition-free public schooling, but undocumented aliens—thus not lawfully residing in the State—are required to pay tuition. The only question is whether *Vlandis v. Kline* applies with full force at the elementary and secondary school levels as well as at the collegiate level.

Justice Brennan's opinion for the Court in *Plyler* sidestepped the problem and disposed of the residency point in a footnote. *Vlandis v. Kline* was not even mentioned:[86]

> Appellant School District sought at oral argument to characterize the alienage classification contained in § 21.031 as simply a test of residence. We are unable to uphold § 21.031 on that basis. Appellants conceded that if, for example, a Virginian or a legally admitted Mexican citizen entered Tyler with his school age children, intending to remain only six months, those children would be viewed as residents entitled to attend Tyler schools. Tr. of Oral Arg. 31–32. It is thus clear that Tyler's residence argument amounts to nothing more than the assertion that illegal entry, without more, prevents a person from becoming a resident for purposes of enrolling his children in the public schools. A State may not, however, accomplish what would otherwise be prohibited by the Equal Protection Clause, merely by defining a disfavored group as non-resident. And illegal entry into the country would not, under traditional criteria, bar a person from obtaining domicile within a State. C. Bouvé, Exclusion and Expulsion of Aliens in the United States 340 (1912). Appellants

---

[84] *Id.* at 452–53.

[85] *Id.* at 453–54.

[86] 102 S. Ct. at 2400 n.22.

have not shown that the families of undocumented children do not comply with the established standards by which the State historically tests residence. Apart from the alienage limitation, § 21.031(b) requires a county to provide education only to resident children. The counties of the State are as free to apply to undocumented children established criteria for determining residence as they are to apply those criteria to any other child who seeks admission.

The Chief Justice's dissent appropriately labeled the analogy to migrating Virginians as "spurious,"[87] but the primary vice of Justice Brennan's view is that it begs the question. The issue is not whether "traditional criteria," "historical[ ] tests," or "established criteria" have been used or ignored here, but whether the actual test adopted by § 21.031 is a "reasonable criteri[on]" within the meaning of the *Vlandis* dictum for establishing bona fide residency. The implication of Justice Brennan's footnote is that a state may not change an established residency requirement or adopt a new residency requirement when faced with a new problem, without raising a constitutional question. If so, the broad acknowledgment of state power in the field contemplated by *Vlandis* would be stood on its head *sub silentio*.

II. The Unanswered Questions

Whatever the precedential weight of the Court's espoused equal protection rationale in *Plyler v. Doe*, it remains to be determined what the Court did to those features of its jurisprudence that it did not address. For a case with some claim to being a constitutional landmark, *Plyler* cut a remarkably messy path through other areas of the Court's jurisprudence. The problem was not so much of unsatisfactory analysis, but of silence. The most important dog that did not bark in the opinion of the Court was *Shapiro v. Thompson*.

A. SHAPIRO V. THOMPSON

In *Shapiro v. Thompson*, the Court invalidated state and District of Columbia laws that required residency within the jurisdiction for one year as one condition of eligibility for welfare benefits. The

---

[87] *Id.* at 2413 n.12.

residency requirements denied putative beneficiaries equal protection of the laws, the Court said, because they impinged on the fundamental right to travel, thus triggering "strict scrutiny," and, under that standard, could not be upheld. To the argument that Congress had sanctioned such residency requirements, the Court replied with what a common lawyer might call traverse, confession, and avoidance: no, Congress had not, but, even if it had, "Congress may not authorize the States to violate the Equal Protection Clause."

"That truism," wrote Professor Kenneth L. Karst several years later, "is unassailable as logic but unhelpful in resolving problems."[88] *Plyler v. Doe* demonstrates that the truism is not only unhelpful but logically problematic as well. Justice Brennan's opinion for the Court concluded that Texas lacked a "substantial state interest" for § 21.031, in part because there was no evidence that Congress wished—as a matter of legislative intent or of national policy—to preserve state educational resources by restricting immigration pursuant to the Immigration and Naturalization Act (INA). Although the relevance of this nonfinding is somewhat ambiguous,[89] the obvious implication is that Texas would have a substantial state interest—or at least would be very close to that elusive goal—if Congress had simply made such a finding or amended the INA to so provide expressly. If Congress had done so, or were to do so in the future, however, the finding would appear to stand on the same footing constitutionally as Congressional approbation of a one-year residency requirement for welfare eligibility.

The situations appear to be identical analytically, but it is no doubt a mistake to assume that Justice Brennan—who also wrote *Shapiro v. Thomspon*—meant to retrench from a "truism" that he did not bother to mention. The cases can be harmonized, if necessary, on a ground suggested by Professor Karst: "the right to travel is based in part on the commerce clause's allocation of powers in the federal system; to this extent, it is obviously not a limitation on Congress but a source of congressional power."[90] Thus, "there is no reason why the right to travel should trigger strict scrutiny of an act

---

[88] Karst, *The Fifth Amendment's Guarantee of Equal Protection*, 55 N.C.L. REV. 541, 559 (1977).

[89] See text at notes 53–56 *supra*.

[90] Karst, note 88 *supra*.

of Congress."[91] The truism is therefore not true unless, as Professor Karst went on, the right to travel "is one of the rights of equal national citizenship included by the fifth amendment's guarantee of equal protection" or if the " 'fundamental' . . . interest in minimum subsistence" is similarly guaranteed by the Due Process Clause of the Fifth Amendment.[92] In *Plyler v. Doe*, Congress's implied power to reconstitutionalize the Texas statute is a function of its plenary power over immigration and naturalization.[93] As with the commerce power, there is no reason why strict or quasi-strict (*i.e.*, middle-tier) scrutiny should be applied here either. But, if the "well-settled principles" that led Justice Brennan to apply a middle tier of scrutiny in *Plyler* are somehow substantively based, then here, too, the truism is intact. If so, the Court's search in *Plyler* for a Congressional purpose to preserve local educational resources was gratuitous. One can obviously read too much into a lacuna. But it is unlikely that *Shapiro's* truism is disturbed by *Plyler v. Doe*, and the decision sounds more and more in substantive due process than in equal protection of the laws. The admonition that Gerhard Casper offered to the Court, in another context, has been learned too well: "The Court cannot first play the role of Galahad and then inform us that the Holy Grail is not that holy after all."[94]

B. ALIENS AS A "SUSPECT CLASS"

Although the classification in § 21.031 was drawn explicitly in terms of (illegal) alienage, the Court declined to follow *Graham v. Richardson*, which viewed such classifications as inherently suspect. It would have been doubly surprising if the Court had done so. First, as the Court had to concede, entry into the class was both volitional and, by definition, unlawful. Second, as two other cases decided during the 1981 Term ably demonstrate, the Court has abandoned *Graham's per se* treatment of alienage as a suspect class. In *Cabell v. Chavez-Salido*,[95] following a retrenchment which began

---

[91] *Ibid.*

[92] *Ibid.*

[93] *Cf.* Hampton v. Mow Sun Wong, 426 U.S. 88 (1976).

[94] Casper, *Jones v. Mayer: Clio, Bemused and Confused Muse*, 1968 SUPREME COURT REVIEW 89, 132.

[95] 102 S. Ct. 735 (1982).

in *Sugarman v. Dougall*,[96] the Court upheld the constitutionality of a California scheme that required a broadly defined group of state "peace officers" (including probation officers, park rangers, and many others) to be citizens. Strict scrutiny may be the general rule, but it is "out of place," said Justice White for the Court, "when the restriction primarily services a political function"[97] such as setting voting qualifications and, to a vague and rather attenuated[98] degree, more generally defining the state's political community and its identity. Justice Blackmun filed an insistent dissent in *Cabell*[99] and a scathing separate opinion a few months later in the third alienage case of the Term, *Toll v. Moreno*,[100] when Justice Rehnquist had the temerity to note that alienage now "cannot always be considered invidious in the same manner as race or national origin."[101]

If the three alienage cases this Term signal the end of the "suspect class–strict scrutiny" lockstep for state classifications based on alienage, then the Term need not be written off as a doctrinal washout in the area despite the fact that *Plyler* and *Toll v. Moreno* were wrongly decided.[102] *Graham v. Richardson*'s conclusion that

---

[96] 413 U.S. 634 (1973). See Note, *The Equal Treatment of Aliens: Preemption or Equal Protection?* 31 STAN. L. REV. 1069 (1979).

[97] 102 S. Ct. at 739.

[98] See Note, note 95 *supra*; T. R. Powell, *Alien Land Cases in the United States Supreme Court*, 12 CAL. L. REV. 259 (1924).

[99] 102 S. Ct. at 744.

[100] 102 S. Ct. 2977, 2987 (1982).

[101] 102 S. Ct. at 2999.

[102] In Toll v. Moreno, the State of Maryland charged nonresident tuition at the University of Maryland to domiciled nonimmigrant aliens who held G-4 visas (officers of certain international organizations and members of their immediate families). The Court held that the tuition policy was preempted by federal law, which exempted G-4 visa holders from federal income taxation. 102 S. Ct. at 2984–85. The State justified nonresident tuition status on the ground that the " 'dollar differential . . . at stake here [is] an amount roughly equivalent to the amount of state income tax an international bank parent is spared by treaty each year.' " 102 S. Ct. at 2985. The Court replied: "The State may not recoup indirectly from respondents' parents the taxes that the Federal Government has expressly barred the State from collecting." *Ibid*. But the federal exemption went only to federal, not state, income taxation. The reason that the plaintiffs and their parents enjoyed state income tax immunity was that State law defined the net taxable income under state law as the taxpayer's federal adjusted gross income. See 102 S. Ct. at 2995 (Rehnquist, J., dissenting). Thus, the indirect recovery that the Court invalidated was a recovery not barred by federal law but created by state law. The Court's opinion obliterates the distinction between federal and state taxing power that Congress expressly recognized. See *id.* at 2995. If the State policy is found to conflict with more generalized federal policies as opposed to discrete federal laws, *cf.* 102 S. Ct. at 2985, then Toll v. Moreno is inconsistent with Plyler v. Doe. See text at notes 56–64 *supra*.

alienage is a suspect classification was gratuitous to begin with, because the Court also concluded that the state requirements in question were preempted by federal law. More important, the basis for the conclusion that "[a]liens as a class are a prime example of a 'discrete and insular' minority . . . for whom . . . heightened judicial solicitude is appropriate" [103] is a prime example of allowing shorthand phrases and the by-products of constitutional interpretation to become and thus displace the document and its historical development.

If it is true that classifications based on alienage are inherently suspect—as Justice Black said of racial classifications in *Korematsu v. United States*,[104] thus requiring "heightened judicial solicitude,"[105] as Justice Stone said in the fine print that now shapes the text of current constitutional theory[106]—then state laws denying aliens the franchise must be unconstitutional. What "compelling state interest" could justify excluding aliens from the polls any more than any other "discrete and insular minority?" Although some have argued that the Equal Protection Clause compels the vote for aliens,[107] the text of section 1 of the Fourteenth Amendment refutes the conclusion.[108] While the Equal Protection Clause, by both its terms and its legislative history, provides some protection to aliens, the first clause of section 1 of the Amendment clearly preserves some distinction between citizens and "persons" generally. There is no suggestion in either the text or historical context of the Amendment that the Equal Protection Clause should override the distinction implicitly drawn in the first clause between citizens and persons. It is true, of course, that noncitizens voted in some places at the time that the Fourteenth Amendment was ratified,[109] but it does not follow that the Equal Protection Clause compelled

---

[103] Graham v. Richardson, 403 U.S. at 372.

[104] 323 U.S. 214, 216 (1944).

[105] United States v. Carolene Products, 304 U.S. 144, 152–53 n.4 (1938).

[106] See ELY, DEMOCRACY AND DISTRUST (1980).

[107] Rosberg, *Aliens and Equal Protection: Why Not the Right to Vote?* 75 MICH. L. REV. 1092 (1977); *cf.* Karst, *Foreword: Equal Citizenship under the Fourteenth Amendment*, 91 HARV. L. REV. 1, 25, 44–46 (1977). See generally Rosberg, *The Protection of Aliens from Discriminatory Treatment by the National Government*, 1977 SUPREME COURT REVIEW 275.

[108] The distinction between citizens and others with specific respect to the vote is made in the Fifteenth, Nineteenth, and Twenty-sixth Amendments.

[109] See note 31 *supra.*

states to make that choice or that depriving noncitizens of the vote at a later date would be a violation of the Amendment. The three cases decided this Term put to rest the constitutional anomaly lurking in whatever was left of *Graham v. Richardson*'s *per se* categorization of alienage as a suspect classification.

C. FEDERAL PREEMPTION

The Term's cases did not, however, clarify the question when federal law or policy on immigration preempts state classifications based on alienage, or what relationship— if any—there is between the federal regulatory scheme and the Equal Protection Clause. The Court avoided the preemption issue both in *Plyler* and in *Cabell v. Chavez-Salido* by resting its decisions on the Equal Protection Clause, thus making it unnecessary to reach the preemption issue. In *Toll v. Moreno*, the Court declined to reach the equal protection issue because it found the Maryland law specifically preempted by federal law. Although Justice Brennan's opinion in *Plyler* reaffirms *DeCanas v. Bica* and analyzes the State's interests in light of the federal immigration scheme, the opinion does not explain why what appears to be preemption analysis is relevant to the Equal Protection Clause.

The question of what role federal laws play in cases of this type is further muddied by a brief and unexplained announcement by Justice Powell in a footnote to his concurring opinion: "If the resident children of illegal aliens were denied welfare assistance, made available by government to all other children who qualify, this also—in my opinion—would be an impermissible penalizing of children because of their parents' status."[110] On its face, Justice Powell's view is inconsistent with both *DeCanas* and *Mathews v. Diaz*, which were decided unanimously within four months of each other in 1976. In *DeCanas*, the Court held that a state statute that "mirrored" federal policy with respect to illegal aliens was not preempted by the federal immigration laws. The denial by states of benefits such as Medicare and food stamps, for example, not only mirrors federal policy but is dictated by federal eligibility requirements established under programs funded wholly or partially by the federal government. In *Mathews v. Diaz*, the Court rejected a

---

[110] 102 S. Ct. at 2406 n.3.

challenge under the Due Process Clause of the Fifth Amendment to a Medicare requirement that denied eligibility to aliens unless admitted to permanent residence and resident in the United States for at least five years. The Court said:[111]

> [T]he fact that Congress has provided some welfare benefits for citizens does not require it to provide like benefits for *all* aliens. Neither the overnight visitor, the unfriendly agent of a hostile foreign power, the resident diplomat, nor the illegal entrant, can advance even a colorable constitutional claim to share in the bounty that a conscientious sovereign makes available to its own citizens and some of its guests. The decision to share that bounty with our guests may take into account the character of the relationship between the alien and this Country: Congress may decide that as the alien's tie grows stronger, so does the strength of his claim to an equal share of that munificence.

The homily may be florid, but the holding is unequivocal. In establishing eligibility requirements for welfare programs, Congress may discriminate against aliens and may discriminate within classes of aliens without violating the Fifth Amendment.

Justice Powell's conclusion appears to turn on his view that the Constitution somehow prohibits the "resident children of illegal aliens" from being penalized for the entry sins of their parents. The constitutional analogy here, as in the majority opinion, is to state classifications based on illegitimacy. Yet Justice Powell wrote for the Court in *Fiallo v. Bell*[112] in 1977, which held that provisions of the Immigration and Nationality Act that had the effect of excluding from preferential admission status the relationship between an illegitimate child and his natural father (as opposed to his natural mother) were not unconstitutional. The decision turned on the deference required by the Court's case law to decisions by the Executive to exclude individual aliens or classes of aliens. Is Justice Powell implying in his *Plyler* opinion that the Court will defer to Executive classifications made at the border but that an alien may temper the Court's deference by resorting to the self-help of illegal entry?

No other member of the Court tipped his or her hand on the applicability of *Plyler v. Doe* to cases that the Court is surely to be asked to decide involving state classifications turning on illegal

---

[111] 426 U.S. at 80.

[112] 430 U.S. 787 (1977).

alienage. The opinions of Justices Brennan, Blackmun, and Powell all emphasize the sympathetic plight of the plaintiff children. The State, on the other hand, is seen as muddled, in not knowing how many illegal alien children there were[113] nor how much it cost to educate them,[114] and disingenuous, in hoping to deter illegal entry by § 21.031 but at the same time conveniently not criminalizing the employment of illegal aliens.[115] If sentiment continues to determine results, then it is a short and foreseeable step to holding that the Constitution forbids states to deny welfare benefits to illegal aliens—at least to "the resident children of illegal aliens." For some, it would be an *a fortiori* case.[116] But it would have less to do with the Equal Protection Clause or cases interpreting it than with the Court's own notions of substantive due process.

D. REQUIESCAT IN PACE RODRIGUEZ?

San Antonio Independent School District v. Rodriguez held that education was not a fundamental right and therefore that state action "impinging" on it did not require strict judicial scrutiny. The decision also held that implicit classifications based on poverty were not suspect either. Of the five opinions filed in *Plyler v. Doe*, only Justice Marshall expressed his (continuing) disagreement with *Rodriguez*. Justice Brennan, for the Court, and the Chief Justice, for the dissenters, both took *Rodriguez* as settled law. Justice Blackmun devoted much of his concurring opinion to showing that the result in *Plyler* was not inconsistent with *Rodriguez*, which he had joined. Justice Powell, the author of *Rodriguez*, spent a long footnote to the same effect.

The final question unanswered by *Plyler v. Doe* is, Why did they bother? The importance of *Rodriguez* at the time it was decided, as Justice Marshall's dissent in the case amply demonstrated, was that it preserved the two-tier model of judicial review of state action,

---

[113] See, *e.g.*, Doe v. Plyler, 458 F. Supp. at 575–77. While the litigation was in progress, the State predicted that 100,000 children would benefit from the District Courts' orders. The day Plyler v. Doe was handed down, the State reported that only 12,000 attended public schools during the 1980–81 academic year and only 18,000 the following year. See THE NEW YORK TIMES, June 16, 1982, p. 15.

[114] See Doe v. Plyler, note 113 *supra*.

[115] *Id.* at 585 & n.21.

[116] See Michelman, *Welfare Rights in a Constitutional Democracy*, 1979 WASH. U.L.Q. 659; but see Bork, *The Impossibility of Finding Welfare Rights in the Constitution, id.* at 695.

and indeed refused to expand the upper tier of strict scrutiny to include education as a fundamental right or poverty as a suspect classification. Three years later, however, *Craig v. Boren* added an intermediate tier—then apparently limited to gender-based classifications—that has proved to be almost as fatal in fact as strict scrutiny. Taken together, *Craig v. Boren* and *Plyler v. Doe* demonstrate that *Rodriguez* is now a constitutional relic whose only significance is its holding; as doctrine, it is irrelevant. The Court's opinion in *Plyler* demonstrates that the middle tier has a sufficiently plastic content so that what formerly could only be accomplished by the controversial finding of a suspect class can now be more easily done by identifying "well-settled principles" that mirror only the case at hand. Whatever the deficiencies of the old two-tier model, it at least provided some predictability and a common ground of discourse. The new three-tier model promises to be nowhere near as predictable, either as to content or result. For example, *Craig v. Boren* and *Mississippi University for Women v. Hogan*,[117] decided this Term, provide evidence that the middle tier will be as "fatal in fact" for gender classifications as strict scrutiny was for racial classification. On the other hand, *Rostker v. Goldberg* (the draft registration case) and *Michael M. v. Superior Court* (the statutory rape case) show that gender-based classifications will occasionally survive middle-tier scrutiny, depending on the circumstances. The upshot is that instead of two rigid and disarmingly predictable tiers of scrutiny, we now have three tiers whose content is indeterminate and unpredictable. In a sense, even the upper tier is no longer as strict as it was when *Rodriguez* was decided. Racial classifications, which once were unconstitutional regardless of the test employed by the Court, now are upheld from time to time,[118] again, depending on the circumstances.

III. Conclusion

The doctrine of *Plyler v. Doe* is so custom-tailored to its facts that it is impossible to predict with confidence its precedential significance. It is tempting to say that the equal protection test

---

[117] 102 S. Ct. 3331 (1982).

[118] See, *e.g.*, Regents of the University of California v. Bakke, 438 U.S. 265 (1978); Fullilove v. Klutznick, 448 U.S. 448 (1980); *cf.* United Steelworkers v. Weber, 443 U.S. 193 (1979).

announced as controlling in *Plyler* amounted constitutionally to zero plus zero equals one; that is, a nonsuspect classification plus a nonfundamental right requires almost strict scrutiny. Nonetheless, the decision helps to clarify a growing pattern in equal protection jurisprudence that is quite different from the dark and bloody ground of *Rodriguez*. To a large extent, there are now not three tiers of judicial scrutiny of the Equal Protection Clause, but one. The demise of strict scrutiny for racial classifications, occasioned by the cases involving affirmative action;[119] the explosive growth of the middle tier of scrutiny since *Craig v. Boren*; and the ten-year-old plea for real "bite" in the "mere rationality" standard[120] have had the combined effect of turning the interpretation of the Equal Protection Clause into an exercise of balancing competing interests whose weights are a function of prior case law only to a limited degree.

The most striking evidence of this development during the Term was not *Plyler v. Doe*, and its expansion of the middle tier of scrutiny, but the invalidation under the Equal Protection Clause of a state statute for failing the once toothless test of rationality. In *Zobel v. Williams*,[121] the State of Alaska enacted a scheme to distribute proceeds from oil reserves developed on State-owned lands. The proceeds were to be paid as annual dividends to the State's adult residents, with the size of each share dependent on the number of years an individual had resided in the State since 1959; the longer the duration of residencey, the larger the premium. The Supreme Court held the plan unconstitutional over only one dissent, because it was not rationally related to a legitimate state purpose. The vice of the plan was not its means, but its goal: to reward those who had presumptively made the greatest contributions to the State since it entered the Union. Putting to one side the institutional question of why a unique case was taking up the Court's precious time for its plenary calendar, the decision is startling, because it appears to be wholly inconsistent with the Court's repeated decisions that classifications affecting eligibility for distribution of gratuitous benefits by the state will be upheld unless they burden a fundamen-

---

[119] *Ibid.*

[120] See Gunther, note 76 *supra*; but see also, *Forum: Equal Protection and the Burger Court*, 2 Hast. C.L.Q. 645, 655–60, 671–72 (1975).

[121] 102 S. Ct. 2309 (1982).

tal right or utilize an invidious classification. (It would be ironic if the Chief Justice's opinion for the Court in *Zobel* were later to be held to have undermined the continuing vitality of, say, *Dandridge v. Williams*.)

Perhaps it is simply not appropriate to subject *Plyler v. Doe* to close analysis. Two of the concurring opinions warn against doing so. If the Court meant what it said as a general rule, we are well on the way to a collapse of three tiers of equal protection doctrine into one. If the Court did not mean what it said, then we can safely ignore its statement, issued less than a week after *Plyler*, that "[a] belief that [a statute] may be inequitable or unwise is of course an insufficient basis on which to conclude that it is unconstitutional."[122]

---

[122] Schweiker v. Hogan, 102 S. Ct. at 2609.

NORMAN DORSEN

JOEL GORA

FREE SPEECH, PROPERTY, AND THE BURGER COURT: OLD VALUES, NEW BALANCES

> When we balance the Constitutional rights of owners of property against those of the people to enjoy freedom of the press and religion, as we must here, we remain mindful of the fact that the latter occupy a preferred position.
>
> *Marsh v. Alabama* (1946)[1]

> It would be an unwarranted infringement of property rights to require them to yield to the exercise of First Amendment rights under circumstances where adequate alternative avenues of communication exist. Such an accommodation would diminish property rights without significantly enhancing the asserted right of free speech.
>
> *Lloyd Corp. v. Tanner* (1972)[2]

I. INTRODUCTION

More than a decade has passed since Lewis F. Powell and William H. Rehnquist were appointed to the Supreme Court by

Norman Dorsen is Stokes Professor of Law, New York University Law School; President, American Civil Liberties Union (ACLU). Joel Gora is Professor of Law, Brooklyn Law School; General Counsel, New York Civil Liberties Union. The views expressed here are personal and not necessarily those of the organizations with which the authors are affiliated. This article is based on Professor Dorsen's 1979 Cooley Lecture at the University of Michigan Law School.

[1] 326 U.S. 501, 509 (1946).

[2] 407 U.S. 551, 567 (1972).

Richard Nixon, bringing to full complement the judicial institution now known as the "Burger Court." Scholars and commentators have begun to assess the Court's work in a systematic way.[3] A few years ago we had occasion to begin our own analysis, focusing on the Court's seemingly disharmonious free speech rulings. In some instances, the Burger Court's free speech decisions seemed to contract earlier rulings of the Warren Court, in others to expand on those decisions. In some cases they dramatically chart new ground.[4]

The Burger Court's commercial speech rulings have now established that substantial First Amendment protection is accorded to speech about goods and services, no matter how commonplace a product may be.[5] A free speech claim has been given heightened protection where it was augmented by the speaker's right to use and control his own items of property.[6] Conversely, where a free speech claim, especially a claimed right to use a particular forum, conflicted with the interests of the private or governmental owner of the forum, the Court has frequently rejected the free speech claim.[7] Further, the Court has upheld restrictions on use of property for sexually oriented speech, in large part because of the impact on surrounding property owners.[8] Finally, the Court has con-

---

[3] See generally Symposium, *The Burger Court: Reflections on the First Decade*, 43 LAW & CONTEMP. PROB. (1980); Galloway, *The First Decade of the Burger Court: Conservative Dominance (1969–1979)*, 21 SANTA CLARA L. REV. 891 (1981). See also the forthcoming selection of essays, edited by Professor Vince Blasi, entitled THE BURGER COURT: CONTINUITY, REACTION, OR DRIFT? (1983). In addition to the four Justices appointed by Richard Nixon, there have been two more recent changes in personnel: Justice Stevens replaced Justice Douglas, and Justice O'Connor replaced Justice Stewart. Three members of the Warren Court—Justices Brennan, White, and Marshall—remain. Although we use the name "Burger Court" to describe the present Court, we are aware, of course, that it is not a monolithic body and that every member has differed with some of the Court's free speech decisions.

[4] For a general discussion of the Burger Court's work in the First Amendment area, see Emerson, *First Amendment Doctrine and the Burger Court*, 68 CAL. L. REV. 422 (1980); Cox, *Foreword: Freedom of Expression in the Burger Court*, 94 HARV. L. REV. 1 (1980).

[5] See, *e.g.*, Virginia State Bd. of Pharmacy v. Virginia Citizens Consumer Council, 425 U.S. 748 (1976).

[6] This has been particularly true, for example, in certain cases involving claims of misuse of the American flag for speech purposes. See, *e.g.*, Spence v. Washington, 418 U.S. 405 (1974).

[7] See, *e.g.*, Lloyd Corp. v. Tanner, 407 U.S. 551 (1972); Greer v. Spock, 424 U.S. 828 (1976); Hudgens v. NLRB, 424 U.S. 507 (1976); CBS v. Democratic National Committee, 412 U.S. 94 (1973); Miami Herald Pub. Co. v. Tornillo, 418 U.S. 241 (1974); FCC v. WNCN Listeners Guild, 101 S. Ct. 1266 (1981). But *cf.* PruneYard Shopping Center v. Robins, 447 U.S. 74 (1980); CBS, Inc. v. FCC, 101 S. Ct. 2813 (1981).

[8] See, *e.g.*, Young v. American Mini-Theaters, 427 U.S. 50 (1976). But see Schad v. Mt. Ephraim, 101 S. Ct. 2176 (1981).

sistently held that speech may not be restricted in order to redress inequalities in the competitive "marketplace of ideas" resulting from disparities in wealth.[9]

These cases suggested a new dimension to free speech rulings which can be summarized by the word "property."[10] With some exceptions, whether free speech claims receive protection in the Burger Court turns on the presence of an underlying "proprietary" interest, private or governmental. Free speech values are protected when they coincide with or are augmented by property interests. Conversely, free expression has received diminished protection when First Amendment claims clash with property interests. To borrow Professor Kalven's useful phrase, when free speech claims are weighed in the balance, property interests determine on which side of the scales "the thumb of the Court" will be placed.[11]

In the 1981 Term the Court's docket contained two pertinent free speech cases. In *Princeton University v. Schmid*,[12] Schmid had been convicted of criminal trespass for distributing political leaflets on a privately owned campus without obtaining the prior approval required by University regulations. The New Jersey Supreme Court overturned the conviction.[13] But the New Jersey court declined to decide Schmid's claimed First Amendment right of access.[14] Instead, encouraged by the *PruneYard* case,[15] the state court turned to the New Jersey constitution to determine whether its free

---

[9] See, *e.g.*, Miami Herald Pub. Co. v. Tornillo, note 7 *supra;* Buckley v. Valeo, 424 U.S. 1, 48–49 (1976); First National Bank v. Bellotti, 435 U.S. 765 (1978). *Cf.* Consolidated Edison Co. v. Public Service Commission, 447 U.S. 530 (1980).

[10] The property element in free speech adjudication is not new. As early as 1919, Justice Holmes employed a commercial metaphor in his first dissenting opinion in a free speech case: "But when men have realized that time has upset many fighting faiths, they may come to believe even more than they believe the very foundations of their own conduct that the ultimate good desired is better reached by free trade in ideas—that the best test of truth is the power of the thought to get itself accepted in the competition of the market." Abrams v. United States, 250 U.S. 616, 630 (1919). But to use a marketplace concept as a formula for protecting speech is very different from the "new dimension" for property in recent First Amendment cases. Nor has Holmes's language of commerce escaped criticism. See TRIBE, AMERICAN CONSTITUTIONAL LAW 576–77 (1978); Baker, *Scope of the First Amendment Freedom of Speech*, 25 U.C.L.A.L. REV. 964, 966 (1978).

[11] See Kalven, *The Concept of the Public Forum*, 1965 SUPREME COURT REVIEW 1, 28 (1965).

[12] 102 S. Ct. 867 (1982).

[13] State v. Schmid, 84 N.J. 535, 423 A.2d 615 (1980).

[14] 84 N.J. at 522, 423 A.2d at 624.

[15] Robins v. PruneYard Shopping Center, 23 Cal.3d 899, 592 P.2d 341 (1979), *aff'd*, 447 U.S. 74 (1980).

speech clause protected the defendant's activity.[16] The court found that such free speech rights were available even upon private property, where the property is in some fashion devoted to a public use. Applying the test to Princeton University, the court concluded that the defendant's activity was consonant with the purposes and institutional integrity of a university and that Princeton's regulations contained no reasonable standards to justify limiting that activity. Princeton vigorously contended that the ruling deprived it of First and Fourteenth Amendment rights of speech and property and appealed the decision to the Supreme Court. The Court dismissed the appeal for lack of a justiciable controversy.[17]

The second case was *Loretto v. Teleprompter Manhattan CATV Corp.*[18] A New York statute required landlords to permit cable television companies to install wires on the landlord's property so that tenants could subscribe to the cable service. The statute was based on the State's speech-related interest in "rapid development of and maximum penetration by a means of communication which has important educational and community aspects."[19] A landlord filed suit, maintaining that the statute authorized a physical trespass on her property and thereby constituted a "taking" without compensation. The New York Court of Appeals, six to one, rejected her claims,[20] but the Supreme Court reversed. The Court held that the trespass sanctioned by the New York statute constituted a traditional taking of property interests which was not justified by the State's concerns with facilitating tenant access to a new medium of communication.

The *Loretto* case provides evidence to support the hypothesis that property concepts are of critical importance in the current Supreme

---

[16] State v. Schmid, 84 N.J. at 563–69, 423 A.2d at 630–33. On the increasingly common resort to state constitutional provisions to protect individual liberty, see Dorsen, *State Constitutional Law: An Introductory Survey*, 15 CONN. L. REV. 99 (1982).

[17] The Court's *per curiam* ruling noted that the State of New Jersey, whose prosecution had been terminated by the state Supreme Court's decision, had not filed an appeal, and there appeared to be no contest between the State and Schmid. The claims of Princeton University, which had intervened in the state appellate proceedings to protect its interests, were found moot because the University had, in the interim, amended its regulations whose violation had prompted the original trespass conviction. See 102 S. Ct. 867 (1982). See discussion in text at notes 147 and 148 *infra*.

[18] 102 S. Ct. 3164 (1982).

[19] *Ibid.*

[20] 53 N.Y.2d 124 (1981).

Court's disposition of free speech interests. This article will test this hypothesis.

II. The Burger Court and Property Rights

"[T]he concept of property never has been, is not, and never can be of definite content."[21] Traditionally, property rights were synonymous with ownership and control of corporeal things such as land and chattels, and certain intangibles such as bills, notes, stocks, and bonds.[22] More recently, the concept has expanded to encompass claimed entitlements to governmental benefits, status, and other economic rights—the "new property":[23]

> Wealth or value is created by culture and by society; it is culture that makes a diamond valuable and a pebble worthless. Property, on the other hand, is the creation of law. A man who has property has certain legal rights with respect to an item of wealth; property represents a relationship between wealth and its "owner."

American law has been torn by ambivalence between viewing property as something over which individuals have "sole and despotic dominion"[24] or as something less than that as defined by community interests. Judge James L. Oakes has described this dualism as follows:[25]

> [O]ne view of "property" emphasizes that we are independent individuals; the other emphasizes that we are parts of a social whole. Obviously, under the former, or "dominion," view of property, the legal system will tolerate a lesser degree of interference from the state by way of taxation or regulation than would be the case under the latter, or "social" view of property. Most judges, including those on the Supreme Court, . . . commence analysis with both views as part of their value apparatus.

---

[21] Philbrick, *Changing Conceptions of Property in Law*, 86 U. Pa. L. Rev. 691, 696 (1938).

[22] *Id.* at 691–92; see Van Alstyne, *Cracks in "The New Property": Adjudicative Due Process in the Administrative State*, 62 Cornell L. Rev. 445, 453 (1977).

[23] Reich, *The New Property*, 73 Yale L.J. 733 (1964); see Oakes, *"Property Rights" in Constitutional Analysis Today*, 56 Wash L. Rev. 583, 587 (1981).

[24] Blackstone spoke of private property as the "sole and despotic dominion . . . over the external things of the world, in total exclusion of the right of any other individual in the universe." Quoted in Powell, *The Relationship between Property Rights and Civil Rights*, 15 Hast. L.J. 135, 139 (1963).

[25] Oakes, note 23 *supra*, at 587.

Although the Burger Court may have included both views of property as part of its "value apparatus," it has pretty firmly resolved the ambivalence by protecting individual "dominion" rather than communal interests. It has done this by extolling economic autonomy and entrepreneurial freedom at the expense of public regulation and movement toward equality. Several lines of decision are instructive.

The first traces to the tentative judicial stirrings during the 1960s that poverty, or lack of wealth, could not constitutionally deprive Americans of certain benefits enjoyed by others.[26] Starting in 1970, the Burger Court rejected the imposition of wealth redistribution as constitutionally compelled in the areas of minimum family assistance, housing, and expenditures on public education.[27] More recently, it has upheld wealth-based obstacles to the exercise of a series of rights that the Court had previously determined to be "fundamental"—access to the courts,[28] voting rights,[29] and abortion.[30] In these cases the Court has made plain that, while the Constitution "does not enact Mr. Herbert Spencer's Social Statics,"[31] neither does it embody John Rawls's A Theory of Justice.

Second, the Burger Court has cramped the development of the Warren Court's constitutional protection for the "new property."[32] The Court has not denied the existence of the new property. It has understood that property interests may include entitlements arising from reasonable expectations and reliances generated by statutory and regulatory schemes.[33] But it has proved stingy in the protection

---

[26] See Harper v. Virginia Board of Elections, 383 U.S. 663 (1966); Kramer v. Union Free School District No. 15, 395 U.S. 621 (1969); Douglas v. California, 372 U.S. 353 (1963); Boddie v. Connecticut, 401 U.S. 371 (1971); Shapiro v. Thompson, 394 U.S. 618 (1969).

[27] See, *e.g.*, Dandridge v. Williams, 397 U.S. 471 (1970); James v. Valtierra, 402 U.S. 137 (1971); San Antonio Indep. School District v. Rodriguez, 411 U.S. 1 (1973).

[28] See United States v. Kras, 409 U.S. 434 (1973); Ortwein v. Schwab, 410 U.S. 656 (1973); Lassiter v. Dept. of Social Services, 452 U.S. 18 (1981). But see Little v. Streater, 452 U.S. 1 (1981). On the criminal side, as well, the Burger Court has tolerated disparities based on wealth in access to legal assistance. See Ross v. Moffitt, 417 U.S. 600 (1974); Fuller v. Oregon, 417 U.S. 40, 53 (1974).

[29] See Salyer Land Co. v. Tulare Lake Basin Water Storage Dist., 410 U.S. 719, 738 (1973) (Douglas, J., dissenting). See also Ball v. James, 451 U.S. 355 (1981).

[30] See Maher v. Roe, 432 U.S. 464 (1977); Harris v. McRae, 448 U.S. 297 (1980).

[31] Lochner v. New York, 198 U.S. 45, 75 (1905) (Holmes, J., dissenting).

[32] See Goldberg v. Kelly, 397 U.S. 254 (1970); Bell v. Burson, 402 U.S. 535 (1971).

[33] See Board of Regents v. Roth, 408 U.S. 564, 576–77 (1972); Goss v. Lopez, 419 U.S. 565 (1975). In Lynch v. Household Finance, 405 U.S. 538, 552 (1972), the Court spoke

of such property interests by imposing two critical limitations on them. First, what constitutes an entitlement would be defined by federal or state law:[34]

> Property interests, of course, are not created by the Constitution. Rather, they are created and their dimensions are defined by existing rules or understandings that stem from an independent source such as state law—rules or understandings that secure certain benefits and that support claims of entitlement to those benefits.

Second, the same source of law that established the "entitlement" could also restrict it, either expressly, as by limiting a faculty appointment to a one-year term, or, indirectly, by circumscribing the procedures available to protect that interest.[35]

The Burger Court has not shown the same parsimonious protection of more traditional forms of property and entrepreneurial interests.[36] Indeed, the Court has dusted off a long disused constitutional provision designed to thwart governmental interference with economic rights—the constitutional prohibition against any state law "impairing the Obligation of Contracts." In 1977, after more than forty years of desuetude, the Clause was invoked to invalidate the statutory repeal of a restriction on the ability of the Port of New York Authority to use revenues and reserves to subsidize mass transit contrary to the terms of the bond indenture.[37] In dissent, Justice Brennan charged that such use of the Contracts Clause created a "constitutional safe haven for property rights embodied in a contract," and "substantially distorts modern constitutional juris-

---

broadly of the important relationship between liberty and rights in property—even "new" property: "[T]he dichotomy between personal liberties and property rights is a false one. Property does not have rights. People have rights. The right to enjoy property without unlawful deprivation, no less than the right to speak or the right to travel, is, in truth, a 'personal' right, whether the 'property' in question be a welfare check, a home, or a savings account. In fact, a fundamental interdependence exists between the personal right to liberty and the personal right to property. Neither could have meaning without the other. That rights in property are basic civil rights has long been recognized."

[34] *Roth*, 408 U.S. at 577; see Perry v. Sinderman, 408 U.S. 593 (1972).

[35] See Bishop v. Wood, 426 U.S. 341 (1976). But see Monaghan, *Of "Liberty" and "Property,"* 62 CORNELL L. REV. 405 (1977); Van Alstyne, *Cracks in "The New Property,"* 62 CORNELL L. REV. 445 (1977); Tushnet, *The Newer Property: Suggestion for the Revival of Substantive Due Process,* 1975 SUPREME COURT REVIEW 261.

[36] See Oakes, note 23 *supra;* Michelman, *Property as a Constitutional Right,* 38 WASH. & LEE L. REV. 1097 (1981).

[37] United States Trust Co. v. New Jersey, 431 U.S. 1 (1977).

prudence governing regulation of private economic interests."[38] The next year, the Contract Clause was used to invalidate a state statute that imposed financial obligations, beyond the terms of labor contracts, on private companies that terminated existing pension plans.[39] Three dissenters insisted that the decision threatened "to undermine the jurisprudence of property rights":[40] "Decisions over the past 50 years have developed a coherent, unified interpretation of all the Constitutional provisions that may protect economic expectations and these decisions have recognized a broad latitude in States to effect even severe interference with existing economic values when reasonably necessary to promote the general welfare."

Finally, the Court has wholly removed many economic activities from the sphere of governmental or "state action" and thereby from potential constitutional restraints. As Professor Nowak has observed:[41]

> The issue in such [state action] cases is whether the actions of nominally private parties should be subject to constitutional restraints. . . . The libertarian Burger Court has reduced government regulation and limitation of property rights by leaving broadcasters free to refuse editorial advertising, private clubs free to discriminate by race, private utilities free to turn off a customer's power, shopping center owners free to exclude picketers and speakers from their property, and creditors free to engage in self-help.

In sum, the Burger Court has restricted the constitutional scope of

---

[38] *Id.* at 33.

[39] Allied Structural Steel Co. v. Spannaus, 438 U.S. 234 (1978).

[40] *Id.* at 260. Outside the Contracts Clause cases, see also Kaiser Aetna v. United States, 444 U.S. 164 (1979); Loretto v. Teleprompter, 102 S. Ct. 3164 (1982); Raymond Motor Transportation, Inc. v. Rice, 434 U.S. 429 (1978); Philadelphia v. New Jersey, 437 U.S. 617 (1978); Hughes v. Oklahoma, 441 U.S. 322 (1979); Kassel v. Consolidated Freightways Corp., 450 U.S. 662 (1981). Where the state in its "proprietary" capacity has entered the market, the Court has allowed it, as buyer or seller, to discriminate against competing business interests. See, *e.g.*, Hughes v. Alexandria Scrap Corp., 426 U.S. 794 (1976); Reeves v. Stake, 447 U.S. 429 (1980); see generally Wells & Hellerstein, *The Governmental-Proprietary Distinction in Constitutional Law*, 66 VA. L. REV. 1073 (1980). The Court has nevertheless stopped well short of a full-scale return to the *Lochner* era and the use of substantive due process or equal protection to protect property interests. See, *e.g.*, Minnesota v. Clover Leaf Creamery Co., 449 U.S. 456 (1981); Hodel v. Virginia Surface Mining & Reclamation Ass'n, 452 U.S. 264 (1981).

[41] Nowak, *Foreword: Evaluating the Work of the New Libertarian Supreme Court*, 7 HASTINGS L.Q. 263, 288 (1980).

government regulation of private economic activity, thereby expanding the "dominion" of owners over their property. Or as depicted by Professor Van Alstyne, the Court has expressed:[42]

> . . . a different, tighter, more conservative view of liberty:
> liberty as security of private property; liberty as freedom of
> entrepreneurial skill; liberty from the impositions of government
> and of third parties from disposing of "one's own." Liberty, in
> brief, more in the mode of John Locke and of Adam Smith and
> somewhat less in the mode of John Mill (or of John Rawls).

It should not be surprising, therefore, that the Court's free speech
cases have revealed a similar sensitivity to private economic
interests.

III. THE BURGER COURT AND FREE SPEECH

What did the free speech landscape look like in early 1972,
when Justices Powell and Rehnquist joined the Court? Even a
casual observer might have been struck by a remarkable series of
free speech decisions rendered toward the end of the Warren Court
era. Two decisions in June 1971 seemed particularly noteworthy.
The first was a characteristically careful analysis by Justice Harlan
holding that California could not punish as disorderly conduct the
public display of the words "Fuck the Draft" in a Los Angeles
courthouse. Justice Harlan said:[43]

> For, while the particular four-letter word being litigated here
> is perhaps more distasteful than most others of its genre, it is
> nevertheless often true that one man's vulgarity is another's
> lyric. Indeed, we think it is largely because governmental
> officials cannot make principled distinctions in this area that the
> Constitution leaves matters of taste and style so largely to the
> individual.

In the other 1971 decision, the Pentagon Papers case, the Supreme
Court defended the First Amendment's basic purposes against a
direct attack. In his concurring opinion Justice Black said:[44]

---

[42] Van Alstyne, *The Recrudescence of Property Rights as the Foremost Principle of Civil Liberties: The First Decade of the Burger Court*, 43 LAW & CONTEMP. PROB. 66, 70 (1980). See also Nowak, note 41 *supra*.

[43] Cohen v. California, 403 U.S. 15, 25 (1971).

[44] New York Times Co. v. United States, 403 U.S. 713, 717 (1971) (concurring opinion).

Only a free and unrestrained press can effectively expose deception in government. And paramount among the responsibilities of a free press is the duty to prevent any part of the government from deceiving the people and sending them off to distant lands to die of foreign fevers and foreign shot and shell.

These two cases capped a number of speech-protective rulings that led free speech partisans to unaccustomed satisfaction. The Court had adopted what appeared to be a rigorous standard for testing restraints on political advocacy and in the process overruled one of the most scorned decisions of an earlier era.[45] It took steps to cope with the "intractable" obscenity problem under normal First Amendment criteria.[46] It accorded the media broad protection against defamation suits arising out of news stories on "matters of public or general interest."[47]

But trouble brewed beneath the surface even then. The precise condition of the First Amendment, if closely inspected, was more uneven and less happy than appeared. First Amendment doctrine was, in the view of one renowned scholar, in "chaos." At the time of the notable free speech victories described above, Professor Emerson decried the lack of a coherent First Amendment policy:[48]

At various times the Court has employed the bad tendency test, the clear and present danger test, an incitement test, and different forms of the ad hoc balancing test. Sometimes it has not clearly enunciated the theory upon which it proceeds. Frequently it has avoided decision on basic First Amendment issues by invoking doctrines of vagueness, overbreadth, or the use of less drastic alternatives. . . . The Supreme Court has also utilized other doctrines, such as the preferred position of the First Amendment and prior restraint. Recently it has begun to address itself to problems of "symbolic speech" and the place in which First Amendment activities can be carried on. But it has totally failed to settle on any coherent approach.

The absence of a "coherent approach," regrettable in itself, also seems pertinent to the use of property concepts in the Court's recent free speech cases, because the more the Court relies on ad

---

[45] Brandenburg v. Ohio, 395 U.S. 444 (1969), *overruling* Whitney v. California, 274 U.S. 357 (1927).

[46] Stanley v. Georgia, 394 U.S. 557 (1969).

[47] Rosenbloom v. Metromedia, Inc., 403 U.S. 29 (1971).

[48] EMERSON, THE SYSTEM OF FREEDOM OF EXPRESSION 15–16 (1970).

hoc First Amendment theories, the more influential can be "unrelated" grounds of decision. Put another way, when the Court persistently balances free speech interests, there is a doctrinal vacuum, and the property "thumb" on the scale can be dispositive.[49]

A. PROPERTY AND SPEECH UNITED

1. *Speech linked to property.* We start with the deceptively simple flag cases. The principal case involved a young man convicted under a statute prohibiting improper use of the American flag for taping a peace symbol on a flag to protest national policies.[50] Although a number of factors were relevant to the decision—absence of a breach of the peace, the impermissibility of punishing the appellant merely because others found his message offensive—the Court treated property concepts as central in overturning the conviction:[51]

> A number of factors are important in the instant case. First, this was a privately owned flag. In a technical property sense it was not the property of any government. . . . Second, appellant displayed his flag on private property.

As the dissenters saw it, private ownership of the flag could not be

---

[49] Scholars have suggested formulations for protecting free speech values from dilution. Professor Tribe's elaborate "two track" theoretical structure attempts to identify all governmental restrictions aimed at the "communicative impact" of expressive activity and treats such restrictions as invalid. TRIBE, AMERICAN CONSTITUTIONAL LAW 580–601 (1978). Professor Baker's formulation protects all speech "that manifests or contributes to the speaker's values or visions—speech which furthers the two key First Amendment values of self-fulfillment and participation in change—as long as the speech does not involve violence or coercion of another." Baker, *Scope of First Amendment Freedom of Speech*, 25 U.C.L.A.L. REV. 964, 1001–02 (1978). Others have suggested a "revitalized" clear-and-present-danger test, Shaman, *Revitalizing the Clear-and-Present-Danger Test: Toward a Principled Interpretation of the First Amendment*, 22 VILL. L. REV. 60 (1976); rules forbidding controls based on content, Bogen, *The Supreme Court's Interpretation of the Guarantee of Freedom of Speech*, 35 MD. L. REV. 555 (1976); the "presumptive unconstitutionality of content discrimination," Karst, *Public Enterprise and the Public Forum: A Comment on Southeastern Promotions, Ltd. v. Conrad*, 37 OHIO ST. L.J. 247, 255 (1976); or a "heavily negative presumption" against control of public speech, Meiklejohn, *Public Speech in the Burger Court: The Influence of Mr. Justice Black*, 8 TOLEDO L. REV. 301, 304 (1977). A thoughtful analysis is found in HAIMAN, SPEECH AND LAW IN A FREE SOCIETY (1981). See generally, DORSEN, BENDER, & NEUBORNE, 1 EMERSON, HABER & DORSEN'S POLITICAL AND CIVIL RIGHTS IN THE UNITED STATES 51–59 (4th ed. 1976).

[50] Spence v. Washington, 418 U.S. 405 (1974); see also Smith v. Goguen, 415 U.S. 566 (1974).

[51] 418 U.S. at 408–9. See Ely, *Flag Desecration: A Case Study in the Roles of Categorization and Balancing in First Amendment Analysis*, 88 HARV. L. REV. 1482, 1483 n.5 (1975).

decisive, because the flag is a "special kind of personality,"[52] "a national property, and the Nation may regulate those who would make, imitate, sell, possess or use it."[53] In this view, the flag as a national symbol may be protected against misuse just as the Coca-Cola insignia as a corporate symbol may be protected against misappropriation. In each instance, there is protection of the intangible property interest in the integrity of a trademark. Thus, the flag use case pitted the tangible property interest in private ownership of a flag against the less tangible interest in public control of the symbol, and the traditional property interest prevailed.[54]

The potency of the property factor can also be seen in a Burger Court decision involving the right *not* to speak, or at least not to have the state appropriate private property as a forum for the state's message. The case involved the right of a Jehovah's Witness to object to the New Hampshire motto, "Live Free or Die," appearing on his automobile license plates. Although the case might have been decided on the established right of persons of conscience to be free from compelled state orthodoxy,[55] the property element was a key factor in the Court's analysis:[56]

> We are thus faced with the question of whether the State may constitutionally require an individual to participate in the dissemination of an ideological message by displaying it on his private property in a manner and for the express purpose that it be observed and read by the public. We hold that the State may not do so. . . .
>
> [The law] in effect requires that appellees use their private property as a "mobile billboard" for the State's ideological message. . . .

The property motifs evident in these cases have been sounded elsewhere. In one case, the Court invalidated a sweeping local ordi-

---

[52] 418 U.S. at 422.

[53] *Ibid.*

[54] This theme of the flag as a national trademark was emphasized by Justice Rehnquist three months earlier in his dissent in Smith v. Goguen, 415 U.S. at 594.

[55] See West Virginia State Board of Education v. Barnette, 319 U.S. 624 (1943).

[56] Wooley v. Maynard, 430 U.S. 705, 713, 715 (1977). In *Wooley*, the Court relied on an earlier case holding that a newspaper could not be compelled to use its property to carry a "reply" message from a political candidate whom the paper had criticized. Miami Herald Pub. Co. v. Tornillo, 418 U.S. 241 (1974). And see Abood v. Detroit Board of Education, 431 U.S. 209 (1977). See generally Gaebler, *First Amendment Protection against Government Compelled Expression and Association*, 23 B.C.L. REV. 995 (1982).

nance that prohibited drive-in movie theaters with screens visible from the street from showing scenes of nudity alleged to be offensive to unwilling viewers.[57] The prevailing opinion emphasized that the speech sought to be regulated emanated from the claimant's property and that the financial costs that drive-in operators would have to incur to shield their screens from passersby would be substantial.[58]

Speech and property were similarly entwined in a 1977 ruling that a municipality, allegedly attempting to stem "white flight" from a residential neighborhood, could not ban the posting of "For Sale" or "Sold" signs on homeowners' property.[59] While the Court's strong free speech opinion applied the traditional doctrine that speech cannot be restricted merely because people may be stimulated to act, the consequence of the decision was to permit use of residential property for speech concerning sale of that property.

The Court has also been impressed with speech claims when an individual or corporation used its funds or property in order to facilitate the speech. In *Buckley v. Valeo*,[60] the campaign finance case, the central issue was stated as whether "money is speech,"[61] that is, whether restrictions on the amount of money that could be spent in political campaigns were restrictions on free speech. Despite powerful countervailing arguments, the Court held that they were:[62] "A restriction on the amount of money a person or group can spend on political communication during a campaign necessarily reduces the quantity of expression by restricting the number of issues discussed, the depth of their exploration, and the size of the audience reached." The Court went on to hold that quantitative

---

[57] Erznoznik v. City of Jacksonville, 422 U.S. 205 (1975).

[58] In *Erznoznik*, the Court left open the question whether the use of property to show sexually oriented movies could be regulated through "a properly drawn zoning ordinance restricting the location of drive-in theaters." 422 U.S. at 212 n.9. A year later, a sharply divided Court held that municipalities could, as part of a zoning plan, single out "adult only" bookstores and movie houses and prohibit them from clustering together in the same areas. Young v. American Mini-Theaters, 427 U.S. 50 (1976). Schad v. Mt. Ephraim, 452 U.S. 61 (1981), invalidated the application of zoning rules to prohibit "live entertainment," including nude dancing, in downtown areas. *Young* was distinguished on the ground that it involved a comprehensive zoning plan aimed at the problem represented by the particular establishments. See also Metromedia, Inc. v. City of San Diego, 453 U.S. 490 (1981).

[59] Linmark Associates v. Township of Willingboro, 431 U.S. 85 (1977).

[60] 424 U.S. 1 (1976).

[61] Transcript of Oral Argument, p. 67.

[62] 424 U.S. at 19. *Cf.* 519 F.2d 821 (D.C. Cir. 1975) (*en banc*).

restrictions on how much money candidates, campaigns, or independent supporters could spend violated the First Amendment.

The Court's protection of the overt use of property and economic resources to facilitate speech was even clearer in a 1978 case where it protected the free speech rights of entities embodying the quintessential modern form of property: the corporation.[63] The Court held that business corporations cannot be prohibited from spending corporate funds to express corporate views on referendum issues, even where those issues do not "materially affect" the corporation's business or property. Although the Court's analysis emphasized the importance of public debate and the emerging First Amendment "right to hear," the specific holding was that speech could not be stripped of First Amendment protection because the source of the speech was a corporation.[64] The dissenters believed that a State may "prevent corporate management from using the corporate treasury to propagate views having no connection with the corporate business."[65]

A final example of the Court's willingness to give heightened protection to speech paid for by the speaker concerned speech by public utilities—corporate entities traditionally subject to comprehensive state regulation. A New York public service commission rule barred utility companies from inserting material that expressed the utility's viewpoint on "controversial matters of public policy" in monthly billing statements to consumers (in this case, the benefits of nuclear power). The Court invalidated the commission ban.[66] After reaffirming broad First Amendment protections for corporate speech, the Court distinguished earlier cases:[67]

---

[63] First National Bank of Boston v. Bellotti, 435 U.S. 765 (1978).

[64] The main line of cases relied on to uphold restrictions on corporate speech involved rulings that corporations and labor unions could be wholly barred from engaging in political campaigns in order "to avoid deleterious influences on federal elections resulting from the use of money by those who exercise control over large aggregations of capital." United States v. Automobile Workers, 352 U.S. 567, 585 (1957). See also Pipefitters v. United States, 407 U.S. 385, 415–16 (1972); United States v. CIO, 335 U.S. 106, 113 (1948). Although the Court indicated that its ruling "implies no comparable right" of corporations or unions to contribute or to become involved in partisan political campaigns, 435 U.S. at 788 n.26, the dissenters thought the decision "casts considerable doubt" upon the constitutionality of such restrictions.

[65] 435 U.S. at 803.

[66] See Consolidated Edison Co. v. Public Service Commission, 447 U.S. 530 (1980).

[67] 447 U.S. at 539–40 (emphasis added). See Greer v. Spock, 424 U.S. 828 (1976); Lehman v. Shaker Heights, 418 U.S. 298 (1974).

Consolidated Edison has not asked to use the offices of the Commission as a forum from which to promulgate its views. Rather, it seeks merely to utilize *its own billing envelopes* to promulgate its views on controversial issues of public policy. . . . [The] Commission's attempt to restrict free expression of a private party cannot be upheld by reliance upon precedent that rests on the special interests of a government in overseeing the use of its property.

Once again, the use of property as a platform for speech validates speech interests.

2. *Speech enhanced by property*. The corporate and campaign speech cases reflect another and perhaps more profound property theme in the Burger Court's decisions: There will be no compelled equalization of the resources to compete in the marketplace of ideas. Time and again the Court has insisted that government cannot limit the free speech rights of the wealthy and powerful in order to afford those with lesser resources the ability to debate on a more equal footing.

During the 1970s, the Court was confronted with litigants seeking price controls and supports in the marketplace of ideas. One set of equalization claims came under the rubric of "access to the media."[68] In *Miami Herald Pub. Co. v. Tornillo*,[69] a candidate for local elective office invoked a 1902 statute to compel a newspaper that had criticized him to publish his editorial reply. The Court sympathetically surveyed the plaintiff's showing that media ownership had become highly concentrated and that the combination of fewer media outlets and the economic barriers to entry had reduced participation in public debate and had constricted the scope of debate.[70] But the Court unanimously rejected an equalizing right of access:[71]

The New York Court of Appeals thereafter held that a utility could, consistent with the First Amendment, be made to bear the expense of informational advertising, by a commission order excluding such costs from the rate base as an allowable expense and thus requiring the cost to be subsidized by the shareholders. See Rochester Gas & Electric Corp. v. Public Service Commission, 51 N.Y.2d 823 (1980), *cert. den.*, 450 U.S. 961 (1981).

[68] See generally Barron, *Access to the Press—a New First Amendment Right*, 80 HARV. L. REV. 1641 (1967); SCHMIDT, FREEDOM OF THE PRESS V. PUBLIC ACCESS (1976).

[69] 418 U.S. 241 (1974).

[70] *Id.* at 247–54.

[71] *Id.* at 254. See also CBS, Inc. v. Democratic National Committee, 412 U.S. 94 (1973); but *cf.* CBS, Inc. v. FCC, 453 U.S. 367 (1981).

. . . [A]t each point the implementation of a remedy such as an enforceable right of access necessarily calls for some mechanism, either governmental or consensual. If it is governmental coercion, this at once brings about a confrontation with the express provisions of the First Amendment.

One might discount this decision on the ground that it reflected a special solicitude for the press. But *Tornillo* previewed the more sweeping issues that surfaced two years later in *Buckley v. Valeo*. The plaintiffs had challenged new statutory restrictions on contributions to federal candidates and expenditures by federal candidates, their campaigns and their independent supporters. The governmental interests alleged to sustain these restrictions were prevention of corruption through unlimited contributions, as symbolized by Watergate, equalization of the ability to compete in the political marketplace, and prevention of "skyrocketing" campaign expenditures.[72] Concluding that the restrictions were consonant with the First Amendment, the District of Columbia Court of Appeals upheld the monetary restrictions in their entirety.[73]

The Supreme Court reversed much of the decision below in an opinion characterized as the "key to understanding the Burger Court's protection of speech connected to economic activity."[74] Initially, the Court rejected the global theory that the application of wealth to subsidize political speech constituted regulable "conduct" rather than speech, or could be subjected to "volume" restraints:[75] "A restriction on the amount of money a person or group can spend . . . necessarily reduces the quantity of expression by restricting the number of issues discussed, the depth of their exploration, and the size of the audience reached." It then turned to particular restraints. After upholding some contribution limitations on anticor-

---

[72] 424 U.S. at 55–57.

[73] 519 F.2d 817 (D.C. Cir. 1975) (*per curiam, en banc*).

[74] Nowak, note 41 *supra*, at 309. Nowak observed that the statutory limitations on campaign expenditures "were based on Congressional adoption of a philosophy like that of Rawls, which required equalized political voices to protect the principles of the social compact." *Id.* at 309. See also Nicholson, Buckley v. Valeo: *The Constitutionality of the Federal Election Campaign Act Amendments of 1974*, 1977 WIS. L. REV. 323; Wright, *Money and the Pollution of Politics: Is the First Amendment an Obstacle to Equality?* 82 COLUM. L. REV. 609 (1982).

[75] 424 U.S. at 15–19.

ruption grounds,[76] the Court sharply rejected the power of government to restrict expenditures by wealthy speakers in order to enhance the voice of others:[77] "[T]he concept that government may restrict the speech of some elements of our society in order to enhance the relative voice of others is wholly foreign to the First Amendment."

Finally, the Court struck down the ceilings on overall expenditures in a campaign by observing categorically that:[78]

> The First Amendment denies government the power to determine that spending to promote one's political views is wasteful, excessive, or unwise. In the free society ordained by our Constitution it is not the government, but the people—individually as citizens and candidates and collectively as associations and political committees—who must retain control over the quantity and range of debate on public issues in a political campaign.

Those whose personal wealth and property permit them a greater opportunity to speak on partisan campaign issues cannot be restricted from doing so in the interests of equality. The decision thus stands as a potent example of wealth and speech uniting to defeat claims based on an equality principle.[79]

The link between property and speech and the refusal to tolerate legislative efforts to "equalize" public discourse by reducing wealth-based differences in the ability to enter the marketplace of ideas were again evident in *Bellotti*. The step from the campaign finance case to the corporate speech case was short in doctrine but long in implication. The issue was whether corporations could be prohibited by statute from spending funds to influence the electorate on a referendum question "other than one materially affecting any of the property, business or assets of the corporation."[80] The

---

[76] *Id.* at 24–29. The Court found that the contribution limits served the compelling interest of preventing the potential and appearance of political corruption associated with unlimited private campaign contributions and that these interests were sufficient to overcome the speech and associational rights implicit in making contributions to candidates.

[77] *Id.* at 48–49, 54.

[78] *Id.* at 57.

[79] Two recent cases under the federal campaign finance laws have generally hewn to the *Buckley* approach. See California Medical Ass'n v. Federal Election Commission, 453 U.S. 182 (1981); Federal Election Commission v. Democratic Senatorial Campaign Committee, 102 S. Ct. 38 (1981).

[80] 435 U.S. at 785.

highest Massachusetts court upheld the restriction on the ground that a corporation's right to speak was a function of—and therefore limited by—its right to protect its property and that the statute allowed corporate speech on issues that affected its economic and property interest.

A sharply divided Supreme Court reversed. Justice Powell's opinion for the Court framed the issue as "whether the corporate identity of the speaker deprives this proposed speech of what otherwise would be its clear entitlement to protection."[81] The Court found that the limitation on corporate speech infringed two First Amendment concerns: (1) prohibiting government from "limiting the stock of information" available to the public and (2) disqualifying government from "dictating the subjects about which persons may speak and the speakers who may address a public issue."[82] The claims that corporate wealth, capital, and power would "drown out" other points of view and exert an undue influence on referendum campaigns were rejected with the observation that there had been no record showing to that effect. More significantly, the Court once again rejected the "concept that government may restrict the speech of some elements of our society in order to enhance the relative voice of others."[83]

It is difficult to avoid viewing *Bellotti* as a Magna Carta for corporate speech on public issues. Taken in tandem with *Buckley v. Valeo*, it provides a broad basis for individuals and corporations to employ aggregations of wealth and property to influence the citizenry on public issues, public questions, and perhaps even candidates for public office. The Court rejected the effort to equalize the debate.[84]

---

[81] *Id.* at 778.

[82] *Id.* at 783, 785.

[83] *Id.* at 790–91. The Court did not foreclose the possibility of a different result where there were "record or legislative findings that corporate advocacy threatened imminently to undermine democratic processes, thereby denigrating rather than serving First Amendment interests . . . " *Id.* at 789. But such a showing may be difficult to make. *Cf.* Citizens Against Rent Control v. City of Berkeley, 102 S. Ct. 434 (1981). See generally Chevigny, *Philosophy of Language and Free Expression*, 55 N.Y.U.L. REV. 157 (1980).

[84] It might be suggested that *Bellotti* should be viewed as a "right to hear" case, reflecting the revival of that free speech interest in the commercial speech cases. But the Court's recognition of a "right to hear" as a discrete First Amendment component has been less than consistent. Compare, *e.g.*, Gannett Co. v. De Pasquale, 443 U.S. 368, 391–93 (1979), with, *e.g.*, Richmond Newspapers v. Virginia, 448 U.S. 555, 576 (1980); Globe Newspaper Co. v. Superior Court, 102 S. Ct. 2613 (1982). For an incisive analysis of *Bellotti*, see Ratner, *Corporations and the Constitution*, 15 U.S.F.L. REV. 11 (1981).

3. *Speech promoting property*. The Burger Court's principal First Amendment innovation has been to incorporate "commercial speech" within the zone of protected speech and, in less than a decade, elaborate an entire doctrine for this purpose. It has done so by explicit reliance on traditional free market models linking the protection of free enterprise and economic interests with the protection of speech. "The relationship of speech to the marketplace of products or of services does not make it valueless in the marketplace of ideas."[85]

In 1942 the Court held that "the Constitution imposes no . . . restraint on government as respects purely commercial advertising."[86] Although this doctrine was subsequently limited,[87] not until 1975 did the Court rule, in the context of advertising of abortion services, that "commercial" speech merited some constitutional protection, the precise extent depending on whether the public interest in the speech outweighed the state's need for regulation.[88]

A year later the Court revised its doctrine by holding that speech which does "no more than propose a commercial transaction" cannot for that reason alone be denied First Amendment protection.[89] The case involved a statutory restriction on price advertising of prescription drugs, where the content of the prohibited message— "I will sell you the X prescription drug at the Y price"—was wholly commercial. The Court rested on three grounds: (1) speech does not lose its protection because it is paid for by the advertiser or flows from an economic motivation; (2) individuals and society have a strong interest in "the free flow of commercial information"; and (3) commercial advertising is indispensable in our "predominantly free enterprise economy." The Court nevertheless disclaimed any suggestion that commercial speech would be as immune from regu-

---

[85] Bigelow v. Virginia, 421 U.S. 809, 826 (1975).

[86] Valentine v. Chrestensen, 316 U.S. 52, 54 (1942).

[87] Pittsburgh Press Co. v. Commission on Human Relations, 413 U.S. 376 (1973).

[88] Bigelow v. Virginia, note 85 *supra*. The case involved a Virginia statutory prohibition on "encouraging . . . the procuring of abortion . . ." applied to the editor of a local weekly newspaper that had run an advertisement for lawful abortion services available in New York. Because the information was of arguable public interest, the Court did not have to address squarely the "purely commercial speech" issues. Two years earlier, in *Pittsburgh Press*, the Court did not cast doubt on the continued vitality of the commercial speech exception where an illegal commercial proposal was concerned.

[89] Virginia State Board of Pharmacy v. Virginia Citizens Consumer Council, 425 U.S. 748 (1976).

lation as other more "protected" forms of speech or that the "commonsense" differences between commercial speech and other forms of speech could not be taken into account in justifying differing kinds of government regulations.[90]

The Court soon extended the protection of commercial speech to "For Sale" signs to sell private homes,[91] to advertisements for contraceptives,[92] and to advertising of low-cost legal services.[93] These cases made clear that *Virginia Board* was to be a powerful precedent for protecting speech promoting goods and services. But they also demonstrated that the "commonsense" distinctions between commercial and political speech had teeth. Such distinctions differentiated the letter solicitation of clients for public interest litigation by ACLU lawyers[94] from in-person solicitation of clients in commonplace personal injury cases.[95] A year later similar distinctions supplied the basis for upholding a Texas statute that, in the interest of avoiding potential consumer deception as to the quality of services, prohibited the practice of optometry under a trade name.[96] The Court revisited these doctrinal problems and reformulated the rules governing commercial speech in a 1980 ruling invalidating a New York Public Service Commission order prohibiting regulated electric utilities from "promoting the use of electricity through . . . advertising."[97]

It has been argued that speech proceeding from economic and profit motives is too remote from the First Amendment values of self-expression and self-governance to warrant protection and that

---

[90] *Id.* at 770–72. Justice Rehnquist, the sole dissenter, took sharp issue with "elevat[ing] commercial intercourse between a seller hawking his wares and a buyer seeking to strike a bargain to the same plane as has been previously reserved for the free marketplace of ideas." *Id.* at 781. He also rejected the consumerist perspective on the Court's opinion, insisting that the First Amendment's primary function is to facilitate public decisionmaking in a democracy, not to facilitate "the choice of shampoo." *Id.* at 787.

[91] Linmark Associates, Inc. v. Township of Willingboro, 431 U.S. 85 (1977).

[92] Carey v. Population Services Int'l, 431 U.S. 678 (1977).

[93] Bates v. State Bar of Arizona, 433 U.S. 350 (1977). See In re R.M.J., 102 S. Ct. 929 (1982).

[94] In re Primus, 436 U.S. 412 (1978).

[95] Ohralik v. Ohio State Bar Ass'n, 436 U.S. 447 (1978).

[96] Friedman v. Rogers, 440 U.S. 1 (1979). Justice Powell observed for the Court that "a property interest in a means of communication does not enlarge or diminish the First Amendment protection of that communication." *Id.* at 12 n.11.

[97] Central Hudson Gas & Electric Corp. v. Public Service Commission, 447 U.S. 557, 566 (1980).

these decisions can only be justified in terms of economic liberty values of the *Lochner* genre.[98] This is a doubtful conclusion. Although the commercial speech doctrine primarily provides succor to economic interests, it is consistent with at least some of the purposes of the First Amendment. Commercial speech provides information of value to private consumers and affects public economic activity. However one resolves the dispute, it is plain that the Burger Court, through the use of the First Amendment, is producing results consonant with free market competition and the maintenance of property values.[99]

4. *Speech and media "property."* The Burger Court's linkage of property rights and speech protection is also reflected in a series of cases that permit owners of mass media to use "their" property for whatever speech they prefer and to refuse access to those who would use their facilities for contrary messages. The cases tend to confirm A. J. Liebling's remark that "Freedom of the press belongs to those who own one."[100]

The Supreme Court's initial encounter with the issue came in 1969 in *Red Lion Broadcasting Co. v. FCC*,[101] where it upheld the personal attack and political editorial branches of the fairness doctrine and thus sustained a narrow form of compelled access to electronic news media. At issue was the broadcasters' asserted First Amendment right to use their allotted frequencies "to broadcast whatever they choose, and to exclude whomever they choose from ever using that frequency."[102] A unanimous Court rejected the

---

[98] See, *e.g.*, Baker, *Commercial Speech: A Problem in the Theory of Freedom*, 62 IOWA L. REV. 1 (1976); Jackson & Jeffries, *Commercial Speech: Economic Due Process and the First Amendment*, 65 VA. L. REV. 1 (1979); Farber, *Commercial Speech and First Amendment Theory*, 74 NW. U.L. REV. 372 (1979); but see Roberts, *Toward a General Theory of Commercial Speech and the First Amendment*, 40 OHIO ST. L.J. 115 (1979); see generally, Symposium, *Commercial Speech*, 46 BROOKLYN L. REV. 389; Note, *Constitutional Protection of Commercial Speech*, 82 COLUM. L. REV. 720 (1982).

[99] Professor Farber, note 98 *supra*, suggests that a commercial message can be broken down into two components: informational and contractual. Where government is seeking to regulate the former, normal First Amendment doctrines are applicable to assess the restriction. Where the regulation is aimed at the contractual component of the message, even though words are used in the transaction, government's broad power to regulate breaches of contract and warranty comes into play. In this view, a false advertisement can be regulated not because it is "bad" speech, but because it is like a breach of warranty. The equation is not easily made.

[100] Quoted in LIEBERMAN, FREE SPEECH, FREE PRESS, AND THE LAW 121 (1980).

[101] 395 U.S. 367 (1969).

[102] *Id.* at 386.

argument, relying on two grounds to uphold limited incursions on broadcasters' rights. First, the Court found that the fairness doctrine advanced the free speech values of "an uninhibited marketplace of ideas in which truth will ultimately prevail," as opposed to permitting "monopolization of that market."[103] That view plainly prefers speech values over the combined property and speech interests of broadcasters. But the Court found it necessary to express a second reason for the fairness doctrine based on a competing "property" interest, public "ownership" of the airwaves: "the First Amendment confers . . . no right to an unconditional monopoly of a scarce resource which the Government has denied others the right to use. . . . Licenses to broadcast do not confer ownership of designated frequencies, but only the temporary privilege of using them."[104] Thus, although *Red Lion* in fact subordinated broadcasters' property rights to First Amendment claims, the Court employed a property metaphor in the form of the public's superior title to the airwaves.[105]

The Burger Court's first encounter with these issues came in *Columbia Broadcasting System, Inc. v. Democratic National Committee*,[106] where it sharply limited *Red Lion* by upholding the right of broadcasters to refuse to accept paid public issue advertisements. Chief Justice Berger's opinion, although noting that the broadcast media "utilize a valuable and limited public resource," found broad Congressional intent to uphold the prerogatives of media owners:[107]

> . . . Congress opted for a system of private broadcasters licensed and regulated by Government. . . . [T]his choice was influenced not only by traditional attitudes toward private enterprise, but by a desire to maintain for licensees, so far as consistent with necessary regulation, a traditional journalistic role.

Thus, principles of journalistic freedom, augmented by congressionally sanctioned concepts of private ownership of broadcast outlets, resulted in protection of the private broadcasters' prerogatives.

---

[103] *Id.* at 390.

[104] *Id.* at 391, 394.

[105] In unanimously rejecting a similar fairness and access claim against privately owned print media, with no comparable public media "ownership" interests affecting the balance, the Court did not even cite *Red Lion*. See Miami Herald Pub. Co. v. Tornillo, 418 U.S. 241 (1974).

[106] 412 U.S. 94 (1973).

[107] *Id.* at 116.

Abuses could be controlled through the fairness doctrine and the license renewal system.[108]

The broadest protection for the journalistic and entrepreneurial freedom of media owners, and the sharpest rejection of access claims, came in *Miami Herald Pub. Co. v. Tornillo.*[109] The Court unanimously overturned a limited statutory form of compelled access by political candidates seeking equal space to reply to personal attacks, notwithstanding a powerful demonstration that "economic factors" have resulted in the concentration of media ownership "in a few hands [with] the power to inform the American people and shape public opinion."[110] Despite the "monopoly of the means of communication," the Court held that any effort to remedy the problem inevitably entailed either government controls or self-censorship, both of which were anathema to free press values.[111] Once again, the First Amendment interests of those whose ownership enhanced their right to speak were to prevail. Compelled access to the pages of their newspapers would not be permitted.[112]

Two cases decided in the 1980 Term reaffirmed the Court's protection of media owners against broad access claims, although in one of these cases it recognized a limited right of access. In the first case a radio station with a particular program format of classical music was sold to a new licensee who planned to change to "popular" musical fare. Access advocates challenged the sale, claiming that the Commission had to take account of the diminution of programming diversity in deciding whether to allow it. The Commission disagreed, reasoning that "market forces" would insure diversity more effectively than "government intervention." The Supreme Court rejected the access claims and upheld the Commis-

---

[108] The Court did observe one flaw in the proposed access scheme for the mandated right to purchase air time for editorial messages: that the statutory public interest standard "would scarcely be served by a system so heavily weighted in favor of the financially affluent, or those with access to wealth. . . . Even under a first-come-first-served system, . . . the views of the affluent could well prevail over those of others, since they would have it within their power to purchase time more frequently." *Id.* at 123.

[109] 418 U.S. 241 (1974).

[110] *Id.* at 249–50.

[111] *Id.* at 254–58.

[112] In FCC v. Midwest Video Corp., 440 U.S. 689 (1979), the Court held that the FCC had exceeded its statutory authority to regulate cable television in promulgating "public access" rules that required cable television operators to set aside a number of cable channels for public use.

sion's policy as consistent with the statute and First Amendment values.[113] The effect of the ruling was a victory for the journalistic and property interests of station owners.

The second decision tested a federal campaign reform statute providing that candidates for federal elective office have a right of reasonable access to the use of stations for paid political broadcasts on behalf of their candidacies.[114] The statute was challenged by the three major networks, which had refused, in late 1979, to make airtime available to President Carter's 1980 reelection campaign. The lower court upheld the statute, and the Supreme Court affirmed.[115] Chief Justice Burger's opinion concentrated on whether Congress had intended to create such a limited right of access and whether the Commission could manageably enforce the requirement. With respect to the broadcaster's First Amendment objections, the Chief Justice acknowledged the tension between journalistic freedom and public control of the airwaves but resolved the conflict by concluding that the facilitating of campaign speech justified the limited right of access:[116]

> Petitioners are correct that the Court has never approved a *general* right of access to the media. [Citations omitted.] Nor do we do so today. Section 312(a)(7) creates a *limited* right to "reasonable" access that pertains only to legally qualified federal candidates. . . .
>
> Section 312(a)(7) represents an effort by Congress to assure that an important resource—the airwaves—will be used in the public interest. We hold that the statutory right of access . . . properly balances the First Amendment rights of federal candidates, the public, and broadcasters.

This *CBS* case hews more closely to *Red Lion* than it does to the first *CBS* decision. In order to enhance campaign speech, it permits a limited incursion on broadcasters' interests that it justifies by reference to public "ownership" of "an important resource." On the other hand, the "limited" right to access will be limited to candidates who can pay for it.[117]

---

[113] FCC v. WNCN Listeners Guild, 450 U.S. 582 (1981).

[114] 47 U.S.C. §312(a)(7) (1971).

[115] CBS, Inc. v. FCC, 453 U.S. 367 (1981).

[116] *Id.* at 396–97 (emphasis in original).

[117] The other instance where the Burger Court allowed some government intrusion upon the property and speech interests of media owners was the 1978 decision upholding FCC "cross-ownership" rules generally prohibiting formation of jointly owned newspaper-

What emerges is that both the First Amendment and property rights that attach to media ownership will generally prevail over broad access and diversity claims. Print media owners cannot be compelled to supply access. In limited instances, electronic media owners are subject to compelled access in a narrow and discrete fashion by virtue of overriding public "ownership" interests.

B. PROPERTY AND SPEECH IN CONFLICT

1. *Speech and the "public forum."* The Court's "public forum" cases supply the most powerful example of a tension between speech rights and property rights. The Burger Court, expressly overruling Warren Court precedent, has held that the First Amendment does not require that facilities open to the public generally must allow speech activity over the objections of the owner—private, corporate, or governmental.

The use of public and private property for First Amendment activities inevitably involves an adjustment of property rights and speech interests. Almost a century ago, Justice Holmes took the position in Massachusetts that property rights would invariably prevail:[118] "For the Legislature absolutely or conditionally to forbid public speaking in a highway or public park is no more an infringement of the rights of a member of the public than for the owner of a private house to forbid it in his house." A different view was taken by Justice Roberts in his oft-cited opinion in *Hague v. CIO*:[119] "Wherever the title of the streets and parks may rest, they have immemorially been held in trust for the use of the public and, time out of mind, have been used for purposes of assembly, communicating thoughts between citizens, and discussing public questions." The Burger Court's adjustment of the interests gives primary weight to property.

a) Private property. In *Marsh v. Alabama*,[120] the Court held in 1946 that corporate ownership of legal title to a "company town" could not override the public's interest "in the functioning of the commu-

---

broadcast outlet combinations in the same locality and requiring divestiture of certain existing combinations. FCC v. National Citizens Committee for Broadcasting, 436 U.S. 775 (1978). See generally Lee, *Antitrust Enforcement, Freedom of the Press, and the "Open Market": The Supreme Court on the Structure and Conduct of Mass Media*, 32 VAND. L. REV. 1249 (1979).

[118] 162 Mass. 510, 511 (1895), *aff'd*, 167 U.S. 43 (1897).

[119] 307 U.S. 496, 515 (1939) (concurring opinion).

[120] 326 U.S. 501, 507 (1964).

nity in such a manner that the channels of communication remain free." The decision overturned the conviction of a Jehovah's Witness for handing out literature on the streets of Chickasaw, Alabama, a community whose buildings and streets were owned by a private corporation. Finding that the town resembled a typical municipality in every way but ownership, the Court held that the property factor should not control:[121]

> Ownership does not always mean absolute dominion. The more an owner, for his advantage, opens up his property for use by the public in general, the more do his rights become circumscribed by the statutory and constitutional rights of those who use it. . .
> When we balance the Constitutional rights of owners of property against those of the people to enjoy freedom of the press and religion, as we must here, we remain mindful of the fact that the latter occupy a preferred position. . . . [T]he circumstance that the property rights to the premises where the deprivation of liberty, here involved, took place, were held by others than the public, is not sufficient to justify the State's permitting a corporation to govern a community of citizens so as to restrict their fundamental liberties. . .

Justice Frankfurter's concurring opinion added: "Title to property as defined by State law controls property relations; it cannot control issues of civil liberties which arise precisely because a company town is a town as well as a congeries of property relations."[122]

In 1968, the Warren Court significantly extended *Marsh* by holding that a state court injunction which prohibited peaceful labor picketers from entering the property of a privately owned shopping center in order to protest the labor policies of a store located in that center violated the First Amendment.[123] The injunction barred the demonstrators from trespassing on shopping center property and relegated them to a public roadway at the entrance to the center parking lot several hundred feet from the supermarket.

Starting from the premise that "peaceful picketing carried on in a location generally open to the public" is presumptively protected

---

[121] *Id.* at 506, 509.

[122] *Id.* at 511. On the same day, the Court invalidated a similar conviction for distributing literature in a company town owned and controlled by the federal government. Tucker v. Texas, 326 U.S. 517 (1946).

[123] Amalgamated Food Employees Union v. Logan Valley Plaza, 391 U.S. 308 (1968).

by the First Amendment, the Court characterized the issue "squarely" presented as "whether Pennsylvania's generally valid rules against trespass to private property" could be applied to bar labor picketing of a store in a shopping center.[124] The Court held they could not. The most striking part of the Court's opinion was its rejection of the shopping center's claimed traditional right to exclude from private property, a right "part and parcel of the rights traditionally associated with ownership of private property."[125] Given the contemporary development of shopping centers as the "functional equivalent" of downtown business districts, the Court concluded that the *Marsh* principles, that ownership does not "always mean absolute dominion" and that the rights of an owner who opens property to the public can be circumscribed, compelled a reversal of the injunction.[126] The shopping center case, taken together with *Red Lion* decided the following year, represented the high point for First Amendment access advocates.

The Burger Court's reversal of this momentum began in 1972 in *Lloyd Corp. v. Tanner*.[127] Responding to property rights arguments, Justice Powell wrote that depriving the private owner of a shopping mall of the right to exclude from its premises people who wished to distribute antiwar leaflets was a violation of the owner's rights to private property and one not required by the First Amendment:[128] "[T]here has been no such dedication of Lloyd's privately owned and operated shopping center to public use as to entitle respondents to exercise therein the asserted First Amendment rights." The record showed that the mall was open to all members of the public, that space in the mall had frequently been made available to civic groups, and that the land upon which the mall was built had originally been publicly owned. Nevertheless, in an elaborate explication of the clash between free speech rights and property interests, the Court found that *Marsh* and *Logan Valley* were not controlling. As time would prove, the grounds upon which those cases were

---

[124] *Id.* at 315.

[125] *Id.* at 319.

[126] *Id.* at 324–25. Justice Black dissented in *Logan Valley Plaza* on the ground that "whether this Court likes it or not, the Constitution recognizes and supports the concept of private ownership of property." *Id.* at 330.

[127] 407 U.S. 551 (1972).

[128] *Id.* at 570.

distinguished were unpersuasive and contained the seeds of the overruling of *Logan Valley*.

In his *Lloyd* opinion Justice Powell insisted that *Logan Valley* was wrong in treating a shopping center as the "functional equivalent" of a municipal business district, since the "invitation extended to the public . . . is to come to the Center to do business with the tenants," and not an "open-ended invitation to the public to use the Center for any and all purposes. . . ."[129] In addition, he maintained that *Logan Valley* could be limited to situations where the First Amendment message was related to an activity at the shopping center because "[i]t would be an unwarranted infringement of property rights to require them to yield to the exercise of First Amendment rights under circumstances where adequate alternative avenues of communication exist."[130]

Finally, the Court addressed the conflict between property interests and speech rights on a broader plane:[131]

> [T]his Court has never held that a trespasser or an uninvited guest may exercise general rights of free speech on property privately owned and used nondiscriminatorily for private purposes only. Even where public property is involved, the Court has recognized that it is not necessarily available for speech, pickets, or other communicative activity . . .

When one compares these observations with the statement in *Marsh* that judicial balancing of property rights against First Amendment rights must be "mindful of the fact that the latter occupy a preferred position,"[132] it becomes clear that the priority of speech over property had yielded to a parity between speech and property, if not a new preference for the latter.[133]

---

[129] *Id.* at 564–65. Thus the Court employed a subject-matter basis for differentiating *Lloyd* from *Logan Valley*, even though less than one week later the Court would observe that "above all else, the First Amendment means that government has no right to restrict expression because of its message, its ideas, its subject matter, or its content." Police Department of Chicago v. Moseley, 408 U.S. 92, 95 (1972).

[130] 407 U.S. at 567. This ground of distinction also contravened settled doctrine: " . . . one is not to have the exercise of his liberty of expression in appropriate places abridged on the plea that it may be exercised in some other place." Schneider v. State, 308 U.S. 147, 163 (1939).

[131] *Id.* at 568–70.

[132] 326 U.S. at 509.

[133] See 407 U.S. at 580 (Marshall, J., dissenting). Similar issues were similarly resolved the same day in Central Hardware Co. v. NLRB, 407 U.S. 539, 543 (1972).

Four years later, the preference for property rights over speech rights was again evident in *Hudgens v. NLRB*.[134] Eschewing pretense of distinguishing *Logan Valley* by expressly overruling it and confining *Marsh* to its facts, the Court held that the First Amendment had no role to play in determining whether union picketers had a right of speech access to privately owned shopping centers. Viewing the issue and the precedents through the prism of the state action requirement, the Court reasoned that while *Marsh* was still sound—since the "company town" was more town than company—*Logan Valley* was out of line in treating the privately owned shopping center as the "functional equivalent" of a business district.[135] Accordingly, the only rights which the union speakers had were those made available by statute.

In dissent, Justice Marshall, joined by Justice Brennan, sharply criticized the Court's property-based approach to the issues and its gratuitous "bypassing of [a] purely statutory issue to overrule a First Amendment decision less than 10 years old."[136] He argued that "courts ought not let the formalities of title put an end to analysis": the important point, underlying *Marsh*, was that "traditional public channels of communication remain free, regardless of the incidence of ownership."[137] The dissent concluded:[138]

> In the final analysis, the Court's rejection of any role for the First Amendment in the privately owned shopping center complex stems, I believe, from an overly formalistic view of the relationship between the institution of private ownership of property and the First Amendment's guarantee of freedom of speech. No one would seriously question the legitimacy of the values of privacy and individual autonomy traditionally associated with privately owned property. But property that is privately owned is not always held for private use, and when a property owner opens his property to public use the force of those values diminishes.

The next decision in the line had an ironic twist, with the Court's

---

[134] 424 U.S. 507 (1976).

[135] *Id.* at 520–21.

[136] *Id.* at 532.

[137] *Id.* at 538, 539.

[138] *Id.* at 542–43. For decisions involving statutory claims by employees to use employers' property for union activity, see Beth Israel Hospital v. NLRB, 437 U.S. 483 (1978); Eastex, Inc. v. NLRB, 437 U.S. 556 (1978); NLRB v. Baptist Hospital, 442 U.S. 773 (1979).

1980 ruling in *PruneYard Shopping Center v. Robins.*[139] The case involved an attempt by a political group to solicit petition signatures at a California shopping center, privately owned but open to the general public. The owners prohibited all such activity at the shopping center. Blocked by *Lloyd's* overruling of *Logan Valley* from asserting a First Amendment right of access, the group persuaded the California Supreme Court that the state constitution's guarantee of "liberty of speech," coupled with the state's police power to regulate private property in the public interest, required a rule permitting access to shopping centers to vindicate state-created free speech rights.[140]

The Supreme Court, speaking through Justice Rehnquist, unanimously affirmed. The Court ruled that the State restriction of property rights in favor of state-recognized free speech rights did not deprive the shopping center owner of federally protected property rights. The Court treated *Lloyd Corp. v. Tanner,* whose continuing validity was not questioned, as having protected private property rights against a First Amendment right of access. But that decision did not limit the state's general police power to regulate property rights:[141]

> In *Lloyd* there was no state constitutional or statutory provision that had been construed to create rights to the use of private property by strangers, comparable to those found by the California Supreme Court here. It is, of course, well-established that a State in the exercise of its police power may adopt reasonable restrictions on private property so long as the restrictions do not amount to a taking without just compensation or contravene any other federal constitutional provision.

Having concluded that *Lloyd* was not controlling, the Court addressed the shopping center's claims that the state restriction of its right to exclude speakers from its premises constituted a "taking" of its property without just compensation and "deprived" it of property without due process of law. Justice Rehnquist observed that "one of the essential sticks in the bundle of property rights is the right to exclude others,"[142] and agreed that there had been such a

---

[139] 447 U.S. 74 (1980).
[140] 23 Cal.3d 899 (1979).
[141] 447 U.S. at 81.
[142] *Id.* at 82.

"taking" by the recognition of a state right to engage in free speech on shopping center property over the owner's objections. But this was not a violation of the Fifth Amendment's Takings Clause, as traditionally interpreted, because it did not "unreasonably impair the value or use" of the property as a shopping center or interfere with "reasonable investment-backed expectations."[143] In addition, the Court found no deprivation of general property rights, given the broad state authority to define and reorder such rights.[144]

At first glance, the shopping center case would appear to confound the thesis that the Burger Court has preferred property rights over free speech interests. On closer examination the decision does not sustain this view.

The Court left undisturbed its holding in *Lloyd* that First Amendment rights of access to private property will be wholly subordinated to state-sanctioned rights to exclude. Except where a State has chosen, as California did, to withdraw the right to exclude from the bundle of property rights, *Lloyd* will control.[145] Had the Court reversed the California court's restriction of the shopping center's right to exclude, it would have had to employ the Due Process Clause to place severe limits on the State's ability to define and condition property rights. Such a ruling would have altered settled doctrine governing the state's police power to regulate property rights and possibly invited a return to the discredited "*Lochner* era."[146]

---

[143] *Id.* at 83.

[144] *Id.* at 85–88. The Court distinguished Wooley v. Maynard, 430 U.S. 705 (1977), the license plate motto case, by reasoning that, unlike the automobile registrant, the shopping center owner had opened his property to the public generally, was not being compelled to carry a specific, state-mandated message on his property, would not be identified with the views expressed by the speakers, and could easily and expressly disavow any connection with or support for the message. Miami Herald Pub. Co. v. Tornillo, 418 U.S. 241 (1974) was held inapposite as an editorial discretion case. See generally Gaebler, note 5 *supra*.

[145] Justice Marshall, the author of the Warren Court's *Logan Valley* decision, reiterated his objection to the Court's approach. *Id.* at 91.

[146] Some members of the Court have hurled the Lochner charge at decisions revitalizing the Contract Clause. See United States Trust Co. v. New Jersey, 431 U.S. 1, 60–61 (1977) (Brennan, J., dissenting); Allied Structural Steel Co. v. Spannaus, 438 U.S. 234, 259–62 (1978) (Brennan, J., dissenting). But the Court has not evinced an inclination to return to *Lochner*. See, *e.g.*, Minnesota v. Clover Leaf Creamery Co., 449 U.S. 456 (1981). See Bishop v. Wood, 426 U.S. 341 (1976); Flagg Bros. Inc. v. Brooks, 436 U.S. 149 (1978); Penn Central Transportation Co. v. New York City, 438 U.S. 104 (1978); Agins v. Tiburon, 447 U.S. 255 (1980); Texaco, Inc. v. Short, 102 S. Ct. 781 (1982). *Cf.* Hodel v. Virginia Surface Mining and Reclamation Ass'n, Inc., 452 U.S. 264 (1981); Donovan v. Dewey, 452 U.S. 594 (1981).

In short, the Court's *PruneYard* decision did not prefer First Amendment rights at the expense of property rights. It upheld the expansive power of states to define, expand, or contract property rights.

The Princeton University case, had it not been mooted,[147] would have permitted the Supreme Court to test the reach of *PruneYard*. In *PruneYard* the state law readjustment of property rights was targeted, in a civil proceeding, on a traditional commercial enterprise which advanced no strong First Amendment interests of its own. In the Princeton case, state criminal law was applied to property owned by a private educational institution claiming both property and speech rights in controlling its premises. In such circumstances, following the *Hudgens* theory, the balance might tilt against allowance of a free speech easement for demonstrators. That was certainly the thrust of the *Loretto* decision,[148] where the Court upheld the rights of landlords to refuse to allow cable television wires to be installed on their property for tenants' use. In finding a "taking" by virtue of "a permanent physical occupation of real property," the Court again manifested its inclination to protect property rights against speech-related claims.

b) "Public" property. Just as *Marsh v. Alabama* is the baseline to examine speech rights on private property, Justice Robert's plurality opinion in *Hague v. CIO* is the standard to measure speech rights on publicly owned property. Rejecting a property-centered conception of the First Amendment, he said: "Wherever the title of streets and parks may rest, they have immemorially been held in trust for the use of the public and, time out of mind, have been used for purposes of assembly, communicating thoughts between citizens, and discussing public questions."[149] The Warren Court was generous in applying this principle to invalidate government restrictions on the use of streets and other public places for First Amendment purposes, including demonstrations before a State House,[150] the home of a mayor,[151] and an Army recruiting station.[152]

---

[147] See text *supra* at notes 12–17.

[148] See text *supra* at notes 18–20.

[149] 307 U.S. at 515.

[150] Edwards v. South Carolina, 372 U.S. 229 (1963).

[151] Gregory v. City of Chicago, 394 U.S. 111 (1969).

[152] Bachellar v. Maryland, 397 U.S. 564 (1970).

These decisions reflect the tension between two approaches to free speech use of publicly owned property. Either government premises open to the public are appropriate forums for speech activity which does not interfere with the functioning of the facility or government may control its property in the same fashion as a private owner to exclude those who would enter for speech activity. The speech-protective approach was demonstrated in *Brown v. Louisiana*,[153] where the Court overturned a breach of the peace conviction of five young black protesters who conducted a silent vigil inside a segregated public library. Justice Fortas found that First Amendment freedoms included "the right in a peaceable and orderly manner to protest by silent and reproachful presence, in a place where the protestant has every right to be, the unconstitutional segregation of public facilities."[154] Justice Black's sharp dissent made the contrary point: "[The First Amendment] does not guarantee to any person the right to use someone else's property, even that owned by government and dedicated to other purposes, as a stage to express dissident ideas."[155] Just a few months later, Justice Black's property views prevailed in a case upholding trespass convictions of civil rights protesters for gathering outside a jail, but upon jail premises. In rejecting the First Amendment claim, Justice Black insisted:[156]

> The State, no less than a private owner of property, has power to preserve the property under its control for the use to which it is lawfully dedicated. For this reason, there is no merit to the petitioners' argument that they had a constitutional right to stay on the property, over the jail custodian's objections, because this "area chosen for the peaceful civil rights demonstration was not only 'reasonable' but also particularly appropriate."

Since the Warren Court was sharply divided in both cases, the Burger Court was free from precedential restraint in determining its approach to governmental control of speech uses of public property. The initial results were inconclusive.

In a 1974 case, *Lehman v. City of Shaker Heights*,[157] the Court split over whether a municipally owned and operated bus company

---

[153] 383 U.S. 131 (1966).

[154] *Id.* at 142.

[155] *Id.* at 166.

[156] Adderley v. Florida, 385 U.S. 39, 47 (1966).

[157] 418 U.S. 298 (1974).

could refuse to accept political advertisements on city-owned buses while allowing commercial messages to be displayed. Justice Black-mun's plurality opinion, finding that no public forum for ideas had been created, characterized the city as acting like a private entrepreneur:[158]

> [T]he city is engaged in commerce. . . . The car card space . . . is a part of the commercial venture. . . . No First Amendment forum is here to be found. The city consciously has limited access to its transit system advertising space in order to minimize chances of abuse, the appearance of favoritism, and the risk of imposing on a captive audience. These are reasonable legislative objectives advanced by the city in a proprietary capacity.

Justice Douglas concurred, observing that the advertising space, if a forum at all, "is more akin to a newspaper than to a park" and, like a newspaper, the city "owner cannot be forced to include in his offerings news or other items which outsiders may desire but which the owner abhors."[159] The dissenters insisted that the city had created a public forum by permitting some advertising and that it was thereby impermissible to deny access on the basis of content or subject matter or to permit commercial messages while prohibiting political communication.

The *Lehman* decision tends to confirm our property thesis in two ways. The Court sanctioned municipal dominion over its property as a sufficient basis to restrict speech and it upheld state discrimination in favor of commercial speech over political speech.[160]

Government's control of its property was solidified in 1976 when the Army prohibited political speeches and leaflet distribution on the premises of Fort Dix, New Jersey, even on portions of the military post generally open to the public. In *Greer v. Spock*,[161] the

---

[158] *Id.* at 303–4.

[159] *Id.* at 306.

[160] In Southeastern Promotions, Ltd. v. Conrad, 420 U.S. 546 (1975), a city had denied the use of its municipal theater to the rock musical *Hair* on the ground that the production was obscene. Justice Blackmun, without reference to his *Lehman* opinion, concluded that the city's action "was no less a prior restraint because the public facilities under their control happened to be municipal theaters. The [facilities] were public forums designed for and dedicated to expressive activities," 420 U.S. at 555. Justice Rehnquist dissented, relying on *Adderley* for the position that the city, as owner of the theater, had broad leeway to decide what productions should be permitted. See Karst, *Public Enterprise and the Public Forum: A Comment on* Southeastern Promotions, Ltd. v. Conrad, 37 OHIO ST. L.J. 247, 248–52 (1976); Stone, *Restrictions of Speech Because of Its Content: The Peculiar Case of Subject-Matter Restrictions*, 46 U. CHI. L. REV. 81, 90–92 (1978).

[161] 424 U.S. 828 (1976).

Court sharply limited a 1972 decision that had permitted such activity on the open portions of a base.[162] It said:[163]

> The Court of Appeals was mistaken . . . in thinking that [the 1972 decision] stands for the principle that whenever members of the public are permitted freely to visit a place owned or operated by the Government, then that place becomes a "public forum" for purposes of the First Amendment. . . . "The State, no less than a private owner of property, has power to preserve the property under its control for the use of which it is lawfully dedicated."

The Court readily upheld the military regulation.[164]

The Court has since applied these principles to permit military commanders broad power to regulate speech activities within a military base even by military personnel properly on the base[165] and to treat prison facilities as "off-limits" to the application of normal First Amendment activities: "A prison may be no more easily converted into a public forum than a military base."[166]

Most recently, in *United States Postal Service v. Council of Green-burgh Civic Associations*,[167] the Court has confirmed its willingness to accord government broad power to restrict speech that impairs governmental control of its property. The issue was whether a postal statute, prohibiting the deposit of unstamped "mailable matter" in a letter box approved as an "authorized depository" by the postal service, violated the First Amendment rights of civic groups which delivered unstamped messages and leaflets in the letter boxes

---

[162] Flower v. United States, 407 U.S. 197 (1972).

[163] 424 U.S. at 836. The Court also observed that excluding the political speakers served the "American constitutional tradition of a politically neutral military establishment under civilian control." *Id.* at 839.

[164] *Greer's* sharp limitation of *Flower* was similar to the Court's analysis two weeks earlier, in Hudgens v. NLRB, 424 U.S. 507 (1976) of the *Logan Valley/Lloyd Center* sequence. Justice Rehnquist has described *Greer* as a case reflecting the "sovereign's" role as "proprietor and owner of property, such as buildings or parks." *The First Amendment: Freedom, Philosophy and the Law*, 12 Gonz. L. Rev. 1, 10–11 (1976). See also Consolidated Edison Co. v. Public Service Commission, 447 U.S. 530 (1980); Board of Education, Island Trees Union Free School District v. Pico, 102 S. Ct. 2799, 2812 (1982) (Blackmun, J., concurring); *id.* at 2827 (Rehnquist, J., dissenting). Justice Rehnquist recently reiterated his views on government's power over its property. Dallas County Hospital District v. Dallas Ass'n of Community Organizations for Reform Now, *cert. denied*, 51 U.S.L.W. 3417 (Nov. 29, 1982) (Rehnquist, J., dissenting).

[165] See Brown v. Glines, 444 U.S. 348 (1980).

[166] Jones v. North Carolina Prisoners' Union, 433 U.S. 119, 134 (1977); see also Bell v. Wolfish, 441 U.S. 520, 548–55 (1979); Houchins v. KQED, 438 U.S. 1 (1978).

[167] 453 U.S. 114 (1981).

of private homes. After canvassing the history and functions of the postal service, Justice Rehnquist concluded that even though the homeowner "pays for the physical components" of the "authorized depository," the homeowner "agrees to abide by the Postal Service's regulations in exchange for the Postal Service agreeing to deliver and pick up his mail."[168] The Court analyzed the case in terms of government ownership of the property in question. In this light, the result was foreordained:[169]

> Indeed, it is difficult to conceive of any reason why this Court should treat a letterbox differently for First Amendment access purposes than it has in the past treated the military base in *Greer* . . . , the jail or prison in *Jones*, . . . or the advertising space made available in city rapid transit cars in *Lehman*, . . . In all these cases, this Court recognized that the First Amendment does not guarantee access to property simply because it is owned or controlled by the government.

The Court determined that it was unnecessary to address "time, place and manner" issues in order to conclude that the postal statute restriction did not violate the First Amendment.

As he had in *Adderley*, *Lehman*, and *Greer*, Justice Brennan adopted a different approach:[170]

> . . . Our cases have recognized generally that public properties are appropriate fora for exercise of First Amendment rights. . . . While First Amendment rights exercised on public property may be subject to reasonable time, place and manner restrictions, that is very different from saying that government-controlled property, such as a letterbox, does not constitute a public forum.

And Justice Marshall maintained in dissent that "[t]he determinative question in each of these [earlier] cases was not whether the government owned or controlled the property, but whether the nature of the governmental interests warranted the restrictions on expression. That is the question properly asked in this case."[171]

Justice Marshall's point is telling. For the Burger Court, the

---

[168] *Id.* at 128.

[169] *Id.* at 129–30.

[170] *Id.* at 136–37. Justice Brennan found the statute a reasonable time, place, and manner rule.

[171] *Id.* at 149 n.7. *Cf.* Heffron v. Int'l Society for Krishna Consciousness, 452 U.S. 640 (1981); Widmar v. Vincent, 102 S. Ct. 269 (1981).

question "whether the government owned or controlled the property" has been central, and the issue "whether the nature of the governmental interest warranted the restrictions on expression" has been marginal. Instead of determining whether the precise nature of the facility rendered the speech activity "anomalous" or "basically incompatible" with the property's primary functions, the Court has permitted formal ownership and control of property to be decisive.

2. *Residential property.* The government won the postal case because it was found to have had the superior property-type interests in the mailbox. Justice Stevens's dissenting opinion was equally steeped in property considerations:[172]

> The mailbox is private property; it is not a public forum to which the owner must grant access. If the owner does not want to receive any written communications other than stamped mail, he should be permitted to post the equivalent of a "no trespassing" sign on his mailbox. A statute that protects his privacy by prohibiting unsolicited and unwanted deposits on his property would surely be valid.

Justice Stevens's concern with "unwanted deposits" of free speech on private property evokes other instances of tension between free speech claims and protection of the value of residential and commercial property.

In a cluster of cases involving diverse issues such as door-to-door canvassing, regulation of pornography and sexually oriented material, and zoning, the Court has approached First Amendment claims with the zeal of urban planners. This tendency was evident in three cases putting homeowners' rights of property and privacy against the rights of free speech of canvassers and picketers. In each instance the Court was able to decide the case without resolving the clash between property rights and speech claims, but it used strong language indicating that homeowners' rights would prevail over speakers'.

In 1976, the Court reviewed an ordinance that required, for "identification" purposes, advance notice in writing to the police by "any person desiring to canvass . . . or call from house to house [for] a recognized charitable [or] political . . . cause."[173] The Court in-

---

[172] 453 U.S. at 152. Justice Stevens dissented because the statute interfered with the homeowners' right to decide whether they wanted to receive the messages.

[173] Hynes v. Mayor of Oradell, 425 U.S. 610 (1976).

validated the ordinance on vagueness grounds. Six Justices concluded that, "vagueness defects aside, an ordinance of this kind would ordinarily withstand constitutional attack."[174] A similar approach was taken in a case involving a local ordinance that prohibited door-to-door solicitation by charitable organizations that devoted more than twenty-five percent of their revenue to organizational expenses. The Court reaffirmed that such solicitation, even though involving political and charitable causes, can be regulated by government in order to protect the privacy of homeowners against fraud, crime, or annoyance.[175] The particular ordinance was invalidated, however, because the twenty-five-percent limitation did not bear a sufficiently substantial relationship to such goals.

The Court also addressed these issues in a case involving residential picketing. A civil rights group challenged an Illinois statute that had the effect of preventing demonstrations on the public sidewalks in front of the home of the Mayor of Chicago. The Court invalidated the statute on equal protection grounds because it exempted certain kinds of labor dispute picketing from the general prohibition on residential picketing.[176] It expressly left unresolved the question "whether a statute barring all residential picketing regardless of its subject matter would violate the First and Fourteenth Amendments."[177] But, in dictum, the majority asserted the broad protection that it would afford to privacy, even against free speech claims, where the ban on residential picketing was content neutral:[178] "The State's interest in protecting the well-being, tranquility, and privacy of the home is certainly of the highest order in a free and civilized society." While the Court's decision invalidated a particular ban on residential picketing at the behest of free speech claimants, its message that homeowners be permitted the quiet use and enjoyment of their property against free speech claims may be its more lasting element.

3. *Property "values."* A series of Burger Court First Amendment rulings reflect basic concern for the protection of property interests.

---

[174] *Id.* at 623. This was Justice Brennan's characterization of the majority opinion.

[175] Village of Schaumburg v. Citizens for a Better Environment, 444 U.S. 620 (1980).

[176] Carey v. Brown, 447 U.S. 445 (1980). Justice Brennan's opinion found the case "constitutionally indistinguishable" from Police Department of Chicago v. Mosley, 408 U.S. 92 (1972).

[177] 447 U.S. at 459 n.2.

[178] *Id.* at 470, 471.

The most important of these relate to sexually oriented speech. For example, the Court rejected a challenge to the notion that there exists a distinct category of "obscene" speech, which can be regulated in ways constitutionally unacceptable for other forms of expression.[179] These decisions also confound normal First Amendment doctrine by permitting plenary regulation of a category of speech causing no demonstrable harm.[180]

In the watershed case, *Paris Adult Theaters I*, the majority relied on the proposition, foreign to First Amendment adjudication, that the Court is not "a super-legislature to determine the wisdom, need and propriety of laws that touch economic problems, business affairs, or social conditions."[181] The preoccupation with commercial, economic, and property matters is particularly noteworthy when it is recalled that the issue was whether government could prohibit the availability of "adults only" sexual ideas to willing adult recipients. A 1969 Warren Court decision had found a First Amendment right to receive such ideas, albeit in the privacy of the home, superior to the claimed harm resulting from access to obscenity.[182] In rejecting that precedent, Chief Justice Burger emphasized governmental interests of a different order:[183]

> [T]here are legitimate state interests at stake in stemming the tide of commercialized obscenity, even assuming it is feasible to enforce effective safeguards against exposure to juveniles and to passersby. . . . [These] include the interest of the public in the quality of life and the total community environment, the tone of commerce in the great city centers, and, possibly, the public safety itself.

It is surprising that such interests, primarily rooted in notions of environmental pollution, aesthetic zoning, and preservation of commercial areas, would be found paramount to free speech concerns. Similarly curious was the Court's insistence that just as government is free to act on the basis of "unprovable assumptions" in the "regulation of commercial and business affairs," it has compar-

---

[179] Miller v. California, 413 U.S. 15 (1973); Paris Adult Theatre I v. Slaton, 413 U.S. 49 (1973).

[180] The Report of the Commission on Obscenity and Pornography (1970); DE GRAZIA & NEWMAN, BANNED FILMS: MOVIES, CENSORS AND THE FIRST AMENDMENT (1982).

[181] U.S. at 64 (quoting Griswold v. Connecticut, 381 U.S. 479, 482 [1965]).

[182] See Stanley v. Georgia, 394 U.S. 557 (1969).

[183] 413 U.S. at 57–58.

ably broad leeway to regulate speech:[184] "Understandably, those who entertain an absolutist view of the First Amendment find it uncomfortable to explain why rights of association, speech and press should be severely restrained in the marketplace of goods and money, but not in the marketplace of pornography." In this view, if government is permitted to regulate speech in the economic marketplace to further the community welfare, it can regulate other forms of speech in the same fashion. Speech interests will be subordinated to the goal of achieving clean, stable, and orderly downtown areas, and the property and economic interests promoted by such developments.

These priorities became more explicit three years later in *Young v. American Mini Theatres.*[185] The Court upheld a Detroit zoning ordinance which differentiated between motion picture theaters and bookstores that exhibited sexually explicit "adult" books and movies and those which did not. The ordinance required that such establishments not be located within 1,000 feet of any two other "regulated uses" or within 500 feet of a residential area. All Justices recognized that the regulated establishments offered materials that were not within the constitutional definition of obscenity. Nevertheless, a five-to-four majority upheld the ordinance, relying in part on a finding of the Detroit Common Council that "some uses of property are especially injurious to a neighborhood when they are concentrated in limited areas."[186] Justice Powell's concurring opinion is even more clearly dominated by property considerations. He viewed the case as "an example of innovative land-use regulation, implicating First Amendment concerns only incidentally and to a limited extent."[187]

In many of these cases property interests conflict—the free speech and property rights of commercial purveyors of books and movies are arrayed against the property owners of the surrounding community. The *Detroit* case curbed the rights of the owners of regulated establishments in the course of protecting the value of the surrounding property against uses which, in the city's words, "ad-

---

[184] *Id.* at 62.

[185] 427 U.S. 50 (1976).

[186] *Id.* at 54.

[187] *Id.* at 73.

versely affect[ed] property values."[188] By contrast, when the proprietor of a drive-in movie showing sexually suggestive films succeeded in invalidating a restrictive ordinance, the counterpoised property interests of the community were not deemed as weighty—the screen was on a busy highway and visible only from two adjacent streets and a little used church parking lot—and the restriction was not imposed as part of a comprehensive zoning plan designed to protect property values.[189]

The concept that speech may be controlled to the extent of its deleterious effect on surrounding property interests also worked its way into a decision that upheld FCC regulation of a radio monologue that was found to be "indecent but not obscene" because it included "dirty words."[190] Although the case can be explained in terms of federal power over the air waves, as well as domestic privacy, Justice Stevens, who wrote the *Detroit* decision, underscored his rejection of the free speech claim by analogy to the zoning power:[191]

> The Commission's decision rested entirely on a nuisance rationale under which context is all important. . . . As Mr. Justice Sutherland wrote, a "nuisance may be merely a right thing in the wrong place—like a pig in the parlor instead of the barnyard." *Euclid v. Ambler Realty Co.* . . . We simply hold that when the Commission finds that a pig has entered the parlor, the exercise of its regulatory power does not depend on proof that the pig is obscene.

Speech and property values clashed again in *Metromedia, Inc. v. City of San Diego*,[192] which tested the validity of municipal zoning restrictions against billboards. Five separate opinions resulted in a narrow invalidation of the ordinance because some forms of bill-

---

[188] *Id.* at 55.

[189] Erznoznik v. City of Jacksonville, 422 U.S. 205 (1975). See also Moore v. City of East Cleveland, 431 U.S. 494 (1977).

[190] FCC v. Pacifica Foundation, 438 U.S. 726 (1978).

[191] *Id.* at 750. Recent Burger Court decisions confirm that local government, at least in some contexts, may subordinate speech interests to property and community values through the careful exercise of the zoning power. Vance v. Universal Amusement Co., 445 U.S. 308 (1980); Schad v. Borough of Mount Ephraim, 452 U.S. 61 (1981). Recently, however, the Court invalidated, on separation grounds, a statute designed to shield churches from close proximity to premises where liquor is sold. Larkin v. Grendel's Den, Inc., 103 S. Ct. ——— (1982).

[192] 453 U.S. 490 (1981).

board advertising were permitted while others were proscribed. But seven members of the Court, relying in part on the ordinance's purpose "to safeguard and enhance property values," would permit broad, nondiscriminatory prohibition of billboards in order to achieve the "twin goals [of] traffic safety and the appearance of the city."[193]

A four-Justice plurality interpreted the ordinance as permitting some "on-site" billboard advertising: "The occupant of property may advertise his own goods or services; he may not advertise the goods or services of others, nor may he display most noncommercial messages."[194] The plurality found it constitutionally permissible for a city allowing on-site billboards to ban "off-site" commercial advertising on billboards, because commercial speech is entitled to lesser protection and thus subject to broader regulation. To that extent, the "city's land-use interests" outweighed "the commercial interests of those seeking to purvey goods and services within the city."[195] The defect in the ordinance was that the city allowed some kinds of commercial billboards but prohibited other kinds of noncommercial messages without adequate justification for the content distinctions.

Justices Brennan and Blackmun, though willing to recognize the validity of some "place and manner" restrictions on billboards, found the ordinance broadly unconstitutional as an unjustified total ban on an important medium of communication:[196]

> . . . the city has failed to show that its asserted interest in aesthetics is sufficiently substantial in the commercial and industrial areas of San Diego. I do not doubt that "[i]t is within the power of the [city] to determine that the community should be beautiful," . . . but that power may not be exercised in contravention of the First Amendment.

Chief Justice Burger's dissent, evoking his opinions in the 1973 obscenity decisions, saw the issues differently:[197]

---

[193] *Id.* at 507.

[194] *Id.* at 503.

[195] *Id.* at 512.

[196] *Id.* at 530.

[197] *Id.* at 557, 559–60. Justice Rehnquist's dissent was even more succinct: "[T]he aesthetic justification alone is sufficient to sustain a total prohibition of billboards within a community." *Id.* at 570.

[W]e are discussing a very simple and basic question: the authority of local government to protect its citizens' legitimate interests
in traffic safety and the environment by eliminating distracting
and ugly structures from its building and roadways, to define
which billboards actually pose that danger, and to decide
whether, in certain instances, the public's need for the information outweighs the dangers perceived.

Justice Stevens also stressed the property theme in his dissent.
Comparing billboards to graffiti, he reasoned that both forms of
expression could be banned:[198]

It seems to be accepted by all that a zoning regulation excluding billboards from residential neighborhoods is justified by the
interest in maintaining pleasant surroundings and *enhancing property values*. The same interests are at work in commercial and
industrial zones. . . . Those interests are both psychological and
economic. *The character of the environment affects property values* and
the quality of life not only for the suburban resident, but equally
for the individual who toils in a factory or invests his capital in
industrial properties.

Finding no censorial motive for the ordinance, Justice Stevens
found it constitutional.

The billboard decision is instructive. When speech interests conflict with property and environmental values protected by government through zoning measures, speech will take second place to the
interests in "enhancing property values" and preventing "ugly" and
"unsightly eyesores." Attractive urban centers and quiet and orderly residential communities are surely important, but they
should not be achieved at the expense of the First Amendment.
Urban planning goals and zoning schemes should not enjoy "talis-
manic immunity"[199] from close First Amendment scrutiny. Moreover, the Court's preference for neat, orderly commercial and
residential environments, wholly uncluttered by "unsightly"
manifestations of free speech, stands in sharp contrast to a different
perception of the untidiness that society must tolerate to maintain

---

[198] *Id.* at 552 (emphasis added).

[199] Young v. American Mini Theatres, 427 U.S. 50, 75 (1976) (Powell, J., concurring);
Schad v. Mt. Ephraim, 452 U.S. 61, 101 S. Ct. 2176, 2187 (1981) (Blackmun, J., concurring).
For an extremely helpful analysis of these issues, see Costonis, *Law and Aesthetics: A Critique
and a Reformation of the Dilemmas*, 80 MICH. L. REV. 355, 446–58 (1972).

the values of free expression. As Justice Harlan stated in *Cohen v. California*:[200]

> To many, the immediate consequence of this freedom may often appear to be only verbal tumult, discord, and even offensive utterance. These are, however, within established limits, in truth necessary side effects of the broader enduring values which the process of open debate permits us to achieve. That the air may at times seem filled with verbal cacophony is, in this sense, not a sign of weakness, but of strength.

IV. CONCLUSION

The apparently close link between the Burger Court's free speech decisions and traditional property interests is consistent with a decade of jurisprudence in the Supreme Court. An older concept that a primary office of civil liberties is to safeguard the liberty of property and contract has reemerged. For most of two centuries the protection of property and contract was viewed as the cornerstone of the protection of liberty. John Adams went so far as to say, "Property must be secured or liberty cannot exist."[201] More recently Justice Stewart observed: " . . . a fundamental interdependence exists between the personal right to liberty and the personal right in property. . . . That rights in property are basic civil rights has long been recognized."[202] And the originator of the "new property" concept believed that property—"new" or "old"—and liberty were inextricably intertwined in providing the individual a buffer against the state.[203]

We do not denigrate the important role of private property as a protector of civil liberties. Nor do we suggest that free speech and property are inherently antithetical. Although they may frequently be in conflict, the values embodied in the two concepts play a complementary role in the maintenance of liberal democracy, however imperfect. As the Court has observed: "[T]he Framers of the

---

[200] 403 U.S. at 24–25 (1971).

[201] ADAMS, DISCOURSES ON DAVILA (1789–90), *quoted in* COKER, DEMOCRACY, LIBERTY, AND PROPERTY 466 (1947). See FREUND, THE SUPREME COURT OF THE UNITED STATES 35–37 (1961).

[202] Lynch v. Household Finance Corp., 405 U.S. 538, 552 (1972).

[203] Reich, note 21 *supra*, at 786–87. See also MICHELMAN, note 36 *supra*.

Constitution certainly did not think these fundamental rights of a free society are incompatible with each other."[204]

By the same token, it is unnecessary to take the position that property interests should always be subordinated to free speech values. Thus, even a low-decibel speaker could not properly assert a right to orate or even to converse in another's living room without permission. Nor is it clear that someone wishing to open a bookstore in a neighborhood zoned for residential use could validly complain that the First Amendment provided a right that overrode a neutrally applied zoning law.

Individual ownership of property is thus closely linked to civil liberty. That is not to say that property concepts must underlie protection of free speech. We see no basis in principle for this in light of the independent values that gird the First Amendment. These purposes are well known and can be briefly summarized. The first is individual fulfillment through self-expression. As Justice Brandeis put it: "the final end of the State [is] to make men free to develop their faculties."[205] The second major justification stresses concepts of self-government and political democracy. This theory of free speech was powerfully formulated by Professor Alexander Meiklejohn and, in a well-known passage, underlined by Justice Brennan, who affirmed the "profound national commitment to the principle that debate on public issues should be uninhibited, robust, and wide-open."[206] The third major purpose of the First Amendment is its purifying quality in advancing knowledge and discovering truth. Or, in Justice Holmes' metaphor, "the best test of truth is the power of the thought to get itself accepted in the competition of the market."[207] And finally, "freedom of expression is a method of achieving a more adaptable and hence a more stable community, of maintaining the precarious balance between healthy cleavage and necessary consensus."[208]

These are the classic purposes of the First Amendment. Each alone may not be compelling, but their sum posits a powerful case

[204] Lloyd Corp. v. Tanner, 407 U.S. 551, 570 (1972).
[205] Whitney v. California, 274 U.S. 357, 375 (1927).
[206] New York Times Co. v. Sullivan, 376 U.S. 254, 270 (1964).
[207] Abrams v. United States, 250 U.S. 616, 630 (1919).
[208] EMERSON, note 48 *supra*, at 7.

for free expression. We see no reason to diminish constitutional protection when property interests clash with free speech values. After considerable exposure to both academic discourse and court-room combat relating to free speech, we have rarely found a person who openly belittles the worth of the constitutional guarantee. To the contrary, everyone professes to support it. Why then the sharp differences among judges and scholars? We suggest that these turn not merely on whether the disputants agree with purposes of the First Amendment but rather on the degree to which they embrace them.[209] The degree of adherence cannot of course be measured, but it is palpable when one reads judicial opinions, law review articles, or even the briefs of lawyers. Like Justice Stewart's approach to hard-core obscenity, one knows it when one sees it. Contrast, for example, Justice Holmes' opinion in *Schenck*[210] with his dissent in *Abrams*.[211] Compare the opinion of Justice Harlan in *Barenblatt*[212] with the Harlan of *Cohen v. California*.[213] Stack up the opinions of Justice Frankfurter against those of Justices Black and Douglas, and the articles of Alexander Bickel and Philip Kurland against those of Thomas Emerson and Harry Kalven, Jr. The differences are intellectual only in part.

The Court's pattern of downgrading free speech when it has appeared to conflict with proprietary rights asserted by individuals, corporations, or even government expresses an erroneous set of priorities. The Court has treated the First Amendment merely as one more factor to be weighed in the constitutional balance rather than as the first among equals in the American pantheon of liberty.[214]

Free speech and property in fact represent different sorts of constitutional liberty. Property is bottomed on protection of wealth

---

[209] Justice Frankfurter was making much the same point when he responded to Justice Holmes's famous dictum that "[g]eneral propositions do not decide concrete cases," *Lochner v. New York*, 198 U.S. 45, 76 (1905), by observing, "Whether they do or not often depends on the strength of the conviction with which such 'general propositions' are held." *Harris v. United States*, 331 U.S. 145, 157 (1947) (dissenting opinion). See Dorsen, Book Review, 95 HARV. L. REV. 367, 384 (1981).

[210] Schenck v. United States, 249 U.S. 47 (1919).

[211] Abrams v. United States, 250 U.S. 616 (1919).

[212] Barenblatt v. United States, 360 U.S. 109 (1959).

[213] 403 U.S. 15 (1971).

[214] See McKay, *The Preference for Freedom*, 34 N.Y.U.L. REV. 1182 (1959).

and "settled expectations," within the larger context of a model of society that is orderly, stable, prudent, and rational. Robust free speech, by contrast, can be untidy, boisterous, and risky. But the alternative of viewing free speech as just another "value" among many presents far greater costs. We cast our lot with the risk takers: Justice Brandeis of *Whitney*,[215] Justice Douglas of *Brandenburg*,[216] and Justice Harlan of *Cohen*, when he expressed his conservative faith in freedom as follows:[217]

> The constitutional right of free expression is powerful medicine in a society as diverse and populous as ours. It is designed and intended to remove governmental restraints from the arena of public discussion, putting the decision as to what views shall be voiced largely into the hands of each of us, in the hope that use of such freedom will ultimately produce a more capable citizenry and more perfect polity and in the belief that no other approach would comport with the premise of individual dignity and choice upon which our political system rests.

---

[215] Whitney v. California, 274 U.S. 357 (1927).

[216] Brandenburg v. Ohio, 395 U.S. 444 (1969).

[217] Cohen v. California, 403 U.S. 15, 24 (1971).

L . A . P O W E , J R .

MASS SPEECH AND THE NEWER FIRST AMENDMENT

I. INTRODUCTION

Our mass society has produced a problem in freedom of speech that appears to be without precedent. Many individuals and organizations that wish to communicate to and to influence others choose to do so through the mass media. These speakers have little or no interest in speaking individually to a handful of people. Instead their First Amendment is one that looks to mass speech, that is, speech where either a broadcasting station or a newspaper is used in order to reach thousands of potential—and often accidental—listeners. Mass speech differs from the paradigm First Amendment situation, that of the lone dissenter, in a number of respects. By definition, the idea of a limited audience is absent. The speech itself wholly lacks spontaneity. What is said is carefully constructed and presented to specification either in a written form

L. A. Powe, Jr., is Hines H. and Thelma Kelley Baker Professor of Jurisprudence, University of Texas.

AUTHOR'S NOTE: I would like to thank David B. Filvaroff, Douglas Laycock, Sanford V. Levinson, and Thomas G. Krattenmaker for their generosity in giving both time and criticisms on earlier drafts of this article. While this article was in press, two additional articles advocating the opposition conclusion appeared: Wright, *Money and the Pollution of Politics: Is the First Amendment an Obstacle to Political Equality?* 82 COLUM. L. REV. 609 (1982); and Lowenstein, *Campaign Spending and Ballot Propositions: Recent Experience, Public Choice Theory and the First Amendment*, 29 U.C.L.A.L. REV. 505 (1982). These articles are richer, more detailed, and a significant improvement over the existing literature. Indeed, had Judge Wright's article been available sooner, it would have been the most frequently cited source in this article. Nevertheless, for precisely the reasons expressed in text, I think Wright and Lowenstein are fundamentally in error in their approach to the First Amendment.

or in a broadcasting spot. It typically is breathtakingly short and deceptively simplistic, demanding amplification and clarification. But mass speech permits no contact between speaker and listener. There is no potential for a dialogue. Indeed, in all probability the speaker does not want one. Like so much else in our modern society, mass speech is wholly impersonal.[1]

The legal problems relating to mass speech are radically new compared to those of the lone dissenter, for two reasons. First, the world of lawyers and judges is the world of judicial opinions. If something is not there, all too frequently it might as well not exist. And problems of mass speech and the mass media during the first 180 years of the Supreme Court have been all but nonexistent in the United States Reports. Those that did sneak in, from Huey Long's unsuccessful effort to silence his urban opposition[2] to Alabama's declaration of war on the *New York Times*,[3] seem too easy—almost sports. Second, television and radio appear to make mass speech look more immediate, more powerful, more effective.

---

[1] Implicitly this paragraph evokes the concept of a Golden Age when things were both different and better. Much of the writing on mass communications opts for this technique and finds a wonderous past: the fifties in television, the thirties in radio, and the time of the ratification of the First Amendment for print. This is nothing short of the equivalent of Adam and Eve in the Garden of Eden and should be taken no more seriously. Furthermore, mass speech is not all that new although television ads are. Use of whatever constituted the more "mass" media has always been the way of more effective opposition to a governmental course of action. If Watergate was not publicized by Woodward and Bernstein taking to a soapbox, neither did the Jeffersonians go at John Adams through solo dissent. Although there are no Supreme Court cases to prove it, Presidents—from George Washington on—were hounded and bothered not by puny anonymities but by people who knew how to use whatever form of mass communication was at hand. And with the exception of John Adams, SMITH, FREEDOM'S FETTERS (1956), Thomas Jefferson, LEVY, JEFFERSON AND CIVIL LIBERTIES 42–69 (1963), and Abraham Lincoln, RANDALL, CONSTITUTIONAL PROBLEMS UNDER LINCOLN 77–81, 176–83, 492–505 (rev. ed. 1951), Presidents did not look to the legal system as a means to handle opposition by mass communication. Once sedition was rejected (politically, if not legally), effective tools did not exist and dissent was tolerated if hardly enjoyed.

Thus Presidents from Washington through Jackson and Van Buren were faced with a politically partisan opposition press that played on the fear of an American monarchy in their free use of the label "King." CUNLIFFE, AMERICAN PRESIDENTS AND THE PRESIDENCY 33, 70–1, 76–80, 89 (1972). When the partisan press gave way to the penny press, Presidents and politicians fared no better, as the 1884 candidates Grover Cleveland and James G. Blaine learned in a campaign of offending jingles. NEVINS, GROVER CLEVELAND 177, 180 (1932); CUNLIFFE, *supra* at 233. Nor did the next change, from the penny press to the new mass newspapers, improve performance, as William Randolph Hearst and Joseph Pulitzer and yellow journalism pushed President McKinley into war with Spain. Tebbel, *The Presidents and the Press*, in DOLCE & SKAU, eds., POWER AND THE PRESIDENCY 242 (1976).

[2] Grosjean v. American Press, 297 U.S. 233 (1936).

[3] New York Times v. Sullivan, 376 U.S. 254 (1964).

Jerome Barron, writing in the Harvard Law Review, focused attention on aspects of the mass speech problem when he labeled the traditional First Amendment concern over suppressing the lone dissenter "The Romantic View of the First Amendment."[4] From Barron's insightful perspective, "when the soap box yields to radio [and television] and the political pamphlet to the monopoly newspaper," the crucial First Amendment issues shift to concerns of private power blocking access to the marketplace of ideas.[5] Barron and others following his lead have attempted to correct the perceived market failure either by guaranteeing individuals some form of access to the mass media or by attempting to restructure the mass media in order to promote diversity.[6] I shall not discuss those important issues. Instead I wish to focus on a different aspect of the perceived problem in the marketplace: the possibility that even if differing viewpoints are present there may be so overwhelming a predominance of communication in support of some of them that other viewpoints simply do not have a chance to be considered on the merits. For those who believe this occurs there is the not unnatural conclusion that the prevailing viewpoint has done so in an unfair way. Had the issue been joined between equals, a differing viewpoint would (or might) have prevailed. Most typically such concerns are expressed in the context of elections, and over the past decade there have been a variety of attempts to even up the potential clash of ideas through either contribution or expenditure limitations on candidates and their supporters.

Since 1976 the Supreme Court has decided cases in the area almost annually. Most recently, in *Common Cause v. Schmitt*[7] it divided evenly on the issue whether the First Amendment protected massive "unauthorized" expenditures by various conservative organizations in support of Ronald Reagan's candidacy in the 1980 election. The structure of argument in the campaign finance cases is fairly simple.[8] Because any contribution or expenditure will

---

[4] Barron, *Access to the Press—a New First Amendment Right*, 80 HARV. L. REV. 1641, 1642 (1967).

[5] *Id.* at 1643.

[6] Much of the literature is collected in Lange, *The Role of the Access Doctrine in the Regulation of the Mass Media: A Critical Review and Assessment*, 52 N. CAR. L. REV. 1, 2–3 n.5 (1973).

[7] 102 S. Ct. 1266 (1982) *affm'ng*, 512 F. Supp. 489 (D.D.C. 1980).

[8] This is taken from Buckley v. Valeo, 424 U.S. 1 (1976), the first of the cases.

be translated into media advertising, a legislative restriction will necessarily limit speech. This is valid only if the government offers very important reasons. Typically, the government has two reasons, both going to the perceived purity of the electoral process. The first is that citizens may view large contributions to candidates as akin to bribery. But this rationale has not been sufficient to sustain all of the legislation. Thus the second justification: an election ought to have the elements of a fair fight, and when one side grossly outspends the other for advertising, a fair fight is impossible. Accordingly the marketplace of ideas is better served, and freedom of speech is enhanced, when one side of an issue is prevented from being repeated so often that it overwhelms rational thought about the merits of the election. This second justification for limiting contributions and expenditures is what I call the enhancement theory of freedom of speech. The theory has developed over the years on foundations that are foreign to the First Amendment; the theory has no place in any sensible treatment of the First Amendment and should, in the future, be summarily rejected.

II. RED LION

Although enhancement came to the fore in argument in *Buckley v. Valeo*,[9] the theory grew out of *Red Lion Broadcasting v. FCC*,[10] the Court's initial entry into the mass speech area. At issue in *Red Lion* were FCC rules that guaranteed an individual who was the subject of a personal attack free air time to make a response. These rules, offshoots of the better known fairness doctrine,[11] were sustained in a sweeping opinion subscribed to by all participating Justices. While I recognize that *Red Lion* is exceptionally well known[12] and deals with access rather than enhancement, the case is essential to understanding the evolution of enhancement.

That a First Amendment case decided in 1969 could support a

---

[9] 424 U.S. 1 (1976).

[10] 395 U.S. 367 (1969).

[11] Briefly, the fairness doctrine requires a broadcaster who presents one side of a controversial issue of public importance to present the other side, albeit with wide discretion about the who, how, and when. The personal attack rules are quite specific and something like a right of reply to a libel. The rules allow a person whose honesty, character, or integrity has been attacked to respond to the attack although there is no right of response if the attack came during a bona fide newscast.

[12] The best article is Van Alstyne, *The Möbius Strip of the First Amendment*, 29 S. CAR. L. REV. 539 (1978), and he cites much of the other literature.

novel First Amendment theory is a tribute to the perceived uniqueness of the issues involved. Even in the late 1960s radio simply seemed different. To hunt through the United States Reports for assistance was an exercise in futility, because the Court had largely let the FCC go its own way for years. Indeed, virtually the only case relevant to the constitutionality of the personal attack rule was Justice Brennan's opinion in *New York Times*.[13] As readers of this journal know,[14] *New York Times* brought the writings of Alexander Meiklejohn[15] to the forefront of First Amendment jurisprudence. Although the Court did not adopt either Meiklejohn's public speech–private speech distinction or his absolute protection of the former, the Court did implement Meiklejohn's primary argument that the State may not penalize controversial speech about public issues. Justice Brennan imaginatively combined his conclusions from *Speiser v. Randall*[16] about the potentialities of mistaken fact-finding to affect speakers' choices adversely[17] with Meiklejohn's basic thesis. The combination resulted in the conclusion that even a civil jury superintending news judgments of what appears in print presented too fearsome a governmental intrusion into public debate, because, unless strictly limited, it was too likely to result in self-censorship rather than vigorous debate. Not surprisingly, the broadcasters in *Red Lion* offered a similar theory to explain why the fairness doctrine cast a pall over broadcast decisions.

Although *New York Times* was only five years old and forcefully proclaimed by Harry Kalven as *the* First Amendment decision,[18] it was to play no role in determining the outcome in *Red Lion*.[19] In-

---

[13] New York Times v. Sullivan, 376 U.S. 254 (1964).

[14] Kalven, *The New York Times Case: A Note on "The Central Meaning of the First Amendment,"* 1964 SUPREME COURT REVIEW 191. As Lee Bollinger so aptly stated, Kalven's article is "one of those rare pieces of legal scholarship that adds content and definition to a decision while purporting to 'interpret' it." Bollinger, *Elitism, the Masses and the Idea of Self-Government: Ambivalence about the "Central Meaning of the First Amendment,"* in COLLINS, ed., CONSTITUTIONAL GOVERNMENT IN AMERICA 99 (1980).

[15] MEIKLEJOHN, FREE SPEECH AND ITS RELATION TO SELF-GOVERNMENT (1948) reprinted as POLITICAL FREEDOM (1960); Meiklejohn, *The First Amendment Is an Absolute*, 1961 SUPREME COURT REVIEW 245.

[16] 357 U.S. 513 (1958).

[17] Only Frederick F. Schauer seems to give *Speiser* the credit it deserves. Schauer, *Fear, Risk, and the First Amendment*, 58 B.U.L. REV. 685 (1978).

[18] Kalven, note 14 *supra*.

[19] I have chosen not to present the *true facts* of *Red Lion* since neither counsel nor the Court was aware of them at the time of decision. They make sobering reading, however, and we are all in Fred Friendly's debt for bringing them to light. FRIENDLY, THE GOOD GUYS, THE BAD GUYS, AND THE FIRST AMENDMENT 1–11, 32–42 (1975).

deed it was cited but a single time, in the company of a citation to Holmes in *Abrams* after a sentence stating the purpose of the First Amendment is "to preserve an uninhibited marketplace of ideas in which truth will ultimately prevail."[20]

It did not follow that, because *New York Times* was to be insignificant to *Red Lion*, Meiklejohn, too, was to be insignificant. Meiklejohn's First Amendment demanded that rational citizen-governors consider fully the options and then "vot[e] wise decisions."[21] Meiklejohn's town meeting analogy[22] focused not on "the words of the speakers, but the minds of the hearers."[23] Thus "[w]hat is essential is not that everyone shall speak, but that everything worth saying shall be said."[24] Because the focus is on listeners rather than on speakers, the state may play a moderating role to ensure that the ideas essential to public decisionmaking were brought forward and redundancies were limited.[25]

New York Times had adopted the citizen-critic emphasis of Meiklejohn. *Red Lion* adopted the town meeting and informed decision-making emphasis.[26] "[T]he people as a whole retain their interest in free speech by radio and their collective right to have the medium function consistently with the ends' and purposes of the First Amendment."[27] At this point one might expect a reference to Brandeis's recitation in *Whitney v. California*[28] of the myriad purposes the Framers had for the protection of freedom of speech. Instead the Court follows with a statement that for someone who had not read Meiklejohn would be jarring indeed: "[I]t is the right of the

---

[20] 395 U.S. at 390. The sentence in text also represents a decided shift in tone from the *New York Times* market description of "free, robust, and wide-open." 376 U.S. at 270.

[21] POLITICAL FREEDOM note 15 *supra*, at 26.

[22] *Id.* at 24–28.

[23] *Id.* at 26.

[24] *Id.*

[25] *Id.* "[The First Amendment town meeting] does not require that, on every occasion, every citizen shall take part in public debate. Nor can it give assurance that everyone shall have opportunity to do so. If, for example, at a town meeting, twenty like-minded citizens have become a 'party', and if one of them has read to the meeting an argument which they have all approved, it would be ludicrously out of order for each of the others to insist on reading it again."

[26] There is a nice exposition of this in Baldasty & Simpson, *The Deceptive "Right to Know": How Pessimism Rewrote the First Amendment*, 56 WASH. L. REV. 365 (1981).

[27] 395 U.S. at 390.

[28] 274 U.S. at 375–77 (concurring).

viewers and listeners, not the right of the broadcasters, which is paramount."[29] With listeners' rights held paramount to broadcasters' rights one could go back to the previous sentence about ends and purposes of the First Amendment with a fuller understanding. Instead of the normal First Amendment concern of governmental interference in the marketplace (or with individual liberty), the Court was taking the marketplace metaphor in a different direction. What happens when the market is malfunctioning and certain ideas are blocked from entry or have far too little chance of reasonable entry? The answer seemed to be that government might selectively intervene in order to overcome barriers to entry and therefore promote better functioning of the market. Instead of being a negative force in the marketplace, the government had a positive role to play.

So, at least, it appeared.[30] As everyone is aware, attempts to extend *Red Lion*'s embrace of the fairness doctrine to access schemes generally failed. It was first rejected as to broadcasters in *CBS v. DNC*[31] and then, in a situation almost identical to *Red Lion*, to major newspapers in *Miami Herald v. Tornillo*.[32] *Red Lion* looked like a latter-day *Shelley v. Kraemer*:[33] it had overwhelming academic and judicial support when decided, but its implications seemed vastly too hot for a judiciary to handle, as *Tornillo* had counseled.[34]

---

[29] 395 U.S. at 390.

[30] Jerome Barron, seeing *Red Lion* as embracing the position that he had been advocating, quickly wrote: "It represents a look at the First Amendment in the light of new social realities of concentration of ownership and control in a few hands that has been produced by the twin developments of media oligopoly and technological change." Barron, *Access—the Only Choice for the Media?* 48 TEX. L. REV. 766, 772 (1970).

[31] CBS v. Democratic National Committee, 412 U.S. 94 (1973).

[32] 418 U.S. 241 (1974).

[33] 334 U.S. 1 (1948).

[34] In 1981 the Court extended *Red Lion*'s access idea to the nation's most favored discreet and insular minority—candidates for federal office. CBS v. FCC. 453 U.S. 367 (1981). Jimmy Carter wanted a half hour of prime time to announce his candidacy (which was no secret) and list all his accomplishments (a well-kept secret) in early December 1979. The networks weren't buying—or selling. The FCC's four Democrats outvoted its three Republicans by a narrow margin and ruled otherwise. The Supreme Court affirmed, finding Congress's § 312(a)(7) conclusion that a candidate for federal office needs the ability to obtain reasonable access to the nation's airwaves was a proper balance of the varied interests at stake. Politicians have access at the broadcaster's bargain basement rates; his opponent then has access on a like basis under the better known § 315(a). The Court's rather terse rejection of any First Amendment arguments to the contrary demonstrated that differential treatment for broadcasting is beyond question and that the Court was not entering into any further explanations. The exact dimensions of the holding will only become clear after a full election

III. Buckley v. Valeo

If access were limited, as *CBS v. DNC* and *Tornillo* held, it did not necessarily mean that *Red Lion* was dying a slow death. Lurking within *Red Lion*'s approval of the fairness doctrine was an idea untested by either *CBS v. DNC* or *Tornillo*. One need not conceive of the fairness doctrine as simply limited to providing access for alternative viewpoints. It also serves to limit the amount of time a broadcaster can spend on one side of an issue without providing additional time for the other side. The fairness doctrine works not only as a limited access mechanism but also as a modest equalization mechanism guaranteeing to consumers that one side of a debate will not be allowed to drown out the other side. While *Red Lion* at first glance seemed like an access case, its true significance could be deeper.

"The right of free speech of a broadcaster, the user of a sound truck or any other individual does not embrace a right to snuff out the free speech of others."[35] This language, intentionally broader than the broadcast context, combined with the rough equalization aspects of the fairness doctrine, would support a proposition potentially more important than access. *Red Lion* might stand for the proposition that government could accept an affirmative obligation to enhance the marketplace of ideas by protecting consumers from those who would speak so often that others could not realistically be heard.

Just as the Court was limiting *Red Lion*'s access possibilities the Congress was dealing with the varieties of abuses of power by Richard Nixon and CREEP. With too much evidence that widespread corruption was causing an erosion in public confidence in government, Congress acted. It attempted to alleviate the corrosive influence of money on presidential elections by amending the Federal Election Campaign Act[36] to prevent huge campaign contribu-

---

season occurs. One can expect that politicians will enjoy the decision, however, as they know how to use the benefits that just happen to come their way. At a minimum, CVS v. FCC puts the scarcity theory of broadcast regulation to rest since no VHF or UHF spectrum space was involved on the facts—regulation of networks *as* networks. See Powe, *American Voodoo*, 59 TEX. L. REV. 879, 900 (1981). See also Polsby, *Candidate Access to the Air: The Uncertain Future of Broadcaster Discretion*, 1981 SUPREME COURT REVIEW 223.

[35] 395 U.S. at 387.

[36] 86 Stat. 3 (1971) amended 88 Stat. 1263 (1974), 2 U.S.C. §§ 431–55.

tions, to limit candidate spending, and to create a meaningful system of public financing of the presidential campaigns. By attempting to equalize the resources of the candidates, Congress sought to ensure that a candidate could not obtain an undue advantage through excessive media exposure. Accordingly, the First Amendment would be enhanced by legislatively imposed equality, since neither side would be in a position to overwhelm the other quantitatively in the mass media.

The 1974 amendments were an integrated whole, but three of them explicitly rested on the theory of enhancement through equalization. One was a Kennedy-Rockefeller provision that limited the amount a candidate or his family could spend from their own fortunes on behalf of the candidate's election.[37] Another was a general provision limiting the total amount of money any candidate could spend to further his own chances.[38] The third related limitation prohibited individuals from spending more than $1,000 in "advocating the election or defeat" of a clearly identified candidate.[39]

These limitations on spending were designed and justified as equalization measures. They flowed from the implicit conclusion of *Red Lion* that in a mass society there is reason to fear the drowning out of voices in the marketplace of ideas. To be sure *Red Lion* had dealt only with access to the market. But what good was entry if the idea could then be overwhelmed by a mere handful of speakers saying the same thing? In the FECA amendments Congress had interfered with the marketplace of ideas, but its intrusion was to enhance speech by limiting the potential power of the wealthy to dominate rather than to elucidate. The challenge to the amendments in *Buckley v. Valeo* provided the first test of the enhancement theory:[40]

> The interests served by the Act include restricting the voices of people and interest groups who have money to spend and reducing the overall scope of federal election campaigns . . . [The Act] is aimed in part at equalizing the relative ability of all voters to

---

[37] 18 U.S.C. § 608(a).

[38] 18 U.S.C. § 608(c).

[39] 18 U.S.C. § 608(e)(1).

[40] 424 U.S. at 17.

affect electoral outcomes by placing a ceiling on expenditures for political expression by citizens and groups.

Even with its benign purpose, the provision limiting an individual's expenditures carried some startling consequences. The $1,000 limitation for individual expenditures relative to a clearly identified candidate criminalized the purchase of a single quarter-page advertisement for or against a candidate in a major newspaper. No meaningful concept of freedom of expression should hold that purchase of a quarter-page ad during the 1976 campaign attacking Gerald Ford's pardon of Richard Nixon was criminal. As with *Tornillo*, the Court was not about to make such a break with tradition. In striking the limitation the Court declared, "[T]he concept that government may restrict the speech of some elements of our society in order to enhance the relative voice of others is wholly foreign to the First Amendment."[41]

When the Court moved from individual expenditures to expenditures by the candidate of his own or family funds, its rejection of enhancement was even blunter: "the First Amendment simply cannot tolerate § 608(a)'s restriction upon the freedom of a candidate to speak without legislative limit on behalf of his own candidacy."[42] Two pages later, in striking down the total spending limitations, the Court simply stated that it found the equalization argument an unconvincing justification "for restricting the scope of federal election campaigns."[43]

While the spending limitations were being struck down and enhancement was being tersely rejected, the Court went on to sustain every other major[44] provision of FECA. In so doing, it approved public financing of presidential elections (at least for major parties); the requirement that a candidate limit his spending if he accepts the public subsidies; extensive disclosure requirements of contributions and expenditures; and limitations on the amount that an individual could contribute to a given candidate and to candidates generally. Thus the Court concluded it is more constitutionally protected to spend than to give. This is not, of course, *a priori* obvious. One

---

[41] 424 U.S. at 48–49.

[42] *Id.* at 54.

[43] *Id.* at 56.

[44] It also invalidated the method of selection of the members of the FEC.

might well conclude, as did Chief Justice Burger,[45] that contributions to a candidate and expenditures by the candidate are but the opposite sides of the same First Amendment coin.[46] But four Justices were able to split them,[47] and they were joined by Justice White who would have sustained the whole works.

Disentangling contributions from expenditures and then sustaining limits on the former was done to the tune of strict scrutiny, but the underlying melody was *ad hoc* balancing. First, the per curiam opinion downgraded the First Amendment interest. Political association was unaffected by FECA. As many individuals as wished could join and pool their resources; only the amount of money an individual could give was limited.[48] And the limitation on contributions "entails only a marginal restriction upon the contributor's ability to engage in free communication."[49] Furthermore the quantity of the contributors' communication does not increase "perceptively" with the size of a contribution.[50] Omitted was any discussion of the contributor who wished to delegate his speech to a more effective communicator, as he freely could under the Court's invalidation of spending limitations if he picked an ad agency rather than a candidate. Next came the upgrading of the state interest. The government has an important interest in preventing not only actual corruption but also the appearance of corruption.[51] The latter point was in answer to a less restrictive alternative argument based on bribery laws and the disclosure provisions.[52]

It is not an easy task to digest all that *Buckley* did: an integrated statutory scheme, taken apart; knowingly adverse treatment of minor parties, allowing the Republicans and Democrats to use the

---

[45] *Buckley* had struck down portions of a fully integrated statute and yet left the surviving portions as the governing law. Not only did the Chief Justice avoid abusing the favorite buzz words of the doctrinalists—compelling, strict scrutiny, less restrictive alternatives—as the *per curiam* so gleefully did, but he alone recognized the impropriety of the Court's imposition of an election scheme controlled by a judicially rewritten statute that had not been, and probably could not be, approved by a single democratically accountable body.

[46] 424 U.S. at 241.

[47] Justices Brennan, Stewart, Marshall, and Powell.

[48] *Id.* at 22.

[49] 424 U.S. at 20–21.

[50] *Id.* at 21.

[51] *Id.* at 26.

[52] *Id.* at 27–28.

federal treasury to enshrine a permanent two-party system with themselves as beneficiaries; authorizing disclosures of even trivial campaign contributions; creating a First Amendment distinction between contributions and expenditures; rejecting instantly and bluntly an argument based on enhancing speech. Rushed to argument and then judgment, perhaps *Buckley* was a sport, another "Nixon" case[53] good for that President and his immediate aftermath, but nothing else.

Unless *Buckley* was a sport, it was important because it did so much. Although the Court refused to adopt enhancement, and in the process labeled it "intolerable," "foreign," and "unconvincing," the provisions held constitutional had been enacted, at least in part, because of a belief in the validity of enhancement.[54] Not surprisingly, the sustaining of the provisions might have been seen as the beginning of a fuller understanding of the enhancement theory. Furthermore, the incongruity in the treatment of contributions and expenditures virtually invited additional litigation as well as the development of a theory that could explain the outcomes.

IV. CORPORATE AND PROXY SPEECH

The first opportunity for the application of *Buckley* came two years later in *First National Bank of Boston v. Bellotti*[55] with a challenge to a Massachusetts ban on corporate spending on referenda issues unless the ballot proposition "materially affected" the business of the corporation.[56] Lest any court attempt to gut the legislative intent, "materially affected" was specifically defined to exclude the proposition of an individual income tax, which, as applied, presented the issue to be determined in *Bellotti*. The law could be sustained either by the application of the enhancement theory or by holding that freedom of speech and the ability to influence election

---

[53] United States v. Nixon, 418 U.S. 683 (1974); Nixon v. Administrator of General Services, 433 U.S. 425 (1977); Nixon v. Warner Communications, 435 U.S. 589 (1978).

[54] See Polsby, *Buckley v. Valeo: The Special Nature of Political Speech*, 1976 SUPREME COURT REVIEW 1, 6, 14–16, and generally, the District of Columbia Circuit's opinion in *Buckley*, 519 F.2d 821 (1975).

[55] 435 U.S. 765 (1978).

[56] *Id.* at 767–68.

outcomes was limited exclusively to human beings.[57] Individual autonomy, guaranteeing to individuals the liberty to speak and think freely so that they may develop their potentiality,[58] had long been recognized as at least one of the important cluster of values protected by the First Amendment. The Court could have said that the impact of the Massachusetts ban would have a minimal effect on individual autonomy, because the officers and shareholders were free to spend and speak without limit on any election issue. Such a holding would not be without problems, however, because a variety of associations such as the ACLU and the NAACP are not individuals. It may well be that this problem of line-drawing immediately made the Court shy away from upholding the ban on the individual autonomy theory.

Furthermore, the Court had never held that individual autonomy was the *sine qua non* of First Amendment jurisprudence.[59] *Bellotti* continued this by concentrating on the town meeting listener-oriented, rather than citizen-critic, view of Meiklejohn. By adopt-

---

[57] A third possibility that is unrelated to the thesis of this paper would be to sustain a ban under some circumstances as a means of protecting shareholders from certain management decisions. See Brudney, *Corporations and Stockholders' Rights under the First Amendment*, 91 YALE L.J. 235 (1981).

[58] As Brandeis said in his *Whitney* concurrence, "Those who won our independence believed that the final end of the State was to make men free to develop their faculties. . . . They valued liberty both as an end and as a means. They believed liberty to be the secret of happiness. . . . " 274 U.S. at 375. See also EMERSON, THE SYSTEM OF FREEDOM OF EXPRESSION 6 (1970); Blasi, *The Checking Value in First Amendment Theory*, 1977 AM. BAR FOUND. RES. J. 521, 544; Baker, *Scope of the First Amendment Freedom of Speech*, 25 U.C.L.A.L. REV. 964 (1978).

[59] Despite the forceful arguments for such a construction by G. Edward Baker, *Scope of the First Amendment Freedom of Speech*, 25 U.C.L.A.L. REV. 964 (1978); *Commercial Speech: A Problem in the Theory of Freedom*, 62 IOWA L. REV. 1 (1976); *Realizing Self-Realization: Corporate Political Expenditures and Redish's "The Value of Free Speech,"* 130 U. PA. L. REV. 646 (1982), I believe the Court was wise to reject them. To some extent, Baker's attempt to compress the purposes of the First Amendment from assisting self-government and promoting individual autonomy into a single purpose is a desire to establish a homogeneous consistency in approach to the First Amendment—an incredibly elusive goal. Furthermore, the elimination of the important First Amendment purpose to promote self-government runs the risk of reworking a large portion of First Amendment jurisprudence. Although Baker's theory might do minimal damage to the general body of the First Amendment, attempts to restrict the first amendment to a single value could eliminate much of the protection that has heretofore been taken for granted. *E.g.*, Bork, *Neutral Principles and Some First Amendment Problems*, 47 IND. L.J. 1 (1971). Finally, I am unconvinced that Baker's necessary conclusion that corporate speech is market-controlled, while individual speech (say that of a candidate) is not, is either accurate or verifiable. See the exchange between Baker, *Realizing Self-Realization*, 130 U. PA. L. REV. 646, 671–77 (1982) and Martin Redish, *Self-Realization, Democracy, and Freedom of Expression: A Reply to Professor Baker* 130 U. PA. L. REV. 678, 686–88 (1982).

ing the marketplace view with its emphasis on the informed voter, the Court could focus on the speech rather than the speaker. Thus the Court could ignore the Massachusetts characterization of the issue as corporate rights and instead define it in terms of speech relating to a functioning democracy. "The inherent worth of the speech in terms of its capacity for informing the public does not depend upon the identity of its source."[60]

Since the Court rejected limiting freedom of speech solely to human beings, the validity of the ban turned on Massachusetts's alternative argument, the enhancement theory. According to Massachusetts, corporate speech presented the risk of one side of a debate so dominating what is heard by the citizenry that alternative viewpoints would be drowned out. Excessive corporate spending might so overwhelm the marketplace that it would unduly influence the outcomes of elections and accordingly shake a citizen's confidence in government. Numerous referenda issues in a variety of states had demonstrated that when corporations thought something impinged on their profitability they would be willing to spend vast sums of money on political advertising to convince the electorate of the validity of the corporate position (or at least of the potential dangers of the action at issue). In a footnote to Justice White's dissent[61]—Justice Powell had treated the facts in *Bellotti* the way majorities typically do in the offensive word cases,[62] that is, not treating them at all—he noted the vast corporate expenditures to defeat a nuclear power issue in California and corporate contributions of $144,000 to defeat a similar measure in Montana where supporters raised but $451.

Justice Powell's response for the Court to the asserted fear of corporations outspending everyone and controlling the outcome on ballot issues is somewhat ambiguous. He seems to answer, "We don't believe you." There is no showing that corporations overwhelm anyone or pose any threat to the confidence of citizens of Massachusetts in their government.[63] The Court did, however,

---

[60] 435 U.S. at 777.

[61] *Id.* at 811 n.11.

[62] *See, e.g.,* Lewis v. New Orleans II, 415 U.S. 130 (1974); Gooding v. Wilson, 405 U.S. 518 (1972) (facts buried in the small print of footnotes).

[63] One might usefully contrast Justice Powell's willingness to ignore Texas and look to Connecticut in San Antonio Ind. School Dist. v. Rodriguez, 411 U.S. 1, 23 (1973). Perhaps Connecticut and Texas are similar, but Massachusetts and California are not.

make a faint nod toward the enhancement theory when it suggested that "[i]f . . . corporate advocacy threatened imminently to undermine democratic processes, thereby denigrating rather than serving First Amendment interests, these arguments would merit our consideration."[64] A "*cf. Red Lion*" followed the sentence. But having made this tentative nod toward enhancement, Justice Powell proceeded in the next paragraph to move from the thought that Massachusetts would be unlikely to make the factual showing necessary to trigger the enhancement theory to the doctrinal conclusion that even with the necessary factual support, the argument was not "inherently persuasive or supported by the precedents of this Court."[65] Everyone agreed that corporate spending might influence the voters. That was its purpose. But unlike candidate elections where corruption or perceived corruption are potentially problems, referenda are issue oriented. And "the fact that advocacy may persuade the electorate is hardly a reason to suppress it. . . . We noted only recently that 'the concept that government may restrict the speech of some elements of our society in order to enhance the relative voice of others is wholly foreign to the First Amendment.' "[66] Naturally *Buckley* was the source of the court's quotation. Were that not sufficient to suggest that the earlier "*cf. Red Lion*" was cosmetic, the Court went on to disassociate itself again from the enhancement theory: "[I]f there be any danger that the people cannot evaluate the information and arguments advanced by appellants, it is a danger contemplated by the Framers of the First Amendment."[67]

Although neither *Buckley* nor *Bellotti* provided support for enhancement, there was a tension in their conclusions about money. That became more apparent in *California Medical Association v. Federal Election Commission* [*CALPAC*],[68] where the Court, consistent with *Buckley*'s holding, sustained a prohibition on individuals and unincorporated associations from contributing more than $5,000 per year to any multicandidate political committee.[69] CALPAC

---

[64] 435 U.S. 789.

[65] *Id.* at 790.

[66] *Id.* at 790–91.

[67] *Id.* at 792.

[68] 453 U.S. 182 (1981).

[69] 2 U.S.C. § 441a(a)(1)(C).

was such an entity, one that receives funds and engages in independent political advocacy. A plurality of the Court reasoned that the contribution limitation in a candidate election presented the same issues of corruption or potential corruption as were present in *Buckley*; therefore, the section was valid. The plurality specifically found that what the contributor was attempting to advocate by means of a "proxy" was different from direct political speech and entitled to less protection.[70] The necessary fifth vote was that of Justice Blackmun, who voted to sustain the provision only by finding that it satisfied strict scrutiny and was necessary to prevent evasion of the limitations approved in *Buckley*, a holding he was "willing to accept as binding."[71]

Where Justice Blackmun disagreed with the plurality was whether the contributions were entitled to full First Amendment protection. He held they were, while the plurality held otherwise because of the "proxy" nature of the speech. The plurality relied directly on *Buckley*'s distinction between contributions and expenditures for the conclusion that proxy speech was not entitled to the same protection as "real" speech, which in turn flows from the conclusion that proxy speech is not the same thing as "real" speech. If this conclusion is incorrect, of course, then proxy speech could be regulated only where a similar regulation of real speech would be sustained. Preventing the appearance of corruption might present such a circumstance, but the plurality's conclusion that proxy speech is less worthy of protection than "real" speech more than suggests that the corruption rationale could not be pressed so far.

But is proxy speech different from "real" speech? What the plurality means by proxy speech is speech by another; no other limiting definition is available on the facts. Yet this definition proves vastly too much, even limited to the circumstances of campaign finance. All of the campaign finance cases involve speech by another. In some circumstances an individual gives to a committee which in turn gives to a professional or to a campaign treasury. In other cases a campaign treasury turns money over to a professional. But let us not lose sight of the speech—that too brief commercial we see or hear. That speech has been prepared by a professional. While the professional might be the candidate himself, more likely

---

[70] 453 U.S. at 196.

[71] *Id.* at 202. *Cf.* Flood v. Kuhn, 407 U.S. 258 (1972).

it is party or campaign officials or an advertising agency. The reason professionals are used is that they are thought to know what is the most efficacious speech. But we do not conclude that a candidate's ad is proxy speech simply because someone else wrote it for him and perhaps delivered it for him. An individual choice to have a message with which he agrees prepared by professionals is no less speech. Proxy speech is simply a pejorative name for a political commercial. It is still speech.

So why must it receive less constitutional protection? Preventing the appearance of corruption (apparently on the Court's own terms) is insufficient, so the only justification that remains is enhancement. Although the enhancement theory is not invoked by name, it necessarily provides the implicit rationale that this less worthy speech should not be allowed to compete as fully as it might.

That a majority of the Justices are uneasy with such a back-door entry into enhancement is illustrated by *Citizens against Rent Control v. Berkeley*,[72] decided last Term. At issue was an ordinance that, as construed, limited only contributions but not expenditures and treated corporations identically with individuals. Quite simply, anyone could spend without limit but could give only $250 to a committee. In an election on rent control nine individuals gave a committee $20,850 to defeat the referendum. Despite the ordinance's facial compliance with *Buckley* and *Bellotti*, and the fact that "proxy" speech was necessarily involved, the Court swiftly and tersely invalidated the law. The Court wasted no time hunting for a constitutional distinction between spending a given amount to buy an ad to influence an election and giving a committee an identical amount to buy an ad to influence an election. As the Court recognized, "[t]o place a spartan limit—or indeed any limit—on individuals wishing to band together to advance their views on a ballot measure, while placing none on individuals acting alone, is clearly a restraint on the right of association."[73] That conclusion was virtually mandated by *NAACP v. Alabama*,[74] which the Court turned to for the important point that "[e]ffective advocacy of both public and private points of view, particularly controversial ones, is undeniably enhanced by group association, as this Court has more than

---

[72] 102 S. Ct. 434 (1981)

[73] *Id.* at 437.

[74] 357 U.S. 449 (1958).

once recognized by remarking on the close nexus between freedoms of speech and assembly."[75]

In relying on *NAACP v. Alabama* to justify collective action the Court left *Buckley* and *CALPAC* quietly on the sidelines. Such picking and choosing among precedents hardly makes for doctrinal stability. The Berkeley ordinance in *Rent Control* had been in perfect compliance with the Court's holdings to that time but was easily invalidated. At a minimum that holding, along with *Bellotti*, separates ballot-issue elections from candidate elections. In ballot-issue cases the corruption rationale is by definition inapplicable— there is no one to be bribed—and enhancement has been found wanting. Accordingly spending restrictions are invalid. With candidate elections there is more ambiguity. First, the corruption (or appearance thereof) rationale is implicated and has justified certain measures.[76] Second, while enhancement has seemingly been rejected, it is not clear that the corruption rationale is sufficient to sustain all the prohibitions. The proxy speech conclusion is so untenable that its use is simply a different methodology for adopting enhancement.

V. COMMON CAUSE V. SCHMITT

The tensions and ambiguities left by the cases might have been resolved to some extent had the Court not split four to four in *Common Cause v. Schmitt*.[77] At issue was the legality of expenditures totaling millions of dollars by several conservative groups to further the election of Ronald Reagan. The organizations that were trying to assist him purported to stand at arm's distance from him. Federal law so required.[78] But in complying with that part of federal law,

---

[75] *Id.* at 460.

[76] Senator Russell Long's famous statement that "when you are talking in terms of large campaign contributions . . . the distinction between a campaign contribution and a bribe is almost a hair's line difference" is quite supportive. U.S. Senate Comm. on Finance, *Hearings on S. 3496, Amendment No. 732, S. 2006, S. 2965 and S. 3014*, 89th Cong., 2d Sess. 78 (1966).

[77] 102 S. Ct. 1266 (1982).

[78] The Presidential Election Campaign Fund Act, 26 U.S.C. §§ 9001–13, prohibits a candidate who accepts public financing from accepting any form of private finnacing to augment the public moneys received and spent other than to compensate for any deficiencies in the federal fund. See 26 U.S.C. §§ 9003(b)(2), 9007(b)(3). Accordingly, there must be strict accounting and only an "authorized committee" may make expenditures on behalf of the candidate. An "authorized committee" is one "which is authorized in writing by such candidates to incur expenses to further the election of such candidates. . . . " 26 U.S.C. § 9002(1).

the organizations ran into another part of federal law, § 9012(f)[79] of the Presidential Election Campaign Fund Act (PECFA).[80] This provision prohibits any unauthorized group (except broadcasters and newspapers in their news and editorial functions)[81] from making independent expenditures of over $1,000 if the expenditures would "further the election" of a candidate who has received public financing of his campaign. The $7.75 million the organizations collectively spent[82] made the $1,000 limitation look like the petty cash it was for each organization. Indeed, even when compared to the $29.4 million spending limits applicable to both candidates,[83] the amount was hardly insubstantial.

At the outset § 9012(f) importantly implicates the corruption rationale, because the expenditures are massive and, even if not given for an explicit *quid pro quo*, carry the appearance that the groups so funding a victory may have acquired a grateful beneficiary.[84] Indeed, Schmitt frankly acknowledged that "some

---

[79] 26 U.S.C. § 9012(f) provides: "(f) Unauthorized expenditures and contributions. (1) Except as provided in paragraph (2), it shall be unlawful for any political committee which is not an authorized committee with respect to the eligible candidates of a political party for President and Vice President in a presidential election knowingly and willfully to incur expenditures to further the election of such candidates, which would constitute qualified campaign expenses if incurred by an authorized committee of such candidates, in an aggregate amount exceeding $1,000."

[80] The Act was first passed in 1966, 80 Stat. 1587 (the dollar income tax return check-off), suspended in 1967 pending the development of Congressional guidelines, 81 Stat. 58, and then implemented in 1971, 85 Stat. 562. Along with the Federal Election Campaign Act, 86 Stat. 3, it was substantially amended in 1974. 88 Stat. 1291.

[81] 26 U.S.C. § 9012(f)(2)(A).

[82] Common Cause Brief at 7.

[83] FEC Brief at 19 n.18.

[84] The potentiality that a candidate will be beholden to large contributors, a conclusion accepted in *Buckley*, does not seem different from the potentiality that a candidate will be beholden to those who spend large amounts of money independently on his behalf. Reagan Kitchen Cabinet member Justin Dart commented that "dialogue with politicians 'is a fine thing, but with a little money they hear you better.'" Common Cause Reply Brief at 16. Maybe with a lot of money they hear you quite clearly. And here the fund-raiser may well be more important than the large contributor. If one assumes that a contributor who gives $250,000 will have some (possibly undue) influence with the candidate, then how much more influence may a committee fund-raiser who can provide ten times that amount?

Even if there is no *quid pro quo*, there may well be its appearance as well as the further appearance that independent committees are simply subterfuges to evade spending limitations. Senator Jesse Helms, who is honorary chairman of a committee that spent $3.3 million, noted that it was awkward to communicate with the candidate but left little doubt that messages could be passed back and forth. Common Cause Brief at 31 n.49. Who would not believe that? The committees in the case were not taken randomly from civics classes to be organized for the occasion. They were permanent bodies of professional politicians who appear to have little naiveté and conducted massive nationwide "shadow" campaigns. Federal Election Commission Brief at 2–3, 25.

measure of loyalty" from the candidate was expected.[85] It is easy to understand how the law might be sustained as a means of eliminating any appearance of corruption in the presidential election process.[86] But the real concern is the arguments dealing with enhancement and how they apply to the facts of *Common Cause*, because no prior case better illustrates the strengths and the weaknesses of the enhancement argument. The arguments on behalf of enhancement, as applied to a context of collecting and spending massive amounts of money on behalf of a candidate who has eschewed private financing, are several: (1) public funding looks to equality in the campaign, and it is unfair to detract from that Congressionally and candidate-determined equality; (2) those who would use their money rather than their voices are attempting to gain an unfair advantage from the fact of their wealth; (3) what is at issue is proxy speech only; (4) the restrictions of § 9012(f) are neutral as to content; and (5) there are ample alternative ways to participate in a campaign. The first two arguments go to fairness; the third attempts to lessen the First Amendment interests; and the last two are designed to show that usual First Amendment concerns are not implicated by the restrictions.

The first of the two unfairness arguments is the distortion of the deliberately created Congressional balance between candidates. If one candidate has no (or few) groups spending independently on his behalf while the other has such supporting groups, then the latter will have the potentiality (and in all probability the likelihood) of more media exposure. Since media exposure is deemed an essential element of a successful campaign, and more is typically better, independent expenditures may give an advantage to one side. Because the goal of public financing is to create a fair and equal campaign, the independent expenditures as such detract from the goal.

---

[85] Schmitt Brief at 9 & 44.

[86] There is an argument that § 9012(f) is a contribution limitation essentially identical to that approved in *Buckley*. While the argument has some surface appeal, there is an important difference that weakens the argument seriously. The convertability of money allows a candidate to turn a contribution "into polling, computerized appeals, professional staff, and media messages." Adamany, *PAC's and the Democratic Financing of Politics*, 22 ARIZ. L. REV. 569, 570 (1980). At a minimum, an independent expenditure by a committee cannot be converted into paying for a candidate's professional staff. Indeed it seems most likely—and *Common Cause* was argued on the assumption—that the independent expenditures will go for media advertising. Under these circumstances it is difficult to argue that any rationale save one that directly allows a restriction on speech could sustain § 9012(f).

Building on the undoing of the Congressionally intended equality is a second and more pervasive concern with unfairness. Speaking of individuals, Paul Freund concluded that those who make
large expenditures for the mass media "are operating vicariously
through the power of their purse, rather than the power of their
ideas."[87] The concept that it is money rather than ideas prevailing is
based on the ability of a single individual who has money to reach
so many people through television and radio. There is almost nothing like it. To be sure, those who have owned newspapers or magazines have been able to reach disproportionately more people than
others in the past, but broadcasting has the seeming ability to reach
everyone. Consider the obvious counterexample of a given individual's devoting all the time he can to convince the voters to elect the
candidate he supports. In theory, at least,[88] everyone can participate equally at this. There are only twenty-four hours in a day and
even correcting for the speed with which various people talk, there
seems to be substantial likelihood that about the same numbers of
people can be reached. I have seen no suggestion that the single
individual could be limited in the amount of time he wished to
devote to a candidate, possibly because it is such a silly idea and
flatly unconstitutional. The trick then is to distinguish time from
money. That distinction is reach. Everyone can reach roughly the
same numbers of people through individual efforts. Those with
money who use it can reach far more, and it is their money, not
their individual energy or message, that gives them their power.

A needed tie between the use of money and the conclusion that
its usage is wrong or unfair is the assumption that the use of money
matters. Here there appears to be substantial agreement that constant repetition of a given message is likely to make potential voters
more prone to vote that way than if there are significantly fewer
times a message is heard. We may not like the thought that the
persuasiveness of a message depends on the number of times it is
heard rather than on its own intrinsic worth, but that is the world
in which decisions about the message must be made.

Intertwining with the unfairness arguments, but in fact separate
from them, is the issue of proxy speech. Common Cause articulated

---

[87] ROSENTHAL, FEDERAL REGULATION OF CAMPAIGN FINANCE 74 (1971) (commentary
by Freund).

[88] In a nice twist on Anatole France, the employed as well as the unemployed are free to
take time away from their jobs.

this both in its brief and in the Foreword to the Harvard Law Review written by the Chairman of its governing board.[89]

> [Ask] whose right of speech is abridged by the restriction. Those who give the money are not engaging in communication. As in the case of a contribution directly to a candidate, there is "only a marginal restriction upon the contributor's ability to engage in free communication" because "the transformation of contributions into political debate involves speech by someone other than the contributor." Those who constitute the committee to raise and spend the money do not engage in speech; their concern is to provide the money . . . [which is] turn[ed] over to one or more advertising agencies to conduct an advertising campaign through the mass media.

The proxy argument was written before the decision in *Rent Control* and is essentially a makeweight to bolster the idea of enhancement, an argument that is essentially complete at this point. Money, so the argument goes, buys access to the mass media and may allow a handful of people an opportunity to use proxies to state and restate their position, thereby increasing the chances that the voters will accept it as the right one for action. It is possible this use of money can create—and maybe maintain—a false political consensus.

Although the argument is complete its proponents have two additional points which they use to rebut the obvious argument that enhancement as applied through § 9012(f) requires people who wish to say more to say less. These surrebuttal arguments are content neutrality and the availability of vast alternatives.

Content control by the government is the "essence" of "forbidden censorship."[90] But § 9012(f) does not attempt to control content. It forbids certain expenditures no matter which viewpoint the individual wishes to support. As Judge Skelly Wright, one of the strongest backers of the enhancement theory, has stated, "[i]t is to say the least, not immediately apparent how ceilings—so long as they apply evenly across the board—could be designed so as to cast a disproportionate burden on minority or disfavored points of view."[91] Yet one might want to ask why there is a need for a limit

---

[89] Cox, *Foreword: Freedom of Expression in the Burger Court*, 94 HARV. L. REV. 1, 62–63 (1980).

[90] Chicago Police Dept. v. Mosley, 408 U.S. 92, 96 (1972).

[91] Wright, *Politics and the Constitution: Is Money Speech?* 85 YALE L.J. 1001, 1009 n.39 (1976).

on the amount that can be spent unless there is some assumption that spending will be unequal. After all, if the spending on each side is likely to be roughly equal, a ceiling may make sense to protect against corruption but is unnecessary to equalize speech on each side. Nor does the idea that a limitation could be justified in order to make door-to-door canvassers feel better about the importance of their efforts seem particularly weighty. It may well be that ceilings only appear to be content neutral. We can well remember that the law in *O'Brien*[92] happily forbade burning a draft card to protest the failure of the United States to bomb North Vietnam back into the Stone Age equally with burning a draft card to protest the war itself. This example alerts one to the possibility that ceilings are useful, because they affect a certain class of people who are much more likely than not to come down on one side of an issue. If this were the case the claim of content neutrality is a facade, and the limitation should be invalidated as an attempt to benefit one side of a public debate.

There is an alternative explanation, however. While people, including the very affluent, may be likely to distribute themselves in a random fashion, those who are likely to spend money may not. Government affects different subclasses of people differently. The President of a computer company or a department store may not care much one way or another about government policy (so long as the economy functions), but dairy farmers, defense contractors, and oil producers care intensely because their profit margins may hinge on government behavior. Because these and others dependent on government largesse, or highly affected by government regulation, may not care which party they support so long as it supports them, the ceilings are possibly as content neutral as Judge Wright and Common Cause assert.

Common Cause also argued that § 9012(f) leaves ample room for the exercise of speech and asociational freedoms. To make this point Common Cause proceeded to list all the ways that a person is free to participate. Individuals could spend as much as they wished. *Buckley* solved that. They may contribute time and energy to work in the election. That allows all kinds of traditional "grassroots" activities from planning strategy to making phone appeals to driving voters to the polls:[93]

---

[92] United States v. O'Brien, 391 U.S. 367 (1968).

[93] Common Cause Brief at 40; Cox, note 89 *supra*, at 60.

Moreover, everyone can find numerous other ways to support publicly financed candidates consistently with Section 9012(f). For example, individuals (acting either singly or jointly) can purchase advertisements in local newspapers; they can purchase local billboard space; they can prepare, reproduce and distribute handbills to their fellow citizens; and they can call in to radio "talk shows" or speak out in other forums to advocate the election of their favorite candidate.

What they may not do is give money to a committee that is receiving money from like-minded citizens in order to promote a cause they hold dear unless the candidate they support gives them written permission to do so.

Neither content neutrality nor the availability of alternatives can be pushed too far. The availability of alternatives not only is a "time, place and manner" concept but typically—although not always—has been held irrelevant to the issue whether the alternative chosen by an individual was valid.[94] And content neutrality is a necessary assertion to avoid what would likely be a *per se* invalidation of a law that did not achieve that; it marks no First Amendment boundaries. Essentially these two points are pleas in mitigation rather than affirmative justifications. The affirmative side must be carried by the enhancement theory.

Common Cause's list of alternatives is a useful beginning point for evaluating § 9012(f). Driving people to the polls may help one's candidate, but it is not speech. The other alternatives are speech, although hearing the response of the harassed citizen answering a phone call about an election may not be as gratifying as one would like, nor is hoping to be lucky or brilliant on a radio talk show. It is quite conceivable that a person who fears nuclear holocaust or is concerned that the ever-expanding government spending will bankrupt the Nation's future or whether there should be constitutional amendments on abortion, school prayer, and so on may want to do more than try a call-in show. Indeed when one talks of federal legislation the decisions of those in New Hampshire can affect those who live in vastly more populous and larger states. One can easily understand why outsiders might wish to communicate with the residents of that State. The Constitution would not allow a limitation on traveling there and hoping to find a noncaptive audi-

---

[94] See Krattenmaker & Powe, *Televised Violence*, 64 VIR. L. REV. 1123, 1266–73 (1978).

ence; nor purchasing a radio station; nor starting a newspaper there. Not surprisingly, an individual might conclude that it would make more sense to join with others of similar views on an issue, pool their dollars, turn it over to professionals who supposedly know better how to communicate with the audience and thus to reach the audience through a media campaign, even one of repetitious slogans. ·

To the extent that the First Amendment protects the individual choice of whether and how to speak, a restriction on how or how often an individual chooses to communicate cuts against that autonomy. This assists in clarifying the issue. If an enhancement theory is to be adopted, it must be because marketplace arguments are so persuasive that they override autonomy concerns.

As we have seen, the concern of enhancement is the potential drowning out of alternative voices. In theory, at least, enhancement need not be concerned with how much time an individual speaking on a street corner spends advocating an idea or a candidate, because time carries its own limits. There appears to be little chance that the marketplace could be overwhelmed or controlled by simple (nonmass media) advocacy. The only way it could happen is if there were sufficient numbers of individuals all taking the same position and too few on the other side. This is hardly a cause for concern, because if the prevailing viewpoint has overwhelming support in the society, then it is only proper that it is in a position to drown out alternatives.

From this perspective the concern of enhancement is that comparatively small numbers of people might drown out much larger numbers by the willingness of the smaller group to spend and spend. This suggests that large spending is quite proper if large numbers of people support it, but not proper if it represents only the few. A statute such as § 9012(f) fails to address this problem, because it equally prevents committees which have large numbers of small contributors as well as those with a few large contributors from spending. Indeed, § 9012(f) prevents thousands of relatively less affluent from banding together to equal what just one very affluent individual might spend.[95] Even if enhancement is a valid theory to override the asserted First Amendment rights of autonomy, § 9012(f) does so with a blunderbuss.

---

[95] Americans for an Effective Presidency Brief at 27.

Overinclusiveness is not § 9012(f)'s only problem. Newspapers and broadcast stations are specifically excluded. Yet if one believes in enhancement, newspapers present a substantial problem, for they allow a wealthy individual to reach vastly more people than he otherwise could. The potential reach of newspapers is great and it may well, as FDR so clearly realized, not represent many voters. The same, indeed maybe more so, could be said for major market television stations. Here, however, unlike newspapers, there is the potentiality of reliance on smothering federal regulation or supervision to prevent the drowning-out problem.[96] But *Tornillo* and the newspaper tradition it represents stands as a bar to the same solution for newspapers. An inability to tone them down is a constitutional given.

This would seem to lead in one of two directions. For the enhancement advocate it is simply that—an unfortunate given, but nothing with which to get carried away. Simply because government cannot prevent newspapers (and magazines) from reaching too many people with too much of the same message is an insufficient reason to prevent government from reaching and limiting what it can. From the other side, the argument is equally obvious. If a newspaper is allowed to reach and propagandize so many readers, why should citizens be prevented from banding together and trying to counter it?

To surrender the interests of individual autonomy and to attempt to tone down a debate (or one side of it) in the interests of enhancing the marketplace is to give up something that is directly traceable to the First Amendment in order to achieve a speculative gain. It is attempted on the speculative basis that a legislature knows at what points the problem of market failure is likely to surface and that enhancement is an effective means of avoiding them.[97] But the solution must recognize that broadcasting is a nicely regulated means of communication, unlikely on the owners' initiative to upset

---

[96] The fairness doctrine nicely does just this. Whatever the original hopes for the fairness doctrine, its modern function is to chill broadcast decisions and to keep the perceived potential power of the medium in check—regardless of individual protestations that the purpose of chilling is inapplicable to the Commissioner's own decisionmaking.

[97] Cox agrees with Justice White in *Bellotti*, 435 U.S. at 804, that expertise of legislators is at its peak and that of judges is at its very lowest in the area of the "political arena," by which he means contributions, but which must, of necessity, implicate the amount of debate. Note 89 *supra* at 69–70.

the market, and that newspapers are an unfortunate outsider, capable of upsetting the market but beyond direct control. Furthermore, it rests on an assumption that less speech may well be better than more, an assumption that appears wildly at odds with the normal First Amendment belief that more speech is better. And more speech is also possible. Although I would not advocate the solution, *Buckley* potentially allows the government to attempt to set some balances in the marketplace. Might not government make available a given amount of funding to each candidate (or each side) and then provide additional funding to the candidate who is being outspent by "unauthorized" committees advertising relative to a clearly identifiable candidate?[98]

VI. SCORECARD ON SPEECH?

While access to the marketplace picked up a majority in *Red Lion*, it fared poorly thereafter. Enhancement has never commanded a majority, and I doubt it will. I would guess the four-to-four split in *Common Cause v. Schmitt* is more likely on the corruption rationale than enhancement, although the latter may have commanded three votes. Indeed we have come this far without being concerned with how any of the justices have been voting. It is time to look.

Table 1 makes it easy to see the extremes. While six justices appear quite ready to strike down most limitations in the expenditure-contribution area, Justices Burger, Blackmun, and Rehnquist are most willing to do so. Indeed, once one remembers that Justice Rehnquist's vote in *Bellotti* flows from a wholly separate premise of state control of corporations,[99] it is apparent that on the mass speech issue he is functionally the same as Burger as the most likely to validate the speech claim. At the other end, Justice White will sustain virtually anything the State passes in this field. Justices Brennan and Marshall are somewhat more discriminating, but they, too, have been willing to embrace access and enhancement and to vote for some of the limitations. Thus, the Justices most likely to support a First Amendment claim are Burger, Rehnquist, and Blackmun, and those most favoring the State are White, Bren-

---

[98] See also Chevigny, *The Paradox of Campaign Finance*, 56 N.Y.U.L. REV. 206 (1981).
[99] 435 U.S. at 822.

TABLE 1
MASS SPEECH

Case	Burger	Blackmun	Rehnquist	Powell	Stewart	O'Connor	Stevens	Brennan	Marshall	White
Tormillo	F	F	F	F	F	...	...	F	F	F
Rent Control	F	F	F	F	...	F	F	F	F	S
CBS v. DNC	F	F	F	F	F	...	...	S	S	F
Buckley:										
Contribution	F	F	F	S	S	...	...	S	S	S
Candidate for self	F	F	F	F	F	...	...	F	S	S
Candidate and										
individual spending ...	F	F	F	F	F	...	...	F	F	S
Bellotti	F	F	S	F	F	...	F	S	S	S
Red Lion	...	...	...	...	S	...	...	S	S	S
CALPAC	O	S	O	O	O	...	S	S	S	S
Total	7-0	7-1	6-1	6-1	5-2	1-0	2-1	4-5	3-6	2-7

NOTE.—F = First Amendment; S = state; O = other ground; ... = did not participate.

nan, and Marshall! Your suspicions that Table 1 cannot seriously reflect the First Amendment are not without force, as Table 2 demonstrates. Table 2 consists of a handful of First Amendment cases I selected on the following criteria: the issue should be instantly recognizable as the First Amendment issue; the vote should have been divided; no two cases should present substantially the same issue. Although other cases might have been selected, I believe the outcomes in Table 2 conform quite closely with what anyone following the Supreme Court would expect. Brennan and Marshall, and to a lesser, more issue-oriented extent[100] Stevens, are more consistently supportive of the speech claim than others. Burger and Rehnquist are by far the least supportive of a simple claim of freedom of speech.

How, then, can one explain this huge discrepancy? One could suggest that Brennan and Marshall are more sensitive to the values peripheral to freedom of speech, especially that of individual autonomy, and that this sensitivity causes them, but not Burger and Rehnquist, to handle cases involving corporate givers—*Bellotti*, to a lesser extent *CALPAC*—more sensibly. This explanation does not work. The individual autonomy argument cannot explain Marshall's reluctance to support it on the candidate expenditure issue in *Buckley*. More fundamentally, individual autonomy is in conflict with the marketplace notions of enhancement in *Common Cause v. Schmitt*. A quick glance at Table 1 will allow one to conclude that Burger, Rehnquist, and Blackmun voted to strike § 9012(f) while White, Marshall, and Brennan voted to sustain it (regardless of whether their basis was the corruption rationale or enhancement). Thus, saying that Brennan and Marshall, but not the others, are sensitive to the whole range of issues around speech may have a nice ring to it, but it is not persuasive.

A more plausible suggestion is that Brennan and Marshall, as stronger First Amendment supporters than others, take more seriously the concept of a marketplace of ideas and an informed self-governing citizenry. By taking the marketplace more seriously, they are more fully aware of the potential pitfalls of the marketplace approach. Thus they, to a greater extent than others, would be conscious of the potential for market failure as well as the possibil-

---

[100] See Young v. American Mini Theatres, 427 U.S. 50 (1976); Krattenmaker & Powe, note 94 *supra*, at 1207–12.

TABLE 2
TRADITIONAL EXPRESSION

Case	Brennan	Marshall	Stevens	Stewart	Powell	Blackmun	White	Burger	Rehnquist
Virginia Board[a]	F	F	F	F	F	F	F	F	S
Schaumburg[b]	F	F	F	F	F	F	F	F	S
Pentagon Papers[c]	F	F	...	F	...	S	F	S	...
Spence[d]	F	F	...	F	F	F	S	S	S
Erznoznik[e]	F	F	...	F	F	F	S	S	S
Nebraska Press[f]	F	F	F	F	S	S	F	S	S
Branzburg[g]	F	F	...	F	S	S	S	S	S
Houchins[h]	F	...	F	F	F	S	S	S	S
Brown v. Glines[i]	F	F	F	S	S	S	S	S	S
Miller[j]	F	F	...	F	S	S	S	S	S
Snepp[k]	F	F	F	S	S	S	S	S	S
Hudgens[l]	F	F	...	S	S	S	S	S	S
Haig v. Agee[m]	F	F	S	S	S	S	S	S	S
Gertz[n]	F	S	...	S	S	S	S	S	S
Total	14-0	12-1	6-1	9-5	5-8	4-10	4-10	2-12	0-13

NOTE.—S = state; F = First Amendment; ... = did not participate.

ᵃ Virginia Board of Pharmacy v. Virginia Citizens Consumer Council, 425 U.S. 748 (1976) (constitutional protection for purely commercial advertising). Justice Stevens did not participate in *Virginia Board*, but in subsequent cases he embraced the doctrine in such a fashion that there is no doubt how he would have voted in the original case.

ᵇ Schaumburg v. Citizens for a Better Environment, 444 U.S. 620 (1980) (ordinance barred door-to-door charitable solicitation by charities where the charity did not use at least seventy-five percent of contributions for charitable purposes).

ᶜ New York Times v. United States, 403 U.S. 713 (1971).

ᵈ Spence v. Washington, 418 U.S. 405 (1974) (flag misuse to protest invasion of Cambodia).

ᵉ Erznoznik v. Jacksonville, 422 U.S. 205 (1975) (banning all nudity at drive-in theaters visible from a public place).

ᶠ Nebraska Press v. Stuart, 427 U.S. 539 (1976) (gag order). I have recast the vote in this case to reflect the positions of the Justices on the issue of a *per se* ban on gag orders. It is quite possible that Justice White's position has thus been miscast.

ᵍ Branzburg v. Hayes, 408 U.S. 665 (1972) (reporter's privilege).

ʰ Houchins v. KQED, 438 U.S. 1 (1978) (press access to prisons). I have "voted" the nonparticipating Marshall and Blackmun as they voted on the same issue earlier in Pell v. Procunier, 417 U.S. 817 (1974).

ⁱ Brown v. Glines, 444 U.S. 348 (1980) (permission necessary before Air Force personnel could circulate petitions on an Air Force base). Of the dissenters only Justice Brennan reached the First Amendment issue. Justices Stewart and Stevens quite sensibly construed the relevant statute to allow petitioning. The majority had to misconstrue the statute in order to reach—and reject—the First Amendment claim.

ᵏ Snepp v. United States, 444 U.S. 507 (1980) (constructive trust remedy on profits from publication of nonclassified material imposed for breach of contractual agreement to submit to CIA prepublication review).

ˡ Hudgens v. NLRB, 424 U.S. 507 (1976) (picketing on private property).

ᵐ Haig v. Agee, 453 U.S. 280 (1981) (passport revocation for activities abroad that are likely to cause serious damage to national security).

ⁿ Gertz v. Robert Welch, 418 U.S. 323 (1974) (public figure, private issue libel).

ity of manipulation. Lee Bollinger[101] has quite perceptively warned that there is an undercurrent of elitism and fear of the "masses" in our current adoption of Meiklejohn.[102]

> Intellectual thought in this century treats such matters as the complexity of the cognitive processes and its extensive irrational components, the rise of the masses and the concomitant break between knowledge and power, and the seemingly innate human impulse for security and release from fear which can open a society to violence and self-destruction. Such intellectual trends have seemingly given birth to a new form of elitism, which casts considerable doubts on the premises of popular sovereignty [since the masses might irrationally "be brought to do things which in a calmer moment they would regard as against their better interests."]

It may well be that, as an empirical matter, the more central Meiklejohn's ideas are to a person, the more the person is called upon to question the premise of a rational self-governing citizenry. And the more the premise is questioned the more one worries about flaws in the marketplace. Furthermore, Meiklejohn's moderator was required to ensure the fairness of the debate. This could lead an individual to conclude that government enhancement of speech is essentially a Meiklejohnian notion and that toning down some participants so that others could be heard better is an appropriate Meiklejohnian methodology for a functioning democracy.

Nevertheless, it is not clear why someone who believes in the marketplace would be more prone to understand its limits than someone who is skeptical about the market. A strong belief in something like the marketplace of ideas need not correlate well with understanding the limitations of the belief, and a skepticism about the market could quite plausibly explain why others do not have

---

[101] Bollinger, note 14 *supra*.

[102] *Id.* at 101. That unease over assumptions of rationality might enter judicial decision-making (if not the decisions themselves) is not surprising. By the time Justice Brennan was enshrining Meiklejohn in the Court's jurisprudence, political scientists and other "political intellectuals" had finished two decades of debate and concern over the underlying component of rationality in citizen participation in a democracy. *The Decline of Classical Democratic Theory* in FOWLER, BELIEVING SKEPTICS: AMERICAN POLITICAL INTELLECTUALS, 1945–64 ch. 6 (1978). "The judgment of many postwar intellectuals, led by prominent social scientists, was the investigation of human nature or typical political behavior did not bear out the faith of classical democratic theory in a rational, informed, interested citizen. . . . " *Id.* at 170. And nowhere did the fear of the masses and demonstration of nonrationality show up more pervasively than in the clinical dissection of the far right wing. See, *e.g.*, BELL ed., THE RADICAL RIGHT (1963), especially the two concluding chapters by Seymour Martin Lipset.

the strong belief in the first place. Without wishing to push this too far, it simply seems to me that there is no substantial reason to conclude that someone who strongly believes in the marketplace will be the person who better understands the limitations of the marketplace. Furthermore, another reason for being skeptical that Meiklejohnian beliefs will be likely to lead to the market enhancement position flows from Bollinger's point about elitism and the current flirtation with Meiklejohn. I agree with Bollinger that there is a subtle but perceptible undercurrent of elitism running through the Court's treatment of the marketplace of ideas. But I do not think this can explain why Brennan and Marshall are more prone to elitism than Burger, Rehnquist, Powell, and Blackmun. Quite frankly, the votes in *CBS v. DNC* and *Pacifica*[103] suggest the opposite.[104]

From this I can see nothing within the normal First Amendment theory or the positions of the Justices that appears to provide a satisfactory First Amendment explanation for the voting patterns in the mass speech cases. Something else appears to be at work here.

As Table 3 assists in illustrating, that something else seems to me to be the fact that the issue in the mass speech cases in one of privileges accruing to wealth: the right to purchase a particular consumption item (in this case a media ad). Although Table 3 consists of seemingly unrelated cases in doctrinal areas ranging from procedural due process to substantive equal protection, what the cases have in common is a wealth transfer claim that follows along the lines of relative affluence.[105] In these cases certain classes

---

[103] FCC v. Pacifica Foundation, 438 U.S. 726 (1978).

[104] Remember the wonderful concern of the Chief Justice that an access scheme in CBS v. DNC would ill serve the marketplace of ideas because it would be "so heavily weighted in favor of the financially affluent, or those with access to wealth," 412 U.S. at 123. It has acquired no additional credibility over the years. CBS v. DNC is a tough case for most of the justices because it presented so many tough issues. It was one type of wealth (broadcasters) versus another type of wealth (those who could afford to buy time); it had state action problems and a tough issue of judicial supervision of administrative inaction. I suspect that it was only easy for Justices Douglas and Stewart, who saw it immediately as a speech case and voted on that basis. For the others it could not have been so easy. Although query if for at least some it may not have been the precursor of Vermont Yankee Nuclear Power v. NRDC, 435 U.S. 519 (1978).

[105] I have included no race cases, such as Griggs v. Duke Power Co., 401 U.S. 424 (1971), Swann v. Charlotte-Mecklenburg, 402 U.S. 1 (1971), Board of Regents v. Bakke, 438 U.S. 265 (1978), or Fullilove v. Klutznick, 448 U.S. 448 (1980), because the race cases seem to me more likely to provide transfers between blacks and nonaffluent whites that between rich and poor.

TABLE 3
ANTI-EGALITARIANISM

Case	Rehnquist	Burger	Powell	Stewart	Stevens	Blackmun	White	Brennan	Marshall
Salyer Land[a]	A	A	A	A	. . .	A	A	E	E
Simon v. E. Kentucky[b]	A	A	A	A	. . .	A	A	E	E
Ross v. Moffitt[c]	A	A	A	A	. . .	A	A	E	E
Spannaus[d]	A	A	A	A	A	. . .	E	E	E
Lassiter[e]	A	A	A	E	A	A	A	E	E
Kras[f]	A	A	A	A	. . .	A	E	E	E
Rodriguez[g]	A	A	A	A	. . .	A	A	. . .	E
Flagg Bros.[h]	A	A	A	A	E	E	E	E	E
Harris v. MCR[i]	A	A	E	E	E	E	A	E	E
Memphis Light[j]	A	A	E	E	A	E	E	E	E
Penn Central[k]	A	A	E	E	A	E	E	E	E
Moreno[l]	A	A	E	E	. . .	E	E	E	E
Maricopa[m]	A	A	E	E	. . .	E	E	E	E
Zablocki[n]	A	E	E	E	E	E	E	E	E
Total	14-0	13-1	9-5	8-6	4-3	6-7	6-8	0-13	0-14

NOTE.—A = anti-egalitarianism: against the poverty claimant or for the more affluent party; E = egalitarianism: for the poverty claimant or against the more affluent party; . . . = did not participate.

a Salyer Land Co. v. Tulare Water District, 410 U.S. 719 (1973) (sustaining voting in a water district election by landowners only in proportion to assessed valuation of the land). See also Ball v. James, 451 U.S. 355 (1981) (same result as applied to a district that in addition to its water functions supplies electricity to hundreds of thousands of people; Stevens joined the majority; White and Blackmun joined Brennan and Marshall in dissent).

b Simon v. Eastern Kentucky Welfare Rights Organization, 426 U.S. 26 (1976) (no standing to challenge IRS elimination of requirement that nonprofit hospitals provide some treatment for indigents in order to qualify for favorable tax treatment). Justices Brennan and Marshall's concurring opinion has been recast as a dissent based upon the distinction between the majority's Article III basis for decision and their conclusion that plaintiffs failed at the proof level.

c Ross v. Moffitt, 417 U.S. 600 (1974) (no right to counsel for discretionary appeal after appeal as of right).

d Allied Structural Steel v. Spannaus, 438 U.S. 234 (contracts clause prevents Minnesota from requiring a funding charge for all ten-year employees in a pension plan when company terminates plan or closes Minnesota part of the business).

e Lassiter v. Department of Social Services, 101 S. Ct. 2153 (1981) (no absolute right to free counsel in parental status termination cases).

f U.S. v. Kras, 409 U.S. 434 (1973) (one can be too poor to be bankrupt).

g San Antonio Ind. School District v. Rodriguez, 411 U.S. 1 (1973) (property tax created funding disparities between rich and poor school districts).

h Flagg Brothers v. Brooks, 436 U.S. 149 (1978) (no state action in statutory private reposition scheme).

i Harris v. McRae, 448 U.S. 297 (1980) (Congress may refuse to fund medically necessary abortions for the poor). Alone among the cases included in this Table, I am uneasy here. I think it is an abortion rather than a wealth case, and I think that explains the votes of Justices Blackmun and White and probably Stevens. For the rest it does not matter.

j Memphis Light, Gas & Water Division v. Craft, 436 U.S. 1 (1978) (due process determination prior to utility termination when issue is nonpayment of disputed bills).

k Penn Central v. New York, 438 U.S. 104 (1978) (historic preservation of Grand Central Station). See also Loretto v. Teleprompter Manhattan CATV, 102 S. Ct. 3164 (1982) (holding a miniscule but permanent occupation of property constituted a taking). Justices Blackmun, Brennan, and White dissented.

l Department of Agriculture v. Moreno, 413 U.S. 528 (1973) (antihippie food stamp provision).

m Memorial Hospital v. Maricopa County, 415 U.S. 250 (1974) (residency requirement as applied to hospital care for indigents).

n Zablocki v. Redhail, 434 U.S. 374 (1978) (right to marry when fettered by preexisting child care obligations).

of people are asking for constitutional help and some Justices seem more willing to provide assistance to the wealthy, while others respond more favorably to the less affluent. Two of the cases, *Penn Central* and *Spannaus*, involve corporations seeking constitutional protection for their current activities; this type of claim would be easily recognizable to the *Lochner*-era Court.[106] Four of the cases, *Salyer Land, Eastern Kentucky Welfare Rights Organization, Flagg Bros.*, and *Memphis Power & Light*, involve attempts by relatively less affluent individuals to interpose the Constitution to their benefit in a private dispute with a larger, more affluent organization. The remainder of the cases are the more "traditional" poverty cases where the constitutional claim is that the government must pick up the tab for the benefit the individual wishes to acquire.

I do not pretend that Table 3 is perfect or comprehensive. What I suggest is that it gives a reasonable approximation of how the Justices are likely to vote in both the poverty cases and their converse (situations where wealthy individuals attempt to protect the perks their wealth can buy). So conceived, Table 3 helps to explain the discrepancy between Table 1 and what one would suspect in a normal First Amendment case such as those shown by Table 2. At the extremes the wealth cases fairly approximate the Justices' votes in the mass speech cases. Justice White does not fit perfectly, as he slips by both Justices Brennan and Marshall. But this is explicable because Justice White sees no conflict between limiting speech and limiting the perks of wealth. As Tables 2 and 3 show, he thinks little of both speech and wealth claims.[107]

---

[106] 198 U.S. 45 (1905).

[107] But see United Steelworkers of America v. Sadlowski, 102 S. Ct. 2339 (1982) where the majority sustained a union rule that prohibits candidates for union office from accepting campaign contributions from individuals who are not members of the union and Justice White dissented. At issue was whether the union rule conformed to the free speech section of the Labor-Management Reporting and Disclosure Act, 29 U.S.C. § 411(a)(2). The majority found that act was not intended to incorporate the entire body of first amendment jurisprudence and sustained the rule. Writing for the dissenters, Justice White found Buckley v. Valeo the most relevant case and would have invalidated the rule. While his vote was the most out of character, he was not alone. Justices Brennan and Rehnquist both flipped from their normal positions. The mind-boggling split: Marshall for Powell, Rehnquist, Stevens, and O'Connor; White for Burger, Brennan, and Blackmun. Beyond saying all bets are off when a labor issue intrudes, compare International Longshoremen's Association v. Allied International, 102 S. Ct. 1656, 1665 (1982) (9–0: "conduct designed not to communicate but to coerce merits still less consideration under the First Amendment") with NAACP v. Claiborne Hardware, 102 S. Ct. 3409 (1982) (8–0: coercive boycott protected); I have no idea what is happening.

It seems that the mass speech cases are really wealth cases masquerading as speech cases. The intellectual drive that produced *Shapiro v. Thompson*[108] in April of 1969 assisted *Red Lion* two months later and has provided the underpinnings of enhancement. Substantive notions of equality were not only informing the Fourteenth Amendment, but they were also being transported into the First Amendment.

VII. CONCLUSION

Once one understands that it is egalitarianism that is the force behind the concern over mass speech issues, then the Court's limiting of access and rejection of enhancement can be intelligibly explained. The current crop of Justices do not find leveling off their affluent peers to be a particularly attractive idea. It is not that they love the First Amendment more; they simply love egalitarianism less. This is hardly the way to build a strong or sensible foundation for the First Amendment to operate in its most widespread context. The mass speech cases of the last decade could and should have an exceptionally strong grounding in traditional First Amendment thought. *Rent Control* is an apt illustration. There the Court turned to *NAACP v. Alabama* rather than *Buckley* and *CALPAC* and accordingly recognized the problem for what it was: individuals banding together to support a common position. Unfortunately it is that recognition in *Rent Control* that sets it apart, because one of the most striking features of the mass speech cases is the implicit assumption that there is something different about the problem. Therefore, instead of turning toward traditional First Amendment methodology, it is appropriate, perhaps imperative, to search for something newer and better, such as enhancement.

The enhancement cases assume that less of a certain type of speech will be better. Yet it has been a given, as the recent majority in *Brown v. Hartlage* noted, that the preferred First Amendment remedy is "more speech, not enforced silence."[109] One would expect not only compelling reasons for determining that less speech is better but also a theory that will operate sensibly in the range of

---

[108] 394 U.S. 618 (1969).

[109] 102 S. Ct. 1523, 1533 (1982) citing Brandeis's concurring opinion in *Whitney*, 274 U.S. at 377.

cases. Enhancement requires determinations of who can talk through the mass media and how often those that can talk may do so before they must stop. Yet enhancement must leave newspapers (and maybe broadcasters) unhappily untouched. As a result, if enhancement is adopted, it would be a back-door entry into the conclusion that the press has the most First Amendment rights of all. Such a conclusion would be a startling turnaround from the Court's intelligent, decade-long resistance to the press' claim that the First Amendment mandates a preferred press position complete with special rights available to the press alone.[110]

The fundamental tenet of enhancement theory that less speech is better at some points seems to rest on two assumptions: first, additional speech on the other side either will not be forthcoming or is not worth the effort, and second, the "reach" of modern mass communications is of such a new order that it needs a different theory to make it function "consistently with the ends and purposes of the First Amendment."[111] Yet just as there is a problem with determining how much is too much, there is also a gap in the explanation of why there will be no further speech on the other side to counter the speech that is being repeated too often. And how "new" is the problem? But for the "mass" communications of newspapers, specifically Pulitzer's and Hearst's, there would not have been a Spanish American War in 1898 to make Theodore Roosevelt next in line to the Presidency in 1900.

Enhancement has been articulated as a rationale only for dealing with the mass media. The soapbox orator, that classic and heroic lone dissenter of so much of the First Amendment case law, seems exempt. He does not fit within enhancement, because he cannot, from his soapbox, create the necessary imbalance. In his case we cannot shut him off because we dislike him, dislike his message, are sick and tired of being bothered, are angry that someone could be so wrongheaded, or feel that he creates such an imbalance in the marketplace that it would be unfair to let him continue. We are stuck with walking away from him or maybe even countering what he says with our own position.

---

[110] See generally Lewis, *A Preferred Position for Journalism?* 7 HOFSTRA L. REV. 595 (1979); *A Public Right to Know about Public Institutions: The First Amendment as Sword*, 1980 SUPREME COURT REVIEW 1.

[111] *Red Lion*, 395 U.S. at 390.

The traditional solution, more rather than less speech, is both possible and desirable in the mass speech area as well. "That the air may at times seem filled with verbal cacophony is . . . not a sign of weakness but of strength."[112] No one has authored a rebuttal to that statement of Justice Harlan, because, as Brandeis recognized over fifty years ago, speech is a part of political liberty. Public discussion is a citizen's duty. As a society we have more to fear from an inert than an active citizenry. Fear and repression menace stable government; speech does not.[113] Thus, the fiftieth, or for that matter the five hundredth, time a message is aired is better than the forty-ninth (or the four hundred and ninety-ninth) time, we have presumed, because with each additional airing it may reach additional listeners.[114] Furthermore, the same message is not necessarily involved. Differences in wording, nuances, or choice of issue may provide the spark that promotes responses in different people. It is not so much that we retain a naive belief that truth is knowable or that the electorate will rationally choose it, as that the simple recognition that no theory requiring people to stop speaking (or stop listening) better fits with our traditions than the one we have adopted. The theory that a speaker has the right to choose his message and the intensity and frequency of its delivery reflects the recognition that a free-for-all on public issues serves both the ideals or self-government and those of maximizing individual choices.

If *Common Cause v. Schmitt* involved a group like Mothers Against Drunk Drivers, the First Amendment issues of mass speech would have looked like traditional ones, and the vote probably would have been eight to White to invalidate the law. The Court would easily have turned to its stored knowledge and concluded that even if the message—politicians had better implement tough criminal sanctions—were repeated so often without adequate opposition that it

---

[112] Cohen v. California, 403 U.S. 15, 25 (1971).

[113] *Whitney*, 274 U.S. at 377 (concurring opinion).

[114] Whether advocates of enhancement are willing to acknowledge this with respect to speech, they rather easily approve a similar idea with respect to the press. Only multimedia owners have opposed FCC rules that have attempted (generally prospectively) to limit media holdings to one within a single market. The rationale, as expressed by the FCC is "that 60 different licensees are more desirable than 50, and even that 51 are more desirable than 50." Multiple Ownership of Standard, FM, and TV Broadcast Stations, 22 FCC2d 306, 311 (1970). The Supreme Court agrees. FCC v. NCCB, 436 U.S. 775 (1978) (upholding the newspaper broadcast co-ownership limitations).

.was likely to be effective and convince people to do that which they otherwise might not, it had to be protected anyway.

Why then is there such a different reaction in the real case? What is the underlying concern about mass speech that causes people to suggest a remedy of enhanced speech, that is, less speech, instead of more speech? One reason seems to be the concern that wealthy individuals (or those with the ability to collect sufficient money) will use their money to buy media messages and create a false and immobilizing consensus.[115] Intertwined with this is the belief that media ads are a noxious simplification of reality and there are members of society who might not understand this, and that they therefore need protection from too much of this speech.

It is hard to dispute that the wealthy seem to enjoy tremendous influence[116]—and not only in this country. But if this is the concern, I would suspect that the best way of dealing with the power of wealth would be to attack its source rather than its consequences. In other words, if the wealthy are too powerful, change the tax and inheritance laws to prevent accumulations of wealth. If that is too extreme, then significant additional public funding can be made available for electoral campaigns, so that the advantages of wealth can either be eliminated or minimized. These are neither easy nor

---

[115] By so doing those in position of wealth and power would avoid the need to relinquish them should the necessity occur. *Cf.* Tushnet, *Deviant Science in Constitutional Law*, 59 TEX. L. REV. 815, 826 (1981).

[116] It is not inconceivable that some who support enhancement may do so because it seems consistent with footnote 4 and heightened judicial scrutiny only for "discreet and insular minorities." United States v. Carolene Products, 304 U.S. 144, 152 n.4 (1938). Justices Brennan, White, and Marshall have already suggested such an application to a Contracts Clause situation in United States Trust Co. v. New Jersey, 431 U.S. 1, 32, 62 n.18 (1977) (dissenting), where they came close to stating that people who can fight a good legislative battle ought not be seeking judicial help if their constitutional rights are violated. See Powe, *Populist Fiscal Constraints and the Contracts Clause*, 65 IOWA L. REV. 963, 969 & n.70 (1980). Whatever the validity of generalizing with footnote 4 in a move from the Fourteenth Amendment to the Contracts Clause, a like application of footnote 4 to the free speech area would be wholly improper. First, footnote 4 excluded freedom of speech from the "discreet and insular minority" rationale for heightened scrutiny. The latter rationale came in the third paragraph of a footnote that discussed First Amendment concepts in the first two paragraphs. Second, Dean John Hart Ely, the ablest modern exponent of footnote 4 and the principle reason for its resurgence, see DEMOCRACY AND DISTRUST (1980), specifically excludes the First Amendment from footnote 4's reach. Ely, *Foreword: On Discovering Fundamental Values*, 92 HARV. L. REV. 5, 14–15 (1978), Third, the specific provisions of the Bill of Rights are designed to place certain rights beyond the majoritarian process, and it makes no sense to say this is so only when the poor or blacks want to exercise their rights, but not when affluent whites wish to do so. Finally, if the First Amendment applied only when legislation affected "discreet and insular minorities," then the Sedition Act would have been constitutional.

cost-free choices, but by not seeking to operate directly on speech
in one case and by adding more speech without limiting anyone in
the other, both are consistent with the traditions of the First
Amendment.[117]

I think it not unlikely that at least part of the impetus to do
something toward limiting mass speech flows from a disdain for
those that would use this type of speech and the message that they
offer as well as the not inconceivable fear that people might listen.
The nice thing about Abrams dropping pamphlets out of an upper
floor window to the street below,[118] or Gitlow distributing that
horribly turgid and dull "Left Wing Manifesto,"[119] or Dennis and
his handful of colleagues reading Marx and Lenin and plotting to
find the proletariat for a revolution,[120] or Brandenburg spouting his
racism and anti-Semitism to the cattle of Hamilton County,[121] was
that we know that even if someone listens, nothing happens. The
speech reaches few people and affects even fewer. But the mass
speech cases involve speech that everyone has seen, and the New
Right mass mailing distortion squads appear to have done what the
lone dissenter never managed to do, convince people to vote the
wrong way. It is easy to defend speech we hate so long as it is
ineffective, but it is much harder to do so when people actually
respond positively. Indeed it represents a perversity in the marketplace, because speech we hate is by definition not the "truth" that a
properly functioning marketplace is supposed to accept. And here
again I find Lee Bollinger's recognition that a distrust of the ability
of the masses to sort out the truth from the slogans, and to make the
type of wise choices intelligent citizens should make, comes into
play to reemphasize the dangers of mass speech as used by dem-
agogic organizations.[122] The sloganeering of mass speech does not
require thought or invite dialogue. It preys on the basest instincts

---

[117] I offer this argument for a less restrictive analysis, not in the belief that it ought to
change a First Amendment result (or indeed, given the elasticity of less restrictive alternatives, that it would change a First Amendment result), nor with assurance that there would
be agreement that what is suggested is really an alternative. Rather I offer it with the
realization that there are those who think such an argument is relevant.

[118] Abrams v. United States, 250 U.S. 616 (1919).

[119] Gitlow v. New York, 268 U.S. 652 (1925).

[120] Dennis v. United States, 341 U.S. 494 (1951).

[121] Brandenburg v. Ohio, 395 U.S. 444 (1969).

[122] Bollinger, note 14 *supra*.

and, unfortunately, may well convince the masses to make our society a less enjoyable place to live.

That is, of course, true of a lot of speech. It was arguably true of the "socialist" FDR and "King Andrew [Jackson] the First." And it is possible that they would have liked a theory that could have toned down the opposition to their administrations in the name of enhancing freedom of speech for all of us. But no such theory was readily available, and until 1969, at least, freedom of speech came to us with but a single tradition: that the "State's fear that voters might make an ill-advised choice does not provide the State with a compelling justification for limiting speech" and if there is concern, more, not less, speech is the best remedy.[123] Thus far the Court's results in the mass speech cases have been reasonably consistent with this tradition. What remains is to strengthen them by recognizing that the mass speech cases present but the modern version of a much older problem to which we have long since known the appropriate remedy.

---

[123] Brown v. Hartlage, 102 S. Ct. 1523, 1532 (1982).

FREDERICK SCHAUER

CODIFYING THE
FIRST AMENDMENT:
NEW YORK v. FERBER

Words and pictures may serve an almost limitless variety of purposes. They may be the instruments with which a political pamphleteer urges a change in government policy, but they may also enable the child pornographer to display for the sexual pleasure of paying customers photographs of children engaged in sexual activity. The former is unquestionably at the core of the First Amendment's protection of freedom of speech and press.[1] The latter is equally clearly some distance from that core.[2] In *New York v. Ferber*[3] the Supreme Court held child pornography to be so far from the core as to be unprotected by the First Amendment. *Ferber*

Frederick Schauer is Cutler Professor of Law, College of William and Mary.

[1] See, *e.g.*, NAACP v. Claiborne Hardware Co., 102 S. Ct. 3409, 3426 (1982); Citizens Against Rent Control v. Berkeley, 102 S. Ct. 434, 437 (1981); Carey v. Brown, 447 U.S. 455, 467 (1980); New York Times Co. v. Sullivan, 376 U.S. 254, 270 (1964); Gilbert v. Minnesota, 254 U.S. 325, 337 (1920) (Brandeis, J., dissenting); MEIKLEJOHN, POLITICAL FREEDOM (1960); BeVier, *The First Amendment and Political Speech: An Inquiry into the Substance and Limits of Principle*, 30 STAN. L. REV. 299 (1978); Blasi, *The Checking Value in First Amendment Theory*, 1977 AM. B. FOUND. RESEARCH J. 521; Bork, *Neutral Principles and Some First Amendment Problems*, 47 IND. L.J. 1 (1971); Kalven, *The New York Times Case: A Note on "The Central Meaning of the First Amendment*," 1964 SUPREME COURT REVIEW 191.

[2] "[F]ew of us would march our sons and daughters off to war to preserve the citizen's right to see 'Specified Sexual Activities' exhibited in the theaters of our choice." Young v. American Mini Theatres, Inc., 427 U.S. 50, 76 (1976) (plurality opinion). Doctrinal or strategic considerations may lead us to treat all or part of the fringe as legally indistinguishable from the core, but this is distinct from identifying a theoretical, prelegal core.

[3] 102 S. Ct. 3348 (1982).

upheld a New York statute[4] proscribing the dissemination of child pornography regardless of whether the materials were legally obscene under the *Miller* standards.[5] Moreover, the Court was unanimous in reaching that conclusion,[6] giving *Ferber* the distinction of being one of very few cases since 1919 in which not a single Justice dissented from a holding that an act of communication was unprotected by the First Amendment.[7]

It would be easy to explain the Court's unanimity of result by reference to the undeniably revolting nature of child pornography and those who trade in it.[8] But this would be too easy. The Court's development of First Amendment doctrine has long been influenced by a willingness to protect that which would, standing alone, command little but condemnation. The course of the First Amendment has been shaped far less by the worthy dissident than by the likes of the Jehovah's Witnesses with their "astonishing powers of annoyance,"[9] Brandenburg and his fellow Klansmen,[10]

---

[4] N.Y. Penal Law § 263.15 (McKinney 1980).

[5] Miller v. California, 413 U.S. 15 (1973). References to the "*Miller* standards" incorporate glosses from other cases. *E.g.*, Pinkus v. United States, 436 U.S. 293 (1978); Splawn v. California, 431 U.S. 595 (1977).

[6] Justice White's opinion of the Court was joined by Chief Justice Burger and Justices Powell, Rehnquist, and O'Connor. Justice O'Connor also wrote a concurrence. Justice Blackmun concurred in the result without opinion. Justice Brennan, joined by Justice Marshall, wrote an opinion concurring in the judgment, and Justice Stevens also wrote an opinion concurring in the judgment.

[7] Although I have not conducted an exhaustive search, the only cases that come to mind are Valentine v. Chrestensen, 316 U.S. 52 (1942), and Chaplinsky v. New Hampshire, 315 U.S. 568 (1942).

[8] Because of the doctrinal focus of this article, I do not deal extensively or critically with the underlying evidence relating to the nature of the child pornography industry. Well-documented discussions can be found in Protection of Children Against Sexual Exploitation: Hearings Before the Subcomm. to Investigate Juvenile Delinquency of the Senate Comm. on the Judiciary, 95th Cong., 1st Sess. (1977); Sexual Exploitation of Children: Hearings Before the Subcomm. on Crime of the House Comm. on the Judiciary, 95th Cong., 1st Sess. (1977); Sexual Exploitation of Children: Hearings Before the Subcomm. on Select Education of the House Comm. on Education and Labor, 95th Cong., 1st Sess. (1977); S. Rep. No. 438, 95th Cong., 1st Sess., reprinted in 1978 U.S. CODE CONG. & AD. NEWS 40; Shouvlin, *Preventing the Sexual Exploitation of Children: A Model Act*, 17 WAKE FOREST L. REV. 535 (1981); Note, *Child Pornography Legislation*, 17 J. FAM. L. 505 (1979); Comment, *Preying on Playgrounds: The Sexploitation of Children in Pornography and Prostitution*, 5 PEPPERDINE L. REV. 809 (1978); Note, *Child Pornography: A New Role for the Obscenity Doctrine*, 1978 U. ILL. L.F. 711; Note, *Protection of Children from Use in Pornography: Toward Constitutional and Enforceable Legislation*, 12 U. MICH. J.L. REF. 295 (1979). Additional materials from the medical and social sciences are cited in *Ferber*, 102 S. Ct. at 3355 n.9.

[9] CHAFEE, FREE SPEECH IN THE UNITED STATES 399 (1941). *E.g.*, Martin v. Struthers, 319 U.S. 141 (1943); Cantwell v. Connecticut, 310 U.S. 296 (1940); Lovell v. Griffin, 303 U.S. 444 (1938).

[10] Brandenburg v. Ohio, 395 U.S. 444 (1969) (per curiam).

Cohen's tasteless jacket,[11] and Frank Collin and the American Nazi Party.[12] People such as this have prevailed under the First Amendment not because what they in particular had to say furnishes the *raison d'être* for free speech, but because they have been the fortunate beneficiaries of a desire to preserve long-run First Amendment values by looking not at isolated instances of speech but at broad categories.[13] They have benefited as well from a great reluctance, even in the face of extreme cases, to permit First Amendment protection to turn on the determination by any official body, even a court, of the comparative worth of particular utterances.[14]

Thus we must look beyond the unique repulsiveness of child pornography to locate an explanation for the Court's unanimity. And what appears on closer inspection of *Ferber* is a growing consensus within the Court on a doctrinal proposition of great importance in First Amendment theory—that the diversity of communicative activity and governmental concerns is so wide as to make it implausible to apply the same tests or analytical tools to the entire range of First Amendment problems. This premise provides the impetus for making First Amendment doctrine more precise and at the same time more complex, developing tools and tests that are greater in number but consequently applicable to increasingly smaller categories of First Amendment issues. And as the size of the categories shrinks, it becomes less necessary to protect that which ideally ought not be protected solely to ensure the protection of the potentially valuable.

From this perspective the virtues of subdividing and thereby

---

[11] Cohen v. California, 403 U.S. 15 (1971).

[12] National Socialist Party of America v. Village of Skokie, 434 U.S. 1327 (1977) (Stevens, J., as Circuit Justice, denying stay); National Socialist Party of America v. Village of Skokie, 432 U.S. 43 (1977) (per curiam); Collin v. Smith, 578 F.2d 1197 (7th Cir.), stay denied, 436 U.S. 953, *cert. denied*, 439 U.S. 916 (1978).

[13] See Scanlon, *Freedom of Expression and Categories of Expression*, 40 U. PITT. L. REV. 519 (1979); Schauer, *Categories and the First Amendment: A Play in Three Acts*, 34 VAND. L. REV. 265 (1981); Shiffrin, *Defamatory Non-Media Speech and First Amendment Methodology*, 25 U.C.L.A.L. REV. 915, 960–61 (1978). For an interesting philosophical contrast to the prevailing legal view, see Dworkin, *Non-Neutral Principles*, in READING RAWLS 124 (Daniels ed. 1975).

[14] See, *e.g.*, Erznoznik v. Jacksonville, 422 U.S. 205 (1975); Chicago Police Dept. v. Mosley, 408 U.S. 92 (1972); Cohen v. California, 403 U.S. 15 (1971). See generally Karst, *Equality as a Central Principle in the First Amendment*, 43 U. CHI. L. REV. 20 (1975); Stone, *Restrictions of Speech Because of Its Content: The Peculiar Case of Subject-Matter Restrictions*, 46 U. CHI. L. REV. 81 (1978). *Cf.* Fried, *Two Concepts of Interests: Some Reflections on the Supreme Court's Balancing Test*, 76 HARV. L. REV. 755 (1963); Rawls, *Two Concepts of Rules*, 64 PHIL. REV. 3 (1955).

codifying the First Amendment seem great. But equally important factors militate against the pull toward smaller categories and more precise tests. Extreme subdivision of the First Amendment magnifies the risk that an increasingly complex body of doctrine, even if theoretically sound, will be beyond the interpretative capacities of those who must follow the Supreme Court's lead— primarily lower court judges, legislatures, and prosecutors.[15] Complex codes may generate numerous mistakes when applied, and First Amendment mistakes are more likely to be mistakes of under-protection than of overprotection.[16] *Ferber*, in carving out yet another distinct category of material unprotected by the First Amendment, and for reasons that are relatively novel in First Amendment theory, is a significant milestone on the road toward elaborate codification of the First Amendment. At the same time it may warn us of the dangers of going much farther.

Although I want to focus on these doctrinal implications of *Ferber*, that is no excuse for ignoring the case's more immediate importance. Child pornography is a matter of great current concern, and *Ferber* establishes the framework for a likely wave of new legislation and litigation. I would be remiss to leap into broad doctrinal speculation without first paying attention to the need for specific analysis of these beginnings of a discrete body of constitutional law relating to child pornography. Justice White's majority opinion in *Ferber* admirably anticipates many of the issues that are likely to arise in its application. That precision and predictability, however, is a product of the Court's willingness to carve out a separate category for child pornography. Thus we cannot completely divorce the particular analysis of the holding from its broader doctrinal premises, and a close look at how the Court treated child pornography will greatly assist in tracing the Court's progress toward codification of the First Amendment.

I. THE CASE

Although forty-seven states and the federal government had at the time *Ferber* was decided enacted legislation specifically ad-

---

[15] See Schauer, note 13 *supra*, at 305–7.

[16] See TRIBE, AMERICAN CONSTITUTIONAL LAW 576–84 (1978); Emerson, *Toward a General Theory of the First Amendment*, 72 YALE L.J. 877, 887–93 (1963); Kalven, note 1 *supra*, at 213.

dressed to the problem of child pornography,[17] not all of these laws presented the constitutional question posed in *Ferber*. Twelve states directed their legislative efforts solely to the *production* of material involving sexual acts by children.[18] Absent any attempt to proscribe the dissemination of the films, books, or magazines so produced, the process of photographing an illegal act for eventual distribution creates no independent constitutional protection for the illegal act itself.[19] The presence of a camera, a pen, or a typewriter does not clothe unprotected acts with First Amendment protection. For example, it would hardly be a defense to a citation for speeding on a public road that the speeding car was at the time being filmed for an episode of *The Dukes of Hazzard*. Conversely, material protected by the First Amendment does not shed that protection merely because it depicts or describes illegal activity.[20] These twelve states thus skirted any constitutional problem by regulating the production but not the dissemination of the material.

Fifteen other states and the federal government did prohibit the dissemination of material depicting children engaged in sexual activity, but limited the prohibition on dissemination to material that was obscene under *Miller*.[21] Because *Miller*-tested obscenity is wholly outside the First Amendment,[22] these statutes also avoided any constitutional problem under current doctrine. With only a rational basis required for dealing with obscenity,[23] imposing special sanctions on child pornography that is also obscene presents no previously unsettled questions.

New York, however, was one of twenty states that desired to go further.[24] Like the previously mentioned jurisdictions, these states

---

[17] The statutes are listed in *Ferber*, 102 S. Ct. at 3351 n.2.

[18] *Id.*

[19] This is merely an instance of the more general proposition that a possible, probable, or even inevitable First Amendment use does not immunize otherwise illegal activity. See, *e.g.*, Branzburg v. Hayes, 408 U.S. 665 (1972); United States v. Reidel, 402 U.S. 351 (1971); Associated Press v. United States, 326 U.S. 1 (1945). *Cf.* Landmark Communications, Inc. v. Virginia, 435 U.S. 829, 837 (1978); New York Times Co. v. United States, 403 U.S. 713, 730 (1971) (Stewart, J., concurring).

[20] So much is implicit in the view that even advocacy of illegal conduct is protected. Brandenburg v. Ohio, 395 U.S. 444 (1969) (per curiam); Yates v. United States, 354 U.S. 298 (1957).

[21] 102 S. Ct. at 3351 n.2.

[22] Paris Adult Theatre I v. Slaton, 413 U.S. 49 (1973); Miller v. California, 413 U.S. 15 (1973); Roth v. United States, 354 U.S. 476 (1957).

[23] Paris Adult Theatre I v. Slaton, 413 U.S. 49 (1973).

[24] 102 S. Ct. at 3351 n.2.

banned the dissemination as well as the production of child pornography. But these states did not require that the material be obscene. New York, for example, made it unlawful to disseminate "any performance which includes sexual conduct by a child less than sixteen years of age."[25] Because a distinct section of the same law provided a separate sanction for material that was also obscene,[26] it was apparent that the first-mentioned section intended to disclaim any necessity for a finding of obscenity.

Paul Ferber was tried for selling two films "devoted almost exclusively to depicting young boys masturbating."[27] Had he been tried only under that section of the New York statute requiring obscenity, Ferber might have been convicted under that constitutionally noncontroversial section. Indeed, Ferber's counsel conceded in oral argument before the Supreme Court that a jury finding of obscenity for Ferber's wares would have been consistent with *Miller*.[28] But Ferber was tried under *both* statutes, enabling the jury to acquit on the obscenity charge while convicting under the section not requiring legal obscenity.[29] Perhaps fortuitously, therefore, the issue was presented starkly: Could Ferber be convicted for selling films depicting sexual acts by children where those films were not legally obscene?

The New York Court of Appeals reversed Ferber's conviction, holding the statute unconstitutional primarily for want of any precedent for denying constitutional protection to nonobscene material.[30] The Court of Appeals also relied on the statute's overbreadth. Even if the statute might constitutionally be applied to Ferber and his films, the statute's potential inclusion of medical and educational materials rendered it fatally overbroad.[31]

---

[25] N.Y. Penal Law § 263.15 (McKinney 1980). I use "disseminate" in place of the statute's comprehensively defined "promote." N.Y. Penal Law § 263.00-5 (McKinney 1980).

[26] N.Y. Penal Law § 263.10 (McKinney 1980).

[27] 102 S. Ct. at 3352.

[28] *Id.* at 3365 n.1 (Brennan, J., concurring).

[29] *Id.* at 3352.

[30] People v. Ferber, 52 N.Y.2d 674 (1981). A federal court had previously relied on similar reasoning to enjoin enforcement of the statute against a particular publication, St. Martin's Press, Inc. v. Carey, 440 F. Supp. 1196 (S.D.N.Y. 1977), but that decision was overturned because the plaintiff had failed to show any real threat of prosecution. St. Martin's Press, Inc. v. Carey, 605 F.2d 41 (2d Cir. 1979).

[31] 52 N.Y.2d at 678.

The Supreme Court's nine-to-zero reversal of the New York Court of Appeals upheld the facial validity of the statute as well as Ferber's conviction under it.[32] Although Justice White's majority opinion acknowledged that the decision of the Court of Appeals "was not unreasonable in light of our decisions,"[33] the Court departed from those decisions to the extent of allowing the states "greater leeway in the regulation of pornographic depictions of children"[34] than existed when juveniles were not portrayed. In reaching this conclusion, the Court relied on a mélange of justifications drawn from diverse strands of existing First Amendment doctrine.

The Court began by acknowledging the "compelling" interest in protecting children.[35] Unlike almost every other free speech case, the focus of state concern was not on the harm that the communication would cause to its recipients or to society. *Ferber* contains not a single word addressed to the effect of child pornography on its viewers, or the effect that a proliferation of child pornography might have on a community. Rather, the concern was for the children used in producing the material.[36]

Although the state interest was therefore in the production and not the dissemination of the material, the Court agreed with New York that this harm could not be dealt with adequately by a restriction limited to the use of children in the production process.[37] Legislation so limited would fail to address the special harm that came to children from knowing that there was a permanent public record of their acts.[38] Moreover, controls limited to production

---

[32] New York v. Ferber, 102 S. Ct. 3348 (1982). For the lineup of the opinions, see note 6 *supra*.

[33] 102 S. Ct. at 3352. The only court outside of New York to confront the issue had held a similar statute unconstitutional. Graham v. Hill, 444 F. Supp. 584 (W.D. Tex. 1978). Two state courts upheld relatively noncontroversial statutes limited to production. Griffin v. State, 396 So.2d 152 (Fla. 1981); Payne v. Commonwealth, 623 S.W.2d 867 (Ky. 1981).

[34] 102 S. Ct. at 3354.

[35] *Id*. On the Court's use of the particular term "compelling," see text accompanying notes 110–15 *infra*.

[36] 102 S. Ct. at 3355.

[37] *Id*. at 3355–56.

[38] *Id*. at 3355. The Court relied in part on the "privacy interests involved." *Id*. at 3356 n.10. But nothing in *Ferber* is helpful in determining the circumstances under which this type of interest in avoiding publicity will be applied in the future. See Posner, *The Uncertain Protection of Privacy by the Supreme Court*, 1979 SUPREME COURT REVIEW 173.

would likely be ineffective. Pornographic materials are produced clandestinely, and attempting to deal with child pornography by going after only the producers would be an exercise in futility.[39] The solution, to New York and other states, was to destroy the market by prohibiting dissemination. The Court agreed with the State that the unquestioned interest in protecting children from exploitation could be served only by a restriction on dissemination.

The Court also agreed that the interest in protecting children could not be met by a dissemination restriction limited to the legally obscene.[40] The Court correctly noted that the *Miller* formulation, directed toward excluding the totally worthless from the coverage of the First Amendment, proceeds from different premises than does the concern for those who will be photographed for films and books. The perceived dangers to the children involved may be equally great if the material contains some serious literary, artistic, political, or scientific value, if it does not as a whole appeal to the prurient interest, or if it does not as a whole offend contemporary community standards.[41] For example, a by-and-large faithful rendition of *Romeo and Juliet* that depicted a fourteen-year-old Romeo engaged in a variety of sex acts with a twelve-year-old Juliet would not be obscene under *Miller*, but might produce the same harms for the child actors that were central to New York's concern.

Having accepted New York's strong interest in restricting material hitherto held to be within the protection of the First Amendment, the Court proceeded to assess the First Amendment implications of the restriction, concluding that:[42]

> The value of permitting live performances and photographic reproductions of children engaged in lewd sexual conduct is exceedingly modest, if not *de minimus*. We consider it unlikely that visual depictions of children performing sexual acts or lewdly exhibiting their genitals would often constitute an important and necessary part of a literary performance or scientific or educational work. . . . [I]f it were necessary for literary or artistic

---

[39] 102 S. Ct. at 3356. See also TRIBE, note 16 *supra*, at 666 n.62.

[40] 102 S. Ct. at 3356–57.

[41] *Id*. Influenced perhaps by the particular result at trial in *Ferber*, the Court implicitly discounted the fact that most child pornography is plainly obscene under *Miller*. See Note, *Child Pornography, the First Amendment, and the Media: The Constitutionality of Super-Obscenity Laws*, 4 COMM/ENT L.J. 115 (1981).

[42] 102 S. Ct. at 3357.

value, a person over the statutory age who perhaps looked younger could be utilized.

This approach is in some tension with *Cohen v. California*.[43] The use
of the word "fuck" might also not have been an "important and
necessary" part of Cohen's message of opposition to the Selective
Service System, but that did not prevent the Court from allowing
Cohen to determine what method of making his statement he determined to be most effective.

Cohen may be distinguised in part because the state's interest in
protecting children against sexual exploitation seems greater than
the state's interest in protecting the public against exposure to vul-
gar language. But the Court relied on the fact that the type of
material employing children engaged in sexual acts is likely to be
less central to the First Amendment. Drawing support from
Young,[44] *Pacifica*,[45] and the defamation cases,[46] the Court reasserted
that an investigation into the content of categories of speech was an
appropriate way of determining that certain categories should be
unprotected by the First Amendment.[47] The Court therefore concluded that because the category of child pornography contained
limited speech value, and because there was a great state interest in
regulating that category, the category would be deemed unprotected by the First Amendment.[48]

> Thus, it is not rare that content-based classification of speech has
> been accepted because it may be appropriately generalized that
> within the confines of the given classification, the evil to be
> restricted so overwhelmingly outweighs the expressive interests,
> if any, at stake, that no process of case-by-case adjudication is
> required. When a definable class of material, such as that cov-

---

[43] 403 U.S. 15 (1971).

[44] Young v. American Mini Theatres, Inc., 427 U.S. 50 (1976).

[45] FCC v. Pacifica Foundation, 438 U.S. 726 (1978).

[46] New York Times v. Sullivan, 376 U.S. 254 (1964); Beauharnais v. Illinois, 343 U.S.
250 (1952). Although the Court cited *Beauharnais* for a methodological rather than substantive
proposition, the reference does keep alive the question of the case's vitality. See Smith v.
Collin, 439 U.S. 916 (1978) (Blackmun, J., dissenting from denial of certiorari).

[47] 102 S. Ct. at 3358. In this respect the Court perpetuated its failure to distinguish
content inquiry directed at determining the boundaries of the first amendment from content
inquiry within those boundaries. See Schauer, note 13 *supra*, at 290 n.114; Stephan, *The First
Amendment and Content Discrimination*, 68 VA. L. REV. 203 (1982). But see Redish, *The
Content Distinction in First Amendment Analysis*, 34 STAN. L. REV. 113, 117 (1981).

[48] 102 S. Ct. at 3358.

ered by § 263.15, bears so heavily and pervasively on the welfare of children engaged in its production, we think the balance of competing interests is clearly struck and that it is permissible to consider these materials as without the protection of the First Amendment.

It remained for the Court to specify the contours of this unprotected category. Curiously, *Ferber* contains no initial description of the category itself, but it is fair to conclude that the category is described by reference to the New York statute—material containing sexual conduct by a child.[49] *Ferber's* other requirements can be viewed as qualifications or elaborations on this basic standard. First among these is that the category is limited to visual portrayals of sexual activity by children. In almost every imaginable case this will be a photographic portrayal.[50] This limitation follows from the particular state concerns involved, because a simulated or linguistic description of sexual conduct would not involve real children in the production. Moreover, the proscribed depictions of sexual conduct must be specifically described in the relevant state law, and the Court clearly had in mind a specificity requirement such as that set forth in *Miller*.[51] Although the Court indicated that the same types of sexual conduct specified in *Miller* would apply to child pornography, it is possible to argue that a more expansive definition of those acts could apply to child pornography. Given that *Ginsberg v. New York*[52] permits an adjusted application of the obscenity standard when materials are sold to children, application of *Ginsberg* by

---

[49] The language quoted in the text accompanying note 48 *supra* supports the conclusion that the Court intended the constitutional definition of child pornography to be coextensive with New York's statutory definition, subject to those qualifications found elsewhere in *Ferber*.

[50] The exact language is "live performance or photographic or other visual reproduction of live performances." 102 S. Ct. at 3358.

[51] 102 S. Ct. at 3358. The relevant age must also be specified, and *id.* at 3358 n.17 implies that any age up to and including eighteen would be constitutionally permissible. The same footnote mentions, with neither approval nor condemnation, statutes that "define a child as a person under age 16 *or* who appears as a prepubescent." *Id.* (emphasis added). Because the Court specifically approved the use of "a person over statutory age who perhaps looked younger," *id.* at 3357, this standard may raise problems. But the lack of an "appearance" alternative might raise substantial proof problems in an action against a distributor or exhibitor. Because puberty tends to have a standard common law meaning of fourteen for boys and twelve for girls, *e.g.*, State v. Pierson, 44 Ark. 265 (1885), there seems nothing wrong with an appearance alternative as long as it is sufficiently below the specified age that there will be no deterrent effect on use of older people to simulate those more youthful.

[52] 390 U.S. 629 (1968).

analogy would seem to permit an adjusted definition of the conduct that may not be portrayed when engaged in by children. Mere nudity is undoubtedly insufficient, but there may be some flexibility with respect to what is to count, for example, as a lewd exhibition of the genitals.

Ferber adopted two other facets of settled obscenity doctrine. The *scienter* requirement of *Smith v. California*[53] is made applicable to child pornography,[54] and thus a defendant must be shown to have had knowledge of the character of the materials.[55] And the Court also made clear that it would engage in independent constitutional review of particular materials found by lower courts to be unprotected.[56] Although commonly associated with obscenity doctrine,[57] independent review applies to the full range of material lying just outside the borders of First Amendment protection,[58] and thus this aspect of *Ferber* breaks no new ground.

The resultant category of child pornography plainly bears little resemblance to the category of obscenity delineated by *Miller*. The Court in *Ferber* explicitly held that child pornography need not appeal to the prurient interest, need not be patently offensive, and need not be based on a consideration of the material as a whole.[59] This last aspect is most important, because it means that the presence of some serious literary, artistic, political, or scientific matter will not constitutionally redeem material containing depictions of sexual conduct by children.

The Court referred to the foregoing factors in terms of having "adjusted" the *Miller* test, but that is like saying that a butterfly is an adjusted camel. The category of child pornography is quite unlike the category of obscenity, although in practice the materials encompassed by the two categories will likely be similar. The dif-

---

[53] 361 U.S. 147 (1959).

[54] 102 S. Ct. at 3358–59.

[55] Hamling v. United States, 418 U.S. 87, 119–24 (1974). See generally SCHAUER, THE LAW OF OBSCENITY 222–26 (1976).

[56] 102 S. Ct. at 3364 n.28.

[57] *E.g.*, Jenkins v. Georgia, 418 U.S. 153, 160 (1974); Miller v. California, 413 U.S. 15, 29–30 (1973); Jacobellis v. Ohio, 378 U.S. 184, 188 (1964) (plurality opinion).

[58] *E.g.*, New York Times Co. v. Sullivan, 376 U.S. 254, 285 (1964); Edwards v. South Carolina, 372 U.S. 229, 235 (1963). Other cases are collected in NAACP v. Claiborne Hardware Co., 102 S. Ct. 3409, 3427 n.50 (1982).

[59] 102 S. Ct. at 3358.

ference in the legal description of the categories, however, will be very noticeable in litigation. The prosecution will prevail in a child pornography case if it proves no more than that the material contains photographic depictions of children engaged in sexual activity, that the conduct is specified in the governing statute, and that the defendant knew the character of the materials. Under such a simple standard, prosecutors will not have nearly the difficulties in proving child pornography as they have had in proving legal obscenity.[60]

The problem with this streamlined definition, however, is that it encompasses material that is hardly pornographic at all. Although the Court held that the material need not be considered as a whole, it emphasized that it was not deciding whether the law could be constitutionally applied to serious works such as medical books or *National Geographic*.[61] This potential reach of the statute suggests overbreadth, but the Court barred *Ferber* from raising the claim, relying on the "substantial overbreadth" standard of *Broadrick v. Oklahoma*.[62] Because the possibility of medical book and similar applications was so remote when compared to the constitutional reach of the statute, the Court held the statute not to be substantially overbroad and thus not subject to a facial attack by one whose own conduct was clearly subject to prohibition.[63]

As Justice Stevens pointed out in his concurrence, the majority's approach to the substantive question made the overbreadth issue easy.[64] By eliminating the "taken as a whole" requirement, thus permitting prosecution of material with some serious value, the majority gave the statute a broad reach. Most of the space that under a narrower holding would be overbroad was thereby filled with constitutional applications. Overbreadth problems are likely to arise when a constitutional rule significantly limits the reach of

---

[60] See Project, *An Empirical Inquiry into the Effects of Miller v. California on the Control of Obscenity*, 52 N.Y.U.L. REV. 810, 910–25 (1977).

[61] 102 S. Ct. at 3363.

[62] 413 U.S. 601 (1973).

[63] 102 S. Ct. at 3359–63. *Ferber*'s restatement of overbreadth principles, as well as its important clarification that *Broadrick* applies to cases other than those containing major nonspeech elements, is more significant than my brief treatment might suggest. A comprehensive and critical recent treatment of overbreadth is Monaghan, *Overbreadth*, 1981 SUPREME COURT REVIEW 1.

[64] 102 S. Ct. at 3367 (Stevens, J., concurring).

state power. Conversely, it is hard for a statute to be overly broad if the constitutional rule permits broad application. Justice Stevens would have preferred a more guarded approach, delaying until it arose the question of material with some serious value,[65] rather than deciding in this case that the presence of some serious value would not prevent a finding of nonprotection.

The question of serious value produced the other two opinions in the case. Justice Brennan, joined by Justice Marshall, would not permit the application of a child pornography statute to "depictions of children that in themselves do have serious literary, artistic, scientific or medical value."[66] And Justice O'Connor emphasized just the opposite—that the Court's holding did not require New York to except from the reach of its statute material with some serious value.[67]

Justice O'Connor's concurrence seems to have been prompted by some ambiguity surrounding the majority's reservation of the question relating to medical books and *National Geographic*. But the majority's explicit holding that the material need not be taken as a whole supports the conclusion that the presence of some serious value will not preclude prosecution. Even this conclusion, however, leaves two situations unaddressed by the *Ferber* majority. In one case a depiction of children engaged in sexual conduct might

---

[65] *Id.* The desire to delay a constitutional ruling may be based on two different but often confused rationales, elements of both of which are found in Justice Stevens's opinion. On the one hand we may wish a case-by-case approach to a particular issue, focusing on the contextual factors found in the particular case. See *id.* at 3366. Apart from this, however, we may still choose a less contextual, more categorical, approach to a particular issue, such as the serious value issue in child pornography cases, but wish to delay specific formulation of that categorical rule until the case arises that presents the issue most clearly. *Id.* at 3367. The former approach goes more specifically to questions of First Amendment approach, while the latter is based on more general considerations relating to the exercise of the function of constitutional review. See Ashwander v. TVA, 297 U.S. 288, 346–48 (1936) (Brandeis, J., concurring). The principle of delaying a constitutional ruling until necessary, although based on undeniably important factors relating to the role of the Court and the necessity of a good record, is too often overestimated. The Court's role as adjudicator should not blind us to its role as guider of lower courts and legislatures and setter of standards. See Schauer, *"Private" Speech and the "Private" Forum: Givhan v. Western Line School District*, 1979 SUPREME COURT REVIEW 217, 217–18. As the Supreme Court gives plenary consideration to a smaller percentage of the cases presented to it, as the number of lower courts increases, as the amount of lower court litigation increases, and as there are greater delays before the Supreme Court finally decides an issue, then to that extent the consequences of a failure to give advance guidance become more severe. If this is true, then the *Ashwander* and related principles should be treated more as suggestive than as dispositive.

[66] 102 S. Ct. at 3365 (Brennan, J., concurring).

[67] *Id.* at 3364 (O'Connor, J., concurring).

itself have serious value,[68] a situation to be distinguished from the case in which a valueless depiction is part of a larger work containing value elsewhere.[69] The other and more likely case is that in which the work is predominantly serious, rather than merely containing some serious value.[70]

One way to resolve these problems would be to establish a *per se* rule prohibiting without exception the use of children engaged in sexual acts. But that solution sacrifices too much of the First Amendment on the altar of predictability, for there *are* situations in which such depictions might serve important artistic or educational goals.[71] If and when presented with such a case, the Court should establish a First Amendment–derived affirmative defense for such material.[72] Under such a defense, a disseminator could avoid conviction by proving by clear and convincing evidence[73] that the material, taken as a whole, is predominantly a serious literary, artistic, political, scientific, medical, or educational work[74] and that the depictions of children engaged in sexual conduct are reasonably necessary[75] to the work as a whole. This affirmative defense would satisfy the most serious First Amendment concerns, especially with

---

[68] Some artistic works might fit this category, as well as material dealing expressly with the sexuality of children.

[69] A clever pornographer, for example, might publish an illustrated version of the *Ferber* opinion, or perhaps of this article. *Cf.* Hamling v. United States, 418 U.S. 87 (1974).

[70] A serious but occasionally explicit version of *Romeo and Juliet* would seem to fit this description.

[71] See notes 68 & 70 *supra*. Where the work is not predominantly pornographic, the humiliation-embarrassment-publicity harm seems to be less. 102 S. Ct. at 3365 (Brennan, J., concurring). Moreover, a predominantly serious publication is not likely to be produced clandestinely, and thus it would be easier to reach the producer for the actual practice of using children, thus eliminating one of the Court's major justifications for permitting actions against dissemination as well as use of children.

[72] Establishing this factor as an affirmative defense, rather than part of the prosecution's burden of proof, creates no due process problems. See Engle v. Isaac, 102 S. Ct. 1558 (1982).

[73] Proof beyond a reasonable doubt would give too little respect to the First Amendment considerations behind the affirmative defense. A simple preponderance standard seems to go too far in the other direction, but this estimate is subject to reevaluation based on experience in actual trials.

[74] The Court's specific mention of medical and educational works, 102 S. Ct. at 3363, suggests that they be specifically included along with the *Miller* list.

[75] "Reasonably necessary" is a compromise standard between "essential" and "reasonably related." The former would get the courts too far into second-guessing literary, artistic, and similar judgments, but the latter might be so relaxed as to be inconsistent with the major tenor of the *Ferber* holding.

independent constitutional review at the trial and appellate levels,[76] while at the same time not presenting the prosecution with the major proof problems that would ensue if the prosecution were required to prove that the material was not predominantly serious.[77]

II. The Paths to Nonprotection

Perhaps the most intriguing feature of *Ferber* is its doctrinal ambiguity. Although it is clear that the Court was determined to reach the result of nonprotection, it is difficult to track the Court's doctrinal route to that destination. I use "nonprotection" in a broad and simple sense merely as a characterization of a result: it is constitutionally permissible to restrict utterance x in circumstances y. But there are numerous doctrinal paths to nonprotection, and the multiplicity of means to the same end reflects the increasing complexity of First Amendment doctrine. *Ferber* is the ideal vehicle for exploring the various paths to nonprotection, because it does not follow any one of them exclusively. Rather, the majority reaches the result of nonprotection by almost randomly picking elements of each of the methods the Court has at times used to justify the conclusion that an utterance is subject to restriction. In sorting out these multiple paths to nonprotection, we may make major progress toward understanding both *Ferber* and the increasingly complex nature of the First Amendment.

A. INCIDENTAL RESTRICTIONS OF SPEECH

Certain instances of communication may be unprotected if their regulation is merely the incidental by-product of a more general state interest. *United States v. O'Brien*[78] and the important commentary it inspired[79] have established that state interests unrelated to

---

[76] See notes 56–58 and accompanying text *supra*. The notion of independent review at the trial level refers to a judge's plainly required task of withdrawing a case from consideration by the jury if a conviction would violate the Constitution.

[77] *Cf.* Miller v. California, 413 U.S. 15, 22–25 (1973).

[78] 391 U.S. 367 (1968). See also Spence v. Washington, 418 U.S. 405, 414 n.8 (1974).

[79] Ely, *Flag Desecration: A Case Study in the Roles of Categorization and Balancing in First Amendment Analysis*, 88 HARV. L. REV. 1482 (1975). See also TRIBE, note 16 *supra*, at 580–601. For criticisms, to me unsuccessful, of this approach, see Emerson, *First Amendment Doctrine and the Burger Court*, 68 CALIF. L. REV. 422, 470–74 (1980); Farber, *Content Regula-*

the communicative impact of the speech may presumptively be served if no less restrictive alternative is available and if there is no excess effect on communication in fact.[80] Determination that a restriction on communication is only incidental to a state regulatory purpose unrelated to communicative impact is therefore one path to nonprotection.

The *Ferber* majority relied on *Giboney v. Empire Storage & Ice Co.*[81] for the proposition that speech may be restricted where it is an integral part of some other plainly regulable act, but this line of argument received little more than an en passant mention.[82] Perhaps this is best explained by the logical flaws of the speech-combined-with-action rationale. All communication has some relation with some course of conduct. Child pornography is an integral part of an illegal act in the sense that an illegal act gives rise to the communication and because the publication exists solely because there is an illegal act to portray. But these cannot be sufficient conditions for nonprotection, for were that the case then both *Pentagon Papers*[83] and *Landmark Communications, Inc. v. Virginia*[84] should have been decided differently. The political content in both of those cases may provide a distinction, but then it is a difference in the value of the speech rather than its connection with illegal activity that justifies nonprotection in *Ferber*.

If the Court in *Ferber* had relied on *O'Brien* rather than *Giboney*, and therefore looked to the State's justification for regulation, this approach may have been more fruitful. The state interest in regulating child pornography is not based on communicative impact. The state is not concerned, for example, with whether viewers of child pornography will as a result set out to exploit or molest children. Nor is the state concerned with the effect that viewing child pornography might have on community environment or morals. Rather, the state is concerned with protecting those children that might be employed in the production process. This is an interest in

---

tion and the First Amendment: A Revisionist View, 68 GEO. L.J. 727, 742–47 (1980); Redish, note 47 *supra*.

[80] United States v. O'Brien, 391 U.S. 367, 377 (1968). The import of the commentary, note 79 *supra*, is that the general *O'Brien* approach is not limited to symbolic speech.

[81] 336 U.S. 490 (1949).

[82] 102 S. Ct. at 3357.

[83] New York Times Co. v. United States, 403 U.S. 713 (1971) (per curiam).

[84] 435 U.S. 829 (1978).

restricting commerce in a product that is created with the use of clearly regulable noncommunicative conduct. Perhaps the most appropriate analogy, therefore, is to the use of child labor in the publication of a newspaper, and to the question of whether a newspaper so produced could be restricted as contraband.[85] If we answer that question in the affirmative,[86] then we must ask whether anything distinguishes the child pornography case.

One quick answer is that a regulatory purpose unrelated to communicative impact is shown in the child labor case by applications of the statute to entities in no way involved with communication.[87] Child pornography is different because the specific sanctions, although not based on communicative impact, are limited to communication. In this sense the analogy might be to the situation where only newspapers were subject to the child labor laws. *Grosjean v. American Press*[88] now comes to mind, but *Grosjean* was in fact a simple viewpoint discrimination case in which the tax was levied solely in reaction to the particular position espoused by the majority of newspapers covered by the new tax.

Although *Ferber* is therefore not controlled by *Grosjean*, its result cannot be justified by a simple reference to *O'Brien*. For *Ferber* as well as *Young* present the special situation in which communicative impact does not explain the state's regulatory purpose, but in which only communication of a certain form is subject to regulation. *Ferber* and *Young* thus present an issue also lurking in the background of *Metromedia, Inc. v. City of San Diego*:[89] How are we to deal with the case in which certain industries or certain formats of communication present problems unrelated to communicative impact but still peculiar to a particular form of communication?[90] Similar prob-

---

[85] *Cf.* United States v. Darby, 312 U.S. 100 (1941).

[86] See Oklahoma Press Publishing Co. v. Walling, 327 U.S. 186 (1946); Mabee v. White Plains Publishing Co., 327 U.S. 178 (1946); Associated Press v. NLRB, 301 U.S. 103 (1937).

[87] Conversely, the absence of such applications would tend to rebut an assumption that no intent to regulate communication existed. *Cf.* Redish, note 47 *supra*, at 145.

[88] 297 U.S. 233 (1936). See Stephan, note 47 *supra*, at 215–18.

[89] 453 U.S. 490 (1981).

[90] I would thus modify the standard distinction between viewpoint discrimination and subject-matter discrimination to include a new and separate problem of format discrimination. The issue is presented by the question reserved in *Metromedia* of whether a total and content-neutral ban on all billboards would be permissible. 453 U.S. at 515 n.20. Implications of a negative answer come from *Metromedia* itself, *id.*, as well as Schad v. Mount Ephraim, 452 U.S. 61 (1981). But a different conclusion might be reached regarding a restriction of all structures of a certain size, where that restriction included all billboards as well as many other structures.

lems would arise if it were found that child labor was a problem only in the motion picture industry, or that newsprint contained a toxic chemical justifying special safety precautions.

Ferber and *Young* are somewhat stickier in that the industry in these cases is characterized not only by its communicative nature but also by the particular nature of the communication. Here an industry-oriented regulation is also a form of content regulation.[91] But where, as in *Ferber*, the state interest is not with the effect of that content on viewers, the special dangers of content regulation are absent, and the case is one more of format discrimination than content discrimination.[92] Although the *Ferber* majority did not follow through with its suggestion that this was more a conduct case than a speech case, it could have arrived at the result of nonprotection by concentrating more closely on the state's interest in controlling an evil unrelated to communicative impact.

B. UNCOVERED SPEECH

Under the *O'Brien* route, state concerns unrelated to communicative impact can produce the result of nonprotection. But even if the state interest is characterized as in some way related to communicative impact, nonprotection may be reached by determining that the type of communication involved is totally unrelated to the purposes of the First Amendment.[93] Some forms of speech are not protected by the First Amendment because they are not even covered by the First Amendment.[94] For such verbal or pictorial acts, the First Amendment's protective devices never come into play. The noncoverage path to nonprotection justifies treating perjury, price fixing, solicitation to nonpolitical crime, and contract law, for example, as outside the First Amendment, for these are all categories of speech in which the state's justification for restriction is not

---

[91] Thus the analogue to *Young* would be a regulation of all theaters, or all bookstores, but based on *Young*'s premises.

[92] See note 90 *supra*.

[93] Because I have previously discussed the matter at length, I will not repeat here the argument that such a methodology can be intellectually justified as well as located in existing doctrine. Schauer, note 13 *supra*, at 267–82; Schauer, *Can Rights Be Abused?* 31 PHIL. Q. 225 (1981); Schauer, *Speech and "Speech"—Obscenity and "Obscenity": An Exercise in the Interpretation of Constitutional Language*, 67 GEO. L.J. 899 (1979).

[94] *Id.* See also BeVier, note 1 *supra*, at 301; Kalven, *The Reasonable Man and the First Amendment: Hill, Butts, and Walker*, 1967 SUPREME COURT REVIEW 267, 278; Shiffrin, note 13 *supra*, at 916 n.17.

measured against a First Amendment standard.[95] In terms of issues actually coming before the Court, this same methodology is present in *Roth-Paris*,[96] in *Beauharnais*,[97] and in *Valentine v. Chrestensen*.[98] It is also supported by some but not all of the language in *Chaplinsky*.[99] Of these cases only the obscenity cases survive today,[100] but we can nevertheless identify a methodology by which the First Amendment is relevant only in the sense that we must look to its boundaries. Once a class of utterance is determined to be outside those boundaries, the First Amendment inquiry ends.

The Court in *Ferber* refers to child pornography as a category outside the First Amendment, and its citation to *Chaplinsky*, *Beauharnais* (!), and the obscenity cases seemingly supports the inference that child pornography is treated as totally uncovered by the First Amendment.[101] But citations and superficial appearances can be deceiving, and closer inspection reveals that the denial of coverage is not the path the Court follows to nonprotection in *Ferber*.

One characteristic of the classic noncoverage cases is that the determination of lack of coverage is made solely on the basis of the First Amendment value of the utterance itself, without regard to possible justifications for restriction.[102] For if the utterances involved are totally unrelated to the purposes of the First Amendment, there is no need to consider, except under a rational basis standard, why the state might want to regulate them. *Ferber*, how-

---

[95] See generally Greenawalt, *Speech and Crime*, 1980 AM. B. FOUND. RESEARCH J. 645; Schauer, note 13 *supra*, at 267–72.

[96] Paris Adult Theatre I v. Slaton, 413 U.S. 49 (1973); Roth v. United States, 354 U.S. 476 (1957).

[97] Beauharnais v. Illinois, 343 U.S. 250 (1952).

[98] 316 U.S. 52 (1942).

[99] Chaplinsky v. New Hampshire, 315 U.S. 568 (1942). To the extent that *Chaplinsky* talks about "classes of speech, the prevention and punishment of which have never been thought to raise any Constitutional problem," *id.* at 571–72, it is consistent with the discussion in the text. But in referring to "no *essential* part of any exposition of ideas" and to a "*slight* social value as a step to truth," *id.* at 572 (emphasis added), and in referring to this slight value as having been "outweighed," *id.*, by other interests, *Chaplinsky* seems of a different genre.

[100] I assume that the original *Chaplinsky* approach is virtually unrecognizable after, *e.g.*, Gooding v. Wilson, 405 U.S. 518 (1972). *Valentine* perished in Virginia State Bd. of Pharmacy v. Virginia Citizens Consumer Council, Inc., 425 U.S. 748 (1976), and *Beauharnais* in a combination of *Brandenburg* and New York Times Co. v. Sullivan, 376 U.S. 254 (1964).

[101] 102 S. Ct. at 3358.

[102] See Greenawalt, note 95 *supra*, at 784.

ever, does not separate the question of speech value from the question of the strength of the state's regulatory interest. The two are considered together, and the Court never determines that child pornography, in isolation, is totally beyond the normative functions of the First Amendment. Moreover, the discussion of state interest in *Ferber* seems premised on emphasizing the particularly overwhelming nature of that interest, and no such showing would be required if child pornography itself were not encompassed by the First Amendment.

The Court's delineation of the category is consistent with the interpretation that the category is not beyond the purview of the First Amendment. If the Court had in fact followed the noncoverage path to nonprotection, we would expect to see, as suggested in *Chaplinsky*[103] and applied in the obscenity cases, a carefully delimited category whose definition was designed to ensure that only material with no First Amendment significance was included. But because there is no necessary connection between the harm at issue here and total First Amendment worthlessness,[104] the category that results from *Ferber* is not defined by the absence of First Amendment value. And so long as there is acknowledged First Amendment value, even if small, in the resultant category, the differences between *Ferber* and the obscenity and other noncoverage cases seem more significant than the similarities.

C. OUTWEIGHING THE FIRST AMENDMENT

The *Beauharnais-Roth-Paris* path to nonprotection proceeds from the assumption that some utterances receive no First Amendment protection at all. Another path to nonprotection proceeds from the opposite assumption—that even the maximum First Amendment protection is less than absolute.[105] Speech that is covered by the First Amendment is not necessarily protected by it, and covered speech will go unprotected if the state can demonstrate a sufficiently strong reason for restriction. Although it might be pos-

---

[103] 315 U.S. at 571 ("certain well-defined and narrowly limited classes of spech").

[104] 102 S. Ct. at 3356–57.

[105] Apart from the especially stringent protection against prior restraints, which is still not absolute, *e.g.*, Nebraska Press Ass'n v. Stuart, 427 U.S. 539 (1976), the maximum protection under the First Amendment is found in the less than absolute protection of Brandenburg v. Ohio, 395 U.S. 444 (1969) (per curiam).

sible to construct First Amendment doctrine so that all covered speech was *eo ipso* protected,[106] we have not followed this strategy of carefully defined absolutes. Even speech at the core of the First Amendment may be restricted if the state interest is sufficiently strong. Although we normally associate this high but not absolute level of protection with the *Brandenburg-Hess*[107] formulation of the clear and present danger standard,[108] it is possible that *Brandenburg-Hess* is representative rather than exclusive. Not every enormous state interest can fit neatly into *Brandenburg's* incitement-immediacy-inevitability formula, and other versions of the general clear and present danger formula may remain viable for special or novel circumstances.[109]

If we accept that there may be dangers so momentous as to outweigh the First Amendment, yet not capable of characterization in *Brandenburg* terms, then *Ferber* can be viewed as partially relying on this "covered but outweighed" path to nonprotection. Although the Court does not cite any cases of the clear and present danger genre, it does describe the interest in protecting children as both "compelling" and "surpassing."[110] It may be that "compelling" means something less here than it does in its more established equal protection context,[111] but it seems more sensible, especially in light of *Globe Newspaper Co. v. Superior Court*,[112] to interpret that language as describing a state interest equal in force but different in kind

---

[106] *E.g.*, EMERSON, THE SYSTEM OF FREEDOM OF EXPRESSION (1970); Frantz, *The First Amendment in the Balance*, 71 YALE L.J. 1424 (1962); Meiklejohn, *The First Amendment Is an Absolute*, 1961 SUPREME COURT REVIEW 245; Nimmer, *The Right to Speak from* Times *to Time: First Amendment Theory Applied to Libel and Misapplied to Privacy*, 56 CALIF. L. REV. 935 (1968).

[107] Hess v. Indiana, 414 U.S. 105 (1973); Brandenburg v. Ohio, 395 U.S. 444 (1969) (per curiam). I take the two together because the force of *Brandenburg's* imminence and likelihood requirements cannot be fully appreciated without the *Hess* application.

[108] See generally Linde, *"Clear and Present Danger" Reexamined: Dissonance in the Brandenburg Concerto*, 22 STAN. L. REV. 1163 (1970); Strong, *Fifty Years of "Clear and Present Danger": from Schenck to Brandenburg—and Beyond*, 1969 SUPREME COURT REVIEW 41.

[109] See especially United States v. The Progressive, Inc., 467 F. Supp. 990 (W.D. Wis. 1979), mandamus denied *sub nom.* Morland v. Sprecher, 443 U.S. 709 (1979), dismissed, 610 F.2d 819 (7th Cir. 1979). See also Van Alstyne, *A Graphic Review of the Free Speech Clause*, 70 CALIF. L. REV. 107 (1982).

[110] 102 S. Ct. at 3354, 3355.

[111] *E.g.*, Shapiro v. Thompson, 394 U.S. 618 (1969).

[112] 102 S. Ct. 2613, 2621 (1982). The suggestion in *Globe Newspapers* is that the "compelling" interest in protecting minors might in some circumstances justify overriding First Amendment considerations more vital than those at issue in *Ferber*.

from the *Brandenburg-Hess* standard. Reports of the demise of *Dennis* may have been premature.[113]

Ferber is therefore important in hinting that interests other than preventing disorder may justify restricting even speech at the core of the First Amendment. But here the Court backed off. For although it has held that speech other than political is entitled to full protection,[114] child pornography is not put in this class. Although technically within the First Amendment, it is held to be much closer to the fringe than the core.[115] With that determination the Court avoided the question of whether the interest in protecting children might outweigh speech at the core of the First Amendment, and thus the references to "compelling" and "surpassing" interests seem more rhetorical than doctrinal.

D. LESS VALUABLE SPEECH

A final path to nonprotection recognizes that not all speech covered by the First Amendment deserves the same level of protection, some forms being subject to control under standards less stringent than clear and present danger in any form. Recognition of these different levels, especially in the offensive speech[116] and commercial speech[117] cases, is one of the most important recent developments in First Amendment methodology.

Within the broad approach of identifying speech entitled to some but not full First Amendment protection, two approaches are possi-

---

[113] Dennis v. United States, 341 U.S. 494, 510 (1951). The first inclinations that there were stirrings in the corpse of *Dennis* came from its employment in Nebraska Press Ass'n v. Stuart, 427 U.S. 539 (1976). For a powerful demonstration that the current standard is the *Dennis* formula subject to a clear and present danger threshold, see Van Alstyne, note 109 *supra*.

[114] See Abood v. Detroit Bd. of Educ. 431 U.S. 209, 231 (1977).

[115] 102 S. Ct. at 3357–58.

[116] FCC v. Pacifica Foundation, 438 U.S. 726 (1978); Young v. American Mini Theatres, Inc., 427 U.S. 50 (1976). For opposing views of this development, compare Farber, note 79 *supra*, with Stone, note 14 *supra*.

[117] *E.g.*, Central Hudson Gas & Elec. Co. v. Public Service Comm., 447 U.S. 557 (1980); Virginia State Bd. of Pharmacy v. Virginia Citizens Consumer Council, Inc., 425 U.S. 748 (1976). Academic criticisms of the offensive speech developments has tended in the direction of objecting to the use of a lower standard, *e.g.*, Stone, note 14 *supra*, but most objections to the commercial speech cases have been along the lines that commercial speech should have remainded outside the First Amendment. *E.g.*, Baker, *Commercial Speech: A Problem in the Theory of Freedom*, 62 IOWA L. REV. 1 (1976); Emerson, note 79 *supra*; Jackson & Jeffries, *Commercial Speech: Economic Due Process and the First Amendment*, 65 VA. L. REV. 1 (1979).

ble. One is to determine *a priori*, without reference to potential justifications for restriction, that speech within a given category is entitled to a particular level of protection. A test is then formulated that applies to any putative restriction within that category. This approach characterizes the recent commercial speech cases, with the four-part standard of *Central Hudson*[118] being applied to a wide range of possible restrictions of commercial speech.

Alternatively, a more particular test may be established by reference not only to the value of the speech within the category, but also to a particular justification for regulating that category. It is this approach that is seen in the fighting words cases,[119] the offensive speech cases,[120] and the defamation cases.[121] Thus the Court has never said that all factually false speech is to be measured against the same standard, or that all offensive speech is to be treated alike. Instead it weighs speech value against the strength of a particular state justification, such as that in protecting reputation in the defamation cases and in preventing urban decay in *Young*. It is tempting to follow the accepted wisdom and say that the Court balances the interests involved, but the balancing metaphor seems inapt, because it suggests, as with real scales, that one side simply does or does not outweigh the other. But this does not seem completely accurate in the First Amendment context, for in none of the cases under discussion does one interest win and the other lose. Rather, the Court attempts to accommodate worthy but conflicting interests in a way that both interests survive to some extent. The resulting accommodation rule, when applied in particular cases, will—as in defamation, fighting words, and offensive speech— often produce the result of nonprotection, but here that result flows from a rule that is in turn premised on the determination that some forms of speech are entitled to only partial First Amendment protection.

Once we recognize this distinction between ways of dealing with

---

[118] Central Hudson Gas & Elec. Co. v. Public Service Comm., 447 U.S. 557, 563–66 (1980). The wording of the test is slightly different in Metromedia, Inc. v. City of San Diego, 453 U.S. 490, 507 (1981).

[119] *E.g.*, Lewis v. New Orleans, 415 U.S. 130 (1974); Gooding v. Wilson, 405 U.S. 518 (1972).

[120] See note 116 *supra*. See also Schad v. Mount Ephraim, 452 U.S. 61 (1981).

[121] *E.g.*, Gertz v. Robert Welch, Inc., 418 U.S. 323 (1974); New York Times Co. v. Sullivan, 376 U.S. 254 (1964).

partially protected speech, the path followed by the Court in *Ferber* becomes apparent. As with commercial speech, some offensive speech, and some factually false speech, the Court holds child pornography to be within the First Amendment, but deserving less than maximum First Amendment protection. Unlike the commercial speech cases, however, the Court does not take this as justification for establishing a general rule applicable to any regulation of that category. Rather, it follows the defamation cases, and to some extent the fighting words cases,[122] in custom tailoring an accommodation rule to a specific state interest.

III. Codifying the First Amendment

Although the *Ferber* methodology thus seems closest to that employed in the defamation and fighting words cases, it takes some effort to isolate this path to nonprotection from the Court's repeated references to cases and standards supporting a number of different doctrinal approaches. In large part this process of extracting bits and pieces from different strands of First Amendment doctrine is explained by *Ferber's* presentation of an issue that was both factually and doctrinally novel. Given this novelty, it is neither surprising nor cause for criticism that the Court felt compelled to rely on many cases and doctrines of only indirect relevance.

The product of this process was the creation of yet another comparatively distinct area of First Amendment doctrine. The rules relating to child pornography now take their place alongside the equally distinct rules relating to obscenity, defamation, advocacy of illegal conduct, invasion of privacy,[123] fighting words, symbolic speech,[124] and offensive speech. Moreover, each of these areas contains its own corpus of subrules, principles, categories, qualifi-

---

[122] I refer not only to the recent cases, note 119 *supra*, but also to the "slight value" interpretation of *Chaplinsky*. See note 99 *supra*.

[123] Although the Supreme Court has yet to decide a pure invasion of privacy case not involving either aspects of falsity or commercial misappropriation, suggestions of a distinct approach are found in Zacchini v. Scripps-Howard Broadcasting Co., 433 U.S. 562 (1977). Moreover, a rather discrete standard of "newsworthiness" can be discerned in lower court cases. *E.g.*, Virgil v. Time, Inc., 527 F.2d 1122 (9th Cir. 1975).

[124] The extent to which symbolic speech is a separate doctrinal category depends on whether the Court is taken at its word in limiting the *O'Brien* test to cases involving symbolic speech. See note 80 *supra*.

cations, and exceptions. There are also special principles for particular contexts, such as government employment,[125] the public forum,[126] and electronic broadcasting,[127] and in addition we have the pervasive tools of First Amendment analysis, such as chilling effect,[128] prior restraint,[129] vagueness,[130] overbreadth,[131] and the least restrictive alternative.[132] Finally, there is the additional overlay of numerous broad approaches to a First Amendment issue. When we take all of this together it becomes clear that the First Amendment is becoming increasingly intricate, which has prompted one scholar to observe pejoratively that First Amendment doctrine is beginning to resemble the Internal Revenue Code.[133] The metaphor rings true, and maybe we are moving toward codification of the First Amendment. Whether this is cause for concern requires a closer look.

In talking about "codification," neither I nor anyone else is suggesting that the First Amendment itself should be codified. It is just fine as written—brief, elegant, and desirably vague, while still eloquently suggesting great strength and breadth. Nor would we want to organize the surrounding doctrine in a form that could be literally codified in a way that the Internal Revenue Code is. That approach would sacrifice too much flexibility for only a slight increase in precision.

It does not follow from the foregoing, however, that First Amendment doctrine should be as simple and vague as the Amendment itself. The arguments for textual simplicity do not apply with

---

[125] *E.g.*, Pickering v. Board of Education, 391 U.S. 563 (1968). See also Mt. Healthy City School District v. Doyle, 429 U.S. 274 (1977).

[126] See generally Stone, *Fora Americana: Speech in Public Places*, 1974 SUPREME COURT REVIEW 233; Kalven, *The Concept of the Public Forum: Cox v. Louisiana*, 1965 SUPREME COURT REVIEW 1. The most recent case is Heffron v. International Society for Krishna Consciousness, 452 U.S. 640 (1981).

[127] Red Lion Broadcasting Co. v. FCC, 395 U.S. 367 (1969).

[128] See generally Schauer, *Fear, Risk and the First Amendment: Unraveling the "Chilling Effect,"* 58 B.U.L. REV. 685 (1978).

[129] *E.g.*, Vance v. Universal Amusement Co., 445 U.S. 308 (1980) (per curiam); Near v. Minnesota, 283 U.S. 697 (1931).

[130] *E.g.*, Smith v. Goguen, 415 U.S. 566 (1974); Interstate Circuit, Inc. v. City of Dallas, 390 U.S. 676 (1968).

[131] See *Ferber*, 102 S. Ct. at 3359–64.

[132] *E.g.*, Globe Newspaper Co. v. Superior Court, 102 S. Ct. 2613, 2622 (1982); United States v. O'Brien, 391 U.S. 367 (1968).

[133] Conversation with William Van Alstyne.

equal or even any force to doctrinal simplicity. A characteristic feature of American law is drafting simple textual instruments with the expectation that courts will use the open-ended text as the touchstone for creating, in modified common law style, a complex and comprehensive doctrinal structure.[134] This feature pervades not only constitutional law but American statutory law as well.[135]

That tradition alone suggests that great complexity in First Amendment doctrine is no cause for surprise. Moreover, taking *Schenck* as the starting point,[136] we have now had sixty-four years' experience with First Amendment problems. As time goes on situations repeat themselves. We are then more able to discern patterns, and these patterns enable us to group recurring features into legal rules and categories. The more we have seen, the less likely we are to be surprised, and open-ended flexibility becomes progressively less important. In the face of this, we must shift the burden and ask whether there is any reason for treating the First Amendment specially in terms of doctrinal simplicity.[137]

The desire for simplicity in First Amendment doctrine is often expressed in terms of a search for "coherence."[138] The contemporary way to praise a theory (especially your own) is to describe it as "coherent," and coherence, in the sense of everything fitting together without inconsistencies, seems on its face to be a worthy goal.[139] But coherence need not produce simplicity. An intricate

---

[134] *Cf.* LEVI, AN INTRODUCTION TO LEGAL REASONING (1949).

[135] Examples of simple and vague statutory language that have generated enormously complex doctrines include Section 1 of the Sherman Antitrust Act, 15 U.S.C. § 1 (1976), and the Securities and Exchange Commission's Rule 10b-5. 17 C.F.R. § 240.10b-5(a) (1981).

[136] Schenck v. United States, 249 U.S. 47 (1919). To take *Schenck* as the starting point seems justifiable, but it is an oversimplification. See Gunther, *Learned Hand and the Origins of Modern First Amendment Doctrine: Some Fragments of History*, 27 STAN. L. REV. 719 (1975); Rabban, *The First Amendment in Its Forgotten Years*, 90 YALE L.J. 514 (1981).

[137] The desire for simplicity need not be unique to the First Amendment. See Craig v. Boren, 429 U.S. 190, 211–12 (1976) (Stevens, J., concurring) ("There is only one Equal Protection Clause. . . . It does not direct the courts to apply one standard of review in some cases and a different standard in other cases").

[138] *E.g.*, HAIMAN, SPEECH AND LAW IN A FREE SOCIETY 425 (1981); Emerson, note 79 *supra*, at 474; Redish, *The Value of Free Speech*, 130 U. PA. L. REV. 591, 592 (1982); Stark, *Book Review*, 17 HARV. C.R.-C.L. L. REV. 271, 272 (1982).

[139] Much of modern legal, political, and moral theory is based on a coherence perspective, in the sense of assuming or arguing that all of our values do, can, or should fit together. *E.g.*, DWORKIN, TAKING RIGHTS SERIOUSLY (1977); RAWLS, A THEORY OF JUSTICE (1971); RICHARDS, A THEORY OF REASONS FOR ACTION (1971); GEWIRTH, REASON AND MORALITY (1978). But maybe our values do not, or can not, fit together. See BERLIN, CONCEPTS AND CATEGORIES: PHILOSOPHICAL ESSAYS (Hardy ed. 1979); Williams, *Conflicts of Values*, in THE IDEA OF FREEDOM: ESSAYS IN HONOUR OF ISAIAH BERLIN 221 (Ryan ed. 1979).

doctrinal structure might still fit together like a jigsaw puzzle, with each principle fitting neatly into the exceptions in another.[140] But that approach requires enormous foresight to produce such precision in rules designed to govern the future. A coherent but complex doctrinal structure, devoid of gaps or inconsistencies, attempts to follow the model of a pure civil law system.[141] Attempting to formulate such a doctrinal system suffers from the same deficiency that has led the pure civil law model to be only a futile dream; no matter how carefully we define our concepts, new situations will arise that just do not fit. First Amendment doctrine serves the normative function of guiding future action, and we cannot incorporate into our standards intended to guide the future every contingency because we just do not know what they will be. Because "we are men, not gods,"[142] we can at best imperfectly predict the future, and the uncertainty of the human condition places insurmountable obstacles in the way of formulating a coherent and complete system of highly specific norms that will cover every situation likely to arise. *Ferber* itself is a perfect example, because the phenomenon of child pornography is so new that it would have been impossible to predict even ten years ago. And there is no reason to believe that ten years from now we will not be presented with First Amendment issues that we have no way of foreseeing today.

But we should not be too quick to dismiss the search for coherence. For coherence is more commonly urged as a simple and unitary principle of the First Amendment,[143] with more specific rules and doctrines being no more than applications of the one unifying principle. If the First Amendment is taken "really" to mean *x*, and *x* is simple, we have a coherent principle by definition. But will any single principle help in deciding cases? One would think, after all, that that is a major purpose of the exercise.

A single principle, defined at a high level of abstraction, certainly assists in terms of flexibility. An abstract single principle will be

---

[140] Such a view is implicit in, *e.g.*, BARRY, POLITICAL ARGUMENT (1965); FRIED, RIGHT AND WRONG (1978).

[141] See BENTHAM, OF LAWS IN GENERAL (Hart ed. 1970).

[142] HART, THE CONCEPT OF LAW 125 (1961).

[143] See note 138 *supra*. See also Baker, *Scope of the First Amendment Freedom of Speech*, 25 U.C.L.A.L. REV. 964 (1978); Richards, *Free Speech and Obscenity Law: Toward a Moral Theory of the First Amendment*, 123 U. PA. L. REV. 45 (1974). The various theories referred to differ in degree of complexity, but they hold in common a commitment to a single strong unifying theme.

able to accommodate almost any foreseeable and unforeseeable change in the nature of First Amendment problems. But that very flexibility is a crippling weakness, for unitary abstract principles can also accommodate any more particularized intuition of the designer or applier of the principle. Use of a single principle to deal with all of our problems produces application that is more likely to be conclusory than principled.

As an example, let us take the single principle of "self-realization," which at the moment is enjoying a good run in the arena of First Amendment theory.[144] Faced with the problem in *First National Bank of Boston v. Bellotti*[145] whether to grant First Amendment protection to corporate speech, one self-realization theorist has argued against the result in that case because self-realization is a right of individuals and does not apply to corporations.[146] But another, starting from the same principle, has reached the opposite conclusion by emphasizing the self-realization goals served by the receipt of information.[147] Similarly, self-realization could produce opposite results in *Gertz*,[148] depending on whether we focused, on the one hand, on the effect on self-realization of being the subject of false statements or, on the other hand, on the self-realization of the defamer in being unfettered in his communicative acts. And self-realization might lead to either of opposing conclusions about *Ferber*, varying with whether we focused on the self-realization of the children or the producers. I have picked self-realization only as an example, for a similar lack of predictive value could be identified in any other single principle of equivalent abstraction.[149]

The problem of excess abstraction does not surround every single-principle theory. A sufficiently narrow principle could serve the function of influencing if not completely determining the deci-

---

[144] *E.g.*, Baker, note 143 *supra*; Redish, note 138 *supra*; Richards, note 143 *supra*. Others take self-realization or a very similar value (*e.g.*, self-fulfillment) as important but not exclusive. *E.g.*, EMERSON, note 106 *supra*, at 6–7; TRIBE, note 16 *supra*, at 578–79.

[145] 435 U.S. 765 (1978).

[146] Baker, *Realizing Self-Realization: Corporate Political Expenditures and Redish's The Value of Free Speech*, 130 U. PA. L. REV. 646 (1982).

[147] Redish, *Self-Realization, Democracy, and Freedom of Expression: A Reply to Professor Baker*, 130 U. PA. L. REV. 678 (1982).

[148] Gertz v. Robert Welch, Inc., 418 U.S. 323 (1974).

[149] *E.g.*, "human rights," "liberty," and "autonomy."

sion of actual cases. Meiklejohn's original theory was both narrow and single-principled,[150] a feature shared by other political interpretations of the First Amendment.[151] But a precise single principle must be consequently narrow, and the problem then is that much seems to have been left out of the First Amendment.[152]

But why must we assume that the First Amendment has a unitary essence? The First Amendment might instead be the simplifying rubric under which a number of different values are subsumed.[153] We wish to prevent government from silencing its critics, but we wish as well to prevent an imposed uniformity in literary and artistic taste, to preserve open inquiry in the sciences and other academic fields, and to foster wide-ranging argument on moral, religious, and ethical questions. This list is representative rather than exhaustive, but it shows that the concept of freedom of speech may not have one central core.[154] And each distinct but interrelated foundational principle may generate its own rules of application. Professor Thomas Emerson identifies several justifications for the First Amendment but then argues that a single principle of application can reflect all of those diverse values.[155] But this seems counterintuitive, for if a number of diverse values are served by the First Amendment, it would seem more likely that an equally diverse doctrinal structure would result.

Although doctrinal simplicity is also thought to minimize the opportunity for interpretive error, this is questionable. As the number of available categories increases, so does the frequency of opportunity for putting a case in the wrong category. But with this comes a decrease in the possibility of error within a category. Larger categories minimize the risk of picking the wrong category, but smaller and more numerous categories lessen the chance of judicial flexibility or manipulation within a category.

---

[150] MEIKLEJOHN, note 1 supra.

[151] See Bork, note 1 supra.. Professor BeVier uses strategic considerations for broadening coverage. BeVier, note 1 supra.

[152] See TRIBE, note 16 supra, at 578-79. Cf. Shiffrin, note 13 supra.

[153] Presumably these different values have some relationship with each other, but that does not mean that there must be one unifying factor or common theme. The relationship may be that of a "family resemblance." See WITTGENSTEIN, PHILOSOPHICAL INVESTIGATIONS §§ 65-72 (2d ed. Anscombe trans. 1958).

[154] See SCHAUER, FREE SPEECH: A PHILOSOPHICAL ENQUIRY 14 (1982).

[155] EMERSON, note 106 supra; Emerson, note 79 supra.

Moreover, a strategy of fewer and larger categories is likely to be less protective of speech. If *Brandenburg* were applicable to utterances within the First Amendment, leaving the courts with a simple "in-or-out, all-or-nothing" choice, recognition of some strong interests, as we inevitably must, would leave large categories of speech totally unprotected by the First Amendment. Defamation, commercial speech, fighting words, and invasion of privacy, for example, would still be on the outside of the First Amendment fighting to get in if the only choice were to give full protection along *Brandenburg* lines.[156]

Categorization, in the sense of treating different forms of speech differently,[157] thus is not necessarily speech restrictive. It is inconceivable that we will ignore such well-established governmental concerns as safety, reputation, protection against fraud, and protection of children. If we try to force all cases within the First Amendment into some sort of a clear and present danger mold, we would likely discover that clarity need not be so clear, immediacy not be so immediate, and danger not be so dangerous. Certain state interests are inevitably going to be recognized, and the alternatives then are diluting those tests that are valuable precisely because of their strength, or formulating new tests and categories that leave existing standards strong within their narrower range.

I do not mean that creating any new category is desirable for its own sake. Unsound categories can be created; the "offensiveness" category of *Young* and *Pacifica* is a prime example.[158] But taking the creation of one bad category as a warrant to condemn all creation of new categories is an exaggerated deployment of the already overused "slippery slope" principle.[159] Some slopes are slipperier than others, and one of the functions of the courts is to place handholds on the slopes for the very purpose of preventing a slide all the way to the bottom.[160] Although it requires a bit of an act of faith, it is

---

[156] With respect to fighting words, however, the standard that emerges after Gooding v. Wilson, 405 U.S. 518 (1972), and its progeny has significant *Brandenburg* overtones.

[157] On the multiple uses of the term "categorization" in First Amendment analysis, see Schauer, note 13 *supra*.

[158] See Gunther, *The Highest Court, the Toughest Issues*, STANFORD MAGAZINE, Fall–Winter 1978, at 34; Shiffrin, note 13 *supra*, at 951.

[159] Overuse of "slippery slope" and "abuse of power" arguments is hardly new, nor is reaction against it. See Martin v. Hunter's Lessee, 14 U.S. (1 Wheat.) 304, 344–45 (1816).

[160] "The power to tax is not the power to destroy while this Court sits." Panhandle Oil Co. v. Knox, 277 U.S. 218, 223 (1928) (Holmes, J.).

possible to create new categories within the First Amendment without entirely eating away the principles of free speech. A narrow but strong First Amendment, with its strong principle universally available for all speech covered by the First Amendment, has much to be said for it. First Amendment protection can be like an oil spill, thinning out as it broadens. But excess precautions against this danger might lead to a First Amendment that is so narrow as to thwart its major purposes.

From this perspective it appears likely that the Court chose the proper approach to *Ferber*. Had it focused more on the "compelling" or "surpassing" interest in children and thus decided the case along clear and present danger lines, *Brandenburg* might have been diluted, with unfortunate consequences if that dilution were then available to assess the probability and immediacy of the danger presented by the Communist Party. And if the Court had focused exclusively on the "noncovered" approach and decided the case along *Beauharnais-Roth-Paris* lines, the current notion of virtually complete worthlessness in a First Amendment sense might similarly have been diluted, with dangers to other forms of speech having some but not central First Amendment value.

Ferber reflects the Court's continuing recognition of the diversity of speech and the diversity of state interests. It is unrealistic to expect that one test, one category, or one analytical approach can reflect this diversity. As the First Amendment is broadened to include the hitherto uncovered, diversity within the First Amendment increases. In addressing different problems separately, the Court is doing nothing more than following the common law model. Contract and tort are distinct because they address different concerns, and changes in the world and the broadening of the First Amendment make it likely that it will encompass problems as diverse as the difference between tort and contract. A unitary approach is likely to be both counterproductive and futile.

It is, of course, possible to go too far. Because no two speech acts or governmental concerns are identical, categorization is in one way artificial.[161] This would suggest an *ad hoc* approach to First Amendment adjudication, with unfortunate consequences. Although it is not a necessary truth that *ad hoc* determinations lead to excess deference to legislative determinations of the dangers posed by speech,

---

[161] See Stephan, note 47 *supra*, at 214 n.49.

such a conclusion is empirically sound.[162] Many First Amendment values are counterintuitive,[163] and many First Amendment litigants are despicable individuals with ridiculous or offensive things to say. Judges are human, and rather large categories still seem the best precaution against First Amendment standards being eroded by the passions of the moment.

Even without case-by-case adjudication, there are dangers in excess complexity. Doctrines can become so complex that they go beyond the interpretive and comprehensive abilities of those who must apply them. We should not become so concerned with doctrinal beauty at the Supreme Court level that we lose sight of the more important role of the Court as provider of guidance for lower courts and legislatures.[164]

Doctrinal complexity inevitably requires the courts to evaluate the relative worth of particular categories of speech. Some degree of this is both necessary and desirable, but again we can go too far. I remain to be convinced that there is a clear line of demarcation between viewpoint and subject-matter discrimination,[165] because subject-matter discrimination can, by entrenching the status quo, be viewpoint discrimination in sheep's clothing. Excess categorization can thus indirectly increase the likelihood of viewpoint discrimination, thereby producing some of the very dangers the First Amendment was designed to prevent.

Finally, excess categorization can reduce flexibility. Any rule or doctrine buys flexibility with the currency of predictability, but the converse is equally true.[166] Making First Amendment doctrine more precise makes it easier both to decide cases and to predict the outcome of First Amendment litigation. But that ease of decision reduces our ability to deal with new forms of communication or new state interests. The *Ferber* approach to novelty was to create a new category, but too much precision in existing doctrine will

---

[162] See Shiffrin, note 13 *supra*, at 961. Compare Gunther, *In Search of Judicial Quality on a Changing Court: The Case of Justice Powell*, 24 STAN. L. REV. 1001 (1972). See generally Bogen, *Balancing Freedom of Speech*, 38 MD. L. REV. 387 (1979); Henkin, *Infallibility under Law: Constitutional Balancing*, 78 COLUM. L. REV. 1022 (1978).

[163] See EMERSON, note 106 *supra*, at 12.

[164] See Corr, *Retroactivity Revisited: A Case Study in Supreme Court Doctrine "As Applied,"* 61 N.C.L. REV. ——— (1983).

[165] See Stone, note 14 *supra*.

[166] See generally HART, note 142 *supra*.

make such a course difficult. In that case the response to novelty may be a dilution of existing standards unless there is sufficient flexibility. If the fringe is not loose, we may discover too late that the core has been jeopardized.

The increasing complexity of First Amendment doctrine, as most recently demonstrated by *Ferber*'s creation of another distinct doctrinal category, is in itself not a cause for criticism, but rather the inevitable by-product of broadening the First Amendment. It is also the expected offspring of the increased sophistication that comes from our increasing familiarity with settled factual patterns in the First Amendment. But it is possible to become so sophisticated that we lose sight of first principles. *Ferber* is an especially noteworthy step on the route to complexity. That is no cause for alarm, but it is time to look a bit further down the road.

PETER M. GERHART

THE SUPREME COURT AND
ANTITRUST ANALYSIS:
THE (NEAR) TRIUMPH OF
THE CHICAGO SCHOOL

Since the Sherman Act was passed in 1890,[1] the Supreme Court has struggled to find an appropriate analytical and methodological framework for applying the federal antitrust laws. For a while, it appeared as if the Court might succeed. In a series of six cases since 1975,[2] the Court seemed to be moving toward a comprehensive, integrated antitrust methodology based on economic analysis and largely following the writing of Chicago school scholars such as Robert Bork[3] and Richard Posner.[4] Last Term, however, in *Arizona v. Maricopa County Medical Society*,[5] the Court missed a

---

Peter M. Gerhart is Professor of Law, Ohio State University College of Law.

[1] 15 U.S.C.A. §§ 1–7 (1980).

[2] Goldfarb v. Virginia State Bar, 421 U.S. 773 (1975); Continental T.V., Inc. v. GTE Sylvania, Inc., 433 U.S. 36 (1977); National Soc'y of Professional Eng'rs v. United States, 435 U.S. 679 (1978); Broadcast Music, Inc. v. Columbia Broadcasting System, Inc., 441 U.S. 1 (1979); Reiter v. Sonotone Corp., 442 U.S. 330 (1979); and Catalano, Inc. v. Target Sales, Inc., 446 U.S. 643 (1980).

[3] Bork, The Antitrust Paradox (1978); Bork, *The Rule of Reason and the Per Se Concept: Price-Fixing and Market Division* (pts. 1–2), 74 Yale L.J. 775 (1965); 75 Yale L.J. 373 (1966).

[4] Posner, Antitrust Law: An Economic Perspective 147–67 (1967); Posner & Easterbrook, Antitrust (2d ed. 1981). See also Easterbrook, *Predatory Strategies and Counterstrategies*, 48 U. Chi. L. Rev. 263 (1981); Easterbrook, *Maximum Price Fixing*, 48 U. Chi. L. Rev. 886 (1981).

[5] 102 S. Ct. 2466 (1982).

significant opportunity to complete its methodological framework, and in doing so, made antitrust analysis once again confused and haphazard.

This development is unfortunate. There is a central analytical model underlying the antitrust laws, and the Supreme Court has a special responsibility to identify and to articulate that model in order to increase the coherence, rationality, and predictability of antitrust analysis. *Maricopa* provided the Court with a splendid opportunity to do so, and the Court's failure to capitalize on that opportunity is dispiriting, even though the plurality decision may be short-lived.

I. The Chicago School and Antitrust Analysis

Sound antitrust analysis must address two interrelated tasks. The first task is substantive: to identify accurately legislative purposes of the antitrust laws. This is difficult enough, but it is complicated by a second, procedural task: to find an appropriate balance between certainty and fidelity to legislative purpose and to fashion rules of conduct that are reasonably clear, precise, and easily applicable without sacrificing substantive antitrust values. Because the search for an accurate definition of antitrust values takes place in a legal system that promotes clarity, precision, and ease of applicability, the tensions between fidelity and certainty are great, creating the danger, evident in the history of antitrust doctrine, that more weight will be given to promoting certainty than is warranted.

Prior to *Maricopa*, the Supreme Court had begun to embrace two postulates suggested by Chicago school scholars that would minimize the conflicts between the goals of certainty and fidelity. The first postulate, one advocated by Robert Bork as early as 1965,[6] is to restore the per se rule as a component of substantive antitrust analysis. This postulate is of immeasurable importance. When per se rules are applicable, issues of the purpose and effect of a person's conduct are irrelevant. Almost since their inception, however, the per se rules have been a source of mystery and misunderstanding. Per se rules were often thought of as if they had self-executing

---

[6] Bork, *The Rule of Reason and the Per Se Concept: Price Fixing and Market Division*, 74 YALE L.J. 775 (1965).

applicability to easily recognizable conduct, or as literal statements whose primary function was to add simplicity and certainty to antitrust law. As a result, antitrust analysis was deflected from a consideration of underlying substantive policies to a largely semantic effort to "characterize" conduct, and courts have had inordinate difficulty making and explaining decisions to apply per se rules.

The postulate that the Supreme Court appeared to embrace prior to *Maricopa* would restore the original conception of the scope and role of the per se rules—one that views the rules as a summation of substantive antitrust policy and hence to be applied only after analysis of policy considerations. Were this postulate fully accepted it would be significant. It would mean that decisions to apply a per se rule must be based on the substantive policies of the Sherman Act, rather than on linguistic compartmentalization, requiring courts to examine and explain the substantive policies, and thus enlivening antitrust analysis with new substantive vigor.

A second postulate of the Chicago school writers—a reorientation of substantive antitrust policy around the consumer welfare model—was also endorsed by the pre-*Maricopa* Supreme Court. The Court said that the only relevant question in evaluating a restraint of trade is whether the restraint promotes or suppresses competition.[7] By implication, "competition" is not to be viewed necessarily as a process of independence and rivalry, but as the outcome of a process. The "promote competition" standard is meant to focus on whether business activity promotes consumer welfare by increasing productive and allocative efficiency, and it is to be guided by economic analysis.[8]

Were this development continued, it, too, would be immensely significant. The promote/suppress standard is an important and relatively objective synthesizing principle that allows antitrust analysis to cut through overlapping verbal categories to a realistic appraisal of the possibility that business conduct will promote efficiency. Indeed, the "promote competition" standard is a simplifying and clarifying concept. As the Supreme Court appeared to recognize, combinations in restraint of trade possibly promote competition under three circumstances—when there is integration to

---

[7] National Soc'y of Professional Eng'rs v. United States, 435 U.S. 679, 691 (1978).

[8] The consumer welfare model is discussed in the text accompanying notes 48–52 *infra*.

efficiency; when the combination overcomes a problem of externalities such as the free-rider problem; and when a combination
reduces transaction costs. These three circumstances define the
range of cases not covered by a per se rule.

II. THE FIRST POSTULATE: THE ROLE OF PER SE RULES

Despite their many benefits, per se rules have been an inadequate component of antitrust analysis, because no coherent theory
has existed for determining when the rules were to be applied. This
significant deficiency reflects confusion about the role of per se
rules and misunderstanding of the substantive antitrust policy that
underlies the rules.

Per se rules, which are said to be applicable to price fixing,
division of markets, horizontal group boycotts, and tying agreements, encapsulate a conclusion that identified conduct is so inherently anticompetitive or so devoid of redeeming virtues that the
conduct is unlawful in and of itself, without regard to the effect of
the conduct or the purpose of those engaging in it.[9] Under per se
rules, both anticompetitive purpose and anticompetitive effect are
conclusively presumed to exist once the forbidden conduct is
proven, so that proof of the forbidden conduct is by itself proof of
an antitrust violation. In contrast, if a per se rule is not applied, the
case must be tried under the rule of reason, which requires the
plaintiff to prove the anticompetitive purpose or effect of the conduct and which permits the defendant to prove that the conduct
achieves legitimate competitive goals.[10]

---

[9] The classic summary of per se rules is from Northern Pac. Ry. v. United States, 356
U.S. 1, 5 (1958): "[T]here are certain agreements or practices which because of their perni-
cious effect on competition and lack of any redeeming virtue are conclusively presumed to be
unreasonable and therefore illegal without elaborate inquiry as to the precise harm they have
caused or the business excuse for their use. . . . Among the practices which the courts have
heretofore deemed to be unlawful in and of themselves are price fixing, . . . division of
markets, . . . group boycotts, . . . and tying arrangements" (citations omitted). There are
many scholarly discussions of the scope and function of per se rules, e.g., Elman, "Petrified
Opinions" and Competitive Realities, 66 COLUM. L. REV. 625 (1966); Loevinger, The Rule of
Reason in Antitrust Law, 50 VA. L. REV. 23 (1964); von Kalinowski, The Per Se Doctrine—an
Emerging Philosophy of Antitrust Law, 11 U.C.L.A.L. REV. 569 (1964); Rahl, Per Se Rules and
Boycotts under the Sherman Act: Some Reflections on the Klor's Case, 45 VA. L. REV. 1165 (1959);
Rahl, Price Competition and the Price Fixing Rules—Preface and Perspectives, 57 Nw. U.L. REV.
137 (1962); Comment, The Per Se Illegality of Price-Fixing—Sans Power, Purpose or Effect, 19 U.
CHI. L. REV. 837 (1952); KAYSEN & TURNER, ANTITRUST POLICY 142–44 (1959).

[10] E.g., Standard Oil Co. v. United States, 221 U.S. 1 (1911); Chicago Board of Trade v.
United States, 246 U.S. 231 (1918).

Because they simplify antitrust doctrine, per se rules often promote such important enforcement goals as ease of application, deterrence, and predictability.[11] The certainty provided by the rules, however, is often illusory. Although the per se rules tell a court that issues of purpose and effect are irrelevant to a case in which the rule is applied, no decision to apply a per se rule can be made until after analysis, however rudimentary, of whether the rule should be applied. In all but the easiest cases, the determination whether to apply the rule has been troublesome, largely because few coherent, consistent standards have existed for making that determination.

Although the per se rules are usually stated as if they were self-executing, they are not.[12] The per se rule covering tying arrangements, for example, is not applied until several issues of purpose and effect are determined.[13] The per se price-fixing rule is strong but not omnipotent: when independent firms agree to reduce competition between themselves, without doing more, their conduct is doubtless unlawful,[14] but not all conduct that might literally or

---

[11] *E.g.*, Northern Pac. Ry. v. United States, 356 U.S. 1, 5 (1958): "This principle of per se unreasonableness not only makes the type of restraints which are proscribed by the Sherman Act more certain to the benefit of everyone concerned, but it also avoids the necessity for an incredibly complicated and prolonged economic investigation into the entire history of the industry involved, as well as related industries, in an effort to determine at large whether a particular restraint has been unreasonable—an inquiry so often wholly fruitless when undertaken."

[12] A similar point is made in Bork, *The Rule of Reason and the Per Se Concept: Price-Fixing and Market Division*, 74 YALE L.J. 775, 777 (1965): "The current shibboleth of per se illegality in existing law conveys a sense of certainty, even of automaticity, which is delusive. The per se concept does not accurately describe the law relating to agreements eliminating competition as it is, as it has been, or as it ever can be. Alongside cases announcing a sweeping per se formulation of the law there has always existed a line of cases refusing to apply it. Doubtless some of the cases in the latter group were wrongly decided, but it would be naive to write them all off as simply incorrect or aberrational. The persistent refusal of courts to honor the literal terms of the per se rules against price-fixing and market-division agreements demonstrates a deep-seated though somewhat inarticulate sense that those rules, as usually stated, are inadequate."

[13] The per se rule is applied only if the seller is selling two separate products, the tying product is unique or has market power, and a not insubstantial amount of commerce in the tied product is foreclosed. Fortner Enterprises, Inc. v. United States Steel Corp., 394 U.S. 495 (1969) *(Fortner I)*; United States Steel Corp. v. Fortner Enterprises, Inc., 429 U.S. 610 (1977) *(Fortner II)*. Moreover, the per se rule is not applied if the combined selling of two products is essential to the seller's goodwill. United States v. Jerrold Electronics Corp., 187 F. Supp. 545 (E.D. Pa. 1960), *aff'd*, 365 U.S. 567 (1961).

[14] The price-fixing per se rule applies to agreements between unintegrated competitors concerning credit terms, Catalano, Inc. v. Target Sales, Inc., 446 U.S. 643 (1980); contractual terms with customers, Paramount Famous Lasky Corp. v. United States, 282 U.S. 30 (1930) (arbitration clauses), United States v. First National Pictures, Inc., 282 U.S. 44 (1930) (completion of existing contracts and cash deposits); discounts, United States v. United Liquors Corp., 149 F. Supp. 609 (W.D. Tenn. 1956), *aff'd per curiam*, 352 U.S. 991 (1957);

even analogically be characterized as price fixing is price fixing subject to the per se rule.[15] Similarly, the per se rule applicable to horizontal group boycotts is so riddled with exceptions that it is difficult to restate the rule in a meaningful way.[16]

The per se rules became defective because they lost touch with the substantive policy that prompted their formulation. As a result, the characterization process—the process of determining whether the conduct challenged in a lawsuit should be characterized as, for example, price fixing subject to the per se rule—is often guided by analytical methods that bear no relationship to relevant substantive criteria.[17] Even those cases that have correctly avoided the heavy hand of the per se rules—and there are many[18]—have been forced

---

United States v. American Smelting & Refining Co., 182 F. Supp. 834 (S.D.N.Y. 1960); markups, Food and Grocery Bureau, Inc. v. United States, 139 F.2d 973 (9th Cir. 1943); trade-in allowances and list prices, Plymouth Dealers' Ass'n v. United States, 279 F.2d 128 (9th Cir. 1960); and trading stamps, United States v. Gasoline Retailers Ass'n, Inc., 285 F.2d 688 (7th Cir. 1961). It applies to agreements between unintegrated competitors not to adver-tise, United States v. Gasoline Retailers Ass'n, Inc. 285 F.2d 688 (7th Cir. 1961); agreements to establish uniform costs on which prices can be based, California Retail Grocers & Mer-chants Ass'n, Ltd. v. United States, 139 F.2d 978 (9th Cir. 1943); and agreement on terms of purchase, National Macaroni Mfgs. Ass'n v. FTC, 345 F.2d 421 (7th Cir. 1965).

[15] *E.g.*, Broadcast Music Industries, Inc. v. Columbia Broadcasting System, 441 U.S. 1 (1979); Evans v. S. S. Kresge Co., 544 F.2d 1184 (3rd Cir. 1976), *cert. denied*, 433 U.S. 908 (1977); United States v. Morgan, 118 F. Supp. 621 (S.D.N.Y. 1953); United States v. Columbia Pictures Corp., 189 F. Supp. 153 (S.D.N.Y. 1960); Department of Justice, Busi-ness Review Letter, August 5, 1980 (granting clearance to cooperative activity with an impact on prices).

The per se rule against vertical price fixing is counterbalanced by the *Colgate* doctrine, United States v. Colgate & Co., 250 U.S. 300 (1919), which permits some refusals to deal with price cutters, and by the doctrine that a seller may determine the prices at which his agents or legitimate consignees sell. Marty's Floor Covering Co., Inc. v. GAF Corp., 604 F.2d 266 (4th Cir. 1979).

[16] Attempts to synthesize the group boycott cases are legion. *E.g.*, SULLIVAN, HANDBOOK OF THE LAW OF ANTITRUST, 229–59 (1977); Bauer, *Per Se Illegality of Concerted Refusals to Deal: A Rule Ripe for Reexamination*, 79 COLUM. L. REV. 685 (1979); McCormick, *Group Boycotts—Per Se or Not Per Se, That Is the Question*, 7 SETON HALL L. REV. 703 (1976); Barber, *Refusals to Deal under the Federal Antitrust Laws*, 103 U. PA. L. REV. 847 (1955).

[17] Without workable criteria for applying the per se rules, antitrust litigation often centers on an elaborate semantic game: for example, a court or advocate wishing to avoid the per se rule against group boycotts must argue either that the conduct is not a boycott (when in fact it is) or that it is a boycott, but not the type of boycott that is subject to the per se rule. *E.g.*, Smith v. Pro Football, Inc., 593 F.2d 1173, 1178 (D.C. Cir. 1978) ("We hold that the NFL player draft is not properly characterized as a 'group boycott'—at least not the type of boycott that traditionally has been held illegal per se"). Neither approach is satisfactory unless the classification decision is based on substantive policy.

[18] *E.g.*, Worthen Bank & Trust Co. v. National BankAmericard, Inc., 485 F.2d 119 (8th Cir. 1973), *cert. denied*, 415 U.S. 918 (1974); Smith v. Pro Football, Inc., 593 F.2d 1173 (D.C. Cir. 1978).

to so torture the relevant doctrine as to make the application of antitrust law appear whimsical,[19] even when it would not be were it freed from the semantic grip of the per se rules. In short, without a theory for determining when the per se rules are to be applied— that is, without attention to the substantive policy that underlies the rules—the rules became formless and opaque.

One of the most ignominious antitrust cases, *United States v. Topco Associates Inc.*,[20] is illustrative. There, the Court applied the per se rule that prohibits division of territories between sellers of different brands (restraints on interbrand competition)[21] to an agreement in which grocery store members of a joint buying agency bound themselves to sell the agency's merchandise (a single brand) in assigned, closed territories (which restrains only intrabrand competition). Despite the district court's thorough rule of reason analysis upholding the restraint,[22] the Supreme Court eschewed any analysis, even analysis to determine whether the per se rule should be applied. The restraint was classified as a horizontal restraint and the Court refused to determine whether the restraint was different from those horizontal restraints subject to the per se rule.[23] The Court should not have applied the per se rule at all. Unlike horizontal interbrand restraints subject to the per se rule, these "horizontal" restraints were primarily intrabrand restraints and were ancillary to the integration of grocery stores in a joint

---

[19] Lower federal courts have been ingenious in creating formulas to blunt the force of literal per se rules. Some courts have established prerequisites for a per se rule. Neeld v. National Hockey League, 594 F.2d 1297, 1299 n.3 (9th Cir. 1979) (*"per se* rules have only been applied in the face of arguably demonstrable anticompetitiveness"); Gough v. Rossmoor Corp., 585 F.2d 381 (9th Cir. 1978), *cert. denied*, 440 U.S. 936 (1979); Hatley v. American Quarter Horse Ass'n, 552 F.2d 646, 653 (5th Cir. 1977) (per se rule not applied in absence of "minimal indicia of anti-competitive purpose or effect"). Still other courts avoid the per se rules by recharacterizing the conduct, *e.g.*, Kentucky Fried Chicken v. Diversified Packaging, 549 F.2d 368, 379 (5th Cir. 1977) ("We deal here not with tie-ins, whose adverse effects and lack of redeeming virtue are by now quite familiar, but instead with approved source requirements"). Other courts practice benign neglect of per se rules, *e.g.*, Eliason Corp. v. National Sanitation Foundation, 614 F.2d 126 (6th Cir. 1980).

[20] 405 U.S. 596 (1972).

[21] *E.g.*, Timken Roller Bearing Co. v. United States, 341 U.S. 593 (1951); Addyston Pipe and Steel Co. v. United States, 175 U.S. 211 (1899), *aff'g*, 85 F. 271 (6th Cir. 1898).

[22] United States v. Topco Associates, Inc., 319 F. Supp. 1031 (N.D. Ill. 1970), *rev'd*, 405 U.S. 596 (1972).

[23] The Court's attempt to rely on United States v. Sealy, Inc., 388 U.S. 350 (1967), as a case "on all fours with this case," 405 U.S. 609, is unpersuasive. In *Sealy*, where the territorial restraints accompanied resale price maintenance, the Court had expressly refused to determine the legality of intrabrand territorial restraints standing alone. 388 U.S. at 356.

buying agency, providing a justification that should have taken the restraints out of the per se rule.[24]

In view of the Supreme Court's decision in *Continental T.V., Inc. v. GTE Sylvania, Inc.*[25] that nonprice intrabrand restraints imposed vertically are to be judged under the rule of reason, *Topco* should be considered as an endangered species,[26] despite the Supreme Court's dogged attempts to retain it.[27] But the *Topco* outcome—which could have been justified under an appropriate analysis[28]—is less troublesome than the Court's perversion of the per se rules. Virtually every statement concerning the per se rules that the majority made in *Topco* is antithetical to sound antitrust analysis.[29]

---

[24] For a fuller discussion of this point, see BORK, THE ANTITRUST PARADOX, 276–77 (1978).

[25] 433 U.S. 36 (1977).

[26] Bork, *Vertical Restraints: Schwinn Overruled*, 1977 SUPREME COURT REVIEW 171 (1977); Posner, *The Rule of Reason and the Economic Approach: Reflections on the Sylvania Decision*, 45 U. CHI. L. REV. 1, 6–10 (1977); Louis, *Restraints Ancillary to Joint Ventures and Licensing Agreements: Do Sealy and Topco Logically Survive Sylvania and BMI?* 66 VA. L. REV. 879 (1980).

[27] *E.g.*, Continental T.V., Inc. v. GTE Sylvania, Inc., 433 U.S. 36, 57–58 nn.27–28 (1977); Arizona v. Maricopa County Medical Society, 102 S. Ct. 2466, 2473 (1982).

[28] Although Topco members were free to expand into one another's territory if they did not use the profitable Topco brand, the Topco brand may have been so integrated into their operations that the members would not expand territories without it. If that were true, the territorial exclusivity for the Topco brand eliminated interbrand as well as intrabrand competition, and that adverse competitive effect might have outweighed the procompetitive effect of the strong Topco brand. Although the findings of the district court undercut this theory (see finding 45, 319 F. Supp. at 1037), the government's brief plausibly challenged that finding. Brief for the United States 30–33.

[29] According to Justice Marshall, "[w]hether or not we would decide this case the same way under the rule of reason used by the District Court is irrelevant," 405 U.S. at 609. This suggests that cases might be decided differently under the rule of reason than under per se rules, a nonsensical suggestion that one of the rules is irrational. Justice Burger expressed the better view in his dissent: "per se rules that have been developed are . . . directed to the protection of the public welfare; they are complementary to, and in no way inconsistent with, the rule of reason." 405 U.S. 621. Justice Marshall also misperceived the relationship between the Court and Congress. "Should Congress," he said, "ultimately determine that predictability is unimportant in this area of the law, it can, of course, make *per se* rules inapplicable in some or all cases, and leave courts free to ramble through the wilds of economic theory in order to maintain a flexible approach." 405 U.S. 609–10 n.10. When Congress passed the Sherman Act, however, it did not legislate predictability as a weightier value than fidelity, nor did it explicitly legislate any per se rules, much less the rule applied by the *Topco* majority.

Justice Blackmun, who found the *Topco* result "anomalous" because it would "tend to stultify Topco members' competition with the great and larger chains," nonetheless concurred in the result on the mistaken theory that "[t]he per se rule . . . now appears to be so firmly established by the Court that, at this late date, I could not oppose it." 405 U.S. at 612–13. The per se rule, however, had never been firmly established as to territorial intrabrand restraints. Paradoxically, Justice Blackmun later joined the majority in overturning the established per se rule applicable to vertical nonprice restraints. Continental T.V., Inc. v. GTE Sylvania, Inc., 433 U.S. 36 (1977).

Most significantly, the existence of a per se rule should not, and logically cannot, preclude a court from determining whether the per se rule should be applied. The applicability of the per se rule is not an issue that is foreclosed by the existence of a per se rule. If the characteristics of a case are so different from previous per se cases that the substantive policy embodied in the per se rule is no longer applicable, the rule should not be applied. It makes little sense to invoke the per se rule, as *Topco* did, solely because analysis under the rule of reason is complicated.[30] Whether the per se rule is applicable is not complicated or beyond judicial capacities; that issue should rarely be decided on the basis of the difficulty of the analysis once the rule of reason is invoked. If the per se rule is inapplicable, it is because the conduct is possibly procompetitive, and, under most circumstances, any rational attempt to assess competitive effects would be better than invoking a per se rule that, by ignoring procompetitive effects, will inevitably lead to incorrect results.

Concededly, per se rules rest in part on a judgment that more extensive analysis would not produce a sufficiently more accurate assessment of competitive effects to outweigh the costs of the analysis, including both monetary costs and the cost of uncertainty.[31] A per se rule can therefore be applied whenever a court determines that alternate analysis is unduly costly. The existence of the per se rule, however, does not relieve the court from evaluating the costs and benefits of a more detailed analysis in the case before it. Moreover, although there are undoubtedly situations in which the alleged redeeming virtues of restraints of trade are incapable of being

---

[30] As Chief Justice Burger said in his *Topco* dissent: "The issues presented by the antitrust cases reaching this Court are rarely simple to resolve under the rule of reason; they do indeed frequently require us to make difficult economic determinations. We should not for that reason alone, however, be overly zealous in formulating new *per se* rules, for an excess of zeal in that regard is both contrary to the policy of the Sherman Act and detrimental to the welfare of consumers generally." 405 U.S. at 624.

[31] *E.g.*, United States v. Container Corp., 393 U.S. 333, 341 (1969) (Marshall, J., dissenting): "Per se rules always contain a degree of arbitrariness. They are justified on the assumption that the gains from imposition of the rule will far outweigh the losses and that significant administrative advantages will result. In other words, the potential competitive harm plus the administrative cost of determining in what particular situations the practice may be harmful must far outweigh the benefits that may result. If the potential benefits in the aggregate are outweighed to this degree, then they are simply not worth identifying in individual cases"). Similar views are expressed in Continental T.V., Inc. v. GTE Sylvania, Inc., 433 U.S. 36, 50 n.16 (1977) and KAYSEN & TURNER, ANTITRUST POLICY, 142–44 (1959).

identified and evaluated efficiently,[32] most forms of procompetitive collaboration can be identified and evaluated without undue cost.[33] In those cases, a per se rule should not be applied until the appropriate analysis has been completed.

The Court's pre-*Maricopa* opinions began to reflect a per se rule that was attuned more to fidelity to antitrust values than to certainty and thus that was in touch with the substantive policy underlying the per se rules. When it reversed the per se rule applicable to nonprice vertical restraints, the Court referred to the "demanding standards"[34] for establishing a per se rule, and noted that although the per se rules provide procedural advantages, "those advantages are not sufficient in themselves to justify the creation of per se rules. If it were otherwise, all of antitrust law would be reduced to per se rules, thus introducing an unintended and undesirable rigidity in the law."[35] Later, when it refused to apply the per se price-fixing rule to the joint licensing of copyright rights, the Court noted that the "easy labels [of per se rules] do not always supply ready answers"[36] and spoke of the importance of examining the substantive policies underlying the rules:[37]

> As generally used in the antitrust field, "price fixing" is a shorthand way of describing certain categories of business behavior to which the per se rule has been held applicable. The Court of Appeals' literal approach [in applying the per se rule] does not alone establish that this particular practice is one of those types or that it is "plainly anticompetitive and very likely without redeeming virtue." Literalness is overly simplistic and often overbroad. When two partners set the price of their goods or services they are literally "price fixing," but they are not per se in violation of the Sherman Act. . . . Thus, it is necessary to characterize the challenged conduct as falling within or without the category of behavior to which we apply the label "per se price fixing." That will often, but not always, be a simple matter.

---

[32] This may be true, for example, of the claim that price fixing between unintegrated competitors leads to lower capital costs by reducing uncertainty. Other examples of theoretically procompetitive price fixing are in SCHERER, INDUSTRIAL ORGANIZATION ECONOMICS 509 (1980), and Mason, *Market Power and Business Conduct: Some Comments*, 46 AM. ECON. REV. 471–81 (1956).

[33] See text accompanying notes 62–115 *infra*.

[34] Continental T.V., Inc. v. GTE Sylvania, Inc., 433 U.S. 36, 50 (1977).

[35] *Id.*, n.16.

[36] Broadcast Music, Inc. v. Columbia Broadcasting System, Inc., 441 U.S. 1, 8 (1979).

[37] *Id.* at 9.

More important, although this aspect of the case is generally overlooked, in *National Society of Professional Engineers v. United States*,[38] the Court made it clear that applying a per se rule is a matter of substantive policy. At issue in *Professional Engineers* was an ethical canon of the National Society of Professional Engineers that prohibited competitive bidding by the Society's members. The Society asserted that the ethical canon was in the public interest, because competitive bidding would lead to unsafe or unethical practices.[39] Its argument rested on a footnote to the Court's prior *Goldfarb* opinion that "[t]he public service aspect, and other features of the professions, may require that a particular practice, which could properly be viewed as a violation of the Sherman Act in another context, be treated differently."[40]

The Court applied a per se rule, however, and refused to allow the Society to prove its assertion. Because Justice Stevens's majority opinion repeatedly invoked the term "Rule of Reason," and because the rule of reason and per se rules are often thought to be separate analytical categories, some have believed that *Professional Engineers* was decided under traditional rule of reason analysis.[41] To Justice Stevens, however, the "Rule of Reason" contains the analysis necessary to decide whether to apply the per se rule and thus covers all antitrust cases. Justice Stevens's "Rule of Reason" is not a rule of reasonableness, but a rule having to do with reasons.[42] All

---

[38] 435 U.S. 679 (1978).

[39] The Court summarized the defense as follows: "[T]he Society averred that the standard set out in the Code of Ethics was reasonable because competition among professional engineers was contrary to the public interest. It was averred that it would be cheaper and easier for an engineer 'to design and specify inefficient and unnecessarily expensive structures and methods of construction.' Accordingly, competitive pressure to offer engineering services at the lowest possible price would adversely affect the quality of engineering. Moreover, the practice of awarding engineering contracts to the lowest bidder, regardless of quality, would be dangerous to the public health, safety and welfare. For these reasons, the Society claimed that its Code of Ethics was not an 'unreasonable restraint of interstate trade or commerce.' " 435 U.S. at 684–85 (footnotes omitted).

[40] Goldfarb v. Virginia State Bar, 421 U.S. at 788–89 n.17 (1975).

[41] Justice Blackmun made this assumption in his concurring opinion. 435 U.S. at 700. See also Redlich, *The Burger Court and the Per Se Rule*, 44 ALBANY L. REV. 1, 36 (1979), and Sullivan & Wiley, *Recent Antitrust Developments: Defining the Scope of Exemptions, Expanding Coverage, and Refining the Rule of Reason*, 27 U.C.L.A.L. REV. 265, 322–23 (1979).

[42] According to Justice Stevens, "the Rule [of Reason] does not open the field of antitrust inquiry to any argument in favor of a challenged restraint that may fall within the realm of reason." 435 U.S. at 688. Rather, "[t]o evaluate [defendants'] argument it is necessary to identify the contours of the Rule of Reason and to discuss its application to the kind of justification asserted by [defendants]." 435 U.S. at 687. After considering these justifications, the Court dismissed them because they "are not reasons that satisfy the Rule." *Id.* at 694.

restraints must be supported by reasons (i.e., justifications) that are legally acceptable; the "Rule of Reason" determines which reasons are legally acceptable and which are not. In effect, the decision in *Professional Engineers* to disallow defendants' asserted reason for their restraint is a decision, under Justice Stevens's "Rule of Reason," to apply the per se rule,[43] one that is based on the substantive policy of the antitrust laws.

Under these pre-*Maricopa* cases, per se analysis functions as the keystone of antitrust analysis. A decision to apply a per se rule should be a decision that the conduct has no redeeming virtues, or at least none worth considering. Conversely, a decision not to apply a per se rule should reflect the substantive content of the rule. It should be based on a conclusion that the conduct in question has redeeming virtues that are worth trying to evaluate, and should thus identify the factors that are relevant in a more extended, factual analysis. These are substantive policy decisions and are not designed merely to simplify antitrust doctrine.

III. The Second Postulate: The Consumer Welfare Model

The Supreme Court's characterization of the per se rules as substantive, not procedural, rules is important. Even more important is that in its pre-*Maricopa* cases the Court restored the original vision of policy-based per se rules by identifying the substantive policies that guide their application.

The Court invoked the familiar promote/suppress standard from *Chicago Board of Trade*[44] as the unifying antitrust standard.[45] Under this standard, if a restraint arguably promotes competition, it is supported by reasons that require analysis of the net effect of the restraint. If, on the other hand, the only reason for the restraint is to suppress competition, it is supported by no acceptable reason and is therefore unlawful per se.

---

[43] Justice Stevens's notion that per se cases are a category of cases under the Rule of Reason has not been repeated by the Court. Indeed, when Justice Stevens wrote the *Maricopa* opinion, note 5 *supra*, he did not capitalize "rule of reason." It is nonetheless clear that a court must examine the reasons advanced to justify a restraint before deciding in which category to place it.

[44] Chicago Board of Trade v. United States, 246 U.S. 231, 238 (1918).

[45] National Soc'y of Professional Eng'rs v. United States, 435 U.S. 679, 691 (1978).

At one level the promote/suppress standard appears paradoxical. If "competition" means business rivalry, then all restraints of trade suppress competition and should be unlawful under the standard. For example, when the seller of a business agrees not to compete with the buyer of the business, competition is suppressed in the sense that the restraint eliminates the potential rivalry of the seller. Hence, if competition is equated with rivalry, a literal interpretation of *Professional Engineers* might "call into question the classic ancillary restraints"[46] or preclude a court from considering ethical or safety norms, even though the Supreme Court has said that those restraints are to be evaluated under the rule of reason.[47]

The explanation for this apparent paradox is that the Court uses the consumer welfare model articulated by Professor Bork[48] to apply the promote/suppress standard. Under this model, competition is seen not as a process of rivalry but as a process that maximizes consumer welfare by maximizing both allocative and productive efficiency. Competition is thus promoted by increasing the efficiency of markets, even if a reduction in rivalry results. The promote/suppress standard thus permits rivalry to be restrained in order to maximize efficiency and consumer welfare.

Although the Burger Court has not explicitly endorsed the consumer welfare model, the promote/suppress standard and the Court's pre-*Maricopa* decisions are intelligible only if interpreted in the light of that model. Moreover, in those decisions the Court often used language suggestive of the consumer welfare model. For example, the Court cited Robert Bork's contention that the Sherman Act is a "consumer welfare prescription"[49] and noted that "an antitrust policy divorced from market considerations would appear to lack any objective benchmarks."[50] Moreover, said the Court, antitrust analysis is to focus "directly on the challenged restraint's impact on competitive conditions"[51] to determine "whether the practice facially appears to be one that would always or almost

---

[46] Robinson, *Recent Antitrust Developments—1979*, 80 COLUM. L. REV. 1, 17 (1980).

[47] National Soc'y of Professional Eng'rs v. United States, 435 U.S. 679, 688, 696 (1978).

[48] BORK, THE ANTITRUST PARADOX (1978).

[49] Reiter v. Sonotone Corp., 442 U.S. 330, 343 (1979).

[50] Continental T.V., Inc. v. GTE Sylvania, Inc., 433 U.S. 36, 53 n.21 (1977).

[51] National Soc'y of Professional Eng'rs v. United States, 435 U.S. 679, 688 (1978).

always tend to restrict competition and decrease output."[52] The last phrase captures the central theme of the consumer welfare model: conduct that restricts output by reducing allocative efficiency is unlawful because it reduces consumer welfare. Conduct that increases productive efficiency without a counterbalancing restriction of allocative efficiency is lawful because it promotes consumer welfare.

By interpreting the promote/suppress standard in the light of the consumer welfare model, the Court made the standard a potentially potent synthesizing principle.

A. SUPPRESSING COMPETITION: THE POLICY UNDERLYING THE PER SE RULES

In *Professional Engineers*, Justice Stevens identified the central substantive policy underlying the per se rules, linking that policy directly to the first case to use the term "per se," *United States v. Socony-Vacuum Oil Co.*[53] As stated by Justice Stevens, antitrust analysis "does not support a defense based on the assumption that competition itself is unreasonable,"[54] so the purpose of antitrust analysis "is not to decide whether a policy favoring competition is in the public interest, or in the interest of the members of an industry. Subject to exceptions defined by statute, that policy decision has been made by Congress."[55] Because competition is always in the public interest, antitrust analysis does not permit "inquiry into the reasonableness of the prices set by private agreement" or "argument that because of the special characteristics of a particular industry, monopolistic arrangements will better promote trade and commerce than competition."[56] Accordingly, the Society's attempt in *Professional Engineers* to justify its restraint "on the basis of the potential threat that competition poses to the public safety and the ethics of its profession is nothing less than a frontal assault on the basic policy of the Sherman Act,"[57] providing no "reasons that

---

[52] Broadcast Music, Inc. v. Columbia Broadcasting System, Inc., 441 U.S. 1, 19–20 (1979).

[53] 310 U.S. 150 (1940).

[54] 435 U.S. at 696.

[55] *Id.* at 692.

[56] *Id.* at 689.

[57] *Id.* at 695.

satisfy the Rule [of Reason]"[58] and thus requiring no factual analysis.

In short, the per se rules wield their power because they express the substantive conclusion that restraints may not be justified by the argument that without the restraint the competitive process would be undesirable, destructive, or contrary to the public interest. Under the consumer welfare model, restraints that are unable to improve efficiency cannot be justified on any other basis.

Justice Stevens also clarified the *Goldfarb* footnote and the relevance of the Society's argument that the professional aspects of engineering require less stringent analytical standards than are normal. The Court denied that the "cautionary footnote" of *Goldfarb* could "be read as fashioning a broad exemption under the Rule of Reason for learned professions."[59] Instead:[60]

> [W]e adhere to the view expressed in *Goldfarb* that, by their nature, professional services may differ significantly from other business services, and, accordingly, the nature of the competition in such services may vary. Ethical norms may serve to regulate and promote this competition, and thus fall within the Rule of Reason. But the Society's argument in this case is a far cry from such a position. . . . [W]e may assume that competition is not entirely conducive to ethical behavior, but that is not a reason, cognizable under the Sherman Act, for doing away with competition.

In other words, special considerations relating to the professions might influence analysis under the rule of reason, but they do not affect analysis of whether to apply the rule of reason. Thus, when competitors "regulate and promote" competition by prohibiting unethical practices, the rule of reason requires a court to consider whether aspects of the professions are relevant to "the nature of competition" within the profession. In contrast, a decision to apply a per se rule depends only upon examining the reasons advanced to justify a restraint to see if they are "cognizable under the Sherman Act,"[61] and that examination is the same for professions as for other business. Because the defendants in *Professional Engineers* restrained competition and not unethical practices, a per se rule was applica-

---

[58] *Id.* at 694.
[59] *Id.* at 696.
[60] *Id.*
[61] *Id.*

ble, and the rule's impact was not changed because the restraint involved a learned profession.

B. PROMOTING COMPETITION THROUGH TRADE RESTRAINTS

Although the "suppress" side of the promote/suppress standard captures the central antitrust principle that consumer welfare is always in the public interest (unless Congress deems otherwise), the "promote" side of the standard is far more interesting and intricate, in part because defendants generally will have the burden of proving that their restrictive agreements promote competition. Analysis of the three ways that trade restraints promote competition shows that the promote competition standard is an economics-oriented theory around which antitrust doctrine can be developed, predicted, and evaluated.

1. *Integration to efficiency.* The predominant form of procompetitive competitor collaboration—and the form that is easiest to recognize and evaluate—is integration to efficiency. The law protects worthwhile integration by permitting restraints that are necessary to facilitate savings of resources or improvements of quality. This strain of the market efficiency theme is pervasive, evident not only in the law applicable to mergers[62] and joint ventures,[63] where it has long been recognized, but also in the law relating to tying arrangements,[64] group boycotts,[65] and price fixing.[66]

---

[62] Williamson, *Economies as an Antitrust Defense: The Welfare Tradeoffs*, 58 AM. ECON. REV. 18, 21 (1968); BORK, THE ANTITRUST PARADOX 198–201 (1978).

[63] *E.g.*, Justice Department, ANTITRUST GUIDE FOR INTERNATIONAL OPERATIONS 13 (Jan. 26, 1977); Pitofsky, *Joint Ventures Under the Antitrust Laws: Same Reflections on the Significance of Penn-Olin*, 82 HARV. L. REV. 1007, 1014–16 (1969).

[64] *E.g.*, Times-Picayune Publishing Co. v. United States, 345 U.S. 594 (1953) (package sale of two items substantially reduces seller's costs and is therefore not unlawful); Dehydrating Process Co. v. A. O. Smith Corp., 292 F.2d 653 (1st Cir. 1961), *cert. denied*, 368 U.S. 931 (1961).

[65] *E.g.*, Instant Delivery Corp. v. Cities Stores Co., 284 F. Supp. 941 (E.D. Pa. 1968) (integrating delivery services of independent department stores and using one carrier is not an unlawful boycott); Interborough News Co. v. Curtis Publishing Co., 225 F.2d 289 (2d Cir. 1955) (no conspiracy when one publisher establishes a distributor and all other publishers shift business to that distributor); Parmelee Transp. Co. v. Keeshin, 144 F. Supp. 480, 186 F. Supp. 533 (N.D. Ill. 1958, 1960), *aff'd*, 292 F.2d 794 (7th Cir.), *cert. denied*, 368 U.S. 944 (1961); Ackerman-Chillingworth v. Pacific Electrical Contractors Ass'n, 405 F. Supp. 99 (D. Hawaii 1975) (joint workman's compensation plan not unreasonable).

[66] Appalachian Coals, Inc. v. United States, 288 U.S. 344 (1933); Evans v. S. S. Kresge Co., 544 F.2d 1184 (3d Cir. 1976), *cert. denied*, 433 U.S. 908 (1977).

Integration occurs when independent firms pool resources to achieve a task; integration results in efficiencies when it permits the firms to avoid costs or to improve quality; integration is worthwhile when firms could not otherwise achieve the efficiencies as quickly. When a restraint is ancillary to an integration that provides efficiencies not otherwise obtainable, a court must apply the rule of reason to determine whether the value of the market efficiency achieved by integration outweighs the adverse effect of the restraint.

Two recent Supreme Court cases nicely illustrate the difference between restraints that are ancillary to integration and those that are not.

Performing rights organizations like ASCAP and BMI were organized by composers to facilitate the enforcement of rights under the copyright laws. Both organizations hold nonexclusive licenses from copyright owners. They sublicense their rights to copyright users and distribute the proceeds to the copyright owners in accordance with a schedule that reflects, among other things, the frequency and nature of use of each copyrighted work. Both organizations refuse to sublicense individual works. They grant only blanket licenses that cover all works in which they have an interest. In *Broadcast Music, Inc. v. Columbia Broadcasting System, Inc.*,[67] CBS challenged the blanket license policy. CBS did not claim that ASCAP and BMI agreed to any term of sale. CBS claimed instead that by establishing a price for its blanket license, each performing rights organization independently engaged in price fixing that is per se unlawful.

The Supreme Court refused to apply a per se rule, finding that "the challenged practice may have redeeming competitive virtues and that the search for those values is not almost sure to be in vain."[68] More particularly, the blanket license "accompanies the integration of sales, monitoring, and enforcement against unauthorized copyright use."[69] The blanket license "is a necessary consequence of the integration necessary to achieve these efficiencies,

---

[67] 441 U.S. 1, 20 (1979).

[68] 441 U.S. at 13.

[69] *Id.* at 20.

and a necessary consequence of [a blanket] license is that its price must be established."[70] Thus, the per se rule was inapplicable.

In contrast, *Catalano, Inc. v. Target Sales, Inc.*[71] involved competitors coordinating, not integrating, their operations. The defendants, competing beer distributors, had agreed to stop selling on credit. Although the per se rule had long been thought to outlaw agreements between independent firms covering any aspect of price,[72] including agreements covering credit terms,[73] both the district court[74] and the Ninth Circuit Court of Appeals[75] refused to apply the per se rule. The Ninth Circuit characterized the credit agreement as a nonprice agreement, akin to product standardization, which "may actually enhance competition."[76]

In a brief per curiam opinion, the Supreme Court reversed this derogation of the per se rule.[77] Holding that credit is an aspect of price, so that a horizontal agreement on credit terms is subject to a literal application of the per se rule, the Court also held that prior cases "foreclose both of the possible justifications"[78] suggested by the Ninth Circuit. The argument that by reducing credit competition the defendants would induce new, procompetitive entry was said to be identical to arguing that competitors should be allowed to make entry attractive by agreeing to raise prices. The per se cases had rejected that argument.[79] Similarly, the argument that by reducing credit competition the defendants might increase price visibility and thus increase overall competition was unacceptable under the per se rule. "Any industrywide agreement on prices will result in a more accurate understanding of the terms offered by all parties

---

[70] *Id.* at 21. On remand, the court of appeals found the blanket license policy to be lawful under the rule of reason. Columbia Broadcasting Sys., Inc. v. American Soc'y of Composers, Authors and Publishers, 620 F.2d 930 (2d Cir. 1980), *cert. denied*, 100 S. Ct. 1491 (1981).

[71] 446 U.S. 643 (1980).

[72] See note 14 *supra*.

[73] United States v. First National Pictures, Inc., 282 U.S. 44 (1930) (agreement to lease only to those making cash deposits).

[74] See 446 U.S. 643 (1980).

[75] 605 F.2d 1097 (9th Cir. 1979).

[76] *Id.* at 1099.

[77] 446 U.S. at 648.

[78] *Id.* at 646.

[79] *Id.* at 649.

to the agreement"[80] but, under the per se rules, no such agreement is permitted. As a result, the defendants' agreement to eliminate credit was unsupported by permissible reasons and was therefore unlawful per se.

The Court's reasoning is sound. *Catalano* involved no integration of functions, only coordination of operations. Moreover, the defendants could not convincingly argue that their agreement integrated the market to make it operate more efficiently. In short, no resource savings counterbalanced the loss of competition flowing from the restraint, and the restraint was therefore per se unlawful.

2. *Externalities, free-riders, and optimal investment.* The second way in which trade restraints may increase market efficiency is by overcoming misallocation of resources caused by externalities—the costs and benefits of economic activity that are not reflected in market prices.[81] Investment decisions made in the market will reflect consumer welfare as long as all social costs and benefits of the activity are included in market prices; all investments that consumers are willing to pay for, but only those investments, will be generated by the market. As a result, in a competitive system it is ordinarily presumed that market forces, not government or private restraints, should govern investment decisions.

The problem of externalities, however, may mean that investment decisions reached through market mechanisms are inappropriate. When the value of commercial activity can be appropriated by consumers (and competitors) without payment, underinvestment in that activity is likely because the rewards of investment are reduced. This is true, for example, for so-called public goods[82]— goods such as national defense that benefit even those who do not pay for them. Conversely, when economic activity imposes costs on the public or competitors that are not included in market prices, too much investment may take place. Under such circumstances, intervention in the market to overcome the resource misallocation caused by externalities may increase market efficiency and thus be procompetitive.

---

[80] *Id.*

[81] *E.g.*, MISHAN, ECONOMICS FOR SOCIAL DECISIONS 85–111 (1975); Bator, *The Anatomy of Market Failure*, 72 Q.J. ECON. 351 (1958).

[82] *E.g.*, Samuelson, *The Pure Theory of Public Expenditure*, 36 REV. ECON. & STAT. 387 (1954); Oakland, *Public Goods, Perfect Competition, and Underproduction*, 82 J. POL. ECON. 927 (1974).

The problem of externalities is an important integrating concept in the laws relating to the competitive system. It serves as a justification for environmental and safety regulation[83] and as the primary economic support for the prohibition on copying and imitation found in the law of copyrights,[84] patents,[85] and unfair competition.[86] In antitrust, the free-rider problem is the externality that has attracted the most attention.[87] It is thus significant that the Supreme Court accepted the free-rider argument as a legitimate justification for nonprice vertical restraints.[88] Nonprice vertical restraints may increase investment in services provided by dealers and distributors, and thus increase market efficiency, by assuring that consumers and competitors will not benefit from such investment without paying for it.

The problem of externalities, however, is not limited to vertical distribution restraints. For example, when Justice Stevens analyzed the venerable *Mitchell v. Reynolds*[89] in *Professional Engineers*,[90] he showed that concern for the free-rider problem is a long-standing antitrust theme. *Mitchell v. Reynolds* approved a noncompetition agreement given by the seller of a business—a classic restraint of trade imposed to overcome a free-rider problem. A person who sells his business is a potential free-rider on the value of the goodwill transferred with the business, because his established business relationships and accumulated know-how permit him to appropriate inexpensively the customer goodwill and business opportunities he transferred to the new owner. The law therefore permits the seller to agree not to compete with the buyer of the business in

---

[83] Breyer, *Analyzing Regulatory Failure: Mismatches, Less Restrictive Alternatives, and Reform*, 92 HARV. L. REV. 549, 555 (1979).

[84] Breyer, *The Uneasy Case for Copyright: A Study of Copyright in Books, Photocopies, and Computer Programs*, 84 HARV. L. REV. 281 (1970).

[85] Machlup, *An Economic Review of the Patent System*, Study No. 15 of the Subcommittee on Patents, Trademarks, and Copyrights of the Committee of the Judiciary, U.S. Senate, 85th Cong., 2d Sess. (1958); Arrow, *Economic Welfare and the Allocation of Resources for Invention*, in THE RATE AND DIRECTION OF INVENTIVE ACTIVITY (National Bureau of Economic Research) 617 (1982); Demsetz, *Information and Efficiency: Another Viewpoint*, 12 J.L. & ECON. 12 (1969); Kitch, *The Nature and Function of the Patent System*, 20 J.L. & ECON. 265 (1977).

[86] KITCH & PERLMAN, LEGAL REGULATION OF THE COMPETITIVE PROCESS 2d ed., 48–53 (1979); International News Service v. Associated Press, 248 U.S. 215 (1918).

[87] *E.g.*, POSNER, ANTITRUST LAW, 147–67 (1976).

[88] Continental T.V., Inc. v. GTE Sylvania, Inc., 433 U.S. 36, 55 (1977).

[89] 1 P. Wms. 181, 24 Eng. Rep. 347 (ch. 1711).

[90] 435 U.S. 679, 689 (1978).

order to overcome this free-rider possibility and protect the value of the business being transferred. Such a restriction, if reasonable, is upheld because "the long-run benefit of enhancing the marketability of the business itself—and thereby providing incentives to develop such an enterprise—outweighed the temporary and limited loss of competition."[91]

Free-rider problems also underlie permissive treatment in some price-fixing and boycott cases.[92] For example, restrictions on hiring by organized athletic teams may be justified as necessary to avoid the possibility that one team will impose costs—in the form of decreased reputation[93] or safety[94]—on the other teams without having to compensate for those costs.

Identifying the problem of externalities as a justification for trade restraints shows the relationship between cases previously thought to be unrelated. The externalities problem is not, however, an acceptable justification in every antitrust context,[95] so care must be taken in its application. Courts should focus their analysis of particular cases on whether circumstances exist that give rise to a genuine problem of externalities; whether the investment induced or saved by the restraint is significant enough to outweigh the restrictive

---

[91] 435 U.S. at 688–89.

[92] Bork, *The Rule of Reason and the Per Se Concept: Price-Fixing and Market Division*, 75 YALE L.J. 373, 457–64 (1966) (analyzing United States v. Columbia Pictures Corp., 189 F. Supp. 153 (S.D.N.Y. 1960) and United States v. Nationwide Trailer Rental System, Inc., 156 F. Supp. 800 (D. Kans. 1957, *aff'd*, 355 U.S. 10 (1957)). See also Eastern Scientific Co. v. Wild Heerbrugg Instruments, Inc., 572 F.2d 883 (1st Cir.), *cert. denied*, 439 U.S. 833 (1978) (price restrictions on sales outside assigned territories should be treated as territorial restrictions).

[93] Molinas v. National Basketball Ass'n, 190 F. Supp. 241, 244 (S.D.N.Y. 1961); Manok v. Southeast Dist. Bowling Ass'n, 306 F. Supp. 1215 (C.D. Cal. 1969) (not a violation to suspend plaintiff, after a hearing, for fraudulent activities intended to manipulate handicaps). *Contra*, Blalock v. Ladies Professional Golf Ass'n, 359 F. Supp. 1260, 1265 (N.D. Ga. 1973).

[94] Neeld v. National Hockey League, 594 F.2d 1297 (9th Cir. 1979) (prohibition on hiring one-eyed hockey player is justified). See also Florists' Nationwide Tel. Delivery Network v. Florists' Tel. Delivery Ass'n, 371 F.2d 263 (7th Cir.), *cert. denied*, 387 U.S. 909 (1967) (restrictions on dealing between florists in integrated network may be necessary to prevent cream skimming). The court appears to have misused the free-rider analysis in Yoder Bros., Inc. v. California-Florida Plant Corp., 537 F.2d 1347 (5th Cir. 1976), *cert. denied*, 429 U.S. 1094 (1977) (restrictions on distribution of unique plant cuttings per se unlawful by analogy to *Fashion Originators' Guild*).

[95] *E.g.*, Fashion Originators' Guild of America v. FTC, 312 U.S. 457 (1941) (secondary boycott not justified to overcome free-riding-style piracy). Compare Cheney Bros. v. Doris Silk Corp., 35 F.2d 279 (2d Cir. 1929) (copying fabric designs is not unfair competition). The author's view that the free-rider problem does not explain or justify resale price maintenance is articulated in Gerhart, *The "Competitive Advantages" Explanation for Intrabrand Restraints: An Antitrust Analysis*, 1981 DUKE L.J. 417 (1981).

features of the restraint; and whether the externalities can be overcome by any less restrictive means.

C. REDUCING TRANSACTION COSTS

Collaborative conduct may also increase market efficiency by
reducing transaction costs—the costs of matching buyers and
sellers.[96] Unlike the model of pure competition,[97] in real markets
information is not ubiquitous or costless. It is costly to search for
goods and for information about goods, to bargain over terms of
sale, and to enforce bargains. Uncertainty is pervasive, and measures to reduce uncertainty or control risks are costly. As a result,
market output is increased when restraints reduce information or
bargaining costs, overcome impediments to the flow of information
and efficient bargaining, or reduce uncertainty. Several examples of
procompetitive restraints that reduce transaction costs are illustrative.

1. *Integration to reduce bargaining costs.* Transaction costs are reduced, of course, when integration of activities eliminates duplicate
bargaining efforts and thus reduces the cost of bargaining, as in
Broadcast Music[98] and several cases upholding joint sales agencies.[99]
The antitrust issues in such cases are similar to those in any cases of
integration, namely, (1) whether the integration is reasonably necessary to achieve the efficiencies, and (2) whether restraints flowing
from the integration are truly necessary to achieve the integration.
When both questions are answered affirmatively, it may safely be
concluded that the procompetitive effects of the integration outweigh any resulting loss of competition.

2. *Organization to reduce search costs.* The amount and quality of
information available about the market significantly affects search
costs—the costs of knowing and evaluating the options the market

---

[96] See generally WILLIAMSON, MARKETS AND HIERARCHIES: ANALYSIS AND ANTITRUST
IMPLICATIONS 20–40 (1975).

[97] *E.g.*, MANSFIELD, MICROECONOMICS 234–35 (2d ed. 1975).

[98] 441 U.S. 1 (1979). See text accompanying notes 67–71 *supra*.

[99] Appalachian Coals, Inc. v. United States, 288 U.S. 344 (1933); Webster County Memorial Hospital, Inc. v. United Mine Workers of America Welfare and Retirement Fund of
1950, 536 F.2d 419 (D.C. Cir. 1976). Compare Virginia Excelsior Mills, Inc. v. FTC, 256
F.2d 538 (4th Cir. 1958); United States v. American Smelting & Ref. Co., 182 F. Supp. 834
(S.D.N.Y. 1960). See also L.C.L. Theatres v. Columbia Pictures, Indus., 566 F.2d 494 (5th
Cir. 1978) (collective surveillance of plaintiff's movie theater to check on alleged underreport-
ing of revenue is permissible).

provides.[100] Efficient amounts of appropriate information may not be generated by the market, however, without competitor collaboration or government intervention, because of the public goods characteristic of information,[101] and because persons will not want to divulge information without a promise that the recipients will reciprocate. As a result, in the absence of a restriction of output, numerous forms of restraint ancillary to information improvement are sanctioned by the antitrust laws—information exchanges among competitors,[102] organized trading exchanges,[103] and product testing and rating.[104]

The problem of search costs and the explanation of the way in which quality, safety, and ethical norms may promote efficiency[105] explain why the Court in *Professional Engineers* said that "[e]thical norms may serve to regulate and promote . . . competition"[106] and thus fall outside the per se rules. When it is costly for consumers to evaluate products, it is difficult for them to reward the products they like with higher prices; prices will reflect the average quality of all interchangeable products, both good and bad. As a result, the

---

[100] See Benham, *The Effect of Advertising on the Price of Eyeglasses*, 15 J.L. & ECON. 337, 338 (1972); Nelson, *Information and Consumer Behavior*, 78 J. POL. ECON. 311 (1970); Stigler, *The Economics of Information*, 69 J. POL. ECON. 213 (1961).

[101] Arrow, *Economic Welfare and the Allocation of Resources for Invention*, in THE RATE AND DIRECTION OF ECONOMIC ACTIVITY 609 (1962); Posner, *Information and Antitrust*, 67 GEO. L.J. 1186, 1193 (1979).

[102] Michelman v. Clark-Schwebel Fiber Glass Corp., 534 F.2d 1036 (2d Cir.), *cert. denied*, 429 U.S. 885 (1976) (exchanging information on plaintiff's creditworthiness is not unlawful where there is no incentive for joint action or uniform conduct); FTC Advisory Opinion (1969); 16 C.F.R. § 15:361 (1980) (permitting trade association credit reporting so long as each member makes own decision and certain protections are afforded).

[103] See, *e.g.*, Silver v. New York Stock Exchange, 373 U.S. 341 (1963); Danville Tobacco Ass'n v. Bryant-Buckner Associates, Inc., 333 F.2d 202 (4th Cir. 1964) and 372 F.2d 634 (4th Cir.), *cert. denied*, 387 U.S. 907 (1967); Mechanical Contractors Bid Depository v. Christiansen, 352 F.2d 817 (10th Cir. 1965), *cert. denied*, 384 U.S. 918 (1966); United States v. Realty Multi-List, Inc., 629 F.2d 1351 (5th Cir. 1980).

[104] Eliason Corp. v. National Sanitation Foundation, 614 F.2d 126 (6th Cir. 1980), *cert. denied*, 449 U.S. 826 (1980); McCann v. New York Stock Exchange, 107 F.2d 908 (2d Cir. 1939); Structural Laminates, Inc. v. Douglas Fir Plywood Ass'n, 261 F. Supp. 154 (D. Ore. 1966), *aff'd per curiam*, 399 F.2d 155 (9th Cir. 1968), *cert. denied*, 393 U.S. 1024 (1969). See Note, *Promoting Product-Quality Information: A Proposed Limited Antitrust Exemption for Producers*, 30 STAN. L. REV. 563 (1978).

[105] See Leland, *Quacks, Lemons and Licensing: A Theory of Minimum Quality Standards*, 87 J. POL. ECON. 1328 (1979); Ackerlof, *The Market for "Lemons": Quality Uncertainty and the Market Mechanism*, 84 Q.J. ECON. 488 (1970); Oi, *The Economics of Product Safety*, 4 BELL J. ECON. 3 (1973).

[106] 438 U.S. at 696.

incentive for any seller to improve the quality of his products is decreased and the incentive to take a free ride on the quality of other products is increased; that is, there will be underinvestment in product quality. When competitors eliminate poor or unsafe products, the average price of products will rise (reflecting the increase in average quality), and the proper investment incentive will be restored. Under such circumstances, restraints of trade may promote consumer welfare by helping to overcome the effects of imperfect consumer knowledge.

This is not an argument that quality or ethical norms always increase efficiency and consumer welfare. Moreover, product norms may be inferior to other, more direct, means of overcoming the problem of insufficient consumer information.[107] But the promote side of the promote/suppress standard is broad enough to permit such sources of consumer welfare to be considered, and the reasonableness test is flexible enough to permit a court to determine whether the prerequisites of this argument have been met—namely, whether the characteristics of the market (particularly the cost of consumer information) are such that quality and safety norms are likely to increase welfare, whether the norms as articulated and applied limit only objectively unsafe and substandard products, and whether other means of overcoming consumer information problems—for example, disclosure requirements—are superior means of achieving the same end.

3. *Transaction costs and product standardization.* Product standardization is a particular form of competitor collaboration that may reduce transaction costs and thus promote competition. Establishing and policing product grading standards,[108] for example, reduces a consumer's cost of evaluating products. Exchanging information about product specifications may reduce the cost of competitive imitation, an important source of consumer welfare.[109] Establishing standard sizes may facilitate handling. And establishing standard

---

[107] For example, disseminating product information to enable consumers to evaluate products may permit greater product differentiation and thus reward and encourage product improvement. Lunsford, *Consumers and Trademarks: The Function of Trademarks in the Market Place*, 64 TRADEMARK REP. 75 (1974).

[108] See, e.g., Tropic Film Corp. v. Paramount Pictures Corp., 319 F. Supp. 1247, 1254 (S.D.N.Y. 1970) (rating motion pictures not unreasonable). *Cf.* Dept. of Justice, Business Review, Transportation Association of America, June 24, 1968 (standardizing terms of reference and tariff formats would enhance transportation competition).

[109] *Cf.* Smith v. Chanel, Inc., 402 F.2d 562 (9th Cir. 1968) (accurately comparing copied product to original is not trademark infringement or unfair competition).

product characteristics may facilitate product interconnection, as when the circuitry of audio components is standardized, or interchangeability, so that, for example, replacement parts can be purchased from any of a number of sellers. For these types of standardization, the risk of anticompetitive harm is small enough and the possibility of economic benefit great enough to support treatment under the rule of reason.

The Court's opinion in *Catalano*,[110] in contrast, exposes the limits that have been placed on the product standardization argument. The Ninth Circuit's refusal to invalidate a horizontal agreement eliminating credit sales was based on its belief that the elimination of credit might be procompetitive, because it would channel rivalry away from nonprice competition and toward price competition by simplifying transactions and eliminating the "distraction" of nonprice terms. Although the Ninth Circuit's characterization of credit as a nonprice term is questionable,[111] the characterization issue is only a semantic quibble: the central issue is whether it is permissible for competitors to channel competition toward one form rather than another.

Channeling competition into particular forms of rivalry, however, does not legitimately reduce transaction costs. The defendants in *Catalano* were not trying to give consumers more information about the market. Their argument was that consumers and the market process would benefit if there were less information about credit terms, because consumers would then focus on information (about prices) that would be more to their advantage. This is not an argument that increasing the amount of information leads to transactional efficiency, but that consumers should be protected from their own misuse of information generated by the market.[112] That argument is inconsistent with consumer welfare. When credit competition is flourishing it is presumably because consumers have chosen credit rivalry over price rivalry.[113] If the consumer sover-

---

[110] 446 U.S. 643 (1980).

[111] See note 14 *supra*.

[112] In applying the First Amendment, the Supreme Court has rejected a similar protectionist argument advanced to justify government restraints on commercial speech. Virginia State Bd. of Pharmacy v. Virginia Citizens Consumer Counsel, Inc., 425 U.S. 748, 769 (1976).

[113] If there were a free-rider problem in the provision of information, one could not be so confident that consumers get the information they really want; but no free-rider problem is apparent in *Catalano*.

eignty underlying a market economy is to be preserved, that decision should be respected and protected.[114]

The distinction between legitimate product standardization and the "standardization" in *Catalano* is clear. The standardization in *Catalano* was not to provide information to make competitive offerings comparable. It was to make them comparable by homogenizing them, reducing them to simplified terms by eliminating some forms of competition. This, as the Supreme Court said,[115] is no different from homogenizing and simplifying transactions by agreeing to sell at a single price and was therefore correctly held to be per se unlawful.

IV. Maricopa: The Court Stumbles

Had the Supreme Court recognized the substantial doctrinal synthesis it achieved in its pre-*Maricopa* cases, it would have written a much different opinion in *Maricopa*. Its *Maricopa* opinion is retrogressive: it champions a wooden, mechanical view of the per se rules and fails to recognize the full range of circumstances in which trade restraints may promote competition.

Maricopa involved an agreement in which nonaffiliated doctors established a maximum price schedule for services they provide patients insured by sponsoring insurance carriers. The plaintiff, the State of Arizona, moved for summary judgment, claiming that the maximum price fixing was a per se antitrust violation. The Ninth Circuit refused to apply a per se rule, noting that too little was known about either the effect of the agreement or the health care industry to permit the per se rule to be invoked.[116]

The Supreme Court, applying the per se rule to invalidate the agreement, reversed. Justice Stevens's opinion for the plurality paid little attention to the economic impact of the maximum price fixing in the context in which it was employed. Instead, the out-

---

[114] Thus, in *Catalano*, the Court rejected the argument that "nonprice" competition is less significant than price competition, just as it earlier rejected the argument that the nonprice competition induced by vertical nonprice restraints is less significant than price competition. Continental T.V., Inc. v. GTE Sylvania, Inc., 433 U.S. 36, 56, n.25 (1977) (an argument "flawed by its necessary assumption that a large part of the promotional efforts resulting from vertical restrictions will not convey socially desirable information about product availability, price, quality, and services").

[115] 446 U.S. at 649.

[116] 643 F.2d 553, 556 (1980).

come rested largely on the longevity and procedural simplicity of the per se price-fixing rule. Thus, Justice Stevens stressed "the costs of judging business practices under the rule of reason"[117] and openly acknowledged the loss of fidelity when per se rules are applied: "For the sake of business certainty and litigation efficiency, we have tolerated the invalidation of some agreements that a fullblown inquiry might have proved to be reasonable."[118] These statements signal a retreat from the promote/suppress standard, because they imply that restraints that potentially promote competition may nonetheless be subject to the per se rules. The Court made that conclusion clear: "The anticompetitive potential inherent in all price-fixing agreements," said the Court, "justifies their facial invalidation even if procompetitive justifications are offered for some."[119]

Justice Stevens's emphasis on the certainty and automatic nature of the per se rules is a throwback to the worst aspects of *Topco*.[120] By implying that per se rules can be applied without considering policy implications whenever something called price fixing is observed, the Court lost sight of the fundamental principle that it had recognized in the cases between *Topco* and *Maricopa*: neither the existence of the per se rules nor the certainty provided by the per se rules enables a court to determine whether to apply the per se rule. The decision to apply the per se rule can be made only after a court determines whether the reasons advanced to justify the restraint are the type of reasons that are acceptable under the promote/suppress standard, that is, whether the restraint possibly promotes competition in one of the three ways described above. To ignore this principle undermines sound antitrust analysis by sacrificing fidelity for certainty.[121]

The Court was no doubt influenced by its belief that the per se

---

[117] 102 S. Ct. 2466, 2473 (1982).

[118] *Id.*

[119] 102 S. Ct. 2466, 2477 (1982).

[120] See text accompanying notes 20–33 *supra.*

[121] Even more remarkable, perhaps, is Justice Stevens's notion, also dredged from *Topco,* see note 29 *supra,* that per se rules "enhance the legislative prerogative to amend the law," because they put the onus on Congress to create exceptions to the per se rules. 102 S. Ct. at 2478. Congress, however, did not enact the per se rules; it enacted a statement of principle— faith in efficiently functioning markets—for the Court to apply. Congress should not be expected to remedy every derogation of that principle that results from a misapplication of per se rules.

rule against maximum price fixing is based on sound policy. The rule arose virtually without examination or explanation at a time when the Court geared its antitrust policy toward protecting the autonomy of businesses rather than toward identifying and protecting business arrangements that promote efficiency.[122] The rule arose, moreover, in cases involving vertical price fixing, rather than the horizontal price fixing in *Maricopa*, so the rule's application in *Maricopa* need not have been automatic.[123] Even the Court's list of the potential anticompetitive dangers of maximum price fixing, which was an exaggeration,[124] could not excuse the Court from determining whether this maximum price fixing promoted or suppressed competition.

When the Court finally reluctantly considered the argument that maximum price fixing by these defendants promotes competition, its analysis was unsatisfactory. Professor Frank Easterbrook has explained how maximum price fixing in the context of *Maricopa* promotes competition by reducing the transaction costs of providing insured medical care.[125] Several factors account for high transaction costs. Because insurers find it difficult to predict the incidence of illness and the cost of treatment, they find it difficult to estimate the medical care costs they must cover under their policies. As a result, their premiums are increased to reflect the risk that their estimates will be erroneous. The difficulty of predicting insurance payouts is exacerbated by the "moral hazard" problem typified by insurance: an insured person has no incentive to shop for low-cost services, because the insurer, not the insured, pays for the services. Although insurers have attempted to ameliorate the problem by agreeing to compensate insureds only for "usual, ordinary, and customary" medical costs, that standard is difficult to apply. It also requires the insurer and the insured to incur the additional costs of determining which fees are "usual, ordinary, and

---

[122] *E.g.*, Kiefer-Stewart Co. v. Joseph E. Seagram & Sons, 340 U.S. 211, 213 (1951) (maximum price "agreements, no less than those to fix minimum prices, cripple the freedom of traders and thereby restrain their ability to sell in accordance with their own judgment"). In *Maricopa* the Court may have reverted to this mode of analysis by concluding that "horizontal agreements to fix maximum prices [are] on the same legal—even if not economic—footing as agreements to fix minimum or uniform prices." 102 S. Ct. at 2475.

[123] Easterbrook, *Maximum Price Fixing*, 48 U. CHI. L. REV. 886, 887–90 (1981).

[124] *Id.* at 900–908.

[125] *Id.* at 896–98 (1981). *Contra*, Kallstrom, *Health Care Cost Control by Third Party Payors: Fee Schedules, and the Sherman Act*, 1978 DUKE L.J. 645, 678–84.

customary." Moreover, both insurers and insureds find it difficult to evaluate the necessity for, and the quality of, medical care, which increases further the transaction costs of an efficient insurance system.

These problems of transaction cost are potentially ameliorated by the maximum price fixing utilized by the doctors in *Maricopa*. Because doctors who subscribe to the plan agree to a maximum fee for covered services, insurers are able to estimate more accurately their liability under their policies and thus reduce premiums. Insureds find the plan attractive, because they are guaranteed that their entire cost of service will be covered if they go to a doctor who subscribes to the plan. With respect to doctors, their maximum fee is fixed, so they have no incentive to inflate costs by providing more services than are required. Minimum quality standards are maintained by physician peer review groups, which check on the medical necessity and appropriateness of treatment provided to insureds.[126]

The Court recognized the strength of these assertions,[127] but rejected them, because it found that the maximum fee schedule challenged in *Maricopa* originated with doctors rather than with an insurer,[128] as is the case with many other types of medical insurance. The Court apparently viewed fee schedules originating with insurers to be a less restrictive, but reasonably substitutable, alternative to fee schedules originating with doctors. The Court was wrong. Doctors may be able to establish maximum prices more efficiently than insurers, because doctors have better information about the cost of various medical services and can more easily determine the maximum prices that will clear the market. If so, insurer-sponsored maximum price schedules are a more expensive, and hence less desirable, alternative to doctor-originated maximum price schedules. The Court recognized this possibility but gave it little weight, because the possibility was "far from obvious" and because any efficiencies from doctor-originated maximum fee

---

[126] The defendants' peer review function, which could be characterized as a form of group boycott, was not challenged in *Maricopa*. 102 S. Ct. 2466, 2471 (1982).

[127] The Court found it arguable "that the existence of a fee schedule, whether fixed by the doctors or by the insurers, makes it easier—and to that extent less expensive—for insurers to calculate the risks that they underwrite and to arrive at the appropriate reimbursement on insured claims." 102 S. Ct. at 2477 n.25.

[128] 102 S. Ct. at 2477–78.

schedules might be offset by the "power of the [doctors] to dictate the terms of such insurance plans."[129]

The Court's reasoning is inconsistent with sound antitrust analysis. Because *Maricopa* came to the Court on plaintiff's motion for summary judgment, there was no factual record, and the Court therefore could not determine whether doctors can establish maximum fee schedules more efficiently than insurers. The only issue appropriately before the Court was whether it is worth the cost to determine at trial the relative efficiency of doctor-originated maximum fee schedules or whether the relative efficiency of doctor-originated fee schedules could be determined from theoretical analysis so as to avoid a trial. The Court refused to address that issue and instead hid behind the procedural fix of the per se rules to avoid the crucial issue. Similarly, the Court's concern that maximum price fixing may enable doctors to "dictate the terms of insurance policies" raises a factual issue that the Court could not appropriately address in reviewing a motion for summary judgment. Although the conspiring doctors in *Maricopa* comprised seventy percent of the doctors in the relevant market,[130] which made it legitimate to question their market power, that is no justification for invoking a per se rule, because the per se rule assumes that the maximum price fixing would be unlawful whatever the market power of the defendants.

The Court should have acknowledged that the maximum price fixing by these doctors might promote competition by facilitating insured medical care, and it should have then identified the factual issues raised by that possibility and openly considered whether an accurate determination of the issues required a trial or whether, given the cost of a trial, an acceptably accurate answer could be given through economic analysis. The Court's approach—avoiding legitimate factual issues in order to shoehorn this case into a per se rule meant for other contexts—only subverts antitrust analysis.

IV. Conclusion

One of the enduring legacies of the Chicago school of antitrust analysis is the identification of a coherent, unified, and consis-

[129] 102 S. Ct. at 2478.
[130] 102 S. Ct. at 2470.

tent framework for analyzing antitrust issues. Prior to *Maricopa*, the Supreme Court appeared to be using that framework in its own analysis. The Court's performance in antitrust cases would improve if it continued to do so.

Antitrust analysis would be improved substantially if the Court would interpret the promote/suppress standard using the consumer welfare model; that is, if it would examine restraints of trade to determine whether they improve productive or allocative efficiency. Under this approach, the per se rules would cease to be viewed as easily applied rules designed to simplify antitrust analysis. Rather, per se rules would be viewed as substantive rules, to be applied when analysis shows that conduct is unable to improve productive or allocative efficiency or that it is costly to determine the efficiency effects of conduct. This approach would not gut the per se rules. Collaboration between nonintegrated competitors that has no possibility of increasing productive or allocative efficiency can be recognized easily; conduct that is now properly subject to per se rules would continue to be subject to per se rules, and just as decisively.

At the same time, rational analysis of conduct that might increase efficiency would be improved. Recognizing that the per se category is separated from the rule of reason category because of the potential for some conduct to promote efficiency, shows the unity of antitrust analysis and focuses attention on the substantive criteria that really matter in evaluating conduct. Moreover, adopting the consumer welfare model would require courts to consider more carefully the efficiency-producing properties of conduct and would thus enliven antitrust analysis with new substantive vigor.

RICHARD A. EPSTEIN

NOT DEFERENCE, BUT DOCTRINE: THE EMINENT DOMAIN CLAUSE

As a matter of practical politics and high political theory, one of the central functions of government is to create a stable legal order in which all individuals may securely use their talents and possessions. In order to meet this minimum condition of social order, it has been seen necessary, at least in the American constitutional system, to develop a complex system of checks and balances to prevent the aggrandizement and abuse of official power by any single group of individuals. Within this framework, the legislature may sometimes change the general rules under which individual rights are both created and protected. Yet the acceptance of the principle of judicial review requires the Supreme Court to determine which legislative initiatives are consistent with the basic constitutional scheme and which are not. While it might be expected that the basic approach to so fundamental a task would have been settled early in our constitutional jurisprudence, today, perhaps as never before, the Supreme Court is still groping for some theory to enable it to distinguish between permissible and impermissible exercises of government power. In many instances, the inquiry is concerned with the rights of speech, religion, or association, or with the power of the state to arrest and prosecute citizens for certain activities. Yet the same inquiry is carried on in connection with various property and economic interests, in cases involving

Richard A. Epstein is James Parker Hall Professor of Law, The University of Chicago.

AUTHOR'S NOTE: I should like to thank Ross Green for his helpful research assistance in the preparation of this article.

the Equal Protection Clause, the Due Process Clause, the Contracts Clause, or the Eminent Domain Clause. This paper will focus on the implications of the Eminent Domain Clause.

The chief problem in economic areas is a simple one. There is a clear collision between the traditional notions of property as a source of individual autonomy and the power of the state to regulate its use and disposition. Even to enter upon the inquiry of determining which government programs pass muster and which do not requires the Court to pass upon the merits of complicated and controversial pieces of public regulation. To avoid many of these problems in areas of economic regulation, the Court has adopted as its watchword "deference" to legislative judgment. Thus in *Usery v. Turner Elkhorn*, Justice Marshall set out the accepted point of departure: "It is by now well established that legislative Acts adjusting the burdens and benefits of economic life come to the Court with a presumption of constitutionality, and that the burden is on one complaining of a due process violation to establish that the legislature has acted in an arbitrary and irrational way."[1] As written, the passage only addresses claims raised under the Due Process Clause, but the pattern of deference developed in due process cases has been carried over to challenges made under the Eminent Domain Clause as well.

The deferential posture of the Supreme Court on matters of economic regulation has without doubt limited the number and types of legislative schemes that may now be subjected to constitutional scrutiny. Ordinary zoning regulations, for example, are largely immune from constitutional attack. But even the present Supreme Court does not view judicial deference as a code word for judicial surrender, and no presumption of constitutionality can spare the Court from making some substantive judgments about the proper scope of government power in economic affairs. Indeed there is a certain irony here. Each effort to relax the applicable constitutional fetters brings in its wake still bolder legislative initiatives, which in turn test the structure of existing constitutional doctrine. No matter where the line is set, some cases will always be difficult.

This past Term followed the pattern of recent years. In two

---

[1] Usery v. Turner Elkhorn Mining Co., 428 U.S. 1, 15 (1976).

important cases, *Texaco, Inc. v. Short*[2] and *Loretto v. Teleprompter Manhattan CATV Corp.*,[3] the Court was asked again to define the limits the Eminent Domain Clause placed on the exercise of state power, but did little to advance the theory or practice of the subject. In *Texaco, Inc.*, the Court, over a persuasive dissent, sustained provisions of a "lapsed mineral statute" that stripped holders of mineral interests of their entire holdings because they did not comply with retroactive filing provisions of which they had no actual knowledge. And in *Teleprompter* both the Court and the dissent muddled the difficult issues under the takings clause in passing on a statute which gave a cable TV firm the right to install its equipment on a landlord's premises without his consent upon payment of a nominal consideration.

Before turning to the particulars of these two decisions, it is important to identify the reasons for the sorry performance of the Supreme Court in these and other eminent domain cases. In my view, the problem stems largely from the Court's wholly mistaken interpretative orientation to the Eminent Domain Clause, which provides "nor shall private property be taken for public use without just compensation." A lawyer not steeped in the Supreme Court tradition would, I think, recognize that the Clause as it is written raises in sequence four issues, three by its express language and the fourth by necessary implication. The first of these is whether the private property of the claimant has been taken. The second is whether the taking, if any, has been for a public use. The third is whether, if for a public use, the taking has been accompanied by just—*i.e.*, full—compensation. Missing from this list of express issues is the question, If the taking so made is not compensated, may it be justified by the police power of the state? The very mention of the police power necessarily restricts the possible application of the Clause. It is therefore not a natural favorite of those who favor an expansive interpretation of the Clause. But the need for the exception arises in a principled fashion, under all but the most uncompromising literalism. Just as private parties can justify taking property without compensation, as when acting in self-defense or in abating a nuisance, the state derives the same right

---

[2] 102 S. Ct. 3164 (1982).

[3] 102 S. Ct. 781 (1982).

when acting as their representative. The police power therefore should be construed to recognize in the state no lesser—but no greater—rights than private individuals have in their relationships with each other.

This straightforward view of the Eminent Domain Clause, it should be stressed at the outset, does not limit the state to the rights that private individuals have against each other. In addition the state is given one vital power that goes far beyond any available to private parties: it is entitled to force the purchase of the property interests for public use, while private parties must always respect as inviolate the property rights of their fellow citizens. For the private individual who wishes to acquire the property of another, it is a case of purchase or nothing; for the state there is a third alternative: condemnation with payment. While a private party may be stymied by a current owner who wishes to hold out for some exorbitant sum, the state can override the owner's wishes, take the property in question, and pay the owner only its highest value for current use. Its power of eminent domain thereby allows it to appropriate for the population at large the surplus value inherent in redeployment of private resources. As holdout questions may loom very large in transactions with many potential participants, the power of the state to have its way when it is prepared to purchase it is very substantial, but often underestimated. An interpretation that presses the Eminent Domain Clause to its logical (and correct) conclusion will place more stringent restrictions upon state power than the current law, but it will still afford the state ample power to do whatever it must do to govern.

The explanatory power of this four-part inquiry into eminent domain issues can be, I think, fully appreciated only when it is contrasted with the dominant view of the Clause. The Supreme Court has repeatedly admonished us that there are no "fixed" rules. On the contrary, takings questions are to be resolved through "essentially *ad hoc* factual" inquiries that have to take into account "such factors as the character of the governmental action, its economic impact, and its interference with reasonable investment-backed expectations."[4] Where the inquiry is framed in this fashion, the Court leaves itself with sufficient degrees of freedom to reach

---

[4] See Penn Central Transportation Co. v. New York City, 438 U.S. 104 (1978); Kaiser Aetna v. United States, 444 U.S. 164, 175 (1979); PruneYard Shopping Center v. Robins, 447 U.S. 74 (1980), for various expressions of the dominant sentiment.

whatever result it wants in any particular case. So read, the text itself places few if any constraints upon the outcome. By holding that the Eminent Domain Clause protects only "investment-backed" expectations, the Court has watered down constitutional requirements, so that it behaves as if only the original cost of a property interest, rather than its current market value, is protected. The looseness of the relevant factors invites, if not requires, the Court to engage in a general balancing test that in turn places no limit on the factors to be considered or the outcome to be reached. Finally, the open-ended nature of its inquiries blocks the development of a rigorous theory with which to harmonize the cases, thereby making each new decision an embarrassment to those that have preceded it.

There is here an instructive analogy to the law of torts. Under the various tests of negligence captured by the "reasonable man" formula, there are no fixed boundaries that determine what defendants are responsible for and what they are not. All is said to depend on the facts and circumstances of the cases, so that some unchecked intuitive response to individual circumstances dominates the application of general rules of decision. This intellectual orientation did much to foster the corrosive anti-intellectualism of legal realism. It also explains in large measure the persistent willingness of the courts to defer to juries on questions of tortious liability. Where there are no rules that matter, how can a court insist that its own views on liability determine the outcomes of particular cases?[5]

With eminent domain, the concern is not with the interplay between judge and jury, but with the higher-stakes game of the interplay between the legislature and the court. Nonetheless the pattern of analysis is exactly the same. If the discussion begins with the idea that there are no fixed rules to guide inquiry, the upshot will be judicial deference, if not to the jury then to the legislature and to its adminstrative offspring. Only where a court has a theory of its subject matter—as for example with political speech under the First Amendment—will it be temperamentally suited to overturn legislative decisions. In short, reasonableness tests lead to amorphous legal structures which in turn foster judicial deference

---

[5] See, for my views on the subject in the area of products liability, EPSTEIN, MODERN PRODUCTS LIABILITY LAW (1980).

across a very broad front. There are for this reason few special
verdicts under a negligence system, while many more are possible
with the more structured inquiry under a theory of strict liability.
The confusion and uncertainty that everywhere mar the law of
eminent domain should not be seen solely as a consequence of the
difficulty of the issues with which the Court must grapple—
although they are hard enough. In part it must be understood as a
failure or an unwillingness to delineate the issues raised with
sufficient clarity so that the parts can all be understood before the
whole is assembled. When the parts are understood and assembled,
the result is greater intellectual confidence and the judicial invalidation of many schemes which at present are thought sufficient to
withstand constitutional challenge.[6] Both *Texaco, Inc.* and *Teleprompter* are apt illustrations of the differences between these two
attitudes of constitutional interpretation, for in both the unwillingness to frame the issues in their proper sequence led to the blurring
of the court's analysis.

In *Texaco, Inc.*, Texaco was the holder of certain mineral interests
under a conveyance from the appellee Short (or her predecessor in
title). The interests in question were not recorded when made,
although it was clear under Indiana law that they were property
interests of equal stature with all other interests in real estate.[7] At
the time these interests were created, there was no requirement that
they be registered in order for the title to be perfected. In 1971,
long after creation of the interests, the legislature passed a statute[8]
which in essence provided that any mineral interest in the state
would lapse and would be reunited with the surface interest from
which it was carved, whenever it could be shown for a twenty-year

---

[6] One illustration of the point is San Diego Gas & Electric Co. v. San Diego, 450 U.S. 621
(1980) (Brennan, J., dissenting at 636), where the question begins with the partial taking
issue and then proceeds step by step through the inquiry without any appeal to the necessity
for *ad hoc* adjudication. The conflict of styles between Justice Brennan's dissent in *San Diego
Gas* and his opinion in *Penn Central* is evident to anyone who cares to read the two opinions.
In *San Diego Gas* he first establishes that there is a partial taking of property because of the
government imposed delay and that this amounts to a taking of an indefinite term. He then
shows that neither compensation nor police power justification is offered for the taking made.
In *Penn Central* the entire inquiry is deflected by his insistence that there is some "fallacy,"
438 U.S. at 130 n.27, in treating any portion of the fee simple as though it were property, a
point wholly inconsistent with his view of property in *San Diego Gas*.

[7] See Ind. Code § 32-5-7-3 (1976). "Interests in oil land gas . . . may be created for life, for
a term of years, or in fee, in such manner and to such extent as are all other interests in real
estate. . . ."

[8] Pub. L. No. 423, approved April 9, 1971.

period that (1) no rent had been paid on the mineral interest, (2) no taxes had been paid on the interest, and (3) no statement of claim had been filed.[9] A grace period of two years for filing after the bill's passage was given to the holders of all mineral interests. The statute further granted owners of ten or more mineral interests within any given county a grace period for filing of sixty days after notice of the lapse had been published, or, in the absence of such publication, after receipt of actual notice.[10] All but one of the appellants in this case were the first individuals who had taken mineral interests from the appellee. One had in turn taken a sublease from one of the other appellants. It was conceded that if the statute governed, the appellee was entitled to a judgment that extinguished the interests of the appellants and vested them in the appellees. In dealing with the claim, the Indiana Supreme Court held the statute constitutional against challenges based upon the Eminent Domain and the Due Process Clauses. Its decision was confirmed by a five-to-four vote of the United States Supreme Court.

In *Teleprompter* the relevant facts were as follows. In 1965 Teleprompter of Manhattan received from the City of New York an exclusive franchise to operate a cable TV system for the upper section of the Borough of Manhattan. The franchise agreement imposed upon Teleprompter obligations to maintain certain performance levels in its business. It also provided that the City of New York was entitled to "a sum of money which shall be equal to five per cent (5%) of all the gross receipts derived either directly or indirectly from the company's operation of the said service."[11] Armed with its franchise the company then proceeded to install its cable in a large number of apartment houses in Manhattan. In order to gain entrance into apartment buildings, Teleprompter typically agreed to pay landlords five percent of the gross receipts for the "exclusive privilege of offering and furnishing CATV or Cable T.V. service to occupants of the premises."[12] Teleprompter also

---

[9] Ind. Code. § 32-5-11-1 (1976): "Any interest in coal, oil and gas, and other minerals shall, if unused for a period of 20 years, be extinguished, unless a statement of claim is filed in accordance with section five hereof, and the ownership interest shall revert to the then owner of the interest out of which it was carved." Ind. Code § 32-5-11-3 (1976) gives the definition of use set out in the text.

[10] Ind. Code § 32-5-11-4 (1976) contains the two-year grace period, while Ind. Code § 32-5-11-5 (1976) allows the holder of ten or more interests in the county to file after notice.

[11] See Resolution No. 53, Board of Estimate, City of New York (Dec. 2, 1965).

[12] See Teleprompter's standard agreement, made Exhibit W in the case before the New

had another standard agreement whereby it paid a fixed fee for certain "crossover" installations (those which went across the property which it did not directly serve). Teleprompter's standard agreement was cancelable at the beginning of each year on ninety days' notice by either side, but only after the agreement had run for an initial five-year period. Mrs. Loretto's predecessor in title had entered into an agreement with Teleprompter which contained the cancellation clause and looked otherwise like the typical agreement for service to occupants, but which paid a one-time fee of $50, with no percentage of the gross.

After Teleprompter had established its standard method of doing business, New York passed Executive Law § 828, effective in January 1973.[13] The structure of the law was clear enough. Under it no landlord was allowed to "interfere" with the installation of cable television facilities on its premises. To this general rule there were several exceptions. One protected the landlord against having to bear the costs of installation. Still another gave it the right to sue the cable company in the event of physical damage to the premises. And the last required the cable company or the tenant to bear the costs of installation. In order to protect the tenants who availed themselves of the service from rent increases, the statute also prevented the landlord from negotiating installation fees with the ten-

---

York Court of Appeals. The five percent figure was a standard figure incorporated in clause 9 of the original document. There is no evidence in the record that any other percentage of royalties was paid by the company, although it did enter into occasional fixed sum agreements, as with Mrs. Loretto's predecessor in title.

[13] N.Y Exec. Law § 828 (McKinney 1982) provides in part:

1. No landlord shall
    a. interfere with the installation of cable television facilities upon his property or premises, except that a landlord may require:

        i. that the installation of cable television facilities conform to such reasonable conditions as are necessary to protect the safety, functioning and appearance of the premises, and the convenience and well-being of other tenants;

        ii. that the cable television company or the tenant or a combination thereof bear the entire cost of the installation, operation or removal of such facilities; and

        iii. that the cable television company agree to indemnify the landlord for any damage caused by the installation, operation or removal of such facilities.

    b. demand or accept payment from any tenant, in any form, in exchange for permitting cable television service on or within his property or premises, or from any cable television company in exchange therefor in excess of any amount which the commission shall, by regulation, determine to be reasonable; or

    c. discriminate in rental charges, or otherwise, between tenants who receive cable television and those who do not.

ant, or from increasing the rent on a discriminatory basis, to fore-
stall it from capturing from tenants the additional benefits of the
cable service. The statute further provided that a Cable Commission should determine what compensation, if any, should be paid to
landlords upon installation of the cable. The Commission in its
own proceedings held that a one-dollar fee to the landlord was the
norm except in those cases in which he could demonstrate some
"greater damage" attributable to the installation of the cable system.[14]

The constitutionality of the scheme was affirmed by the New
York Court of Appeals. Five judges held that the scheme fell within
the "elastic" provisions of the police power[15] and therefore was not
a taking. One concurring judge found that there was a taking but
thought that the compensation provided under the scheme was
sufficient.[16] There was a lengthy dissent by Cooke, C.J., who
found the statute an unconstitutional taking of private property
without just compensation.[17] The United States Supreme Court
reversed by a six-to-three vote. The majority of the Court, speaking
through Justice Marshall, found that there was a taking of property
and ordered the case remanded to consider the "amount of the
compensation due."[18] Justice Blackmun, writing for himself, Justice Brennan, and Justice White, dissented on the familiar ground
that, as there was "no set formula" to answer takings questions, the
balance of interests in the case required affirmation of the decision
of the New York Court of Appeals.

On their faces little unites *Texaco, Inc.* and *Teleprompter*. Nonetheless the two cases do exhibit a common failure of approach that
is best revealed by setting them against the fourfold framework of
analysis set out above: Was there a taking of private property? Was
it for a public use? Was the taking justified by the police power? If
not, Was proper compensation paid? It might be objected that this
form of analysis does not pay sufficient attention to the equal protection and due process issues that are discussed by the various

---

[14] 102 S. Ct. at 3170.

[15] Loretto v. Teleprompter Manhattan CATV Corp., 53 N.Y.2d 124, 143, 423 N.E.2d
320, 329, 440 N.Y.S.2d 843, 852 (1981).

[16] See Gabrielli, J., 53 N.Y.2d at 155, 423 N.E.2d at 336, 440 N.Y.S.2d at 859.

[17] 53 N.Y.2d at 156, 423 N.E.2d at 336, 440 N.Y.S.2d at 859.

[18] 102 S. Ct. at 3179.

opinions. In my view, however, they are, and can be shown to be, variations of the deeper eminent domain questions that are explicitly addressed. The so-called due process questions, including the procedural issue of the appropriate notice, can be understood not as some *ad hoc* shared intuitions but as necessary corollaries of a systematic eminent domain analysis of these same issues.

I. TAKING OF PRIVATE PROPERTY

The first issue raised by a uniform interpretation of the Eminent Domain Clause is whether the private property of the complainant has been taken by the state. To find for him on this question is not to require compensation, as there are still the police power and (implicit) compensation questions. The conclusion, however, is of no little importance, for it does draw the state action under the scrutiny of the Eminent Domain Clause. In both *Texaco, Inc.* and *Teleprompter*, moreover, there seems nothing that can be said against the finding of a taking. Neither situation presents the very considerable complexities that arise when challenges are made to taxes or regulations that only limit in part the use and control of property.[19] Instead, these situations have a common feature: before the enactment the claimant was in exclusive possession of the property in question, while afterward that possession rested, in whole or in part, in some other private individual. Thus in *Texaco, Inc.* the matter seems straightforward enough. The effect of the statute upon the claimant was to transfer his entire interest to the owner of the surface. Justice Stevens, writing for the Court, does not deny that the claimant has lost his property. Nonetheless, he disputes the application of the takings clause on the following ground, which is brief enough to be set out in full:[20]

> In ruling that private property may be deemed to be abandoned and to lapse upon the failure of its owner to take reasonable actions imposed by law, this Court has never required the State to compensate the owner for the consequences of his

---

[19] For my views on this subject, see Epstein, *Taxation, Regulation and Confiscation*, 20 OSGOODE HALL L.J.———(1982), where for example I argue that the following programs are unconstitutional under the proper interpretation of the Eminent Domain Clause: the black lung disease programs, see Usery v. Turner Elkhorn Mining Co., 428 U.S. 1 (1976); the windfall profits tax on crude oil and gas; and the Montana Severance Tax on coal, Commonwealth Edison v. Montana, 453 U.S. 609 (1981).

[20] 102 S. Ct. at 792.

own neglect. We have concluded that the State may treat a mineral interest that has not been used for 20 years and for which no statement of claim has been filed as abandoned; it follows that, after abandonment, the former owner retains no interest for which he may claim compensation. It is the owner's failure to make any use of the property—and not the action of the State—that causes the lapse of the property right: there is no "taking" that requires compensation. The requirement that an owner of a property interest that has not been used for 20 years must come forward and file a current statement of claim is not itself a "taking."

The argument cannot bear the weight that is given to it. The question whether the property has been abandoned or has been taken cannot be governed solely by state legislation. The whole point of the distinction, as introduced by Justice Stevens, is to determine the reach and application of the Eminent Domain Clause. If the state can simply declare that property is abandoned when in fact it is not, then it can by persuasive redefinition evade a constitutional provision designed to limit its power. What is needed therefore is a further normative inquiry[21] as to whether the state's standards for abandonment adopted by the legislature conform to constitutional dictates. One possible approach to the question is to ask whether the test conforms to the usual tests for abandonment developed at common law. Here, of course, human nature being what it is, the initial presumption is that no person ever abandons anything of value unless shown to have done so. In order to prove abandonment, it is normally required that there be, in addition to the loss of possession, an intent on the part of a prior owner to abandon whatever rights he has previously enjoyed in the property. One might quarrel with some applications of the common law rules on the subject, but it is difficult to see that they vary in any material way from the ordinary usage of the term, or that it would be possible, especially as a constitutional matter, to come up with some alternative account of abandonment that rejects either the initial presumption or the definitional insistence upon the mental and the physical elements.

With these principles in mind, the treatment of the mineral rights in question seems unproblematic. Even if they are unused,

---

[21] See, *e.g.*, PruneYard Shopping Center v. Robins, 447 U.S. 74, 89 (1980) (Marshall, J., concurring).

the value is evident. There was in this case no physical act that approximated abandonment and no intention to abandon either. To the contrary, the passive behavior of the owners after the passage of the statute is attributable not to an intention to abandon, but to their abiding ignorance about the legal consequences attached by the State to their inaction. To sustain the statute we must accept a new constitutional conception of abandonment that rejects both the traditional mental and physical elements of the act. The nonuse and the nonpayment of taxes may be evidence of abandonment in some contexts. But surely it is not conclusive evidence, especially when it is known from other sources that neither the mental nor the physical requirements of the act have been satisfied. To make matters worse, the State of Indiana, with the blessing of the Supreme Court, also attributes to this ersatz abandonment not only its usual common law consequence of the loss of title by the mineral holder but also the acquisition of title by the surface owner, a distinct consequence properly associated not with neglect but with transfer. It is to indulge in a Pickwickian use of the English language to speak of the "owner's failure to make any use of the property"—and not the action of the State—as the "cause" of the loss of his property right. All that can be said in this case is that the claimants did not register because they did not know they had to. The further assertion, that they "failed to make any use of the property," presupposes that the State may impose at will a novel duty of use or registration upon pain of forfeiture when none existed before. Yet surely no legislature can avoid its constitutional obligations by first imposing duties upon individuals at its own pleasure, only to make loss of property the consequence of nonperformance of the duty so imposed. It is as though the State said, "If you do not pay $1,000 to X, we shall take your property." The nonpayment of the money is not the cause of the loss of the property. It is the State legislation that compels this draconian consequence.

The same analysis can be made even if the decisive issue in the case is transformed into due process, with the claimant's chief objection being that he did not receive adequate notice under the doctrine of *Mullane v. Central Hanover Bank & Trust Co.*[22] The Due Process Clause applies only where the State has deprived an individual of life, liberty, or property without due process of law;

---

[22] 339 U.S. 306 (1950).

where deprivation of property is the issue, the deeper concerns of the Eminent Domain Clause will also be implicated. But if the property may be deemed abandoned, then there is simply no deprivation by the State, and hence no occasion to determine whether the Due Process Clause imposes substantive limitations upon State action that the Eminent Domain Clause does not. Again, by deft recharacterization of common law doctrines the State defeats the constitutional obligations under which it is obliged to labor. As a matter of principle, no matter how one looks at the case, there is no cheap and easy victory for the State. The takings clause is clearly implicated. The real difficulty in *Texaco, Inc.* is with the other three issues on the eminent domain agenda.

A similar analysis can be made of the threshold issue in *Teleprompter*. Here it seems at first blush simply incredible that the question of whether private property has been taken can at this late stage be the subject of a serious discussion by the Supreme Court of the United States. The issue only gives the appearance of difficulty if it is assumed that once the taking of private property is established, the right of compensation necessarily follows. Yet in my view, we are only at the first stage of a very complex inquiry. That first stage is, moreover, an easy one given the physical intrusion and permanent use of the claimant's land that was authorized by the statute. To be sure, the state legislation did not authorize the condemnation of the entire fee. It only allowed that access and use which was necessary for the installation of the Cable TV hookups. There is a long line of cases that recognize, however, that partial takings are subject to the Eminent Domain Clause.[23] And while cases involving destruction of property by the state have caused some difficulty under the Clause, and so too others that have been concerned with the loss of access, there are no cases to my knowledge that have ever disputed the application of the clause when the state (or its grantee) is in permanent possession of the property. The dissent seeks to defeat this conclusion by appealing to the general rules governing the "temporary" taking of private property, where it notes that the accepted rule measures their compensability

---

[23] See, *e.g.*, United States v. Causby, 328 U.S. 256 (1946); San Diego Gas & Electric Co. v. San Diego, 450 U.S. 621 (1980). *San Diego* is of special interest for the dissent of Brennan, J., who was in the dissent in both *Texaco, Inc.* and *Teleprompter.* It was the utter unwillingness to recognize the force of this doctrine in connection with air rights that makes *Penn Central* such an indefensible decision. See note 4 *supra.*

by reference to the general balancing tests of the sort that it champions here.[24] Moving from these cases, it then argues that even where the taking is permanent, the adoption of a *per se* rule is wholly inappropriate where the level of intrusion is small, the gain to the tenants in question is great, and the social importance of the matter is self-evident.[25] All of these things may be true but none is relevant to the limited inquiry here. The dissent is clearly correct when it says that there is no principled constitutional distinction between a temporary and a permanent taking, just as there is no principled distinction between a life estate and a fee simple. But from that correct premise it follows that in both instances there is a taking *simpliciter* by the government when it has cut off any recognized property right of an owner, which is the result urged by Justice Brennan in *San Diego Gas*. The differences between one class of takings and another may well be relevant on the other issue: for example, it may be easier to develop a police power justification for limited takings than for permanent ones. But what the dissent cannot do is to rely upon the differences between various types of property rights to bar wholesale the application of the Eminent Domain Clause. None of the factors it points to can, save by deliberate distortion of the English language, deny the taking by the state, which is a very different affair from an affirmative defense, which admits the truth and sufficiency of the complaint, while introducing new matter to justify or excuse the conduct found *prima facie* unlawful. In *Teleprompter* the denial route will not work. There is a taking and, with that established, it is then incumbent upon the dissent to explain how all of the various economic and social factors it identifies relate not to some undifferentiated social concern but to any of the three specific issues that remain open for resolution. We begin that inquiry by turning to the second question: Is the taking for public use?

---

[24] 102 S. Ct. at 3184.

[25] In this it echoes the language of the 1970 report to the Public Service Commission of New York, by Commissioner William K. Jones, Regulation of Cable Television by the State of New York: "This proposal involves some intrusion upon the property interest of the landlord. But the interest intruded upon is a wholly abstract one—given the conditions specified, the landlord's interest consists entirely of insisting that some negligible unoccupied space remain unoccupied. The tenant's interest clearly is more substantial, consisting of a right to receive (and perhaps send) communications from and to the outside world. In the electronic age, the landlord should not be able to preclude a tenant from obtaining CATV service (or to exact a surcharge for allowing the service) any more than he could preclude a tenant from receiving mail or telegrams directed to him." Report at page 207.

II. PUBLIC USE

As written, the public use limitation in the Constitution requires at the very least that certain takings not be permitted the state even if it is prepared to pay just compensation.[26] The great challenge in the area is to mark out that class of cases in which the public use language bites. Here it is clear that the limits will not be reached, or even tested, where the property in question is taken for the traditional functions of government: the operation of a military base, a public park, a post office. In each of these cases the property in question is used to generate a public good—one in which the entire public shares—either because the good itself is nondivisible in its nature (as with military protection) or because it is rendered nondivisible in its administration (as with public parks open by law to the public generally). But to find many cases in which the public use requirement is no impediment to government action is not to identify those cases where it does restrict government power. While this is not the place to explore the precise boundaries of the public use question, it is interesting that both *Texaco, Inc.* and *Teleprompter* present troublesome questions on this score. The issue was not even raised in *Texaco, Inc.*, in large part because the Court, having decided that there was no taking, thought that it could evaluate the matter under the Due Process Clause, which (the vagaries of incorporation notwithstanding) contains no public use language.[27] And in *Teleprompter* the issue itself received a casual,

---

[26] As a literal matter it could be argued, but only faintly, that the public use language means that the Constitution simply places no limitation upon takings made for private purposes. But this conclusion would allow greater state power for an illegitimate purpose than it would allow for a legitimate purpose. To avoid that embarrassment the phase must be construed as doubtless it was meant. Takings for private use (assuming that they are authorized elsewhere in the Constitution, itself doubtful) cannot be coerced by the government. Even so there are cases that suggest that the just compensation clause did not reach takings undertaken for private purposes, even if done without compensation. See, e.g., Harvey v. Thomas, 10 Watts 63,67 (Pa. 1840), discussed in HORWITZ, THE TRANSFORMATION OF AMERICAN LAW 65–66 (1977).

[27] Indeed the application of the full text of the Eminent Domain Clause against the states is probably better achieved through the Guaranty Clause—"The United States shall guarantee to every State in this Union a Republican Form of Government"—Art. IV, § 4. Note also that in Chicago, Burlington & Quincy R.R. v. Chicago, 166 U.S. 227 (1897), Harlan, J. in arguing for the incorporation of the Just Compensation Clause (with its public use language) into the Due Process Clause of the Fourteenth Amendment says "It [the forced transfer of property from one person to another] would be treated not as an exertion of legislative power, but as a sentence—an act of spoliation. Due protection of the rights of property has been regarded as a vital principle of republican institutions." *Id.* at 235–36. No reference is made to the Guaranty Clause which this passage evokes.

not to say cavalier, treatment, which once again showed the enormous reluctance of the Supreme Court to face seriously the implications of the Eminent Domain Clause.

In *Texaco, Inc.* the public use question arises as follows. Before the passage of the statute, the property in question vested in the mineral owner. After the passage of the statute, it vested in the surface owner. By what possible reason could the shift in the ownership of the land from A to B—both private parties—serve some kind of a public use? The closest to an answer that one finds in Justice Stevens's opinion is the explanation, to be considered later, that the statute is proper under the police power, because it is intended to eliminate uncertainties in the title of mineral interests and thereby to facilitate the discovery and development of fossil fuels. These goals in turn were described by the Indiana court as the "public nature of these purposes,"[28] itself an oblique reference to the public use requirement.

The implications of this analysis are disturbing. If this line of argument is regarded as acceptable, then in every case some indirect benefit to the public at large will authorize a forced transfer of property from A to B by state intervention. In any event it seems proper to ask the further question whether the purported gains derived from these essentially private transfers will materialize. Here the owners of the interests were experts in mineral development: surely Texaco has at least some claim to the entrepreneurial skills and initiative attributable to Mrs. Short. Why then will the transfer provisions of the statute move the resources from worse to better hands? A voluntary transaction could have been arranged if Mrs. Short had been best able to exploit the minerals. If so, can the public use requirement be satisfied whenever a coerced transfer of wealth between private parties might possibly have attenuated public benefits? Surely it is far too large a leap from those cases where high transaction costs block the provision of some public, *i.e.*, indivisible, good such as defense or police protection.

A different approach must be taken to uphold the statute on this ground without perverting the sense of the public use requirement. Here it is useful to put the initial question as follows. Can the public use requirement be satisfied for the ordinary system of recordation which is only prospective in effect? Whether a system is

---

[28] See Short v. Texaco, Inc., 406 N.E.2d 625, 630 (1980).

prospective or retroactive does not affect the question of public use. If the answer turns on the consequence of noncompliance, then the standard recordation system must also fail under the public use language, for the only way the integrity of titles under recordation can be recorded is to prefer the ownership claims of those who claim through the system over those who do not. It therefore seems more sensible by far to avoid deciding the public use question in light of what happens in the odd case of noncompliance: there is no system of fines for nonrecordation that will allow the system to discharge its central purposes if unrecorded titles are still regarded as valid against the world. Instead, the proper approach must be to ask whether the recordation system as a whole is open for the use of the public, which in its normal operation is its *raison d'être*. Everyone must record and must examine the records. As long as no person is excluded from participation in the system, the public use requirement is satisfied, even if the only sensible sanction requires a transfer between private parties in the rare case of noncompliance.[29] We are therefore a long way from the ordinary case in which property is simply taken from A and given to B. The constitutional doctrine can be well understood to comport with sensible intuitions.

If the public use issue is raised in somewhat oblique form in *Texaco, Inc.*, it is dealt with in explicit but wholly unsatisfactory fashion in *Teleprompter*. There the entire discussion of the Supreme Court was an uncritical endorsement of the Court of Appeals' view that "§ 828 serves the legitimate public purpose of 'rapid development of and maximum penetration by means of communication which has important educational and community aspects,' 53 N.Y.2d at 143–144."[30] The subject in fact deserves a far more serious constitutional scrutiny. Thus *Teleprompter* shares with *Texaco, Inc.* the obvious fact that the title to the property in question does not vest in the State at the conclusion of the transaction. Instead, the ownership rights over the limited space occupied by

---

[29] This does suggest a possible ground for distinction between the retroactive and prospective schemes. If the default rate were very much higher under retroactive schemes, then perhaps the case of noncompliance could be treated as typical, so that the public use requirement would not be satisfied. But my own inclination is to enjoin the scheme on public use grounds only where it is designed to procure these transfers—a very narrow category of cases.

[30] 102 S.Ct. at 3170–71.

the equipment vest in Teleprompter, along with the necessary ease-
ments to service and to maintain the installed equipment. As
fashioned by the Court, the public use argument—here transformed into the somewhat broader "public purpose"—again appeals solely to the indirect benefits generated by the use in question. There is still no explanation of how any taking could fail on
public use grounds when such indirect benefits are taken into account. In addition, there is no explanation as to why government
action was needed to secure the benefits to "education and community" that are identified by the Court, given that Teleprompter had
had marked success in selling its packaged benefits without any
legislative assistance at all.

We do not deal here with any serious holdout situation. There
was no evidence in the record that any private landlord refused its
standard five percent offer or received a higher percentage of the
gross. And there was some evidence that in certain cases—that of
Mrs. Loretto's predecessor in title—Teleprompter was able to acquire the rights in question for a lesser sum than the standard five
percent figure. In a world of standard contracts with rapid penetration into the market, there is every reason to believe that CATV
would have become commonplace even without the intervention of
the statute.[31] The transaction costs were not high, and the gains
from trade were manifest to all concerned. As with *Texaco, Inc.*,
more than a benefit to Teleprompter and its subscribers must be
shown in order to satisfy the public use requirement.

As with *Texaco, Inc.*, it is possible to construct a more powerful
argument. The decisive inquiry is whether the company is under
an obligation to extend its services in the manner of any traditional
common carrier to all the individuals that come within its service
territory, here at nondiscriminatory rates.[32] Where that is done the

---

[31] Indeed, perhaps before it recognized the potential windfall that lay behind the Commission's power to regulate the fees that landlords could charge cable companies, the New York
State Cable Television Association opposed passage of the bill creating the Commission,
largely on the ground that an extra layer of governmental regulation would be unproduc-
tively intrusive. See Memorandum of New York State Cable Television Association in
Opposition to Assembly Bills 12001-A and 12378 Proposing to Create a State Commission
on Cable Television, May 20, 1972.

[32] See, N.Y. Exec. Law § 825 (McKinney 1982), which provides in part: "3(b) any rate or
rates found by the commission, after public notice and opportunity for hearing, to be
discriminatory or preferential as between subscribers similarly situated shall thereafter be
void. Reduced rates or free service to government, education or charitable institutions shall
not be considered unduly discriminatory or preferential."

statute will pass muster under public use, as well as indicate the proper limits on the principle. The public use requirement is not met where the power of eminent domain is given to a company that retains the usual prerogatives of a private party to exclude members of the public at will. But by the same token the phrase "public use" does not require public ownership at the conclusion of the transaction. It should therefore be quite sufficient that Teleprompter labored under common carrier obligations under the terms of the statute, so that no person could simply be excluded from participation in the system. Given the legal relationships that existed under the Act it is quite irrelevant that there may have been as an economic matter no holdout problems or transactional barriers that warranted the substitution of coerced for voluntary transactions. When the power of eminent domain is exercised is a question for the legislature and not for the courts to decide. The public use requirement is met because the private ownership thereby created is impressed with a public trust. No more is required.

III. POLICE POWER

Notwithstanding the apparent difficulties of the question, we can conclude that the government schemes in both *Texaco, Inc.* and *Teleprompter* pass inspection under the public use doctrine. The next question is whether the government can avoid the payment of compensation by referring to its exercise of the police power. The matter was considered in *Texaco, Inc.* Justice Stevens expressly noted that the Court held that the statute was a "permissible exercise of the police power," because it helped "to remedy uncertainties in titles and to facilitate the exploitation of energy sources and other valuable mineral rights."[33] This conclusion was not necessary to the decision, because the Court had already made the unsound determination that there was no taking at all. A correct analysis of the case demands that it be considered.

In dealing with asserted claims of justification under the police power for private takings, it is always necessary to make certain that the power itself is not rendered so expansive a construction as to nullify the application of the Eminent Domain Clause. In particular the question of whether a taking is justified under the police

---

[33] See 102 S. Ct. at 789 n.15, quoting 406 N.E.2d at 630–31.

power is very different from the previous inquiry whether the taking may go forward under the public use requirement. The police power question is designed to ask whether the state may go forward without paying at all; the public use requirement asks whether it may go forward if it is prepared to pay. It is therefore wholly improper to allow the very broad tests of public use to play any role in answering the more stringent police power question. Condemnation of private lands for a post office is a taking for a public use, but it certainly cannot be justified under the police power no matter how great the contribution of a sound and efficient post office to the safety and security of the nation as a whole. When it is claimed that the Indiana statute is justified by the police power because it promotes the certainty of title and the development of mineral resources, the entire point should be viewed with some caution. Suppose, for example, the state thought that it was an enormous mistake to allow the severance of mineral interests from surface interests and that it was imperative to reunite the fee in the hands of the surface holders, who would not be required therefore to pay compensation for what they received. Is there any reason to think that this statute would be justified under the police power notwithstanding its—at least under received doctrine (however unsound)—admitted public purpose? Clearly an account of the police power requires some limited class of ends that it is proper to achieve without compensation. Whatever their weaknesses, the traditional antinuisance justifications of the police power at least had this desirable characteristic. What is troublesome about *Texaco, Inc.* is that the question of police power ends is not even considered.

But let us suppose that we find that organization of a sensible system of titles is a proper end of the police power. There is still the question whether the means chosen fit that end. It is at this level that the Indiana statute is subject to the most severe criticism: it is difficult to think of a worse way to scramble the titles to mineral interests. A system of recordation, to be workable, must have at least two features. First, all the interests of a given type must come under the system so that potential purchasers will know that there is a single place to look to validate title. Second, the question whether the title in question is marketable must be determined by an examination of the paper record, without more.

Yet note what the Indiana statute does. It exempts from recordation those interests that have been mined or upon which royalties have been paid in the last twenty years. The statute therefore is only partially inclusive and raises two issues, each of which in the normal course of events requires a determination of matters outside the paper record. After the statute, every title will be under a cloud unless the disagreements between mineral and surface owners are resolved by an explicit agreement or, where buyers are fastidious, perhaps even by a court decree. Thus, suppose that after the statute the surface owner wants to reconvey the mineral interest. No buyer will deal with him without an assurance that no rents and no taxes have been paid for the last twenty years. By the same token the holder of the mineral interest cannot obtain clear title unless he too can show that he comes within the statute, a task that will be greatly complicated if the surface owner ever lays title to the interests in question.

The only way out of this situation is to have universal recordation of all interests regardless of their previous history. But to achieve that particular result, it is not necessary in the least that the interests be taken from mineral holders without actual notice. The Indiana statute created no complications when actual notice had to be served by the surface owner upon the mineral owner. Indeed, the statute could have dispensed with the assistance of the surface owner by requiring the recorder of deeds to publish general notices in newspapers of the new filing requirement, or even by sending actual notice to each person known to have paid taxes within the state on mineral interests within, say, the last three or five years, given the possibility that he has other interests on which taxes have not been paid. Or a general rule could have been made to require all new transfers of mineral interests to be recorded in order to be perfected. My point is not to determine the ideal way to introduce a recordation system in midstream. It is to note that there is no reason whatsoever to allow the taking of private property to accomplish an end that could—to revert to a familiar constitutional theme—be accomplished by far less restrictive means. Indeed, what is so disturbing about the decision in *Texaco, Inc.* is that the Court, conceding that the ends themselves were legitimate, did not even think it appropriate to ask the question whether the means fit the ends. Once that question is considered, it does not take a rigorous or strict scrutiny of the type found in First Amendment cases to condemn the statute. A far less intrusive test upon state discretion—Was there any reasonable fit between the means and the ends?—would have made it quite impossible to justify this statute under the police power.

With all this said, there is very little need to tarry over the treatment of the police power issue in *Teleprompter*. That notion was not relied upon by the Supreme Court, which found only that there was a *prima facie* taking. But the issue was extensively treated by the New York Court of Appeals. The error in its analysis should be evident from the statement of the police power justification that the New York Court of Appeals offered: "Here the purpose sought to be achieved, as stated by the Legislature (§ 811) is rapid development of and maximum penetration by a means of communication which has important educational and community aspects."[34] If that language looks strangely familiar, it is because it is the precise sentence that the Supreme Court used (apparently without noting the change in function) to explain why the proposed legislation met the public use requirement. The confusion between the two doctrines could not be made more explicit.

The irony cuts deeper. Later in its opinion, the Court of Appeals quotes the famous phrase of *Penn Central Transportation v. New York City*,[35] when it says that the state, in the interest of education and development of a new system of communication, seeks to adjust "the benefits and burdens of economic life to promote the common good."[36] Yet far from showing that the statute falls within the police power, it only shows that the rhetoric of *Penn Central* does nothing to answer the hard questions when and how the Eminent Domain Clause applies to economic regulation—including that which authorizes what would otherwise be explicit trespasses. It is probably no wonder that the dissent in *Teleprompter* did not follow the lead of the New York Court of Appeals. Once it is admitted that the taking has occurred, the police power defense will not work. It is therefore better to cloud the issue with the rhetoric of "no set formula" than candidly to face the issues raised by the Clause in their proper intellectual sequence.

IV. COMPENSATION—EXPLICIT OR IMPLICIT

The final question raised by these two cases concerns the matter of compensation. At first glance it may seem odd that the

---

[34] 53 N.Y.2d at 143–44, 423 N.E.2d at 329, 440 N.Y.S.2d at 852.

[35] 438 U.S. 104 (1978).

[36] 53 N.Y.2d at 145, 423 N.E.2d at 330, 440 N.Y.S.2d at 853.

issue is even addressed here. In the usual case issues of compensation are thought to involve two separate questions. First, where there is an admitted taking, are all items of loss suffered by the owner compensated?—a point which has raised no small questions in connection with loss of good will or attorneys' fees incurred either in opposing the taking or, more typically, in resolving the question of valuation. Second, where the item taken is admitted to be compensable, how is it to be valued?—a branch of law of enormous importance in the day-to-day administration of the eminent domain law but of little relevance to the theoretical issues raised by both *Texaco, Inc.* and *Teleprompter.*

What the above account misses, however, is an entire branch of eminent domain law—implicit in-kind compensation—first analyzed in detail by Professor Frank Michelman in his classic article on the subject.[37] This doctrine is a powerful if ill-defined limitation upon the reach of the takings clause, which to some extent has had a role even in the traditional cases of private parcels of land taken for public improvements. The nineteenth-century cases on special assessments, for example, often addressed the issue of how compensation for land taken should be reduced by the increments in value of the land retained by the original owner. The issue in question, however, is of renewed importance given the wide range of modern regulations, which typically impose limited burdens on a broad class of property holders. Here the central point is that even if the restrictions in question constitute a taking—a point far from clear under the current law—the compensation for the property taken may be in the form of the parallel restrictions placed upon the property of others. An easy illustration of the principle is a general ordinance for a downtown shopping area that limits the size, location, and color of signs. As all are restricted, each is compensated by the increased visibility of his own signs by virtue of the restrictions that are placed upon others. To understand both *Texaco, Inc.* and *Teleprompter,* it is necessary to see whether the doctrine of implicit in-kind compensation reaches so far as to spare the State of the need to render explicit compensation.

One of the common points between the Court and dissent in *Texaco, Inc.* is that a general system of recordation of prospective

---

[37] Michelman, *Property, Utility, and Fairness: Comments on the Ethical Foundations of "Just Compensation" Law,* 80 HARV. L. REV. 1165 (1967).

application escapes constitutional challenges under the Contracts Clause, the Eminent Domain Clause, or the Due Process Clause. Under the Eminent Domain Clause the soundness of this analysis is clear. The insistence that titles be recorded in order to be fully protected imposes a set of burdens upon all owners of land. *Prima facie* these constitute a taking of private property. Before the statute, the land was wholly unencumbered; afterward, the owner had to pay some cost to keep his title in its original condition. The burden of those precautions operates like a lien upon the property and measures as a first approximation the value of the interest taken.

Nonetheless, there is no requirement for explicit compensation equal to the expected costs of registration, as each landowner receives in exchange an important set of implicit benefits by the operation of the system as a whole. In the first instance recordation increases the value of all land holdings, for, as the Indiana Court noted, the usual recordation system makes it possible to identify the parties with whom potential purchasers must deal and thus facilitates the movement of real estate to higher-value uses. In addition each individual owner of land shares in the overall gains created by a recordation system. His own ability to dispose of the property in question is enhanced by his ability to deliver clear title to a purchaser. And so too his own general abilities to acquire the property of others. The reason why recordation is used everywhere is that its gains so outweigh its costs, both for the system as a whole and for each of its participants. To require explicit compensation from all to all is to demand of the state that it perform the mindless administrative tasks of moving dollars back and forth by taxing the very individuals who receive the payments in question. To allow the system to go forward on the ground of implicit in-kind compensation is to recognize what is an undoubted truth—the benefits received are the just compensation for the restrictions imposed.

The situation is radically transformed once the rule is applied on a retroactive basis. The major effect of the retroactive application of the general rule is that it skews the relationship between benefits and costs under the recordation system so that the doctrine of implicit compensation no longer spares the state the duty to make explicit compensation. As noted above, the requirement that one register his property to protect it is still a taking of private property.

It is also the case that the individual owner receives the general benefits of a system of registration, which we can assume for these purposes to be positive notwithstanding the major flaws in the Indiana plan detailed above. While the size of the benefits is unchanged by the retroactive nature of the program, the associated costs of the taking are sharply increased. In the prospective case the costs to every owner were the very minor costs of complying with the statute in question. Transactions are done by lawyers, and recordation is a routine part of what is done, so that the likelihood of nonrecordation is virtually nil. Here the costs to Texaco and others similarly situated were the loss of the full value of the property. As there is no transfer, there is no occasion to call in a lawyer, so that now the probability of nonrecordation is far greater. The broad and diffuse general gain does not offset, at least as a first approximation, the very large and special loss with which it must be matched. If one could argue that there was no taking to begin with, then the question of compensation would never arise. But as it has arisen, explicit compensation is required because the implicit compensation is inadequate. To be sure, the State can make the payments if it wishes (and perhaps can even charge them to Mrs. Short, who is the sole beneficiary of the government program). But if that compensation is not forthcoming then the operation of the system must be enjoined.

What might the State argue in order to overcome this imbalance between the property taken and the benefit received? Here its strategy was to argue that the losses to the original owner are not measured by the value of the property taken but, as in the case of prospective registration, the costs of registration. It is precisely on this point that the issue of notice raised in explicit form in *Mullane v. Central Hanover Bank & Trust Co.*[38] fits into the constitutional equation, even when that case is analyzed in eminent domain terms. Where there is actual notice, the landowner is placed in a position to mitigate the losses by complying with the demands of the statute. For him the balance between costs and benefits, between property taken and benefits received, is restored to that found in the ordinary case of recordation. Simple steps in mitigation allow him to limit his own losses. He cannot therefore call upon the State to pay him for the preventable losses that were not in fact prevented.

---

[38] 339 U.S. 306 (1950).

The Court through Justice Stevens recognizes the relevance of the notice argument but insists that the notice provided by publication of the statute met the constitutional standards. But the very fact that an institutional owner like Texaco, Inc. did not discover the statute[39] suggests that the possibilities of mitigation simply were not there. While there were low-cost steps that could have allowed mineral holders to gain the necessary knowledge, the burden must be on the State to take those precautions, just as the burden is on the State to provide adequate compensation in any other takings case. This conclusion is fortified when we examine both statutes of limitations and adverse possession rules, which were relied upon by the Court to show that the notice requirements of *Mullane* were satisfied. In both these instances there is clear notice of the risk of loss from the basic transaction itself. Adverse possession can be acquired only where the occupation has been open and notorious.[40] A cause of action in the usual case only accrues after the occurrence of injury, which is an effective form of notice.[41] In both cases the party whose rights are lost can protect himself on the strength of what in most cases is the actual notice provided by the underlying events, without the independent investigation of an unknown hazard demanded under the Indiana statute.

Although the dissent does not cast the argument in eminent domain terms, it does expose with both power and clarity the weaknesses of the Court's analogy to cases involving adverse possession and statute of limitation. In its view the decisive precedent is *Lambert v. California*,[42] where it was held that actual notice was required under the Due Process Clause to impose criminal sanctions on convicted felons who upon arrival in Los Angeles did not

---

[39] The treatment of the section by Indiana may in part explain the confusion. In the 1971 Acts of Indiana, P.L. No. 423 can be found in the index under minerals, but not under "oil and gas." In the index to the 1976 Indiana Code, the lapse statute is found under "oil and gas"; in the compiled code, however, the statute forms a chapter entitled "lapse of mineral interest," separated by a chapter on highways from the chapters on "oil and gas."

[40] 3 AM. JUR. 136 (2d ed. 1962).

[41] In some cases, notably those involving drug and chemical injuries, the harm itself may be manifest only long after the exposure. And in these cases the statute of limitation doctrine is usually adjusted to take into account the want of knowledge at the time of injury. Thus either it is said (as is consistent with ordinary usage) that the injury occurs only when the harm is manifest, see Urie v. Thompson, 337 U.S. 163 (1949); or special rules are adopted to toll the operation of the statute of limitation until the harm itself is reasonably discoverable.

[42] 355 U.S. 225 (1957).

register with the Chief of Police. The Court does not confront the *Lambert* analogy but seeks to evade it by noting that the notice demanded by Texaco is required if the property is transferred in a judicial proceeding but not if the result of purely private action. The point is profoundly misguided. Where the loss of property takes place in the context of a trial, the aggrieved party receives at least some legal protection against state aggrandizement. Where it takes place without any legal proceedings, there is no protection at all against the private abuses of state power. At the very least the eminent domain analysis suggests that the losses sustained through the retroactive statute are not matched by the gains. If anything I should be more prepared to uphold the statute if a judicial proceeding were required before title to the mineral interests was extinguished, but the statute seems fatally defective no matter what procedures are used to effectuate the taking. When retroactively applied, the benefits received do not equal in value the property taken.

This is not to say that the dissent is immune to criticism. One weakness of the opinion is that it fails to explain why the notice question is relevant to the case as a matter of first principle. A still deeper problem is that it does not confront the full implications of its own analysis of the retroactivity point, now relevant textually to the question whether the compensation received is adequate for the property taken. The dissent cites general language from *Turner Elkhorn* to the effect that very close scrutiny should be given to any forms of retroactive legislation,[43] but it never asks the question whether its disapproval of retroactive legislation in the instant case can be reconciled with the Court's approval of it in *Turner Elkhorn*. In *Turner Elkhorn*, it will be recalled, the Court sustained against challenges under the Due Process Clause a tax upon the production of coal which was designed to provide on a retroactive basis compensation for victims of black lung disease. The companies against whom the tax was imposed had complied with all their obligations under the workmen's compensation statutes and the tort law, and any direct action by the individual employees was unquestionably barred by statutes of limitations. The tax was simply a prelude to the imposition of a disproportionate burden upon the firms in re-

---

[43] 102 S. Ct. at 799.

turn for which—in contradistinction, say, to special assessments—they received no disproportionate benefits.

How could that tax be sustained and the Indiana statute be struck down? One possible line is that *Turner Elkhorn* did not involve questions of notice and therefore has on its particulars nothing to do with the case at hand. Yet that misses the fact that notice itself is not the ultimate question but simply evidence of the total burden placed upon a given class of persons. Where there is notice there is the opportunity to mitigate, which reduces the losses for which compensation must be provided. Now what is distinctive about *Turner Elkhorn* is that even after the notice is provided there is very little that the company taxed can do to avoid a disproportionate burden: the only way to avoid the tax is to eliminate future production, which is to throw out the baby with the bathwater. The taxes imposed therefore represent a far more massive intrusion upon private rights than the legislation involved in *Texaco, Inc.*, where notice if given is of real benefit to the party affected. It follows therefore that as the dissent is correct on *Texaco, Inc.*, then *Turner Elkhorn* is *a fortiori* wrong. There is no easy way to distinguish the two cases by placing each in its own narrow box—taxation in the one case, procedural due process in the other.[44] Both cases squarely raise eminent domain issues, and both require invalidation of the government program.

The analysis of compensation is also important to the complete understanding of *Teleprompter*. In the view of the dissent the only interest that the landlord had was the use at its highest value of the small volume of space necessary for the installation. Given that the statute protected him against any incidental losses, the nominal compensation figure was therefore regarded as appropriate. The effect of this analysis is to argue that all the possible gains created by the adoption of the new technology should be shared solely by the CATV companies on the one hand and the tenants on the other, on the ground—to use the language of the original commission report—that the landlord had no "legitimate" interest in the gains.[45] The same argument might be restated: the value of the premises as a whole was not diminished by the installation of the CATV equipment, so why should the landlord be in a posi-

---

[44] For a more extended criticism of the case, see *Taxation, Regulation and Confiscation*, note 19 *supra*.

[45] Report, note 25 *supra*, at 206.

tion to complain against coercion that has not left him worse off than before?

In order to understand the weaknesses of this alluring argument, it is necessary to determine the appropriate baseline against which to measure the claim for compensation. To make the discussion more concrete, consider the case where the government wants to install expensive equipment on a given plot of land, which would render the land far more valuable than it is in its current use. The usual theory behind the Eminent Domain Clause is that the individual owner is not entitled to share in that appreciation that occurs due to governmental conduct. That argument also explains why, in the context of condemnation for highway purposes, the state should not have to pay any substantial value if it at the same time condemns the right to erect billboards on abutting land. The value of that right for condemnation purposes must be its value before the land was used for a highway and not afterward. The state need not pay a private owner for the very benefit that its own conduct has conferred upon the retained lands.

Yet this was not the situation in *Teleprompter*, as the government action did not make any apartment house suitable for CATV. There it was established that before the statute the company had as a general practice paid royalties in the amount of five percent to landlords for the privilege of laying its cables. The ability of the landlord to demand, and get, that benefit was in no way created by the state legislation. In *Teleprompter* therefore it is not correct to view the interest of the landlord as the right to use some small fraction of his property; it also includes the right to exclude others from its use and to charge them whatever price he sees fit for its use. Before the condemnation the landlord could have yielded the use and exacted the five percent charge in exchange. Now his power to do so is gone. The Supreme Court has long recognized what common sense dictates—that property includes the right to possess, use, and dispose of a given thing.[46] An award that ignores the value of exclusion in essence says that if the state pays for possession and use, then it may have the right of disposition for free.

It follows that there is no need to remand the case for further determination on the compensation issue. The problem below was that New York never took into account the right of disposition in

---

[46] See United States v. Petty Motors Co., 327 U.S. 372 (1945).

valuing the interest taken. Any recalculation of the proper damages for the loss of use or possession simply repeats the same error that brought the case to the Supreme Court in the first place. Since there is a clear pattern of negotiation that establishes the value to the landlord of the right to exclude, there is nothing left which calls for a remand. As a common carrier satisfies the public use test, the state can still allow Teleprompter to force the purchase of the necessary property interest and spare it perhaps some additional transaction costs and the occasional holdout problem. But in the guise of forcing a transaction, it cannot convert what was once a bargain into a gift. There is in this instance no implicit compensation to the landlord to defeat the obligation to pay explicit compensation. The issues in *Teleprompter* are important, but when the whole is broken down into its parts they are not difficult, even if they were misunderstood by both the Court and the dissent.

CONCLUSION

I hope that I have done more than show the errors that have infected two particular cases. The larger purpose is to indicate that many doctrines—*e.g.*, abandonment, notice, taxation, and so forth—that seem to wander about the landscape without any clear constitutional home can be incorporated into a single theory of eminent domain that tests each government initiative against a four-fold program that asks in sequence: Is this a taking of private property? Is it for a public use? Is there a police power justification? Is there just compensation, explicit or implicit? The purpose of this program is to lend intellectual coherence to the current body of eminent domain law, which even the defenders of the Supreme Court's performance have regarded as undisciplined, if not unprincipled. The extended discussion of these two cases gives some hint of the power of the method. More work is needed to show how the same program can be applied to the myriad of other government programs that have been challenged under the takings clause, or for that matter under the Contracts Clause or the Due Process Clause as well.